FIRE AND SWORD
IN THE
SUDAN

HER MOST GRACIOUS MAJESTY

THE QUEEN OF GREAT BRITAIN AND IRELAND

AND

EMPRESS OF INDIA

WHO HAS EVER SHOWN DEEP SOLICITUDE FOR AND GRACIOUS
SYMPATHY WITH THE EUROPEAN PRISONERS
IN THE SUDAN

THIS RECORD OF HIS LIFE IN CAPTIVITY

IS BY PERMISSION HUMBLY DEDICATED BY HER MAJESTY'S
MOST DEVOTED AND GRATEFUL

RUDOLF C. SLATIN.

FIRE AND SWORD
IN THE
SUDAN

A Personal Narrative of
Fighting and Serving the Dervishes
1879–1895

by

Colonel Sir R. Slatin Pasha,
CB, KCMG

Greenhill Books, London
Presidio Press, California

This edition of *Fire and Sword in the Sudan*
first published 1990 by Greenhill Books, Lionel Leventhal Limited,
Park House, 1 Russell Gardens, London NW11 9NN
and in 1991 by
Presidio Press,
31 Pamaron Way, Novato, Ca.94949, U.S.A.

British Library Cataloguing in Publication Data
Slatin Pasha, Rudolf, Freiherr von
Fire and Sword in the Sudan: Personal Narrative
of Fighting and Serving the Dervishes, 1879–1895.
Popular ed.
1. Sudan. Dervish Empire
I. Title   II. Feuer und Schwert in Sudan. *English*
962.403092
ISBN 1-85367-082-0

Publishing History
Fire and Sword in the Sudan was first published
in 1896 (Edward Arnold) and is reproduced now exactly
as the revised 1897 edition, complete and unabridged.

In reprinting this book for a modern audience any
imperfections in the original Victorian typesetting are
inevitably reproduced, and the quality falls short of
the high standards normally to be expected in a modern book.

Printed by Biddles Limited, Guildford, Surrey.

PREFACE

PROMPTED by the earnest entreaties of my friends rather than by any wish of my own to relate my experiences, I have written these chapters.

The few months which have elapsed since my escape have been so much occupied in resuming my official duties, compiling reports, and satisfying the kindly interest displayed by a large number of people in my strange fate, that any attempt at quiet and steady literary work has been almost impossible.

During my captivity I was unable to make any notes or keep any diaries; in writing, therefore, the following pages, I have been dependent entirely on my memory, whilst the whirl of the busy European world, and the constant interruptions to which I have alluded, have given me little time to collect my scattered thoughts.

When, therefore, after having been debarred for so many years from intercourse with outside affairs, and entirely out of practice in writing down my ideas, I find myself urged to lose no time in publishing an account of my adventures, I must beg my readers to excuse the many defects they may notice.

My experiences have no pretence to being of any literary or scientific value, and the personal episodes I have described can lay claim to little importance ; I have merely attempted to give to those interested in Sudan affairs a true and faithful account of my life whilst fighting and serving the Mahdists.

RUDOLF SLATIN.

LONDON,
  October, 1895.

TRANSLATOR'S NOTE

IN preparing the edition in English of Slatin Pasha's experiences in the Sudan, I have followed the system adopted in Father Ohrwalder's ' Ten Years' Captivity in the Mahdi's Camp.'

F. R. WINGATE.

LONDON,
  October, 1895.

INTRODUCTORY NOTE

BY

FATHER DON JOSEPH OHRWALDER,

LATE PRIEST OF THE AUSTRIAN MISSION STATION AT DELEN,
IN KORDOFAN, AND FOR TEN YEARS A CAPTIVE
IN THE MAHDI'S CAMP.

THE joy at meeting my dear friend and former comrade in
captivity, Slatin Pasha, in Cairo, after his miraculous escape,
was indeed great ; and it is with extreme gratification that
I comply with the wishes of those friends who are interested
in his experiences to preface them with a few remarks.

To have been a fellow-sufferer with him for many years,
during which the closest friendship existed between us—a
friendship which, owing to the circumstances of our captivity,
was necessarily of a surreptitious nature, but which, interrupted as it was, mutually helped to alleviate our sad lot—
is, I think, a sufficiently good reason for my friends to urge
that I should comply with their wishes.

Apart, however, from these purely personal motives, I
need only refer to the fact that the small scraps of information which from time to time reached the outside world
regarding Slatin Pasha excited the deepest sympathy for
his sad fate; what wonder, then, that there should have
been a genuine outburst of rejoicing when he at length

escaped from the clutches of the tyrannical Khalifa, and emerged safely from the dark Sudan ?

It is most natural that all those interested in the weal and woe of Africa should await with deep interest all that Slatin Pasha can tell them of affairs in the former Egyptian Sudan, which only a few short years ago was considered the starting-point for the civilization of the Dark Continent, and which now, fallen, alas! under the despotic rule of a barbarous tyrant, forms the chief impediment to the civilizing influences so vigorously at work in all other parts of Africa.

Slatin Pasha pleads with perfect justice that, deprived all these years of intellectual intercourse, he cannot do justice to the subject; nevertheless, I consider that it is his bounden duty to describe without delay his strange experiences, and I do not doubt that, whatever literary defects there may be in his work, the story of his life cannot fail to be both of interest and of value in helping those concerned in the future of this vast country to realize accurately its present situation.

It should be remembered that Slatin Pasha held high posts in the Sudan; he has travelled throughout the length and breadth of the country, and, a perfect master of the language, he has had opportunities which few others have had to accurately describe affairs such as they were in the last days of the Egyptian Administration; whilst his experiences during his cruel captivity place him in a perfectly unique position as the highest authority on the rise, progress, and wane of that great religious movement which wrenched he country from its conquerors, and dragged it back into an almost indescribable condition of religious and moral decadence.

Thrown into contact with the principal leaders of the revolt, unwillingly forced to appear and live as one of them, he has been in the position of following in the closest manner every step taken by the Mahdi and his successor, the Khalifa, in the administration of their newly-founded empire.

Sad fate, it is true, threw me also into the swirl of this

great movement; but I was merely a captive missionary, whose very existence was almost forgotten by the rulers of the country, whilst Slatin Pasha was in the vortex itself of this mighty whirlpool which swamped one by one the Egyptian garrisons, and spread far and wide over the entire Sudan.

If, therefore, there should be any discrepancies between the account published some three years ago of my captivity and the present work, the reader may safely accept Slatin Pasha's conclusions as more correct and accurate than my own; the opinions I expressed of the Khalifa's motives and intentions, and of the principal events which occurred, are rather those of an outsider when compared to the intimate knowledge which Slatin Pasha was enabled to acquire, by reason of his position in continuous and close proximity to Abdullahi.

In concluding, therefore, these remarks, I will add an earnest hope that this book will arouse a deep and widespread interest in the fate of the unhappy Sudan, and will help those concerned to come to a right and just decision as to the steps which should be taken to restore to civilization this once happy and prosperous country.

That the return of Slatin Pasha from, so to speak, a living grave should bring about this restoration is the fervent prayer of his old comrade in captivity and devoted friend,

DON JOSEPH OHRWALDER.

SUAKIN,
June, 1895

CONTENTS

CHAPTER I.

INTRODUCTORY.

CHAPTER II.

RESIDENCE IN DARFUR, AND EARLY HISTORY OF THE PROVINCE.

CHAPTER III.

THE GOVERNMENT OF DARFUR.

CHAPTER IV.

CHAPTER V.

CHAPTER VI.

CHAPTER VII.

LIST OF ILLUSTRATIONS

———◇———

Appearing between pages 22 and 23

Slatin Pasha
Gessi Pasha's Troops advancing to the attack on "Dem Suleiman."

Appearing between pages 38 and 39

Zubeir Pasha
A Rizighat Warrior

Appearing between pages 198 and 199

Bedayat praying to the Sacred Tree
Surrender of the Bedayat to Slatin
Fight between the Rizighat and Egyptian Troops
A Dervish Emir
The Death of Hicks Pasha
Bringing Gordon's Head to Slatin
An Abyssinian Scout
A Slave Dhow on the Nile
The Mahdi's Tomb, Omdurman
The Execution of the "Batahin"
Famine-stricken
The Khalifa inciting his Troops to attack Kassala
The Khalifa and Kadis in Council
Slatin Pasha flying from Omdurman
Slatin in hinding in the hills
A Camel Corps Scout

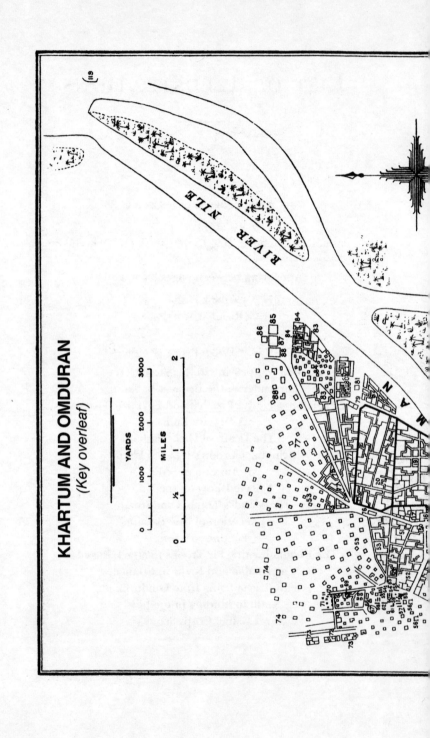

KHARTUM AND OMDURAN
(Key overleaf)

YARDS

0   1000   2000   3000

MILES

0   ½   1   2

RIVER NILE

[115]

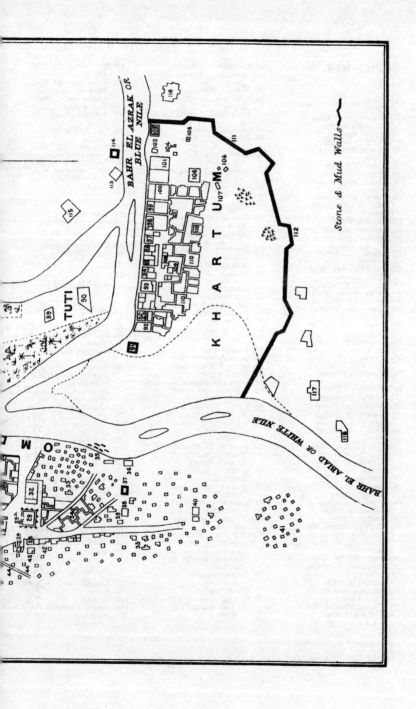

BAHR EL AZRAK OR BLUE NILE

TUTI

KHARTUM

BAHR EL ABIAD OR WHITE NILE

Stone & Mud Walls

OMDURMAN.

1. The Mosque
2. Mihrab
3. Kubbet el Mahdi (Mahdi's tomb)
4. The tin Mosque
5. Khalifa's enclosure
6. Khalifa's special court
7. Khalifa's Palace
8. Khalifa's Harem
9. Khalifa's kuran school
10. Houses of Khalifa's Mulazemin (body guard)
11. House of Mahdi's son
12. Khalifa's stables
13. Khalifa's stores
14. Mahdi's Harem
15. House of Mahdi's family
16. Khalifa Ali Wad Helu's house
17. Houses of Khalifa Ali Wad Helu's Mulazemin & relations
18. House of Khalifa's son (Osman)
19. Great stone wall of Omdurman
20. Mud wall of Omdurman
21. House of the Khalifa's relations
22. Slatin's new house
23. } Houses of Kadis
24.
25. Yakub's old house
26. Yakub's new house
27. Houses of Yakub's katebs
28. Slatin's old house
29. Beit el Amana
29a. Flags & drums stores
30. Other houses of Khalifa's relations
31. Prison
32. Arms Factory
33. Quarters of the Western people
34. Quarters of Borgo & Takarna people
35. Mashra (Ferry)
36. Khalifa's house on the Nile
37. Old fort of Omdurman
38. House of the commandant of Jehadia
39. Quarters of the Black Jehadia
40. Khalifa's house in Dem Yunes
41. Hillet (village) of the Fetihab Arabs

42. Quarters of Bornu, Fellata & Gowama people
43. House of Nur Angara
44. Quarters of Homr Arabs
45. Quarters of Kababish and other camel-owning Arabs
46. Quarters of Hamar Arabs
47. Quarters of Habbania Arabs
48. Quarters of Rizighat Arabs
49. Quarters of Kanana Arabs
50. House of Abdulla Wad Ahmed
51. Quarters of Degheim Arabs
52. Quarters of White Nile tribes
53. Quarters of Jaalin Arabs
54. Carpenters' shops
55. Market courts of justice
56. Scaffolds
57. Salt Market
58. Linen & cloth market
59. Barbers' shops
60. Tailors' shops
61. Vegetable market
62. Butchers' shops
63. Forage market
64. Grain & date market
65. Grain & date stores
66. Wood market
67. Women's market
68. European cook shops
69. The Muslimania quarter
70. Old house of Father Ohrwalder
71. Cemetry
72. Houses of Ahmed Sharfi & family of Khalifa Sherif
73. Quarters of Kunuz Barabra
74. Quarters of the Danagla
75. Quarters of the Beni Jarrar Arabs
76. Tombs of the Martyrs
77. Quarters of different tribes
78. Tombs of the Mahdi's family & relations
79. Powder factory
80. Beit el Mal
81. Slave market.
82. Commissariat stores of the Mulazemin & Katebs

83. Quarters of the Fur tribes
84. Quarters of the Egyptians (Ibrahim Pasha Fauzi, Said Bey Guma, Yusef Effendi Mansur & others)
85. Khalifa's Hejra house
86. Khalifa Ali Wad Hulu's Hejra house
87. The Hejra Mosque
88. Quarters of the Wad el Besir & Hellawin Arabs

TUTI ISLAND.

89. Powder Magazine
90. Tuti village

KHARTUM.

91. Mukran fort
92. Gardens
93. Church
94. Sanitary Department
95. Post and Finance offices
96. Austrian Consulate
97. Government House (Hekemdaria)
98. Governor's palace (Saraya)
99. Grain stores
100. Arsenal
101. Barracks
102. Hospital
103. Fort Burri
104. Small arms, ammunition stores
105. Artillery ammunition stores
106. Cartridge factory
107. A place of worship
108. French Consulate
109. Italian Consulate
110. Houses of the natives
111. Bab el Messallamia
112. Fort Kalakla
113. The Eastern palace (Saraya)
114. North Fort

115. Khojali
116. Burri
117. Kalakla
118. Shagaret Muhhi Bey
119. Halfaya

FIRE AND SWORD
IN THE
SUDAN

FIRE AND SWORD IN THE SUDAN

------◇◇------

CHAPTER I.

INTRODUCTORY.

My First Journey to the Sudan—Return to Austria—My Second Journey—Corruption in the Sudan—Appointed Governor of Dara —Zubeir Pasha and his Son Suleiman—The Gellabas, Jaalin, and Danagla.

IN July, 1878, when serving as lieutenant in H.I.H. the Crown Prince Rudolph's regiment, the 19th Foot, on the Bosnian frontier, I received a letter from General Gordon inviting me to come to the Sudan and take service with the Egyptian Government, under his direction.

I had previously, in 1874, undertaken a journey to the Soudan, travelling by Assuan, Korosko, and Berber, and had reached Khartum in the month of October of that year thence I had visited the Nuba mountains, and had remained a short time at Delen, where a station of the Austrian Roman Catholic Mission had just been established. From here I explored the Golfan Naima and Kadero mountains, and would have made a longer stay in these interesting districts but the revolt of the Hawazma Arabs broke out, and, being merely a traveller, I received a summons to return forthwith to El Obeid, the chief town of Kordofan. The Arab revolt, which had arisen over the collection of the excessively high taxes imposed by the Government, was soon suppressed; but, under the circumstances, I did not think it worth while returning to the Nuba districts, and therefore decided to travel in Darfur.

At that time the Governor-General of the Sudan, Ismail Pasha Ayub, was staying at El Fasher, the capital of Darfur, and on reaching Kaga and Katul I found, to my great disappointment, that an order had just been issued prohibiting strangers from entering the country, as it had been only recently subjugated, and was considered unsafe for travellers. I returned, therefore, without further delay to Khartum, where I made the acquaintance of Emin Pasha (then Dr. Emin), who had arrived a few days previously from Egypt in company with a certain Karl von Grimm.

At that time General Gordon was Governor-General of the Equatorial Provinces, and was residing at Lado, so to him we wrote asking for instructions. Two months afterwards the reply came inviting us to visit Lado, but in the meantime letters had reached me from my family in Vienna urging me to return to Europe. I had been suffering considerably from fever, and, besides, I was under the obligation of completing my military service the following year. I therefore decided to comply with the wishes of my family.

Dr. Emin, however, accepted Gordon's invitation, and he started soon afterwards for the south, while I left for the north. Before parting, I begged Emin to recommend me to General Gordon, which he did, and this introduction eventually resulted in my receiving the letter to which I have already referred, three years later.

Emin, it will be remembered, was, soon after his arrival at Lado, granted the rank of Bey, and appointed Governor of Lado; and on Gordon's departure he was nominated Governor-General of Equatoria, in which position he remained until relieved by Mr. Stanley, in 1889.

I returned to Egypt by the Bayuda Desert, Dongola, and Wadi Halfa, and reached Austria towards the close of 1875.

Gordon's letter, received in the midst of the Bosnian

campaign, delighted me. I longed to return to the Sudan
in some official capacity; but it was not till December,
1878, when the campaign was over, and my battalion had
gone into quarters at Pressburg, that I received permission,
as an officer of the Reserve, to set out once more for Africa.

My brother Henry was still in Herzegovina; so, remaining only eight days in Vienna, to bid the rest of my family
farewell, I left for Trieste on 21st December, 1878, little
dreaming that nearly seventeen years would elapse, and
that I should experience such strange and terrible adventures, before I should see my home again. I was then
twenty-two years of age.

On arrival in Cairo, I received a telegram from Giegler
Pasha, from Suez; he had just been appointed Inspector-
General of Sudan Telegraphs, and was on his way to
Massawa, to inspect the line between that place and
Khartum. He invited me to travel with him as far as
Suakin, and I gladly availed myself of his kind offer. We
parted at Suakin, he proceeding by steamer to Massawa,
while I made preparations to cross the desert to Berber
on camels. I received every assistance from Ala ed Din
Pasha, who was then Governor, and who subsequently, as
Governor-General of the Sudan, accompanied Hicks Pasha,
and was killed with him when the entire Egyptian force was
annihilated at Shekan, in November, 1883.

On reaching Berber, I found a dahabia awaiting me there
by General Gordon's orders, and, embarking immediately,
I arrived at Khartum on 15th January, 1879. Here I was
shown every kindness and consideration; Gordon placed at
my disposal a house situated not far from the palace, and a
certain Ali Effendi was directed to attend to all my wants.
In the course of our daily meetings, General Gordon used
often to talk of the Austrian officers whom he had met at
Tultcha, when on the Danube Commission, and for whom
he entertained a genuine friendship. I remember his saying
to me that he thought it was such a mistake to have changed
our smart white jackets for the blue uniform we now wear.

Early in February Gordon appointed me Financial Inspector, and I was instructed to travel about the country and examine into the complaints of the Sudanese who objected to the payment of the taxes, which were not considered unreasonably heavy. In compliance with these orders I proceeded *via* Mesallamia to Sennar and Fazogl, whence I visited the mountain districts of Kukeli, Regreg, and Kashankero, in the neighbourhood of Beni Shangul; and then I submitted my report to General Gordon.

In this report I pointed out that, in my opinion, the distribution of taxes was unjust, and resulted in the bulk of taxation falling on the poorer landed proprietors, whilst those who were better off had no difficulty in bribing the tax-gatherers, for a comparatively small sum, to secure exemption. Thus enormous quantities of land and property entirely escaped taxation, whilst the poorer classes were mercilessly ground down in order to make up the heavy deficit which was the result of this most nefarious system.

I further pointed out that much of the present discontent was due to the oppressive and tyrannical methods of the tax-gatherers, who were for the most part soldiers, Bashi-Bozuks, and Shaigias. These unscrupulous officials thought only of how to enrich themselves as quickly as possible at the expense of the unfortunate populations, over whom they exercised a cruel and brutal authority.

In the course of my journey I frequently observed that the property of the Sudan officials—for the most part Shaigias and Turks—was almost invariably exempted from taxation, and on inquiry I was always told that this privilege had been procured owing to the special services they had rendered the Government. When I remarked that they received pay for their services, they appeared greatly offended and annoyed. However, on my arresting some of the principal delinquents, they admitted that their taxes were justly due. In Mesallamia, which is a large town situated between the Blue and White Niles, and a considerable trade centre, I found an immense collection of young women, the property of the wealthiest and most respected merchants, who had procured them and sold them for immoral purposes, at high prices. This was evidently a most lucrative trade; but how were the establishments of these merchants to be taxed, and what action was I to take? I confess that ideas and experience on this point quite failed me; and feeling my utter inability under these circumstances to effect any reform, and having at the same time little or no financial experience, I felt it was useless to continue, and therefore sent in my resignation. Meanwhile, Gordon had gone off to Darfur, with the object of inquiring into the circumstances connected with the campaign against Suleiman, the son of Zubeir Pasha; but before leaving he had promoted Giegler to the rank of Pasha, intrusting him with the position of acting Governor-General during his absence. I therefore took the occasion to send him my report and resignation by the same post, and soon afterwards received a telegram from Gordon approving my resignation of the position of Financial Inspector.

It was an immense relief to me to be free from this hateful task; I had no qualms of conscience, for I felt my utter inability to cope with the situation such as I found it —radically wrong, and corrupt through and through.

A few days later I received a telegram from Gordon appointing me Mudir of Dara, comprising the south-western districts of Darfur, and ordering me to start at once, as I was required to conduct military operations against Sultan Harun, the son of a former Sultan, who was bent on endeavouring to wrest back his country from his Egyptian conquerors. Gordon further instructed me to meet him, on his return journey, somewhere between El Obeid and Tura el Hadra, on the White Nile. Having despatched my camels to this spot, where Gordon's steamer was waiting for him, I embarked without further delay, and on landing at Tura el Hadra I proceeded west, and after two hours' ride reached the telegraph station of Abu Garad, where I learnt that Gordon was only four or five hours distant, and was on his way to the Nile. I therefore started off again, and in a few hours found him halted under a large tree. He was evidently very tired and exhausted after his long ride, and was suffering from sores on his legs. I had fortunately brought some brandy with me from the stock on board his own steamer, and he was soon sufficiently revived to continue his journey. He asked me to come back with him to Tura el Hadra, to discuss the Darfur situation with him, and to give me the necessary instructions. He also introduced me to two members of his suite, Hassan Pasha Helmi el Juwaizer, formerly Governor-General of Kordofan and Darfur, and to Yusef Pasha esh Shellali, who was the last to join Gessi in his campaign against Suleiman Zubeir and the slave-hunters. We were soon in the saddle, but Gordon shot far ahead of us, and we found it impossible to keep up with his rapid pace. We soon reached Tura el Hadra, where the baggage camels, which had previously been sent on ahead, had already arrived. As the steamers were anchored in mid-stream, we were rowed out in a boat. I found myself sitting in the stern, next Yusef Pasha esh Shellali, and, as a drinking-cup was near him and I was thirsty, I begged him to dip it into the river and give me a drink. Gordon, noticing this, turned to me, smiling, and said in French, ' Are you not aware that Yusef Pasha, in spite of his black face, is very much your senior in rank ? You are only the Mudir of Dara, and you should not have asked him to give you a drink.' I at once apologized in Arabic to Yusef Pasha, adding that I had asked him for the water in a moment of forgetfulness ; to which he replied that he was only too pleased to oblige me or anyone else to whom he could be of service.

On reaching the steamers, Gordon and I went on board the *Ismailia*, while Yusef Pasha and Hassan Pasha went on the *Bordein*. Gordon explained to me in the fullest detail the state of Darfur, saying that he hoped most sincerely the campaign against Sultan Harun would be brought to a successful close, for the country for years past had been the scene of continuous fighting and bloodshed, and was sorely in need of rest. He also told me that he believed Gessi's campaign against Suleiman Zubeir would soon be over; before long he must be finally defeated or killed, for he had lost most of his Bazinger troops (rifle-bearing Blacks), and it was impossible for him to sustain the continual losses which Gessi had inflicted on him. It was past ten o'clock when he bade me ' Good-bye.' He had previously ordered the fires to be lighted, as he was starting that night for Khartum, and, as I stepped over the side, he said, in French, ' Good-bye, my dear Slatin, and God bless you; I am sure you will do your best under any circumstances. Perhaps I am going back to England, and if so, I hope we may meet there.' These were the last words I ever heard him utter; but who could have imagined the fate that was in store for both of us? I thanked him heartily for his great kindness and help, and on reaching the river-bank I stopped there for an hour, waiting for the steamer to start. Then I heard the shrill whistle, and the anchor being weighed, and in a few minutes Gordon was out of sight—gone for ever!

On the following morning, mounted on the pony which Gordon had given me, and which carried me continuously for upwards of four years, I started off for Abu Garad, and, travelling thence by Abu Shoka and Khussi, reached El Obeid, where I found Dr. Zurbuchen, the Sanitary Inspector. He was about to start for Darfur, and we agreed to keep each other company as far as Dara. We hired baggage camels through the assistance of Ali Bey Sherif, the Governor of Kordofan; and just as we were about to set out, he handed me a telegram which had been sent from Foga, situated on the eastern frontier of Darfur; it was from Gessi, announcing that Suleiman Zubeir had fallen at Gara on 15th July, 1879: thus was Gordon's prediction verified that Suleiman must soon submit or fall.

I should here mention that soon after Zubeir Pasha's conquest of Darfur he left for Cairo, leaving his son Suleiman in charge of his affairs at Shakka. In 1877 Gordon had appointed Suleiman Governor of Bahr el Ghazal, but a quarrel soon sprang up between him and a certain Idris Ebtar, who was a native of Dongola, and to whom Zubeir Pasha had also confided some of his affairs; the Zubeir family, it should be remembered, belonged to the powerful Jaalin tribe, between whom and the Danaglas there had always been great jealousy, and in this fact lies, I think, the secret of much of the subsequent trouble in the Sudan.

The Bahr el Ghazal province is inhabited by an immense variety of negro tribes, who were more or less independent of each other until the Danagla and Jaalin Arabs, advancing from the Nile Valley in their slave-hunting expeditions, gradually settled in the country and took possession of it. The Jaalin trace their descent back to Abbas, the uncle of the Prophet. They are very proud of it, and look down with the greatest contempt and scorn on the Danagla, whom they regard as descended from the slave Dangal. According to tradition, this man, although a slave, rose to be the ruler of Nubia, though he paid tribute to Bahnesa, the Coptic Bishop of the entire district lying between the present Sarras and Debba. This Dangal founded a town after his own name, Dangala (Dongola), and gradually the inhabitants of the district were known as Danagla. They are, for the most part, of Arab descent, but, having mixed freely with the natives of the country, have somewhat lost caste. Of course they, too, insist on their Arab descent, but the Jaalin continually refer to their Dangal origin, and treat them with contempt and derision. The relations between these two tribes must be fully recognised, as they play a large part in the subsequent events in the Sudan.

The quarrel between Suleiman and Idris soon came to blows; the latter appealed to Khartum, obtained the assistance of Government troops under Gessi Pasha, and then followed that series of campaigns in the Bahr el Ghazal which ended in the capture of Suleiman, who, though promised his life by Gessi, fell a victim to an intrigue of the Danaglas, and was executed. Not so, however, his companion in arms, Rabeh, who, fearing the vengeance of the Danaglas, voluntarily left Suleiman prior to his surrender, and, marching in a north-westerly direction with a portion of Suleiman's army, began that series of strange and wild adventures which have placed him to-day, in the neighbourhood of Lake Tsad, a conqueror of a large portion of Central Africa, and a figure of considerable importance in the destinies of the Dark Continent.

There is also one other point I should mention in connection with tribal dissensions which bears largely on the subsequent events in the Sudan, and for this reason must be explained in some detail.

In this his second visit to Darfur, Gordon had ascertained that the Sudanese merchants of El Obeid had been selling arms and powder to the rebel Suleiman, with whom they naturally sympathized for their own selfish purposes; this contraband of war had been secretly despatched to Bahr el Ghazal through the intermediary of the Gellabas (petty traders), who obtained enormous prices from Suleiman : for instance, six to eight slaves would be exchanged for a double-barrelled gun, and one or two slaves was the price of a box of caps. The officials at El Obeid made some attempt to check this trade, but the difficulties were great. The districts between Kordofan and Bahr el Ghazal were inhabited principally by nomad Arab tribes, such as the Rizighat, Hawazma, Homr, and Messeiria; it was, moreover, an easy matter for small parties of Gellabas to traverse, without fear of detection, the almost uninhabited forests with which the country abounds; and even if an Egyptian official came across them, he was, as a rule, quite amenable to a small bribe.

Gordon was fully cognisant of all this, and therefore gave the order that trade of every description was to be stopped between El Obeid and Bahr el Ghazal. The merchants were, in consequence, ordered to quit all districts lying to the south of the El Obeid, Et Toweisha, and Dara caravan road, and to confine their trade entirely to the northern and western countries whilst active operations were going on in Bahr el Ghazal. But, in spite of the strictness with which these orders were enforced, the chances of gain were so enormous and so enticing that the merchants grew almost insensible to the risk of discovery; and, in fact, the Government had not at hand the means of checking the trade in an adequate manner—indeed, in spite of the Government restrictions, the trade rather increased than decreased. Gordon therefore had to resort to very drastic measures. He ordered the Sheikhs of the Arab tribes to seize all Gellabas in their districts, and forcibly drive them to Dara, Toweisha, Om Shanga, and El Obeid, and at the same time held them responsible for any Gellabas found in their countries after a certain date. This order was welcomed by the greedy Arabs, who seized the occasion to pillage not only the wandering traders, but even those who had been settled amongst them for years, and who had nothing to do with this illicit commerce; they gathered the wheat and the tares together, and cast out both indiscriminately, making considerable profit over the transaction. Gordon's order was now the signal for a wholesale campaign against the traders, who not only lost their goods, but almost every stitch of clothing they possessed, and were driven like wild animals in hundreds, almost naked, towards Dara, Toweisha, and Om Shanga. It was a terrible punishment for their unlawful communication with the enemies of the Government.

Many of these traders had been residing amongst the Arabs for years. They had got wives, children, concubines, and considerable quantities of property, which in turn fell into the hands of the Arabs. The fates, indeed, wreaked all their fury on these wretched slave-hunters, and the retribution—merited, as it undoubtedly was, on the principle of an eye for an eye, and a tooth for a tooth—was painful enough to witness, and had consequences which were more far-reaching; for it must be remembered that the majority of these petty traders were Jaalin from the Nile Valley, and between them and their Arab oppressors there now arose the most implacable hatred, which has continued up to the present time, and which shows signs of increase rather than of diminution.

In point of humanity, this attack on the Gellabas may be open to question ; but, on closer investigation, it will be apparent to all that it was not possible to deal with an anomalous situation, such as then existed, by political or philanthropic methods—drastic and violent measures could alone be effective. The Arab himself says, ' Nar el ghaba yelzamba el harika '—' Against a prairie-fire, fire must be used ' ; and the proverb was peculiarly applicable in this case.

Now, these traders being for the most part Jaalin, Shaigias, and Danagla, had, of course, relations and friends in the Nile Valley ; and, indeed, many of the latter were their intermediaries in the commercial and slave transactions which took place. Gordon's orders therefore were scarcely less unpopular amongst these Nile-dwellers, who could not understand why such severe measures were necessary.

CHAPTER II.

RESIDENCE IN DARFUR, AND EARLY HISTORY OF THE PROVINCE.

Arrival at Om Shanga—Matrimonial Difficulties—A Sudanese Falstaff —Description of El Fasher—I take up my Duties at Dara—Zogal Bey, the Sub-Governor—I undertake a Campaign against Sultan Harun—Niurnia, Harun's Stronghold in Jebel Mara—I defeat the Sultan at Rahad en Nabak—Death of Harun—My Meeting with Dr. Felkin and the Rev. Wilson—My Boy Kapsun—Gordon's Letter from Abyssinia.

I LEFT El Obeid early in July, 1879, in company with Dr. Zurbuchen, the Sanitary Inspector-General, whom I had met in Cairo ; our route took us through Foga, the telegraph terminus, and here I found a telegram from Gordon, telling me that he was proceeding on a mission to King John of Abyssinia.

We reached Om Shanga to find it crowded with Gellabas who had been turned out of the southern districts, and were really in a pitiable condition. Curiously enough, the news had spread far and wide that I was Gordon's nephew (I suppose on account of my blue eyes and shaven chin), and in consequence I was looked upon with some apprehension by these people, who considered him as the cause of all the troubles which they were now justly suffering. I was over-whelmed with petitions for support; but I told them that as Om Shanga was not in my district, I could do nothing for them—and even if I could have spared them something from my private purse, I had neither the desire nor inclina-tion to do so.

In one case, however, I confess to having broken the rule; but, before relating this little episode, I should explain that my action must not be judged from the standpoint of purely Christian morality. In this case I admit to being guilty of even greater moral laxity in regard to the Moslem marriage law than is enjoined in the Sharia or religious law; but when my readers have finished the story I think they will perhaps share the feelings which prompted me to act as I did. Several of the merchants who had travelled from the Nile called upon me, and begged me to interest myself in the case of an unfortunate youth, a native of Khartum, and only nineteen years of age. They related that, before quitting Khartum, he had been betrothed to his beautiful but very poor young cousin; the parents had consented to the marriage, but he was to first take a journey, and try to make some money. On his arrival at Om Shanga, a very rich old woman took a violent fancy to him. Whether the youth had been overcome by her riches my informants did not say; but the old woman would have her way, and had married him, and now, finding himself comparatively wealthy, he had no particular desire to give her up. The sad news had reached Khartum, the poor girl was distracted, and now I was asked to solve the difficulty. What was I to do? I called up the youth, who was unusually good-looking, and, taking him aside, I spoke to him with as serious a countenance as I could preserve; I pointed out how very wrong it was of him, a foreigner, to have married a strange old woman, while his poor *fiancée* was crying her eyes out at home, and that even if his cousin's dowry was small, still, in honour bound, he should keep his promise. He hesitated for a long time, but at length decided to go before the Kadi (judge of the religious law), and get a divorce. I had previously seen the Kadi, and had instructed him that, should the youth seek a divorce, it was his duty to break the news as gently as he could to the old wife, as I was most anxious the separation should be carried out with as little commotion as possible; and, taking a guarantee from the young man's relatives that they would be responsible that he should go direct to Khartum, I warned the Government official of Om Shanga that the youth was to be banished at two days' notice! I also told him that he might say what he liked about me to the old woman, and that I was quite ready to bear the blame, provided he could get her to give him some money for the journey. Little did I imagine what a storm I had brought on my devoted head! It was about four o'clock in the afternoon, and I was lying on my angareb (native couch) in the little brick hut, when I heard the voice of an angry woman demanding to see me instantly. I guessed at once who it was, and, bracing my nerves for the fray, told the orderly to let her in. Dr. Zurbuchen, who was in the room with me, and whose knowledge of Arabic was very limited, was most desirous to leave me; but I was by no means anxious to be left alone with an angry woman, and at length persuaded him to stay. No sooner was the divorced wife admitted than she rushed up angrily to Dr. Zurbuchen, whom she mistook for me, and shrieked, in a tone of frantic excitement, ' I shall never agree to a divorce. He is my husband, and I am his wife; he married me in accordance with the religious

law, and I refuse to let him divorce me.' Dr. Zurbuchen,
thoroughly startled, muttered in broken Arabic that he had
nothing to do with the case, and meekly pointed to me as
the hard-hearted Governor. I could not help being amused
at the extraordinary figure before me. She was a great
strong woman, with evidently a will of her own; and so
furious was she that she had quite disregarded all the rules
which usually apply when Eastern ladies address the opposite
sex. Her long white muslin veil had got twisted round
and round her dress, exposing her particoloured silk head-
dress, which had fallen on her shoulders: she had a yellowish
complexion, and her face was covered with wrinkles, while
her cheeks were marked by the three tribal slits, about half
an inch apart; in her nose she wore a piece of red coral,
massive gold earrings in her ears, and her greasy hair was
twisted into innumerable little ringlets, which were growing
gray with advancing age. I thought I had never seen a
more appalling-looking old creature; but my contemplations
were cut short by her screeching voice, which was now
directed on me with renewed fury, and I was confronted
with the same question she had addressed to the terrified
doctor. Giving her time to recover her breath, I replied:

'I quite understand what you say, but you must submit
to the inevitable: your husband must leave; and as you
are a native, I cannot permit you to go with him. You
appear undesirous of having a divorce; but you must
remember that, in accordance with the Moslem law, it is
for the man to give the woman her divorce papers, and not
the woman the man.'

'Had you not interfered,' she shrieked, 'he would never
have left me! Cursed be the day you came here!'

'I beg of you, do not say that,' I answered; 'you are a
woman of means, and I should not think you would have
any difficulty in securing another and perhaps older husband.'

'I want no other,' she literally screamed.

'Silence!' I said somewhat sharply. 'The relatives of
your former husband wish him to leave you; they com-

plained that it was only your money which bound him to you ; and now, whatever you may say, he is to leave to-morrow. Besides, do you not think it is outrageous that an old woman like you should have married a young lad who might have been your grandson ?'

These last words drove her into a state of perfect frenzy ; and, losing all control over herself, she threw up her hands, tore off her veil, and what else might have happened I know not, but my kavass (orderly), hearing the noise, rushed in, and quietly but forcibly removed her from the room, caution-ing her that her conduct was disgraceful, and that she had made a laughing-stock of herself. The following day her husband left, and I do not doubt her grief was considerable; but some years later I had the satisfaction of meeting the youth, married to his early *fiancée*, and already the father of a family ; he thanked me profusely for having got him out of the clutches of the old woman, and brought him to his present happy state. It is needless to relate that I slept soundly that night, convinced that I had done a good piece of work, and that it had cost me nothing.

Two days later we left Om Shanga, and halted for the night at Jebel el Halla, where we were met by Hassan Bey Om Kadok, the Sheikh of the northern Berti tribes, who had shown great loyalty, and had been granted by Gordon the rank of Bey. He was a middle-aged man, very stout, with great broad shoulders, and a round, smiling face; he might well have been called the Sudan 'Falstaff.' Some years later, when the tables were turned, and masters became servants, he and I found ourselves together as orderlies in the Khalifa's bodyguard, where his cheerful disposition and genial nature brightened an existence which at times was almost unbearable. His brother Ismail was exactly the opposite—tall, thin, and serious ; and the two brothers never by any chance agreed, except on one point, and that was their inveterate love of marissa (Sudan beer) : to have each a large jar (made of pottery, and known in Darfur as the *Dulang asslia* or *Um bilbil*) of this marissa, and to vie with one another in emptying it first, was to them the greatest pleasure in life.

They invited us to sup with them, and for our evening meal an entire sheep, baked on charcoal, was served up, besides a quantity of roast fowls and a dish of asida (the latter is somewhat like the Italian polenta, and is eaten with all the courses); there were also several jars of marissa. We thoroughly enjoyed the food, leaving the marissa to our hosts, and substituting for it some of our own red wine. Hassan and Ismail, however, freely regaled themselves with wine as well as marissa, the effect on the former being to make him extremely talkative, while the latter became more and more silent. Hassan related many little incidents about Gordon, for whom he had the greatest admiration and regard. He was much grieved to hear he was going to Abyssinia. 'Perhaps,' said he sadly, 'he will go back to his own country, and never return to the Sudan again.' Curiously enough, he was partially correct. He then left the room, and returned almost at once, carrying a magnificent saddle and sword. 'Look!' said he; 'these are the last presents General Gordon gave me when I accompanied him to El Fasher; he was most kind and generous.' Then Ismail showed us a rich, gold-embroidered robe which Gordon had presented to him. 'Pride,' said Hassan, 'was unknown to Gordon. One day, on our way to El Fasher, one of the attendants shot a bustard; and when we halted at noon, the cook at once boiled some water, and threw the bird into the pot so as to take off its feathers. Gordon, seeing this, went and sat himself down by the cook, and began helping him to pull out the feathers. I at once rushed up, and begged him to allow me to do this for him, but he answered, " Why should I be ashamed of doing work ? I am quite able to wait on myself, and certainly do not require a Bey to do my kitchen work for me." '

Hassan continued chatting till a late hour. He related his experiences during Zubeir's conquest of Darfur, then of the subsequent revolt and the present situation, frequently reverting to Gordon, whom he held in great honour. 'Once, travelling with Gordon,' he remarked, 'I fell ill, and Gordon came to see me in my tent. In the course of conversation I told him that I was addicted to alcoholic drinks, and that I put down my present indisposition to being obliged to do without them for the last few days. This was really my indirect way of asking Gordon to give me something; but I was mightily disappointed, and, instead, received a very severe rebuke. "You a Moslem," said he, "and forbidden by your religion to drink wines and spirits! I am indeed surprised. You should give up this habit altogether; every-one should follow the precepts of his religion." I replied, "Having been accustomed to them all my life, if I now gave them up my health must suffer; but I will try and be more moderate in future." Gordon seemed satisfied, got up, shook hands with me, and bade me good-bye. The following morning, before leaving, he sent me three bottles of brandy, with injunctions that I should use them in moderation.'

Meanwhile Hassan's lanky brother sat in complete silence, leaning on his elbows and solemnly filling up and swallowing glass after glass of marissa, with an almost clockwork re-gularity. When he had stopped talking, he got up in a very deliberate manner, solemnly wiped his mouth with his hand, and said in a melancholy tone, 'Yes, brandy is very good; it is not an alcoholic drink, it is medicine. Gordon is a great and benevolent man; we shall never see him again.'

It was very late before our hosts left us, and, having ordered our baggage camels to start before daybreak, we had a few hours' sleep. The next morning at sunrise our riding camels were ready, and Dr. Zurbuchen and I looked about for our hosts, to wish them good-bye. At length we saw Ismail hurrying towards us; his head was evidently suffering from the effects of the previous night. 'Masters,' he shouted, 'we have always been told that in your country justice exists; I am sure that there guests never wrong their hosts. Last night, when your baggage camels started, your people carried off my best rug, which I had laid out for you to lie down on yesterday.' I made inquiries, and had no doubt that one of my men must have made off with the precious rug, so, ordering one of my kavasses to mount his camel and overtake the caravan, I patiently awaited his return. In due time he came back with the stolen rug, and, tied on behind him, one of my eight Black soldiers, who belonged to our escort. On being interrogated, the man said he had taken it by mistake, but as I had no doubt of his guilt I had him flogged and sent back a prisoner to the nearest military post at Om Shanga. I was much upset by the occurrence, for I knew that these people were apt to conclude that as the master is, so is the servant, and had I not acted with severity on this occasion I should probably have had a frequent recurrence of such thefts.

With profuse apologies to our hosts, we set off for El Fasher, and passing through Brush, Abiat, and Ergud, reached there after five days' march.

For the last century El Fasher had been chosen as the capital of Darfur. It is built on two sandy hills running north and south, and separated by a valley some four hundred yards across, known as the Wadi Tendelti. The fort is situated on the western hill, and consists of a square, mud-brick enclosure, about three feet thick, built on the slope, and surrounded with a ditch fifteen feet deep ; at the corners were four small towers, manned with guns which fired from embrasures.

This enclosure embraces the Government buildings, Governor's house, officers' quarters, and men's barracks; but the quarters of the irregular cavalry are outside. The wells are down in the valley, about one hundred and fifty yards distant from the walls of the fort.

At this time Messedaglia Bey, an Italian, was Governor of El Fasher ; he gave Dr. Zurbuchen and myself a cordial welcome, and allotted us quarters in the Government buildings. We had both suffered somewhat from fever during our wet march, and therefore decided to rest here for a few days.

After a short rest at El Fasher, Dr. Zurbuchen and I continued our journey to Dara, and were accompanied a short distance along the road by Messedaglia Bey, who told us that his wife was coming to Khartum, and that he was asking for leave of absence to go and meet her there and bring her to El Fasher. I suggested that it would be advisable to wait till Sultan Harun had been dealt with before bringing his wife so far; but Messedaglia replied there was not the least cause for fear, and that there were now quite sufficient troops in the country to suppress any local difficulties. I had heard, however, that Harun's influence was considerable, and that there was some apprehension that the now reduced Government forces might be hard pressed. Having only just come to the country, and having had no previous experience, it was of course impossible for me to judge; I therefore accepted Messedaglia's views on the situation, and bidding him and Said Bey Gumá, the commandant, farewell, we hurried on towards Dara, our road taking us through Keriut, Ras el Fil, and Shieria.

Zurbuchen was a very much older-looking man than myself, with a long black beard and spectacles, whilst I looked perhaps even younger than I was. The hair on my upper lip had scarcely begun to sprout, and altogether I had a most boyish face; consequently, wherever we went, he was invariably taken for the Governor, and I for the doctor or apothecary. As we approached the end of our journey, the doctor, who was suffering from fever, had to ride slowly, and to save time for official work, I rode on slightly ahead, and happened to reach the village of Shieria (a day's march from Dara) a little before the appointed time. I found the villagers busily preparing for our reception, the houses were being swept out, straw mats laid down, and the Kadi and Sheikh had spread out their carpets, on which the new Governor was to repose. Making my camel kneel down, I got off, and to inquiries as to who I was, I answered, 'One of the new Governor's escort,' having previously warned the rest of my escort to say nothing. The inquisitive villagers now assailed me with innumerable questions. ' What sort of man is the new Governor ?' said one. ' Oh,' I replied, ' I think he will do his best, and I believe he is inclined to be just and easy-going.' ' But is he brave and kind-hearted ?' said another. This was rather a puzzling question to answer, so I replied guardedly, ' He does not look as if he were afraid, but I haven't yet heard much about his courage; he has a manly appearance, and I believe he is kind-hearted; but of course it is impossible for him to satisfy everyone.' ' Ah !' said another, ' if we only had a governor like Gordon Pasha, then the country would indeed be contented ; he never ceased to distribute money and presents, and never sent the poor and needy away without giving them something. I only once heard him say some harsh words, and that was when Suleiman Zubeir was at Dara, and when he turned to the Kadi, saying that there were several bad characters amongst the Sudanese, and that it did not always do to treat them leniently.' ' Yes,' chimed in the Kadi, ' I heard him say so myself; but he referred only to the Gellabas and traders who came from the Nile, and who were implicated with Zubeir and his son in every description of unlawful trade by which they could benefit themselves.'

' Gordon was indeed a brave man,' said the Sheikh of the village, who introduced himself as Muslem Wad Kabbashi; ' I was one of his chiefs in the fight against the Mima and Khawabir Arabs : it was in the plain of Fafa, and a very hot day. The enemy had charged us and had forced back the first line, and their spears were falling thick around us ; one came within a hair's-breadth of Gordon, but he did not seem to mind it at all, and the victory we won was entirely due to him and his reserve of one hundred men. When the fight was at its worst, he found time to light a cigarette. Never in my life did I see such a thing ; and then the

following day, when he divided the spoil, no one was forgotten, and he kept nothing for himself. He was very
tender-hearted about women and children, and never allowed
them to be distributed, as is our custom in war; but he fed
and clothed them at his own expense, and had them sent to
their homes as soon as the war was over. One day,' continued the Sheikh, 'without letting him know, we put some
women aside; but if he had found us out, we should have
had a bad time of it.'

After a short pause, I inquired about affairs in Dara, and
about the qualifications of the various officials; for I had
already heard that they were very unreliable, and I was
now told that they looked on my advent with no friendly
eye.

Meanwhile Dr. Zurbuchen and the rest of the caravan
had arrived, and at once the Sheikh, Kadi, and other village
dignitaries lined up in a semicircle to receive him, while I,
concealing myself as much as possible, awaited with amusement to hear what Muslem Wad Kabbashi would say. He
began with warm welcome to the new Governor, praised his
qualifications, and eloquently described the joy of all his
people at his arrival. Poor Dr. Zurbucnen, whose com
prehension of Arabic was very slight, became more and
more perplexed. 'Indeed I am not the Governor,' he
urged, 'I am only the Sanitary Inspector. The Governor
must have arrived long ago; but as he had only a few
people with him, perhaps he has been mistaken for someone
else.' I now thought it time to step forward, and laughingly thanked the villagers for their kind reception, assuring
them that I would do all in my power to satisfy their wants,
and that at the same time I looked to them to assist me
in seeing my orders carried out. Of course they made the
most profuse apologies for the mistake; but I assured them
there was not the least necessity for their doing so. I was
anxious, I said, to be on the most intimate and friendly
terms with all of them, and I hoped they would allow the
same friendly relations to continue. From that day forth,

Sheikh Muslem Wad Kabbashi became one of my most faithful friends, and continued to be so, in times of joy and sorrow, until I left the country.

This little episode had given us all a hearty appetite, and we sat down to an excellent meal of roast mutton; and that over, we were again in the saddle, bivouacking for the night under a large tree about two hours' march from Dara. At sunrise the next morning I sent on a messenger to announce our approach, and on reaching the outskirts we were given a great military reception, the garrison was drawn up in line and a salute of seven guns fired, after which the troops filed off to their barracks, and, accompanied by Major Hassan Helmi, the commandant, Zogal Bey, the Sub-Governor, the Kadi, and some of the principal merchants, we proceeded to the fort in which the Government buildings are situated. The inspection lasted about half an hour, and I then went to my own quarters, in which I had ordered rooms to be prepared for Dr. Zurbuchen, who was to be my guest for a few days.

Scarcely had we settled down to dinner that evening, when a great hubbub arose amongst the servants, who were evidently trying to prevent two men from pushing their way into our circle. They were messengers carrying a document which proved to be a letter from Ahmed Katong and Gabralla, the two chiefs of an irregular corps which garrisoned the station of Bir Gowi, some three days' march south-west of Dara: this was to say they had just received information that Sultan Harun was going to attack them, and that as they had only a small force, they proposed to evacuate their station, unless reinforcements could be sent at once; but they said that if they left the district, all the villages would be plundered.

There was no time to be lost, so I ordered Hassan Effendi Rifki to select two hundred regulars and twenty horsemen to be ready to start with me at once for Bir Gowi.

By midnight all was ready, and, bidding Dr. Zurbuchen

Rudolph C. Slatin

Gessi Pasha's Troops advancing to the attack on "Dem Suleiman."

good-bye, I started off for the south-west, saying that I hoped
to see him again in four or five days.

I was young, strong, and keen to have some fighting
experience, and I well remember my delight at the thought
of a brush with Sultan Harun. The idea of difficulties and
fatigue never crossed my mind; all I longed for was a
chance of showing my men that I could lead them. At
sunrise I halted my little party, which consisted of two
hundred Blacks—the officers also being Sudanese—and the
horsemen (Turks and Egyptians), and addressed them in a
short speech, saying that at present I was an entire stranger
to them, but they should see I was ready to share fatigue
and discomfort with them on all occasions, and that I hoped
we should march rapidly forward with a good heart. Simple
as my harangue undoubtedly was, I saw that it had made an
impression, and when I had finished, they raised their rifles
above their heads, in Sudanese fashion, and shouted that
they were ready to conquer or die.

At noon we halted near a village, and I then carefully
inspected the men. They were all well armed, and had a
plentiful supply of ammunition ; each man was also provided
with a water-bottle made out of goat or gazelle skin, known
as ' sen ' (pl., siun); but they had brought no rations with
them. On inquiry, I was told, ' Wherever you go in
Darfur you will always find something to eat.' I therefore
made my way to the Sheikh of the village, and asked him
to supply some dukhn. This corn is generally soaked in
water, then pressed, mixed with tamarind fruit, and eaten
in this condition, the bitter-sweet water being an excellent
thirst-quencher. This food Europeans usually find indi-
gestible; but it is very nourishing, and is eaten almost
exclusively by the Sudanese soldiers when campaigning. I
gradually got accustomed to it, taking it almost invariably
when out on such expeditions ; but I found that unless one
was feeling very well, it generally brought on most painful
indigestion. The Sheikh now brought us the corn, and
also a large dish of asida, which was divided amongst the

men; and whilst they were having their meal, I asked the officers to share with me a tin of preserved meat, which they admitted was much superior to the asida and dukhn. I then called up my clerk, and told him to write out a receipt for the corn, which he was to give the Sheikh, to be his voucher for the remission of taxation equivalent to the value of the dukhn supplied. But the good man, when he understood my orders, refused to accept the receipt, adding that it was not only his duty to give the corn, but that the rights of hospitality demanded it. I told him, however, that I was well aware the natives of Darfur were most generous; but to impose the feeding of two hundred men on him quite exceeded the bounds of hospitality, and that it was only just he should receive payment. He at length agreed, and this conversation appeared to give him confidence; for he admitted that if this principle were always carried out, the natives would greatly appreciate it; but, unfortunately, it was the usual custom for troops arriving at a village to enter the houses, and take anything and everything they wanted, with the result that the inhabitants dreaded their approach, and at once tried to hide all they had. I thanked the Sheikh for telling me this, and promised I would do all I could to rectify the evil.

At sunset we reached Bir Gowi, which was a military post garrisoned by some one hundred and twenty irregulars under two chiefs—Ahmed Katong and Gabralla—who told me they had sent out spies to ascertain Harun's movements, but they thought he had not yet descended from Jebel Marra into the plains; so, thoroughly tired and sleepy after my long journey, followed by the two days' hard marching, I went to bed; but my head ached, and the incessant beating of drums in my honour kept me awake all night, and the following morning I felt really unwell. Ahmed Katong came to see me, and I told him I had a bad headache. 'We can easily cure that,' said Ahmed cheerfully. 'I have a man here who can stop headaches at once; he is a much better man than the doctor at Dara—indeed, there is no doctor at Dara; he is really only an apothecary, with the courtesy title of doctor.'

'All right,' said I; 'but how is he going to cure me?'

'Oh! it is very simple,' he answered. 'He places both his hands on your head, and repeats something; then you get perfectly well—in fact, better than you were before.'

'Then let him come at once,' I cried.

I was young and ignorant in those days, and I thought that possibly one of these wandering Arabs might have visited Europe and learned something of the magnetic cure, and had given up the pleasures of life in order to make himself useful to mankind. I confess to feeling a little mistrustful when I thought of what Ahmed had said; but then, after all, doctors in Europe speak, so why should not he? In a few minutes Ahmed ushered into my presence a tall dark man with a white beard, who appeared to be a native of Bornu, and introduced him as 'the doctor who will cure your headache.' Without a moment's hesitation, the doctor placed his hand on my head, pressed my temples with his thumb and forefinger, and, muttering a few words I could not understand, to my horror, spat in my face. In a moment I had jumped up and knocked him down; but Ahmed, who was standing by, leaning on his crutch, begged me not to take it in this way. 'It was not really meant for rudeness,' he said; 'it is merely a part of the cure, and will do you much good.' But the poor doctor, whose confidence had been somewhat shaken, and who was still standing at a distance, muttered: 'Headache is the work of the devil, and I must drive it out; several passages from the Kuran and the sayings of holy men direct that it should be chased away by spitting, and thus his evil work in your head will cease!' In spite of my annoyance, I could not help laughing. 'So I am supposed to be possessed of a devil,' I said; 'I trust he was only a little one, and that you have really driven him out.' I did not, however, let him make a second experiment, and, giving him a dollar as compensation, I bade him good-bye, and he left me, calling down the blessings of Heaven on my poor head, which was still aching sadly.

As there was still no news of Harun, I remained that day in bed and received frequent visits from my friends Katong and Gabralla. The former offered me his horse, which I refused, whilst the latter pressed upon me one of his maid-servants. 'She is young and pretty,' he said, 'and has been well brought up in my house; she knows how to pre-pare native food, is good at housework, and is above all a good and careful nurse, and thoroughly understands all the ailments of the country.' Again I was obliged to refuse this proffered kindness; so poor Gabralla went away some-what downcast with his failure. But having already had a rather painful experience at the hands of the doctor, I was not particularly anxious to intrust myself to the tender mercies of even a dusky maiden, however proficient a nurse she might be.

The next morning I arose feeling quite myself again, and when I met Ahmed and told him that I had recovered, he at once answered, 'Of course, I knew you would get quite well; Isa' (the name of my doctor) 'has never yet put his hands on anyone and failed to cure him.'

Another day passed, and still no news of Harun. On the following day, about noon, one of Gabralla's messengers returned with the news that Sultan Harun had collected his men, but still had not moved down from his summer resort in the hills. On the fourth day after our arrival at Bir Gowi, a second messenger came in and stated that when Sultan Harun heard from the natives that I had left Dara for Bir Gowi with the intention of fighting him, he had at once disbanded his men, who had dispersed over Jebel Marra.

Thoroughly disappointed with my first failure, I returned crestfallen to Dara, but by that time Dr. Zurbuchen had gone, leaving behind him a letter in which he wished me all success. I also found that during my absence my un-fortunate Arab clerk, who had accompanied me when I was

Financial Inspector, and had come with me to Dara, had become crazy ; they had put him in a house next my own, and when I went to see him, he sprang forward to embrace me, crying out, ' Thank God ! Sultan Harun has done no harm to you ; but Zogal Bey is a traitor, beware of him. I have ordered the fires in the engine to be lighted, in order that the train may take you to Europe, where you will be able to see your relations again. I shall come with you ; but we must be careful about Zogal, he is a scoundrel !' Evidently the poor man's mind was quite unhinged ; nevertheless, crazy people sometimes speak the truth. I quieted the poor old man, and induced him to lie down till he heard the engine's whistle warning us to be off, and commending him to the care of the servants, I went away. Five days later the whistle had sounded, and the poor man had been carried off to his long home—his death was, I suppose, due to a rush of blood to the brain.

I now busied myself with the administrative affairs of the province of Dara, and about a month after my return I received a letter in French from Messedaglia, telling me that he had determined to put an end to the Harun trouble ; and for the purpose he ordered me to move secretly *via* Manawashi and Kobbé, with a division of regular troops, towards Jebel Marra, and attack Niurnia, the Sultan's residence. At the same time, he wrote, he was despatching troops from El Fasher, *via* Tura, and from Kulkul, *via* Abu Haraz, to rendezvous at a certain spot and co-operate in the attack.

In compliance with this order I left Dara with two hundred and twenty regulars and sixty Bazingers, and marching *via* Manawashi reached Niurnia, Harun's stronghold in Jebel Marra, to find it evacuated. The morning after my arrival, I started off with a portion of my force in search of Harun, but had been gone only a few minutes when I heard rapid firing from the direction of Niurnia, and galloping back, found the party I had left behind heavily engaged with a hostile force, which I soon recognised as the detachment of troops sent to my assistance from El Fasher, but which had failed to arrive in time at the rendezvous; and advancing on Niurnia, which they had seen was occupied, they had opened fire, little thinking that they were showering bullets on their comrades. I had no small difficulty in stopping the firing, which had already resulted in a loss of seven killed and eleven wounded, whilst a bullet had passed through my coat and my horse had been wounded in two places.

We remained ten days at Niurnia, and as I could get no accurate news of Harun's movements I decided to return. On our way back we passed through several villages and took the people entirely by surprise, for they had not expected us from the west. Most of the men had been collected by Sultan Harun, and those who could escape to the hills did so; but my men captured about thirty women, whom we took along with us for a short distance. In one village the people were so completely surprised that few of them had time to fly, and seeing that they were only women I sounded the halt, in order to give them a chance of getting away. I then formed up the men on the road, so as to prevent them scattering through the village, and in this formation we marched on. One poor woman, I noticed, in her hurry to escape, had left her two children on a rock, while she herself fled like a gazelle up the mountain side. Going to the rock, I found two pretty babies quite naked, but with strings of coral round their waists and necks. They were as black as ravens, and probably twins about eighteen months old. Dismounting, I went up to them, and they began to cry and cling to each other, so taking them in my arms, I told my servant to bring me some sugar from my travelling-bag. This pacified them at once, and, smiling through their tears, they munched what to them was probably the nicest thing they had ever tasted in their little lives. Then, taking two of the red handkerchiefs (a supply of which I generally carried about to offer as presents), I wrapped the babies up in them, laid them down on the rock again, and moved on some distance. Looking back, I saw a human being, evidently the mother, creeping down the rocks. Then joyfully seizing her little ones, whom she thought perhaps she had lost for ever, she fondled them most lovingly. She had got back her naked treasures clothed in lovely garments, and licking their little black lips all sticky with their feast of sugar.

A few days after this little episode, and when we were still some distance from Dara, news reached me that during my absence Harun had suddenly descended on the town, which he had pillaged, and had made off again towards the hills with a quantity of spoil and many women captives. Ascertaining that he could not be far off, and procuring guides from the neighbourhood, I set off in pursuit, and when about two days' march south-east of El Fasher, came up with his force, little suspecting they were pursued. I succeeded in approaching almost unnoticed, and falling upon them suddenly, I utterly routed them, capturing quantities of arms, besides liberating all the women captives. Harun's horse was shot under him, but he himself, with a few followers, escaped, only to fall a few days later at the hands of the Kulkul troops under Nur Angara, and with his death the revolt speedily died out, and peace was once more restored to the country.

On my return to Dara I received a letter from Gessi Pasha, in Bahr el Ghazal, informing me that Dr. R. W. Felkin and the Rev. C. T. Wilson, of the English Church Missionary Society, were on their way from Uganda to Khartum, *viâ* Dara, and with them were some Waganda envoys sent by King Mtesa to Her Majesty the Queen of England. Gessi begged me to give them all help on their journey, and said that they were leaving for Dara on the date he was writing. They reached Dara a few days later, and I greatly enjoyed their short stay with me.

All they told me was of immense interest, and I, too, was able to give them the latest information from Europe, which, though months old, was news to them.

One morning I was told, much to my amusement, that the sight of a camel had caused Mtesa's envoys such alarm that they had fled. 'Well,' said I to Dr. Felkin, 'as you have to make the rest of your journey on camel-back, it is advisable your men should get into the way of it; so if you will get them together I will send for a camel and put their courage to the test.' He went off, and I sent for a camel belonging to one of the merchants, which was very big and fat. By this time the envoys and others had arrived, and the camel, appearing suddenly round a corner, caused almost a stampede. It was only the sight of the unconcern of Dr. Felkin and myself which kept them from bolting as hard as their legs could carry them. Dr. Felkin explained to them that the camel was a most patient and docile animal, on which they would have to make the remainder of their journey to Egypt, and that there was no cause for fear; still they kept a respectful distance from the alarming beast, and when I told my kavass to mount and make it get up and sit down, their astonishment was boundless. At length one, more courageous than the rest, volunteered to mount; timorously approaching the animal, he was assisted into the saddle, and having safely got through the operation of rising, with a beaming countenance he surveyed his friends from his lofty seat, and proceeded to make a speech to them on the pleasures of camel-riding. Apparently he had invited them to share these pleasures with him, for suddenly, without a moment's warning, they rushed at the poor animal in a body, and began to swarm up it. Some tried to mount by the neck, others by the tail, and half a dozen or so clung to the saddle-trappings. For a moment the camel seemed stupefied by this sudden attack, but recovering its presence of mind, it now lashed out in all directions, and in a moment had freed itself completely from every unfortunate Waganda who had been bold enough to approach it. I do not think I ever laughed so much in my life. These people evidently took the poor animal for a mountain, but the shocks they experienced when the mountain began to heave so terrified them that for long they would not come near it. However, first one and then another summoned up courage to mount, and by the time they left Dara they were all fairly proficient in the art of camel-riding.

I had in my household several young boys who had been taken from the slave-traders, and as Dr. Felkin had no servant to attend on him personally, I suggested he should take one of them. He accepted the offer gladly, so I handed over to him a bright little Fertit boy called Kapsun, whom he agreed to bring up in Europe. Two years and a half later I received, at El Fasher, a letter written in English by little Kapsun, thanking me for allowing him to go with Dr. Felkin ' to a country where everyone was so good and so kind,' and saying that he had adopted the Christian religion, and was ' the happiest boy in the world '; he also sent me his photograph in European clothes.

The time for the departure of my two friends came all too soon for me, but they were anxious to get on, and mounted on their camels they left for Khartum *viâ* Toweisha.

Some time later I received a letter from Messedaglia telling me that he was leaving for Khartum to fetch his wife. No sooner had he reached that place than he got into some difficulty with the authorities and was discharged, and his place as Governor-General of Darfur was taken by Ali Bey Sherif, formerly Governor-General of Kordofan.

It was about the close of 1879 or early in 1880 that I received a letter from General Gordon, written in French some two months previously from near Dabra Tabor, in Abyssinia. Although this letter was destroyed many years ago, I can remember almost the exact words, which were as follows :

' DEAR SLATIN,
    ' Having finished my mission to King John, I wanted to return the same way that I came, but when near Gallabat I was overtaken by some of Ras Adal's people, who forced me to go back, and I am to be taken under escort to Kassala

and thence to Massawa. I have burnt all the compromising documents. King John will be disappointed when he finds he is not master of his own house.

‘Your friend,

‘ C. GORDON.’

CHAPTER III.

THE GOVERNMENT OF DARFUR.

Government Administration in Dara—My Visit to Khartum—Arrival of Gessi in Khartum—I return West with Bishop Comboni and Father Ohrwalder—Am appointed Governor-General of Darfur—Hostilities between the Maheria and Bedeyat Arabs—I proceed to the Bedeyat Country—Strange Manners and Customs of the Bedeyat—Saleh Donkusa and the Heglik Tree—The Ceremony of taking the Oath of Fidelity—Return to El Fasher—Troubles at Shakka and Death of Emiliani—I leave for Dara.

I WILL now pass over the events of the year 1880, which proved to be a fairly peaceful one in the Dara district. During that period I busied myself principally with the administrative affairs of the province, personally visited almost every village, and made the acquaintance of all the powerful Arab tribes who were constantly on the verge of war with each other, and between whom I had frequently to act as mediator.

Towards the close of 1880, I found I had so many important matters requiring the decision of the Governor-General that I applied for permission to come to Khartum, and see Rauf Pasha, who, on Gordon's departure, had succeeded him. My request was approved, and at the beginning of 1881 I quitted Dara, and reached Khartum a fortnight later.

Here I found Zurbuchen, who welcomed me heartily, and carried me off as his guest to a house near the Roman Catholic Mission, which had belonged to the late Latif Debono, a Maltese, and a well-known slave-dealer.

During my stay in Khartum, I had frequent talks with

Rauf Pasha on the state of my province, and I suggested that a more just and lenient form of taxation should be introduced in the Fasher and Kebkebia districts. I also asked him to allow me to order the Arab tribes to supply annually a certain number of young slaves, who should form a contingent from which the vacancies caused by sickness, deaths, and other casualties amongst the troops could be filled up ; and I further proposed that the Arabs should be allowed to pay their tribute in slaves instead of cattle, as by this means I hoped to win back Suleiman Zubeir's Bazingers, who were scattered amongst the tribes, and whose knowledge of the use of firearms was, in my opinion, a continual source of danger to the Government. Rauf Pasha concurred in all these suggestions, and gave me written orders to this effect.

When I arrived in Khartum, a certain Darfuri named Hassan Wad Saad en Nur, whose father had been killed with Vizir Ahmed Shata in Shakka, came to me, and begged me to intercede for him to be permitted to return to his country ; meeting Rauf Pasha shortly afterwards, I begged him to allow this, and he gave instructions for his discharge to be at once made out. A few days later, however, he sent for me, and explained that, after further inquiry, he had decided to cancel Nur's discharge. I explained that he had only acted like the rest during the revolt, and that now it was not possible for him to do any further harm. Rauf Pasha, however, remained resolute, and I, feeling annoyed, retorted that, as I had given Nur my word that he should return with me, it remained for Rauf Pasha to decide whether he would let him go, or whether he would discharge me, and, bidding him good-bye, I marched off. Two days later he again sent for me, and said that I was wrong in having given Nur my word so quickly. I fully admitted the justice of this censure, and, to my surprise, he then said that he had reconsidered the matter, and had decided to let Nur go ; and, as regards myself, he thought me a stubborn but capable official, and had in consequence requested his High-

ness the Khedive, Mohammed Tewfik Pasha, to appoint
me Governor-General of Darfur, with the title of Bey. I
thanked him for his kind words, and assured him that I
should do my utmost to justify his confidence in me.

Rauf Pasha now asked me to state in writing that I would
be responsible for the future good behaviour of Nur; and
this I did gladly, feeling convinced that, after all my trouble
on his behalf, the man would prove loyal and faithful. On
returning to my house, I sent for Nur, who had spent two
days of suspense, dreading that his discharge would be
refused; and when I told him the good news, he fell at my
feet, and poured out his gratitude in the most voluble terms.
I felt that he was a man of honour, and that I could trust
him : little did I know that I had taken a snake into my
bosom.

My short stay in Khartum passed rapidly in the company of my many friends. Bishop Comboni and Fathers
Ohrwalder and Dichtl had arrived from Cairo towards the
end of January, 1881, as well as Hassan Pasha, the chief
of the Financial Department, Busati Bey, Consul Hansal,
and others. Ohrwalder and Dichtl put up in my quarters,
and many a long talk used we to have over our own beloved
country.

On 25th January, 1881, Gessi arrived at Khartum very
seriously ill. During his journey from Meshra er Rek, he
had been hemmed in by the ' Suds,' or barriers of floating
vegetation, through which travellers must at times cut their
way with axes. For three months and more he had struggled
hopelessly to make his way through them, and the terrible
sufferings undergone by him and his men through famine
and sickness are almost indescribable. He lost the majority
of his men and crew, and acts of cannibalism were of daily
occurrence. He was at length rescued by Marno in the
steamer *Bordein*, and brought to Khartum, where he was
most carefully tended by the Mission sisters ; but the shock
to his system had been so great that he could not recover
his strength, despite every effort made by Dr. Zurbuchen.

It was at length decided to try and send him to Egypt, and we made all arrangements to make his journey as comfortable as possible. He was particularly anxious to take with him his servant Almas, who happened to be a eunuch; but Rauf Pasha, fearing that it might create a scandal, and that strictures might be passed on his government of the Sudan, for a long time refused permission for him to go. Yielding, however, to the persistence of Zurbuchen and myself, he at length authorized it, and on 11th March we carried poor Gessi in a sort of litter to the Governor's dahabia, in which he was towed to Berber; thence he was carried across to Suakin, where he arrived on 10th April, and, embarking a fortnight later, reached Suez on the 28th, too weak almost to move. He was taken to the French hospital, where he expired two days later.

Meanwhile, matters in Darfur had not been progressing very satisfactorily. Zogal Bey wrote that Omar Wad Darho had been conducting himself very badly at Shakka, and I showed the report to Rauf Pasha, who telegraphed that he was to return at once to El Fasher.

There being nothing to keep me, I decided to return and take up my new duties as soon as possible. Rauf Pasha placed a steamer at my disposal, and, accompanied by Bishop Comboni and Father Ohrwalder, whom I promised to mount on my camels as far as El Obeid, we quitted Khartum on 29th March. Consul Hansal, Marcopoli Bey, Zurbuchen, and Marquet, travelled with us in the steamer as far as Tura el Hadra, and here we bade them good-bye. Little did I think that one only of that company should I ever meet again, and under what strange circumstances I was once more to return to the capital of the Sudan. I was very young, the heavy responsibilities of my new and important position occupied all my thoughts, and I was full of high hopes for the future; but fate had a strange and terrible destiny in store for me.

After five days' march we reached El Obeid, and from here the Bishop made a tour through Jebel Nuba, while

Father Ohrwalder remained at El Obeid, and was eventually sent to the mission station of Delen, in southern Kordofan. I stayed in El Obeid a few days only, and, having received telegraphic orders to proceed to Foga, I bid my two friends farewell. One of them—the good Bishop—I was destined never to see again ; he died in Khartum on 10th October, 1881. The other—my dear friend Ohrwalder—like myself, was soon to go through many strange and horrible experiences before we were again to meet as fellow-captives of the as yet unknown Mahdi, who was shortly to overthrow every vestige of Government authority in the Sudan.

On quitting El Obeid, I proceeded with all despatch to Dara, and thence to El Fasher, where I arrived on 20th April. Here I found the Government administration in a state of great confusion, and it took me some months to establish even a semblance of law and order in my new Governorate ; but by continually travelling about, and personally seeing into matters, I attained some measure of success, and was full of hope for the future.

Hitherto, I had been unable to visit the north-western part of the province, and the news of a fight having occurred between the Maheria and Bedeyat Arabs furnished a good pretext for a journey to these almost unknown districts. About the middle of December, 1881, I left El Fasher with two hundred infantry and some irregular Shaigia cavalry, under Omar Wad Darho.

The first night after leaving El Fasher we camped near the Migdob wells, about half-way to Kobbé ; and when it was dark, I happened to stroll towards the wells, accompanied by one of my attendants. I was dressed in much the same way as the soldiers, and it was too dark for me to be recognised ; I therefore came close to the well, and watched the women drawing water. Some Shaigia now came up to water their horses, and asked the women for their buckets, which they refused to give. ' We shall first fill our jars,' they said, ' and then you can use the buckets.' ' Your words are as a punishment sent from God,' replied one of the Shaigia ; 'this is the result of bringing liberty into the country. By Allah ! were it not so, and were not Slatin with us, you and your vessels would very soon be our property.' 'God grant him a long life !' was the retort ; and I strolled quietly away, thoroughly pleased to have heard with my own ears an admission from the mouths of Sudanese that they were thankful to the Europeans for having released them from the oppression and violence which had hitherto characterized the system of government in this country.

When about half a day's march beyond Kebkebia, we were overtaken by some mounted messengers, despatched by Adam Omar with a French cipher message from Marcopoli Bey, in the Governor-General's name, which had been sent to Foga, whence it had been posted on to Kebkebia *viâ* El Fasher. It ran as follows : 'A Dervish named Mohammed Ahmed has, without just cause, attacked Rashed Bey near Gedir. Rashed Bey and his troops have been annihilated. This revolt is very serious. Take the necessary steps to prevent malcontents in your province from joining this Dervish.' I sent an immediate answer, as follows : 'Your message received. I shall take the necessary steps to comply with your orders.'

Some time previously I had been told privately that a religious Sheikh had been causing difficulty to the Government by calling on the natives to resist authority. As, however, I had heard nothing of the matter officially, I concluded it had been satisfactorily settled ; but now this annihilation of the Mudir Rashed Bey and his troops was evidently a matter of grave import. The movement must have suddenly assumed large dimensions ; but who would have dreamt the results would have been so terrible and so widespread !

Having started on this expedition, I could not now well give it up without exciting mistrust ; but I determined to bring it to a successful issue with the least possible delay.

It is a strange fact that the Bedeyat, although completely

surrounded by Moslem states and peoples, are almost the
only tribe in this part of Central Africa who still adhere to
their old heathen customs. If their chiefs are asked by
Mohammedans to repeat the creed, they can say, 'There
is no God but God, and Mohammed is his Prophet.' But
beyond this they know nothing ; they are utterly ignorant
of the precepts of the Kuran, and never pray as Moslems.

Under the widespreading branches of an enormous heglik-
tree, and on a spot kept beautifully clean and sprinkled with
fine sand, the Bedeyat beseech an unknown god to direct
them in their undertakings, and to protect them from danger.
They have also religious feasts at uncertain dates, when
they ascend the hills, and on the extreme summits, which
are whitewashed, they offer sacrifices of animals. They
are a fine, stalwart race, very dark in colour, with straight
features, a thin nose and small mouth, and resemble Arabs
more than negroes. The women are famed for their long
flowing hair, and there are some great beauties amongst
them, as one often finds amongst the free Arab tribes.
They generally wear skins of animals round their waists
and loins ; but the higher class and their women dress in
long flowing robes made of white Darfur cotton cloth.
Their food is very plain. Corn does not grow in their
country, and is almost unknown to them. They take the
seeds of the wild pumpkin, which grows there in abundance,
and they soak them in wooden vessels made from the bark
of trees. After taking the outer shells off, they leave the
seeds to steep until they lose their bitterness, and then,
straining them off and mixing them with dates, they grind
them into a sort of flour, which is cooked with meat, and
forms the principal food of the country.

They have also most strange customs as regards inheri-
tance and succession. The cemeteries are generally situated
at some distance from the villages, and when a father dies
the body is taken by all the relatives to be buried. The
ceremony over, on a given signal they all rush together at
the top of their speed to the deceased's house, and he who

Zubeir Pasha.

A Rizighat Warrior.

THE GOVERNMENT OF DARFUR

arrives first and fixes his spear or arrow in it is considered
the rightful heir, and not only becomes possessor of all the
cattle, but also of his father's wives and other women, with
the exception of his own mother. He is at perfect liberty
to marry them if he wishes, or he can set them free. A
man's female household is entirely regulated by his financial
position. It is great or small according as the lord and
master is rich or poor.

We at length arrived at Kamo, where the great Zaghawa
Sheikh Saleh Donkusa informed me that the Bedeyat chiefs
would arrive the next day. In concert with him I selected
the heglik-tree as the place of meeting, which was to be
held one hour after sunrise, and in which he was to act as
the intermediary between myself and the Bedeyat. I then
ordered our tents to be moved to within less than half a mile
of the tree, and early the next morning I had the troops
drawn up in line ready to receive the Bedeyat chiefs, whose
approach Saleh now announced. Standing with my officers
and sanjak, Omar Wad Darho, about one hundred yards in
front of the line, with our servants holding the horses, we
prepared to receive our distinguished visitors, who, guided
by Saleh, were now seen advancing, with their hands
crossed on their chests and heads bowed low. They had
brought an interpreter with them, and through him we
exchanged mutual greeting. I then ordered carpets to be
spread on the ground, and asked them to be seated, whilst
I and my officers sat on small field-chairs; and, having
partaken of sugar and water and dates, we began our
palaver.

The four Bedeyat Sheikhs were tall, fine-looking, middle-
aged men, with good features, and dressed in long white
robes, which no doubt our friend Saleh had prepared for
them ; they also wore the usual straight Arab sword. Their
names were Gar en Nebbi, Bosh, Omar, and Kurukuru ;
but I am not quite sure that these high-sounding Arab
names were not assumed for the occasion. Their attendants,
numbering between sixty and seventy men, dressed in shirts,

and skins, stood some way behind, while Saleh Donkusa
seated himself close to the Sheikhs and the interpreter. The
spokesman, Gar en Nebbi, now addressed the interpreter
with the words ' Kursi Sellem,' to which the latter answered
' Sellem,' indicating that he was ready to translate ; and he
then began : ' We belong to the Bedeyat tribe, and our
fathers and grandfathers have paid tribute to the Sultans
of Darfur every two or three years when an officer was sent
to collect it. You Turks have now subdued the Furs and
have conquered the country, and you have never before
asked us to pay tribute. You [Slatin]—as our friend and
brother Saleh Donkusa has informed us—are the ruler of
this country, and in token of submission we have brought
you ten horses, ten camels, and forty cows. Do you, therefore, fix the amount of tribute to be paid by us.'

It was now my turn to speak, so, repeating the ' Kursi
Sellem,' I began : ' I thank you for your submission, and I
am only going to demand a small tribute ; but I have
specially come here to call on you to return the camels you
stole from the Maheria, and release the prisoners you
captured.' Gar en Nebbi, after a short pause, replied :
' Since the time of our forefathers we have been in constant
feud with the various Arab tribes. If we fight and take
prisoners, it is our custom to allow them to be ransomed.
We have often before released Maheria captives.' I referred
to Sheikh Hasaballa to ask if this was so, and he answered
in the affirmative ; and then I asked whether he had ever
done so since the Egyptian Government had taken possession of the country, or whether he referred to the period in
which they were ruled by the Darfur Sultans. ' Before you
conquered the country,' he answered, ' but only two years
ago, the Maheria invaded our country ; we repulsed them
and drove them out, so that they returned empty-handed.'
I looked at Hasaballa, and saw from his silence that the
Bedeyat was telling the truth. ' That may be so,' I
answered, ' but at that time I was not governing this
country. I am well aware that in those days you did what

you thought was right, and I do not in any way blame you for it ; but as I am now your master, I wish you to act in accordance with my orders. You should, therefore, hand over your prisoners ; but as the Maheria previously attacked you, then I order that instead of returning them all the camels you took, you can retain half, as a reward for your bravery in having prevented them from pillaging your country.' A long pause now took place, and the four Sheikhs discussed the matter between themselves. Gar en Nebbi then answered, ' We shall comply with your orders ; but as it will take a long time to collect the camels, which are scattered throughout the country, it will be easier for us to release the captives.' ' Then look sharp,' said I, ' and carry out these orders as soon as possible ; and when you have done so, I will release you from the payment of this year's tribute. I can quite understand that it may cause you some difficulty to return the camels and pay your taxes as well.'

This arrangement apparently quite satisfied them, and they thanked me profusely ; so I asked them to stay with us till the following day, and Saleh would look after all their wants. Then, mounting our horses, I gave the command to the troops to fire three volleys, which terrified the poor Bedeyat, who had scarcely ever seen firearms. Telling Saleh to bring the Sheikhs before me the next morning at the same hour, I galloped off with my escort to the camp.

During the day I busied myself in considering how best to get back to El Fasher without endangering the success of my present expedition ; I could not wait until the Bedeyat had collected and handed over their captives ; moreover, I was disturbed about the condition of the water-skins supplied by the Maheria, and blamed Hasaballa severely for furnishing such bad equipment. Next morning, when the Sheikhs arrived, I asked them if they had yet despatched men to collect the prisoners and camels ; and when they answered ' No,' I replied in an irritated tone that I could not possibly wait to see my orders carried out. To this Gar en Nebbi answered, ' Master, we are here to carry out your orders; you can return, and we shall deliver over the men and animals to Saleh Donkusa and Hasaballa, who is remaining as his guest.' ' I have another proposal to make,' said I. ' I do not doubt your sincerity and loyalty, but I am anxious to know you better personally; I wish, therefore, you and any others you may desire to bring with you should accompany me to El Fasher, and at the same time tell your representatives to collect the men and animals, and hand them over to Hasaballa, who is staying with Donkusa. When I hear at El Fasher that this has been done, I shall then send you back to your country laden with rich presents. You have never visited El Fasher yet, and you will be interested to see the seat of Government and understand its power, and I sincerely trust that you and Saleh will concur with my proposal; you will be so pleased with all you will see that in future I know you will always comply most readily with my orders.'

Saleh at once answered that he thought the proposal a very good one, and that he was content to stay behind, as he had already seen El Fasher. I saw by the faces of the Bedeyat that the idea pleased them, and, after a long palaver amongst themselves, they made up their minds to accompany me. Knowing that the sooner they carried out my orders about the return of the captives and camels the sooner they would start, they lost no time in nominating good men as their representatives with the tribe, and, selecting six men as their attendants, they announced they were ready to leave; but, before starting, they wished to swear the oath of fidelity, in which, of course, I readily acquiesced. The ceremony was performed as follows: A horse's saddle was brought and placed in the midst of the assembly, and on this was laid a large earthenware dish filled with burning charcoal; a lance was then fixed to the saddle, and the head Sheikhs, with their attendants, now came forward, and, stretching out their hands over the lance and burning charcoal, they recited the following words with great solemnity, ' May my leg never touch the saddle, may my body be smitten with the lance that kills, and may I be consumed by the burning fire, if I ever break the solemn oath of fidelity which I now make to you.'

After this solemn declaration, I had now no doubt of the loyalty and honesty of these people.

That afternoon I gave the order to start, and, accompanied by the four Bedeyat chiefs and their attendants, we left Kamo, having given Saleh and Hasaballa most strict injunctions to inform me without delay when the tribe had complied with my instructions. Anxious to reach El Fasher without further delay, I left the Sheikhs in charge of the infantry, telling the officers to do all that was possible to make their journey comfortable; and then, accompanied by Omar Wad Darho and my Shaigia escort, I set off at a rapid pace.

The first information I received on arrival at El Fasher was the sad news of the sudden death of Emiliani Danziger at Shakka. He had formerly been Mamur of Kobbé, but I had sent for him to represent the Government in Southern Darfur. He had been suffering from heart disease for years, and at last it had carried him off; his officials, who did not understand the suddenness of the disease, thought they might be suspected of poisoning him, and had at once brought his body on a camel to Dara, where the apothecary held a rough *post mortem* examination, and certified that death had occurred from natural causes. His body was buried at Dara, and I afterwards had a stone erected to commemorate my poor countryman who had died in this distant land.

I next learnt that some trouble had arisen at Shakka which would oblige me to go to Dara for a few days. Disquieting rumours also reached us of the state of affairs in Kordofan and Khartum; however, it was generally thought in Government circles that the revolt would be speedily crushed by the military expedition despatched for this purpose.

A few days later the troops with the Bedeyat Sheikhs

arrived, and in order to impress them, I ordered out all the garrison, and in the evening we had a grand firework display in their honour. I entrusted the Mudir with looking after the comfort of my guests, but unfortunately I was not able to stay long with them. As soon as the horses were sufficiently rested I started off again for Dara, accompanied by Darho and his two hundred Shaigias, leaving Said Bey Guma as commandant and representative of the Government during my absence.

CHAPTER IV.

THE KHALIFA'S PERSONAL ACCOUNT OF THE RISE OF THE MAHDI.

Early Life of Mohammed Ahmed, the Mahdi—The religious Tarikas—Mohammed Ahmed quarrels with his Religious Superior—He is refused Forgiveness, and joins a rival Sheikh—He is joined by Abdullahi et Taaishi—The Mahdi secretly tells Abdullahi of his Divine Mission—The Failure to seize Mohammed Ahmed on Abba Island—The Mahdi's Hejira to Jebel Gedir—He nominates his Khalifas—The Defeat of Rashed Bey and Yusef Pasha Shellali—Effect of the Mahdi's Victories in Kordofan—The Mahdi's Intrigues with the Inhabitants of El Obeid—Futility of the Steps taken by the Government to cope with the Revolt.

THE revolt raised by the so-called Dervish proved to be of a very serious nature.

This man, Mohammed Ahmed, was born near the Island of Argo, in Dongola, and was of a poor and obscure family, but who claimed to be 'Ashraf,' or descendants of the 'Prophet.' Their claims to this dignity, however, were not inquired into or acknowledged by anyone. In general he was known as a Dongolawi. His father was an ordinary fiki, or religious teacher, and had given him his early instruction in reading the Kuran and in writing, and when still a child had taken him to Khartum, but he himself had died on his journey, near Kerreri, and here his son subsequently erected a tomb to him, known as the ' Kubbet es Sayed Abdullahi ' (the dome of Sayed Abdullahi).

Young Mohammed Ahmed was now left entirely to his own resources. He studied assiduously, and being of a deeply religious disposition, he became a great favourite with his master, who taught him to learn the Kuran by heart, and gave him his early instruction in theology ; he subsequently went to Berber, and became the pupil of the well-known Mohammed el Kheir (formerly Mohammed ed Dekkeir), who completed his religious education. He remained for several years in Berber continually studying, and his unassuming nature, intelligence, and religious zeal made him a great favourite with his instructors. When he arrived at manhood he quitted Berber and went to Khartum, where he became a disciple of the celebrated and highly revered Sheikh Mohammed Sherif, whose father, Nur ed Dayem, and grandfather, Et Tayeb, had been the principal exponents of the Sammania Tarika, or doctrine.

The meaning of the word ' tarika ' is literally ' way '; hence ' Sheikh et Tarika ' signifies ' the guide to the way.' The duties of these holy personages consist in writing a certain number of prayers and texts of the Prophet, which the devotees are called upon to repeat a certain number of times, and thus facilitate the ' way ' to those heavenly mansions which are the goal of all true believers. The Sheikhs et Tarika are therefore exponents of various doctrines, and each one bears the name of the original founder of the order, such as the ' Khatmia,' the ' Khadria,' the ' Tegania,' the ' Sammania,' etc. They are held in high respect by their disciples, who are their most devoted and obedient adherents.

Mohammed Ahmed soon showed himself a most zealous and ardent supporter of the Sammania tarika, and became very devoted to its head, Sheikh Mohammed Sherif. He now went to live on the Island of Abba, on the White Nile, near Kawa, surrounded by several devoted disciples. They earned a livelihood by cultivating the lands, and received frequent gifts from religious persons who passed up or down the Nile. Mohammed Ahmed's grand-uncle, Mohammed Sharfi, had resided on the island for some years, and the young zealot had married his daughter. His two brothers, Mohammed and Hamed, also lived there, drove a good trade in boat-building, and supported the young fiki, who had hollowed out for himself a cave in the mud-bank, and lived here in almost entire seclusion, fasting often for days, and occasionally paying a visit to the head of the order to assure him of his devotion and obedience.

One day it fell out that Mohammed Sherif, as is the custom on such occasions, had gathered together his Sheikhs and disciples to celebrate the feast of the circumcision of his sons; he had also given out that his guests might amuse themselves by singing and dancing as they liked, and that as such feasts were occasions of rejoicing, he would pardon, in God's name, any sins that might be committed during the festivities which were contrary to the religious law. But the godly fiki, Mohammed Ahmed, pointed out to his friends that singing, dancing, and playing were transgressions against the laws of God, and that no man, be he even Sheikh et Tarika, could forgive such sins. These views reached the ears of Mohammed Sherif, who, entirely disagreeing with Mohammed Ahmed's arguments, and being withal very angry at this assumption on the part of his disciple, called on him to justify himself. Consequently Mohammed Ahmed, in the presence of all the inferior Sheikhs and fikis, came in the most humble manner before Mohammed Sherif and besought his forgiveness. Sherif, however, abused him roundly, called him a traitor and a sedition-monger who had broken his vow of obedience and fidelity, and ignominiously struck him off the list of disciples of the Sammania order.

Thoroughly humbled and subdued, Mohammed Ahmed now went to one of his relatives and asked him to make a sheba,* and with this on his neck, and his head besprinkled

---

* A sheba is a piece of forked wood which is fixed on the neck by way of punishment, and in this position is very painful.

with ashes, he again returned in deep repentance to Mohammed Sherif, begging his forgiveness. The latter, however,
utterly refused to have anything further to say to him, and
in despair Mohammed Ahmed returned to his family in
Abba. He held the founders of the Sammania order,
Sheikhs Nur ed Dayem and et Tayeb, in the greatest
respect, and to be removed with ignominy from his beloved
tarika was a disgrace too hard to be borne. Shortly afterwards Mohammed Sherif happened to be in the neighbourhood, and again Mohammed Ahmed appeared before him
in the sheba and ashes, and once more implored forgiveness. ' Be off, you traitor !' shouted Mohammed Sherif.
' Get away, you wretched Dongolawi, who fears not God
and opposes his master and teacher ! You have verified
the words of the saying, " Ed Dongolawi Shaitan mugalled
bigild el insan " (The Dongolawi is the devil in the skin of
a man). By your words you try to spread dissension
amongst the people. Be off with you ! I shall never forgive you !'

Kneeling in silence, his head bowed low, Mohammed
Ahmed listened to these scathing words, then rising, he
went sadly away. Tears streamed down his cheeks, but
they were not now tears of repentance. Rage and anger
burned within him, and these feelings were heightened by
the knowledge of his powerlessness to do anything by which
to wipe out this disgrace and insult. Boiling over with
indignation, he returned to his home and announced to his
faithful disciples that he had been finally abandoned by
Mohammed Sherif, and that he now intended to apply to
Sheikh el Koreishi, who lived near Messallamia, to receive
him into his order. This Sheikh had succeeded the holy
Sheikh et Tayeb, the grandfather of Mohammed Sherif, and
was one of those authorized to maintain and teach the
Sammania doctrines as he considered right, and on this
account there was considerable jealousy between him and
Mohammed Sherif.

In due time Sheikh el Koreishi's reply was received,

saying that he would accept him gladly. Mohammed Ahmed and his disciples now made all preparations to proceed to Messallamia, and were on the point of starting when a message was received from Mohammed Sherif directing him to appear before him, when he would give him a full pardon, and permit him to resume his old functions; but to this Mohammed Ahmed sent back a dignified answer that he felt perfectly innocent of any crime, and sought no forgiveness from him, and that, moreover, he had no desire to lower him in the eyes of the world by bringing about a meeting between him and ' a wretched Dongolawi.'

Sheikh Koreishi now received him with open arms, and the incident between the godly but cunning Mohammed Ahmed and his late spiritual guide spread far and wide in the Sudan. That an inferior in a religious order should have refused the forgiveness of his superior was an unheard-of proceeding; but Mohammed Ahmed did not hesitate now to proclaim openly that he had left his late superior because he could no longer have any respect for a master who acted contrary to the religious law. And in this way he secured an immense amount of public sympathy, which brought his name prominently forward, and added considerably to his prestige. Even in distant Darfur the matter was the principal topic of conversation, and his refusal to accept forgiveness made him the hero of the hour.

He obtained Sheikh Koreishi's permission to return to Abba, where he received visitors from all parts, who sought the blessing of this holy man ; and common people now crowded to the island, seeing in him a sympathetic leader who was bold enough to openly defy his superiors. He received quantities of gifts, and these he openly distributed amongst the poor, thus earning the epithet of ' Zahed ' (the renouncer, or one who has renounced the good things of this life). He then made a journey through Kordofan, where the towns and villages abound with religious fikis of the most ignorant and superstitious description. Amongst them he had an enormous success. He also wrote a pamphlet, which he distributed amongst his specially trusted adherents, summoning them as true believers to do all in their power to purify the religion, which was becoming debased and insulted by the corruption of the Government, and the utter disregard of the officials for the tenets of the true faith.

A few months later the Sheikh el Koreishi died, and Mohammed Ahmed and his disciples lost no time in going at once to Messallamia, where they erected a tomb, or dome, to his memory.

It was while here that a certain Abdullahi bin Mohammed, of the Taaisha section of the Baggara (cattle-owning) tribe of south-western Darfur, presented himself to Mohammed Ahmed, and sought permission to be admitted into the Sammania Tarika; his request was granted, and Abdullahi swore eternal fidelity to his new master. This man was the eldest of the four sons of Mohammed et Taki, of the Juberat division of the Taaisha tribe, which in its turn was descended from the 'Aulad um Sura.' His three other brothers were Yakub, Yusef, and Summani; he also had a sister named Fatma. The father was on bad terms with his relatives, and determined to proceed on pilgrimage with his whole family to Mecca, where he resolved to settle, and end his days in close proximity to the birthplace of his Prophet. Those who knew Et Taki described him as a good man, scrupulous in his attendance to his religious duties, and capable of curing diseases and insanity by means of heggabs, or religious charms; he was also a teacher of the Kuran. Of his sons, Abdullahi and Yusef were the most unmanageable, and the father had the greatest difficulty in making them learn by heart even the few passages from the Kuran necessary for the ordinary prayers. Yakub and Summani, on the other hand, had more of their father's quiet disposition, and, having learnt their verses and commentaries, were able to help him in his religious duties.

The family had, it appears, joined the Furs in combating Zubeir's entry to Darfur, and the latter relates how, during the fight at Shakka, he took Abdullahi prisoner, and was about to have him shot, when some of the Ulema craved pardon for him, which he granted. Abdullahi, in his grati- tude, subsequently sought out Zubeir secretly, and an- nounced to him that he had had a dream, in which it had been shown to him that he was the expected Mahdi, and that he (Abdullahi) was to be one of his faithful followers. 'I told him,' relates Zubeir, 'that I was not the Mahdi; but that when I became aware of the wickedness of the Arabs, and how they blocked the roads, I came to open them and establish trade.'

Et Taki and the family quitted their home when Zubeir had concluded peace, and, travelling *viâ* Kalaka to Shakka, they had remained there two years, and had proceeded thence *viâ* Dar Homr and El Obeid to Dar Gimr, where they re- mained the guests of the head Sheikh for some months, and where Et Taki died, and was buried by the head Sheikh, Asaker Abu Kalam, at Sherkéla. Before his death he urged on his eldest son, Abdullahi, to take refuge with some religious Sheikh on the Nile, then immigrate to Mecca, and never return again to their country.

Leaving his brothers and sister under the care of Sheikh Asaker Abu Kalam, in accordance with the dying wishes of his father, Abdullahi set out for the Nile Valley; and, when making inquiries along the road, he heard of the dissension between Mohammed Ahmed and his Sheikh, Mohammed Sherif, and he resolved to go to the former, and ask him to allow him to join the order. 'It was a very troublesome journey,' said Abdullahi bin Sayed Mohammed, Khalifat el Mahdi (his full name), to me some years later, when he first became ruler of the Sudan; for at that time he used to talk openly to me, and had not learnt to mistrust me, as he did latterly. In those days, as I shall subsequently relate, he would send for me, and chat with me alone by the hour, seated on his beautifully-made angareb, over which a palm- mat was spread, whilst I sat beside him on the ground, with my legs tucked up under me. 'Yes, indeed, it was a very troublesome journey,' he repeated. 'At that time my entire property consisted of one donkey, and he had a gall on his back, so that I could not ride him; but I made him carry my water-skin and a bag of corn, over which I spread my rough cotton garment, and drove him along in front of me. At that time I wore the wide cotton shirt, like the rest of my tribe. You remember it, do you not, Abdel Kader? For you have only recently come from my beautiful country' [he always used to call me 'Abdel Kader,' unless there happened to be present another man of the same name, when he would call me 'Abdel Kader Saladin,' *i.e.*, Slatin]. 'My clothes and my dialect at once marked me out as a stranger wherever I went; and when I crossed the Nile, I was frequently greeted with, "What do you want? Go back to your country; there is nothing to steal here." The Nile people do not think well of us,' he continued, 'because the merchants going west to Zubeir, in Bahr el Ghazal and to our countries, were frequently maltreated by the Arabs; and when I asked them where the Mahdi, who was known as Mohammed Ahmed, lived, they gazed at me incredulously, saying, "What are you going to him for? He would not soil his lips by even mentioning the name of your race." Everyone, however, did not treat me in this way; some would take pity on me and direct me. Once, when passing through a village, the people wanted to take my donkey away, saying that it had been stolen from them the year before; and they would have succeeded, had not an elderly and God-fearing man interposed, and allowed me to pursue my way. I was continually mocked and hooted at during my long journey; and had not a few people out of sheer pity occasionally given me some food, I must have starved. At length I reached Messallamia, and here I found the Mahdi busily engaged in building the tomb of the late Sheikh el Koreishi. On seeing him I entirely forgot all the troubles I had suffered on my journey, and was content to simply look at him and listen to his teaching. For several hours I was too timid to dare to speak to him; but at length I plucked up courage, and in a few words told him my story,

and about the sad condition of my brothers and sister, and
I begged him, for the sake of God and His Prophet, to
allow me to become one of his disciples. He did so, and
gave me his hand, which I kissed most fervently, and I
swore entire submission to him as long as I lived. This
oath I kept most scrupulously until the angel of death overtook him ; and some day he will overtake us, and therefore
we should ever be ready to meet him.'

Pausing for a moment, he gazed at me, and I at once
said, ' Yes, indeed, sire, you have faithfully kept your
promise, and the Lord God Almighty has rewarded you;
for you, who at one time were despised and rejected, have
now become absolute lord and sovereign of this land. Those
who insulted you at that time should indeed be thankful
that you have not wreaked vengeance on their heads. A
man capable of such restraint must indeed be the successor
of the Prophet.' Abdullahi, I knew, loved praise and
flattery, and on this occasion I perhaps almost exceeded the
limits ; but I was most anxious that he should continue to
tell me his story.

' When I had taken the oath,' continued Abdullahi, ' the
Mahdi called one of his disciples, named Ali, and said to
him, " You are brethren from this day ; give each other
your mutual support, trust in God, and do you, Abdullahi,
obey the orders of your brother." Ali was very good to
me ; he was as poor as myself, but when the Mahdi sent
him any food, he always shared it fairly with me. During
the day we carried bricks required for building the tomb,
and at night we slept side by side. In a month the dome
was complete. At this time the Mahdi received hundreds
of visitors, and had little time to look at or think of me ;
still, I knew that I had found a place in his heart, and he
appointed me one of his flag-bearers.* When we left
Messallamia, people flocked around us to gaze at the Mahdi,

* When religious sheikhs go out to preach, they are generally preceded by men bearing flags, on which texts from the Kuran are
inscribed.

whom they at that time called only Mohammed Ahmed, and
listen to his teachings and seek his blessing.

'It was in this way that we marched to the Island of
Abba. My sandals were worn out, and I had to give my
donkey to a Mukaddum [superior disciple] to carry a sick
man ; but at length we reached the Mahdi's house, and now
I fell very ill with dysentery. My brother Ali took me to
his little straw hut, which was scarcely large enough to hold
two people, looked after my food, and, as I was in bed, he
used to fetch water from the river to enable me to perform
my " wadu " [religious ablution].

'One evening he went to fetch the water, but did not
return ; and the next day I was told that he had been
attacked and killed by a crocodile—Allah yerhamu ! Allah
yeghfurlu ! (May God be merciful ! may God forgive him
his sins !)' I repeated these words after the Khalifa, adding,
' Sire, how great is your patience ! and therefore has God
exalted you. Now may I ask you if, during your illness,
the Mahdi paid any attention to you ?' ' No,' replied
Khalifa Abdullahi, ' the Mahdi wished to try me. It was
not till after Ali's death, and when I lay helpless in the hut,
that he was told I was ill. One evening he came to see me.
I was too weak to get up, so he sat beside me, and gave me
some warm medida [a sort of meal pap which, mixed with
melted butter, is used as a stimulant] out of my pumpkin
gourd, saying, " Drink that, it will do you good ; trust in
God." He then left me, and shortly afterwards some of
the brethren arrived, and took me, by his order, to a cottage
near his own hut. He himself lived in a simple tukul
[straw hut]. From the moment I had taken the medida
which he had given me, I felt better ; he had said it would
do me good, and the Mahdi always speaks the truth, and
cannot lie.' ' Yes, indeed,' I interposed, ' the Mahdi is
faithful and true, and you, as his successor, have followed
exactly in his footsteps.' ' Once near him,' continued the
Khalifa, ' I recovered rapidly, for I saw the Mahdi daily ;
he was as the light of my eyes, and my mind was at rest.

He used to ask about my family, and said they had better remain in Khordofan for the present. " Trust in God" was always the last thing he said to me. He now used often to come and talk privately with me, and one day he intrusted me with the secret of his divine mission. He was appointed as Mahdi by God, he said, and had been taken by the Prophet into the presence of the apostles and saints. But long before he intrusted me with his secret—indeed, from the first moment I beheld his face—I knew that he was the messenger of God—el Mahdi el Muntazer [the expected guide]. Yes, these were indeed happy days, and we had then no cares or troubles ; and now, Abdel Kader, as it is getting late, you had better go to bed.' ' May God grant you a long life, and may He strengthen you to lead the true believers into the right path,' said I, and I quitted his presence with the usual salute.

In Abdullahi, the Mahdi had a ready instrument at hand for this great work. It is strange to think that this man might never have risen to any importance had he not quarrelled with Mohammed Sherif ; but now the reputation he had already gained amongst the inhabitants of the Gezira (the country lying between the Blue and White Niles) raised hopes in his mind that he was destined for a high position. He now began to secretly tell his special adherents that the time had come when religion must be purified, that this was to be his work, and that those of them who wished might join him in it. But he always called himself the slave of God, and made believe that he was acting entirely on inspiration from above. Abdullahi was able to give him full information about the western tribes, who, he said, being powerful and courageous, would gladly seize an occasion to fight for the religion of God and His Prophet, and to conquer or die. To secure their adherence he advised Mohammed Ahmed to make a tour through Kordofan, and setting out, they proceeded to Dar Gimr, where Abdullahi's family immediately joined them and became his faithful adherents. He told them, however, that the time had not yet come for them to leave their homes ; for the present they would be more useful in inciting the local inhabitants.

From Dar Gimr he proceeded to El Obeid, where he visited all the principal chiefs and Sheikhs, religious and other, and by inquiring carefully into their views and opinions, he gradually laid the foundations for his great design. In the strictest secrecy he told those of whose fidelity he was assured that he had a divine mission to cleanse and purify the religion, already polluted and debased by corrupt officials. In El Obeid his most trusted confidant was the Sayed el Mekki, the head of the religious Sheikhs; but he advised that for the present no active steps should be taken, as the Government was very powerful, and the tribes were too split up and disunited to be able to raise a revolt. Mohammed Ahmed took a more sanguine view, and between them it was agreed that Mekki should observe absolute secrecy, and should take no steps until Mohammed Ahmed should begin the movement, when he promised him his entire support.

After leaving El Obeid, he proceeded to Tagalla, where he interviewed Mek Adam Um Daballo, the ruler of the district, who received him very kindly, but who, on the advice of his Kadi, refused to make any promises of assistance. He now returned to Abba, *via* Sherkéla.

During this tour Mohammed Ahmed had full opportunities of seeing for himself the state of the country, and he was soon convinced that there was a spirit of the most bitter hostility against the authorities on the part of the poorer population, who, as I have already pointed out, were taxed out of all proportion to their property, and who suffered terrible oppression and tyranny at the hands of the self-seeking and unscrupulous tax-gatherers who infested the country. Amongst the latter, there were now a considerable number of Sudanese, who lost no opportunity of enriching themselves and of putting their relatives in positions of secondary importance, to help them to this end.

As a case in point, Gordon's nomination of the wealthy Sudanese merchant Elias as Pasha and Governor-General of Kordofan created an immense amount of illfeeling in the country; and the same might be said of his assistant, Abderrahman ben Naga, also a wealthy Kordofan merchant. Both of them were capable men, and understood the management of the people, but they worked entirely for their own interests and those of their relatives. Moreover, a spirit of jealousy became rampant amongst other Sudanese of high rank, who considered themselves quite as capable of filling high positions as those who had been selected in preference to them. Consequently, when Elias Pasha sent orders to Mek Adam to pay his taxes, he refused point blank, as he was of royal descent. 'I pay for goods I buy from merchants, but I do not pay tribute to them,' said Mek Adam proudly to the officials who had been sent to him. At the same time he sent to El Obeid to inquire if all the Turks and other 'Whites' had died, as the Government had now given high positions to men who were merely merchants, instead of to persons of high descent. These were the reasons for the subsequent discharge of Elias Pasha and Abderrahman from their official positions, and their substitution by Turks and Egyptians.

As regards the Europeans, there were very few of us; but, as a rule, we were liked and respected, because the people trusted our word; but I do not doubt that we also gave them cause to be dissatisfied with us. With probably the best intentions in the world, we would issue rules and regulations entirely at variance with the manners, customs, and traditions of the Sudanese. There is also no doubt that our attitude in regard to the slave question caused wide-spread discontent. The religion permitted slavery, and from time immemorial the ground had been cultivated and the cattle tended by slaves. That slave-hunting and slave-driving led to the perpetration of the most horrible cruelties and bloodshed, I do not for a moment hesitate to admit; but this was a matter of very little concern to the slave-buyers, who, as a rule, did not illtreat their slaves. Now we, by our activity and energy, had not only made the export of slaves from the Black countries almost impossible, but we listened to the complaints of slaves against their masters, and invariably set them free.

Mohammed Ahmed cleverly seized the occasion of all this discontent to act ; he was well aware that religion was the only possible means of uniting all these discordant elements and widely diversified tribes who were at continual feud with each other; he therefore declared himself the ' Mahdi el Muntazer,' thus at once creating himself a personality which must be superior to all others, and hoping by this means to drive out of the country the hated Turks, Egyptians, and Europeans. But still he thought the time for an open declaration was not yet ripe ; he therefore continued to increase the number of his trusted adherents, till at length the nature of his divine mission became an open secret.

Some time previous to this, Rauf Pasha, Governor-General at Khartum, had been secretly told by Mohammed Sherif of Mohammed Ahmed's intentions ; but it was known that the early differences between the two religious Sheikhs had greatly embittered Sherif, and consequently the authorities did not lay much store by his statements, and merely concluded that Mohammed Ahmed was a holy man who had obtained a certain hold over the people, owing to his superior sanctity.

But now the Government learnt from quite another source that this man was a danger to the public peace, and therefore they determined to put an end to the matter, once and for all.

For this purpose Rauf Pasha sent for Mohammed Bey Abu es Saud, who was known to Mohammed Ahmed, and despatched him in a steamer to Abba with orders to bring the Sheikh to Khartum. Mohammed Ahmed's friends, however, gave him timely warning, and told him that if he came to Khartum he would in all likelihood be kept there,

through the intrigues of Mohammed Sherif. When, therefore, Saud appeared at Abba, he was welcomed by Abdullahi
and Mohammed Ahmed's brother, who conducted him to
the Sheikh. Abu Saud now informed him of the reports—
false, he admitted—which had been circulated about him,
and strongly advised him to come to Khartum and justify
himself before his master, the Governor-General. 'What!'
shouted Mohammed Ahmed, rising suddenly, and striking
his chest with his hand, 'by the grace of God and His
Prophet, I am master of this country, and never shall I go
to Khartum to justify myself.'

Abu Saud drew back terrified; he then tried to calm him
by soft words ; but Mohammed Ahmed, who had previously
planned this scene with Abdullahi and his brother, continued
to talk vehemently, and urged Abu Saud to believe in the
truth of what he said.

Abu Saud was now, however, much concerned about the
safety of his own person, and as soon as he could beat a
safe retreat, he did so, and returned to Khartum to inform
the astonished Governor - General of the failure of his
mission.

Mohammed Ahmed now realized that there was no time
to be lost ; his future depended entirely on his own immediate exertions, and he did not hesitate to instantly write to
his adherents throughout the length and breadth of the
Sudan, stirring them up against the Government, while he
directed his own immediate followers to prepare forthwith
for the Jehad.

In the meantime Rauf Pasha was not idle. Realizing,
after his interview with Abu Saud, that the matter was very
serious, he resolved to despatch two companies, each under
the command of an adjutant-major, to seize this fanatic ;
and thinking to create emulation between them, he promised
that the officer who succeeded in capturing him should be
promoted at once to the rank of major. But this plan only
ended in creating discord, and the consequences were direful
in the extreme. The troops, under the chief command of

Abu Saud, were embarked in the steamer *Ismaïlia*, which had been armed with a gun, and, quitting Khartum early in August, 1881, they proceeded to Abba; but on the journey dissensions arose between the two officers and Abu Saud. Meanwhile Mohammed Ahmed, who had news of the despatch of the steamer, collected his people, and, obtaining help from the Degheim and Kenana tribes near him, whom he summoned to join in a Jehad, he made all preparations to offer resistance, stirring up religious enthusiasm by declaring that the Prophet had appeared to him and announced that all persons taking part in this religious war should earn the title of ' Sheikh Abdel Kader el Gilani ' and ' Emir el Aulia,'* titles highly prized amongst Moslems. Now, however, that matters had become really serious, those who came forward and offered to give up their property and lay down their lives for the great cause were not numerous.

The steamers arrived off Abba at sunset, and, in spite of Abu Saud's appeals, the two officers determined to disembark at once. But the commander, into whose heart fear had entered when he heard Mohammed Ahmed declaring that he was ' master of the land,' remained on board with his gun, and anchored in mid-stream. Both officers, entirely ignorant of the locality, and each jealous of the other winning the tempting reward, advanced by different paths in the dead of night along the muddy banks towards Mohammed Ahmed's settlement. The latter, with his adherents, had quitted the huts, and, armed with swords, lances, and clubs, had hidden themselves in the high grass, whilst the troops, arriving from opposite directions, now opened a hot fire on the empty village, with the result that each inflicted considerable loss on the other; and in the midst of this hopeless confusion the villagers leapt from their ambush and created terrible havoc amongst the

* Favourites of God. The expression occurs in the Kuran in the following verse : ' Are not the favourites of God those on whom no fear shall come, nor shall they be put to grief ?' (Surah x. 73).

already demoralized men, who fled in all directions. A few
only succeeded in reaching the bank and swimming out
to the steamer; and Abu Saud, now thoroughly terrified,
wished to return to Khartum, but was at last induced by
the captain to stay till the following morning, in the hope
of picking up fugitives. None, however, came, and at
dawn he steamed back at full speed with his direful news.

The effect of this success on Mohammed Ahmed and his
adherents can be readily understood; they had suffered
little or no loss, though he himself had been slightly
wounded in the arm, and Abdullahi, who dressed the
wound, counselled that this little accident should be kept
secret from the rest. Still, the number of his followers was
not largely increased, as the local people were convinced
that Government would take strong measures to suppress
the revolt, and they would not risk the losses which they
felt certain would ensue.

Mohammed Ahmed, strongly urged by Abdullahi and his
brothers to increase the distance between himself and the
Khartum authorities, now resolved to retreat to southern
Kordofan; and to avoid this move being considered a flight,
he announced to his adherents that he had received an
inspiration to proceed to Jebel Masa,* and there await
further Divine instructions. Before quitting Abba, he
appointed, also in accordance with the Divine Will, his four
Khalifas. The first of these was Abdullahi, who (the
precedent of the Prophet being adopted) represented the
Khalifa Abu Bakr es Sadik; Ali Wad Helu, of the
Degheim tribe (White Nile), was chosen to represent the
Khalifa Omar ibn el Khattab; and the representative of
the fourth Khalifa, Ali el Karrar, was Mohammed esh
Sherif, one of Mohammed Ahmed's relatives, who was then
only a boy. The chair of the third Khalifa, Osman ibn

* The Mahdi is supposed to come from Jebel Masa, in North Africa;
but the astute Mohammed Ahmed did not hesitate to call Jebel Gedir,
which was to be his destination in Kordofan, by this name, and thus
fulfil one of the principal conditions of a ' Mahdi.'

Affan, was not filled for the moment, but was subsequently offered to and refused by the great Sheikh Es Sennusi, of Northern Africa.

To move this large following across the river was now a matter of some difficulty, for the people who owned boats, fearing that they might be accused of complicity, at first refused; but at length all—including a large contingent of Degheim and Kenana Arabs, who joined at the last moment — were transferred to the west bank; and, advancing into the Dar Gimr country, Mohammed Ahmed summoned the inhabitants of the districts through which he passed to follow him to Jebel Masa. The greatest enthusiasm now prevailed amongst his followers, who lost no opportunity of telling the credulous and superstitious populations through which they passed of the wonderful miracles performed by the Mahdi. On one occasion, quite ignorant of any danger, he halted with only a few followers in close proximity to the camp of a certain adjutant-major named Mohammed Guma, who, with a party of sixty soldiers, was collecting taxes. The latter, fearing the responsibility he might incur by attacking him without orders, referred to El Obeid for instructions; but long before they arrived the Mahdi had rejoined the bulk of his people and had continued his march; so this golden opportunity was lost. Years afterwards I met the unfortunate Guma in a sad and miserable plight in Obdurman. ' Ah !' said he, ' if I had only known then that I should be reduced to walking about barefoot, and begging my bread, I should not have asked for instructions, and so allowed that wretched Dongolawi to escape; it would have been better to have been killed than to have endured the miseries of this wretched existence.'

Another excellent opportunity of capturing him was also lost. It happened that Giegler Pasha had been ordered to come to El Obeid to represent the Governor-General in connection with a case of embezzlement by a district inspector and wealthy Sudan merchant named Abdel Hadi; hearing

that the so-called Mahdi was in the neighbourhood, he
despatched, towards the end of September, Mohammed
Said Pasha with four companies to arrest him and bring
him to El Obeid. But, either by design or through carelessness, the expedition failed in its object; the troops,
apparently, halted during the day at the place in which the
rebels had slept the previous night, and after thus uselessly
wasting three days, they returned to El Obeid, the result
being that they were discredited as being afraid to attack,
and the Mahdi's prestige rose proportionately.

It had been Mohammed Ahmed's intention to stay for a
time at Jebel Tagalla; but Mek Adam, learning of this,
sent one of his sons to him with a gift of corn and sheep,
bearing a message that he thought he had better retire
further into the interior. He was therefore obliged to continue his journey, and after a long and troublesome march
at length reached Jebel Gedir, where, in addition to the
local inhabitants, a section of the Kenana tribe now resided.

At this time Rashed Bey was Governor of Fashoda; and,
being fully informed of the Mahdi's movements, resolved to
attack him before he became more powerful. A German
named Berghof was also in Fashoda. He was formerly a
photographer in Khartum, but Rauf Pasha had sent him up
the river as an inspector for the suppression of slavery.
Rashed now advanced, accompanied by Berghof and Kaiku
Bey, king of the Shilluks, towards Gedir. Entirely under-
rating the enemy with whom he had to deal, he marched
with no military precautions, fell into a carefully prepared
ambush, and some fourteen hundred of his men were annihilated. So sudden was the attack that there was not even
time to fire a rocket. Rashed and a few of his personal
attendants made a gallant defence, but were soon overpowered by superior numbers and killed.

This defeat occurred on 9th December, and Mohammed
Ahmed no longer hesitated to call himself the Mahdi. His
prestige, especially in the eyes of the Arabs, rose enormously;
nevertheless, his relations with his immediate neighbours

were not of the best. Khalifa Abdullahi, in subsequent conversations with me in Omdurman, referred to this period, as far as I can recollect, in the following words: ' We arrived at last at Gedir, thoroughly tired out after our long and troublesome journey. The Mahdi had only one horse, and that of the inferior Abyssinian breed, while I had to walk almost the whole distance; but God grants strength to those true believers who are ready to lay down their lives for the faith. My brothers, Yakub, Yusuf, and Sammani had joined us with their families, also my stepmother, who was nursing my baby at her breast. My brother Harun, too, would not stay behind, so he also joined us. I was always greatly concerned about my wife, stepmother, and child, who is Osman Sheikh ed Din, whom you now see before you. It did not so much matter for us men; troubles and afflictions are sent us by God, and we bear them, only too thankful that we should be chosen by Him to raise the faith which had been trodden down to the dust, and to teach our brethren. But,' said he, smiling, ' teaching won't bring us food for our women and children. People flocked to us in crowds, it is true; but most of them were even more destitute than ourselves, and came to us for support. Those who were well off shunned us,—riches are the curse of this world,—and those who have them will be deprived of the joys of Paradise. The people whose countries we crossed did not give us much help; but the little he got the Mahdi graciously offered to the pilgrims, whom he considered as his guests. When I heard the women and children weeping, I felt sometimes that my heart would break; but when I gazed at the Mahdi's face I trusted in God and became at rest. Patience, Abdel Kader, is the highest virtue. Practise that, and God will reward you.'

The defeat of Rashed Bey awakened the Government to a sense of the serious nature of the revolt, and an expedition was at once organized and placed under the command of Yusef Pasha Shellali, who had greatly distinguished himself in Gessi's campaign in Bahr el Ghazal, and was noted for

his courage and resource. A reinforcement of a battalion
of infantry and some volunteers, under the command of
Abdalla Wad Dafalla (the brother of Ahmed Wad Dafalla),
with Abd el Hadi and Sultan Dima, was also to be sent
from Kordofan.

Meanwhile the Mahdi despatched letters in all directions,
proclaiming his victories and his Divine mission. He summoned all to join the Jehad, giving the name of Ansar* to
his followers, and promising them four-fifths of the booty
taken in war (the remaining fifth he reserved for himself),
while to those who should fall fighting for God and His
religion he held out the certainty of the fullest enjoyment of
the pleasures of Paradise. Thus did he pander to the main
characteristics of the Sudanese, viz., fanaticism and greed.

Yusef Pasha Shellali's force, which numbered some four
thousand men, was composed of regular infantry under
Mohammed Bey Suleiman and Hassan Effendi Rifki, whom
I had previously discharged ; the irregular cavalry were
placed under the courageous Shaigia Melek, Taha Abu
Sidr, and leaving Khartum on 15th March, 1882, they proceeded to Kowa, where they awaited the reinforcements
expected from El Obeid.

Abdalla Wad Dafalla, however, found it no easy matter
to collect volunteers. There was a general feeling that it was
wrong to fight against a man of piety, and, moreover, as the
Mahdi and his followers were little else than beggars, there
was no enticement of rich plunder to allure them. Besides
all this, Elias Pasha, the richest merchant in Kordofan and
the ex-Governor, was the deadly enemy of the Dafalla
family, and exercised all his influence, which was still considerable, in preventing men joining him. However, Abdalla
had agreed with the authorities to proceed, and, including
regulars, the force with which he left El Obeid numbered
some two thousand men ; and joining with the remainder
at Kowa, the entire expedition of six thousand strong pro-

* That is, the ' Helpers '—a term given by the Prophet Mohammed
to the early converts of El Medina.

ceeded to Fashoda, which was reached in the middle of May.

After a short rest, Yusef Pasha advanced west, and camped, on the evening of 6th June, at Mesat, near Jebel Gedir, confident of success. Why should such men as Yusef Pasha, Mohammed Bey, and Abu Sidr fear a starving crowd of sickly, half-famished, and almost naked Arabs? Had they not won victories on the White Nile at Duffilé? Had they not conquered Bahr el Ghazal, and brought the proud Sultans of Darfur to submission? What could this ill-armed and ignorant fiki do? Abdalla Wad Dafalla alone raised a note of warning that they should not underrate the danger. He had had a fall from his horse when marching out of El Obeid, which is considered a bad omen in the Sudan; but who was going to listen to this preacher in the wilderness? They did not even think it worth while to cut down a few thorn bushes to make a zariba, but merely picked up a little of the scrub lying close by, and formed a rough enclosure, utterly inadequate for defence; so the Mahdi's sickly, half-famished, and almost naked Arabs fell on Yusef Pasha's army in the early dawn of the 7th June. Dashing through the slight inclosure, they were on the sleeping soldiers in a moment, and made short work of them. Yusef Pasha and Abu Sidr were killed in their night-shirts at the doors of their tents, and in a few minutes there was scarcely a man left alive. Abu Sidr's concubine rushed at her master's murderers, and shot two of them with a revolver, but she fell prone over his body, stabbed to the heart. Abdalla Wad Dafalla, with a few of his attendants, alone made a short stand, but they soon shared the fate of their companions.

When anything unusual happens in uncivilized countries, it is always considered by the natives as supernatural; and this was exactly the effect of Yusef Pasha's disaster on the credulous and superstitious minds of the Sudanese. For sixty years the country had been governed by the Turks and Egyptians. If the tribes refused to pay their taxes, they were invariably punished; and no one dared to question for a moment the right of the authorities to do so. Now this holy fiki, Mohammed Ahmed, had suddenly appeared on the scene. With a crowd of ill-armed and undisciplined men he had inflicted several crushing defeats on the well-armed and well-equipped Government troops. There could now be no doubt he was the ' Mahdi el Muntazer,' the expected Mahdi!

The defeat of Yusef Pasha placed the whole of southern Kordofan in his hands, and now he was in a position to make good his deficiencies. He had gained money, arms, horses, and loot of all sorts, and these he distributed amongst the chiefs of tribes who now flocked to him. They believed most firmly that he was the true Mahdi, whose only intention was to uphold the faith, and who had no regard for wealth and property.

The news of the Mahdi's victories now spread far and wide, and amongst an uneducated population such as that of Kordofan the accounts were exaggerated to a quite ridiculous extent. Roused by the spirit of fanaticism, numbers of them quitted their homes and marched to Jebel Gedir, which was now openly renamed Jebel Masa, while others, gathering round the local chiefs, prepared to fight against the various Government posts and stations scattered throughout the country.

This condition of affairs was eminently favourable to the ruling passions of the nomad Arabs. Under the cloak of a religious war, which owed its existence to them, they massacred, plundered, and robbed the natives, who, they said, were loyal to the hated Turks; and at the same time they shook themselves free from the taxation imposed on them by a Government they detested.

The Mahdi now placed himself in communication with the merchants of El Obeid, who, through their wealth and connection with the people, virtually ruled the town and a considerable part of the country. They thoroughly understood the situation. None knew better the weakness and effeteness of the Government, and many were prepared to side with the Mahdi. Elias Pasha was the chief amongst these malcontents, and detested Ahmed Bey Dafalla, who was a great friend of Mohammed Pasha Said. He was well aware that these two would, in the event of the defeat of the rebels, do him all the harm they could. Elias Pasha, therefore, employed himself actively in secretly collecting adherents for the Mahdi. Many of the less wealthy merchants anticipated better times should the Government be overthrown, whilst there were not a few who, though disinclined to the Mahdi, were driven to espouse his cause by the fear that, should he prove successful, their wives and property would fall into the hands of his victorious followers.

As for the religious Sheikhs, this movement was one which held out the highest prospects of promotion for them. They prided themselves that one of their number had successfully dared to proclaim himself a Mahdi, and they looked to the time when he or his sons should drive out the hated Turk, and rule the land. A few—only a very few—sensible people foresaw the danger which would threaten the country should the Mahdi prove successful, and these did all they could to prepare the Government for the coming storm; but their numbers were too small to have any effect.

Elias Pasha now sent his son Omar to acquaint the Mahdi with the situation, and to beg him to come forthwith to El Obeid; while Mohammed Pasha Said, realizing that this would undoubtedly be the next step, and deluded with the idea that the people would be prepared to stand a siege with him, began to dig an enormous ditch round the town, and, at the suggestion of Ahmed Bey Dafalla, he put the Government buildings in a state of defence, and built a parapet around them. His parsimonious ideas, however, led him into a grave error. Instead of laying in large stores of corn, which the merchants, seeking only their own interests, were perfectly ready to provide, he refused to pay more than peace prices. It was, in consequence, rapidly bought up at a higher rate by those who were already beginning to feel the effects of the disturbed state of the country, and so he lost the favourable moment to buy.

Meanwhile, massacres in the districts were of almost daily occurrence. Tax-collectors, detached military posts, and Government officials, fell an easy prey to the blood-thirsty Arabs. The Bederia tribe attacked and almost annihilated the inhabitants of Abu Haraz, which was a day's march distant from El Obeid, and only a few men, women, and children succeeded in reaching the capital; the rest were all killed or taken prisoners during the flight along the waterless track. Young girls were, of course, looked upon as valuable booty, and were given water by their captors; but the older women suffered the most horrible mutilation. Arms and legs were ruthlessly cut off merely to gain possession of the bracelets and anklets they wore. A few days later, the town of Ashaf, in Northern Kordofan, was attacked and plundered by the Arabs, though a defence was made by Nur Angara, who was living there at the time, and who assisted Sanjak Mohammed Agha Japo, formerly one of Gordon's kavasses. They were, however, eventually forced to retire on Bara. This Japo was an old Kurdi, and during the retreat he performed prodigies of valour. Collecting all the women and young girls in the centre of his square, he bade them sing songs of victory, saying that such music drove fear out of all hearts; and, making constant counter-attacks, he succeeded in bringing almost all the fugitives in safety to Bara.

This town was now attacked, and the Arabs repulsed; but, collecting in greater numbers under Sheikh Rahma, they completely invested it, and cut off all supplies.

A mass of Arabs had also collected at Kashgeil, and against these Mohammed Pasha Said dispatched a battalion of regulars, who succeeded in temporarily dispersing them; but, in doing so, the troops lost so heavily that virtually it was little short of defeat; and, collecting again, these Arabs attacked Birket, where the entire garrison of two thousand men was put to the sword. A similar disaster overtook the troops at Shatt, on the White Nile, where two hundred were massacred; but their subsequent attack on Duem was repulsed, with a loss of two thousand men.

Meanwhile, the emissaries sent by the Mahdi to the Gezira had not been idle. The Gehena, Agaliyin, Hawazma, and Hammada Arabs, under Abu Rof, had attacked and invested Sennar; but the town had been subsequently relieved by Sanjak Saleh Wad el Mek, who had been dispatched thence with a large force of Shaigia.

The town of Abu Haraz, on the Blue Nile, had been invested by Sherif Ahmed Taha; and Giegler Pasha, who was acting Governor-General in place of Rauf Pasha, had arrived in the neighbourhood, and had directed Melek Yusef of the Shaigia to attack the rebels with an inferior force, which was defeated. Melek Yusef, disdaining flight, had got off his horse, and, seating himself cross-legged on his farwa (sheepskin), had ordered one of his slaves to kill him. Giegler had at once proceeded to Khartum, and, procuring reinforcements, had returned and attacked Ahmed Taha, who had been killed, and his head sent to Khartum. He had then cleared the neighbourhood of Sennar of rebels without suffering any serious loss. In spite, however, of these temporary successes, troubles increased, and the Government daily received alarming accounts of the disasters which had overtaken troops and inhabitants in various parts of the country. In consequence, Abdel Kader Pasha had been dispatched to the Sudan as Governor General. He had arrived at Khartum on 11th May, 1882, and had busily set to work to place the town in a state of defence. These measures had some effect on the natives, and it was evident to them that the Government intended to act resolutely; but, at the same time, it was perfectly clear to them that these steps were not merely precautionary, but were rendered absolutely necessary by the very serious position of affairs. The arsenal and dockyard, ammunition stores, magazines, and Government archives, must be safeguarded against all eventualities. Besides, one of the first

acts of the new Governor-General was to withdraw to
Khartum a portion of the garrisons of Gallabat, Senhit,
and Gera, in which districts there was at present complete
tranquillity.

Meanwhile, Mohammed Ahmed fully realized that to
kindle the smouldering fire into a blazing flame his presence was absolutely necessary. He therefore accepted
Elias Pasha's invitation to come to El Obeid, and, leaving
his uncle, Mahmud Sherif, with a few followers, to look
after his wives and children in Jebel Masa, he descended
into the plains, and marched with his forces towards the
wealthy capital of Kordofan.

CHAPTER V.

SPREAD OF THE REVOLT IN SOUTHERN DARFUR.

I arrive at Dara—Despatch of an Officer to Shakka—Return to El
    Fasher—I make Dara my Headquarters—The Power of a Woman's
    Tongue—Sheikh Madibbo threatens Shakka—Cowardly Conduct
    of Mansur Helmi—I proceed to his Assistance—I commence my
    Campaign against the Southern Arab Tribes—The Night Attack
    on Madibbo's Camp—Mansur Helmi's cowardly Retreat from
    Shakka—Courageous Conduct of Ali Agha Juma.

WHEN I quitted El Fasher for Dara, early in 1882, I was
accompanied by three hundred and fifty mounted men, under
Omar Wad Darho. This large escort was quite unnecessary, but I thought it advisable to show the Arabs that the
Government had plenty of troops at its disposal to suppress
any trouble on their part.

On arrival at Dara I visited poor Emiliani's grave, and
put up a stone to his memory. Zogal Bey was administering affairs here as Acting-Governor in his place, and the
general aspect looked very troubled. The southern Arab
tribes—the Rizighat, Habbania, and Maalia—were in revolt; they held constant meetings, in which it was declared

that Dervishes were flocking to the standards of the Mahdi, who had been sent by God to raise the Faith. I therefore ordered Mansur Effendi Helmi to proceed at once to Shakkah to restore order with two hundred and fifty regulars and twenty-five horsemen.

He marched off *viâ* Kalaka, whilst I returned forthwith to El Fasher to collect the various detachments of troops which were out in the district gathering taxes, and prepare for all eventualities. Before leaving Dara, I had a long and serious interview with Zogal. I had known this man well when I had been Governor here, and it had come to my ears that he and Omar Wad Darho had had several talks about the Mahdi and his doings, and had agreed that should he continue to be victorious they would join him. These two men were the richest officials in Darfur, and exercised great influence in the country : their secession would have been very serious ; I therefore thought my best plan was to show them great friendliness, and do all that was possible to avoid a breach occurring between us. In my conversation with him I therefore made no allusion to his meetings with Darho, but confined myself to pointing out that he being a relative of the Mahdi, and at the same time a high Government official, it behoved him to support lawfully constituted authority to his utmost.

In saying good-bye to the officers and officials, I pointed out the absolute necessity of strict attention to their duties, and told them I would return from El Fasher as soon as possible; and, leaving the mounted troops in Dara, I departed for the capital, where I arrived after three days' march. Here I learnt that the telegraph station at Foga had been taken by the rebels, and in consequence I gave orders for reinforcements to be sent to Om Shanga.

The postal system was now completely interrupted, and I was obliged to send any communications to El Obeid and Khartum concealed in hollowed-out lance-staves, between the soles of boots or sandals, or sewn into the bearer's clothing. The extra ammunition I had ordered when in

Khartum had, owing to the negligence of the officials, been delayed; it had reached El Obeid late, and now, the roads being cut, it could be sent no further.

From Dara I learnt that Madibbo, chief of the Rizighat tribe, refused to come in. There was now no doubt that all the southern tribes were in a state of active revolt, and had every intention of joining the Mahdi. I therefore thought my headquarters should now be at Dara, so, taking two hundred infantry and seventy-five of the newly-arrived cavalry, I proceeded thither.

On my arrival news reached me that an incident had occurred which, though in itself insignificant, led to very serious consequences. I previously mentioned that on my way to Khartum I had been met by Sheikh Ali Wad Hegeir, of the Maalia tribe, who had accompanied me there. He had proved loyal and faithful to the Government, and I had appointed him chief of the southern Maalia Arabs. Hearing that a meeting of the Rizighat Arabs under Sheikh Belal Nagur, with a view to joining the Mahdi, was about to be held, he resolved to attend the meeting and arrest this sedition-monger. Accompanied by his father-in-law and a few of his friends, he presented himself at the meeting, and, seeing some of his own tribe amongst the number, he called on them to separate themselves from the rest and come to him. His summons was left unheeded, and a disturbance took place, in which Hegeir and his friends, being far in the minority, were severely handled, and barely escaped with their lives. The news of the fray had, however, preceded them, and had been distorted, so that on reaching their home Hegeir was greeted by his wife with the words: 'Rageli hidlim wa Abuyi Rabta; Safar yomein sawuhum fi Gabta' (My husband is a male ostrich, and my father a female ostrich; they made a two days' journey in a moment). Belal Nagur, however, pursued the fugitives, and, joined by the Maalia, attacked Hegeir's house. The latter was urged by his friends to flee for protection to Mansur at Shakka; but, smarting under his wife's sarcastic verses, he refused,

saying, ' I shall never fly to save my life. Better is it to
fall under the sword than to be laughed at by a woman.'
And, true to his word, he defended himself against fearful
odds until a spear split his head in twain, and he sank down
to die, repeating his creed with his last breath. His father-
in-law fell dead close to him, and his wife, who was the
cause of this sad catastrophe, and had thus lost husband
and father, was captured and enslaved.

Mansur Helmi, being now anxious to conclude arrangements with the tribes, begged that I should come to Shakka,
as, being the representative of Government and well known
to the Arabs, I would have greater weight with them; he
also expressed his opinion that a strong fort should be made
in Shakka, and manned with a couple of guns. As it was
most important to conclude terms with the Arabs, I resolved to comply with his request, and, taking one hundred
and fifty regulars, twenty-five horsemen, and one gun, I
started for Shakka.

During my march I received frequent confirmation of the
spread of the revolt, and of the Mahdi's successes, and on
arrival at Madibbo's village at Dein, a messenger brought
me the startling news that Mansur had attacked that sheikh
near Shakka, had lost a considerable portion of his force,
and was practically invested in Murrai. I at once decided
to order reinforcements from Dara to join me, and pending
their arrival I remained at Dein, where I had no doubt
Madibbo would shortly attack me, and my conjecture
proved correct. I was also joined by Sheikh Afifi, of the
Habbania tribe, with twenty horsemen, and the subsequent
exploits of this loyal chief are worthy of record.

One evening, just before sunset, when my men were out
collecting wood, we were suddenly attacked by Madibbo's
horsemen, who were seen in hundreds some distance off
galloping towards the zariba. Sheikh Afifi instantly
saddled his horse, mounted, and, standing before me with
poised spear, shouted, ' Arifni zen ! ana thor et tokash, abu
galb min adem, ana bidaur el mot !' (You know me well !

I am the pushing ox, the man who has a heart of bone. I seek death!) And with this he dashed out of the zariba, and, disappearing amongst the trees, returned in a few minutes, his spear dripping with blood, and leading after him a captured horse; the two other Sheikhs and their men also had a slight skirmish, losing one horse and capturing another. In a few moments we heard some rifle-shots, and fearing that Madibbo's main body had arrived, I called the mounted Arabs into the zariba and prepared for defence. However, I soon ascertained that a small party only had come, and had taken up a position in a clump of trees; I therefore sent fifty men to drive them out, and they retired, leaving behind them three killed.

The next morning, however, the enemy were seen advancing again, and I at once sounded the 'alarm,' and everyone went to his post. The attack came from the north-west, where there was a small wood which gave considerable cover. In the centre of our zariba was a mound, on the top of which I placed an old bench found in one of Madibbo's huts, and which an Egyptian had turned into a chair. Seated in this position, I obtained a good view of the surrounding country, as well as of all that was going on in the zariba. The enemy now advanced within rifle-range, and the bullets began to whistle about our ears. Getting up from the chair to give some order and have a better view, a shot whizzed past and struck the back of the chair in which I had just been sitting and shivered it to pieces. After this I thought it advisable to take up a less exposed position. The enemy's fire now became very hot, but the men were well protected in the trenches, and our loss was trifling. The horses and camels, however, suffered severely, and feeling that if kept huddled up in the zariba we might lose them all, I selected fifty men, and, making a sortie from the southern entrance, we turned west, and, opening suddenly on the enemy's flank, inflicted considerable loss on him by a murderous cross-fire, eventually driving him from the position. However, we did not secure this success without paying for it. As far as I can recollect, we lost twelve killed.

By the evening, thoroughly tired out, most of the men had dropped off to sleep, and we anticipated a quiet night, but at about eleven o'clock we were startled by a brisk rifle-fire. Fortunately it was a very dark night, and the fire was ill-directed. So I ordered the men not to reply, and in consequence it slackened, and eventually ceased altogether.

Summoning Sheikh Afifi, I now asked him to send out some of his men to discover Madibbo's position, promising them they would be well rewarded if they brought back reliable information. In about two hours they returned, and reported that Madibbo was in his village with his Bazingers, while the Arabs were encamped to the south and west of it. They were in considerable force, but had taken no precautions for defence, and our spies, who had crept up quite close to their camp-fires, had overheard them laughing and joking at our not having replied to their fire, saying we must have been too frightened to do so.

Waiting for half an hour, I called up seventy men, and told them, before the officers, I wanted them to surprise Madibbo's camp; that if we fought an action in the open against superior numbers, we should probably lose heavily; but we had now ascertained the Arabs were quite unprepared, and a sudden night attack might completely demoralize them, and give us a chance of returning to Dara for reinforcements. The plan was thoroughly approved, and all the officers at once volunteered to join, but this I could not permit. So, leaving behind two officers, four buglers, and seventy men, I quitted the zariba, accompanied by Afifi, who refused to leave me. Suspecting that possibly some of Abu Salama's people might get out and betray us, I gave the officers who remained behind strict injunctions that during our absence no one should leave the zariba, and that a most careful look-out should be kept; and advancing cautiously, guided by the spies, in the space of about an hour we found ourselves close to the enemy's camp. Our spies proved thoroughly trusty, and, besides, I had previously travelled in these districts, and knew the country well. Dividing up, therefore, into two parties, I placed one under the command of a very brave officer named Mohammed Agha Suleiman, a native of Bornu, and leading the other party myself, we crept up to within six or seven hundred yards of the unsuspecting foe, when I ordered the bugler to sound 'Commence firing.' The confusion in the enemy's camp was now indescribable. Madibbo's Bazingers, leaving their arms, fled. The horses, terrified by this sudden commotion in the dead of night, became restive, broke their ropes, and bolted in all directions, chased by the Arabs. In a few minutes every one of Madibbo's huts was deserted, and in the distance could be heard the sounds of the terrified crowds, fleeing from our little band of seventy men. We had been completely successful, and it took Madibbo some days before he could collect his men again. I burnt his village, and the blazing flames, shooting to the sky, lighted up the deserted camp. Only two of my men had been wounded by thrown spears. We captured a large number of saddles, which I ordered to be thrown into the flames, as well as a quantity of old guns and matchlocks ; but we kept the forty Remington rifles taken, and now marched back to the zariba, where we had a most enthusiastic welcome from the others, who had been awaiting our return with great anxiety.

Being still without news from Dara, I decided to return there, and, after three days' march, reached the town, where I found the reinforcements and ammunition all ready to leave, and as the men I had brought back were tired, I determined to change them also, and return with a completely fresh force to help Mansur Helmi ; but to my surprise, at daybreak the next morning, I received a letter saying that Mansur was on his way to Dara, and would arrive the following day. This was to me most unsatisfactory news, for it meant that my difficulties in re-occupying Shakka would be considerably increased. The next morning he arrived, accompanied by a few slaves, who were ready to drop down with fatigue ; and I then learnt that he had disgracefully abandoned his men, and in sheer terror had deserted his command in order to seek safety in Dara. I at once placed this cowardly officer in arrest, and then sent off spies in all directions to discover the whereabouts of the column, and for the moment abandoned all idea of an expedition to Shakka. Ten days later I received the joyful news that the missing troops were close to Dara. It transpired that their commander—a certain Ali Agha Guma —after Mansur's desertion, had carried out a most masterly retreat, and, although continually harassed and attacked on the road, had succeeded in safely bringing in all the wounded and a number of Shakka merchants who had sought his protection.

At this period Said Bey Guma was governor of El Fasher, and I had frequently written to him to send me more troops and ammunition ; but finding that he either could not or would not heed my orders, I set off for Hashaba, where it had been arranged the various friendly tribes would meet me.

CHAPTER VI.

THE SIEGE AND FALL OF EL OBEID.

Said Pasha, Governor-General of Kordofan, prepares to defend El Obeid—The Mahdi attacks the Town, but is repulsed with Great Loss—The Missionaries at Delen fall into the Mahdi's Hands— The Siege and Fall of Bara—The Horrors of the Siege of El Obeid —Said Pasha is forced to Surrender—His Interview with the Mahdi—His Execution.

INSPIRED by his numerous victories, and encouraged by Elias Pasha's urgent appeal that he should proceed to El Obeid, the Mahdi left Gedir, and, joined by thousands upon thousands of fanatical Arabs and slave-hunters, he advanced to Kaba, a village on the outskirts of the town.

From here he despatched horsemen to reconnoitre and summon all those who were willing to join his banners. He also wrote to Mohammed Pasha Said, calling on him to submit. His letter was read out before the officers; and at the suggestion of Mohammed Bey Skander and the majority of the officers the bearers of the letters were sentenced to be shot. Said Pasha himself was averse to this decision, but eventually gave way and confirmed the sentence, which was immediately carried out.

Mohammed Ahmed now spared no effort to rouse the fanatical spirit of the masses by whom he was surrounded. He preached day and night to a rapt audience on the heavenly joys in store for all those who joined the Jehad, and on Friday morning, September the 8th, this seething mass of human beings, armed only with swords and spears, rolled like the waves of the sea towards the town. All the arms taken in Rashed's and Shellali's expeditions had been left behind at Jebel Gedir, and the rifle fire of the defenders soon began to play with deadly effect on the crowd, who, utterly undeterred, and seeking only for blood and plunder, continued their advance, swarming into the ditches and up the parapet, and entering the deserted town. At this critical moment Major Nesim Effendi told his bugler to sound the advance; and the signal being taken up by the other buglers, the soldiers, clambering up on to the tops of the walls and houses, brought a murderous fire to bear on the assailants. Slowly the surging mass, under this hail of lead, was driven back, leaving behind them thousands of killed and wounded. Once more they rallied and attempted again to storm; but again were they driven back with still greater slaughter, till at length the survivors retired out of range, and the gallant garrison was completely victorious.

In this assault the Mahdi's brother Mohammed, Khalifa Abdullahi's brother Yusef, the Kadi, and a host of Emirs were killed. The Mahdi himself, during the attack, took up a position out of range, behind a small house; and had Said Pasha taken Ahmed Bey Dafalla's advice to pursue after the Dervishes had been routed, in all probability he would have been taken, and the subsequent bloodshed and horrors thus avoided.

But Said Pasha contented himself with this temporary success, believing that the Mahdi was too crushed to again attempt an attack, and that this defeat would probably destroy his influence. The Mahdi's relatives and near friends also realized this, and on their advice he removed his camp to Gianzara, a hill lying beyond range to the north-east of the town ; and in this position maintained an open investment, while awaiting the arrival of the arms and ammunition for which he had sent to Jebel Gedir.

The mission station at Delen, which had been founded some eight years before, and which was guarded by eighty men of the slave guard, had long been in a critical position. Whilst on his way to El Obeid, the Mahdi had sent one of his adherents, Mek Omar, with instructions either to capture or kill all persons found there. The missionary Fathers, Joseph Ohrwalder and Luigi Bonomi, had arranged to flee with the troops and all the mission to Fashoda ; but their plan fell through, owing to the cowardice of the captain commanding the troops. They were eventually obliged to submit, were robbed of all they had, and were marched as prisoners to El Obeid. Here the Mahdi and Khalifa Abdullahi made every effort to convert them and the sisters who were with them, but they remained firm. The following day they were taken, accompanied by thousands of howling Dervishes, to an open space, where a great review was held. After momentarily expecting death, they were at length told their lives were spared, and they were handed over to the care of a Syrian named George Stambuli, who had joined the Mahdi from El Obeid.

At this time a most wonderful comet appeared, which was taken by the Sudanese as a sign from heaven that the Government was about to be overthrown, and that the true Mahdi had appeared on earth.

An expedition sent under Ali Bey Lutfi to relieve Bara

and El Obeid, when on the march and suffering from thirst, was attacked by the Gowama Arabs under Fiki Rahma ; of the two thousand men of which it was composed, two hundred only succeeded in escaping to Bara. Soon after this Tayara was attacked, and its little garrison, after resisting manfully, was obliged to submit at the end of September.

Bara fell next, after a long and well-sustained siege. The garrison had inflicted considerable loss on the rebels, but a fire had broken out and burnt up almost all the corn. Hunger and disease had done their work, and, hopeless of any succour, Surur Effendi, the commandant, Nur Angara, and Mohammed Agha Japo, at the urgent request of the garrison, were forced to submit, early in January, 1883, to Abderrahman Wad en Nejumi, and were conducted by him to Gianzara.

The Mahdi celebrated the capture of Bara with a salute of one hundred guns, and the unfortunate garrison of El Obeid, hearing the sounds, thought that a relieving army was approaching, but when they learnt that Bara had fallen, they became greatly disheartened. For months they had been suffering all the horrors of famine ; food had risen to fabulous prices ; no steps had been taken to lay in a stock of provisions, and there was a great scarcity of corn. A month before the capitulation dukhn had risen to four hundred dollars the ardeb ; only the most wealthy could supply themselves with a little meat. The price of a camel rose to fifteen hundred dollars, a chicken might be had for thirty or forty dollars, and an egg for a dollar to a dollar and a half. But my comrades in captivity, Fathers Ohrwalder and Rosignoli, have already described the horrors of that long and terrible time, and I need not repeat them here ; suffice it to say that after a five months' siege, during which the most terrible privations were endured, and in which a very large proportion of the remaining population and garrison died of starvation, Mohammed Pasha Said was at last forced to capitulate. He wished to blow up the powder magazine, but the officers begged that their wives and children might be spared, and he was obliged to give way. He therefore wrote to the Mahdi that he was prepared to surrender the town. The Mahdi replied that he and his officers need have no fear, and the following morning sent a deputation of leading merchants, under Mohammed Wad el Areik, to Said Pasha, with instructions that he, the superior officers of the garrison, and the chief merchants, should present themselves before him. The deputation had brought with them jibbas (the patched shirt adopted as a uniform by the followers of the Mahdi), which had now to be worn, and, mounting on horses, the sad cavalcade, led by Said Pasha, filed out of the fort which they had defended so long and bravely. With him were Mohammed Bey Skander, the commandant, Major Nesim Effendi, Ahmed Bey Dafalla, Mohammed Bey Yasin, and several other officers. Seated on his angareb, on which a goat's skin was spread, the Mahdi received them kindly, gave them his hand to be kissed, and pardoned them. He told them that he of course understood they had been deceived in regard to him, having doubted his Divine mission; but that he forgave them, and now required them to take the solemn oath of allegiance, and complete submission to him and the cause. This formality over, he gave them dates and water, and urged them to renounce the pleasures of this world and think only of the world to come. Turning to Said Pasha, he then said: 'I do not blame you as a Turk for having done all you could to defend the post confided to you; but you did not do well to kill my messengers, for it is not right that messengers should be punished.' Before Said Pasha could reply, Skander Bey quickly answered, 'Master and Mahdi, Said Pasha did not do this, but it was I, in my capacity as commandant of the fort, who ordered the execution, as I considered them rebels, and in this I did not do well, as you truly say.' 'I did not mean by my question to ask you to justify yourself,' said the Mahdi. 'My messengers have obtained what they most desired; when they took the letters from me they sought the death of martyrs, and their wish was fulfilled. The merciful God has granted them their hearts' desire, and now they are in the enjoyment of all the pleasures of Paradise. May God grant that we may follow in their footsteps!'

During this conversation, according to a plan prepared beforehand, Abu Anga and his men had occupied the fort, powder magazine, and Government buildings, whilst the Emirs installed themselves in the officers' quarters. The Mahdi now told Wad el Areik, who happened to be a personal friend of Said Pasha, to take him and his officers back to their houses; but on their return they found them occupied, and were given to understand that their property had now been confiscated. Soon afterwards the Mahdi himself entered the town to inspect it, and ordered the garrison to quit the entrenchments. The women and children, who had so patiently waited for relief, were now ordered out to the Mahdi's camp, and were allowed to take nothing with them. Even the women were searched to the skin, in a most revolting manner, and anything found was instantly taken off to the Beit el Mal (Mahdi's treasury), where the property was subsequently distributed amongst the Emirs and other high personages. In searching for gold and treasure the most heart-rending scenes were enacted, and weeping and wailing was heard on all sides, as the unfortunates were flogged to make them disgorge.

Said Pasha himself was called upon by Ahmed Wad Suleiman, the Mahdi's Emin Beit el Mal (or treasurer), to hand over all his money, but he replied that he had none. It was well known that he was a very wealthy man, but he obstinately denied he had anything. When the Mahdi heard this, he instructed Wad Suleiman to make every inquiry of Said Pasha's servants, and while he was occupied in doing this, the Mahdi continued conversing with Said Pasha on the precepts of religion, and frequently asked him, before the assembled masses, why he refused to disclose the hiding-place of his treasure, and Said Pasha as persistently denied that he had any money whatever. In this way some time passed, and at length Wad Suleiman, who had meanwhile succeeded in getting one of the female servants to admit that her master had concealed the treasure in the wall, returned to the Mahdi, and whispered in his ear that they had found it. The latter, beckoning him to sit down, continued to talk of the vanities of this world, and the great necessity of renouncing them; and then, turning suddenly to Said Pasha, he said, 'You swore a most solemn oath of allegiance; why, then, do you refuse to say where your money is? Money is the root of all evil. Do you now expect to gather more riches?' 'Oh, sire,' replied Said Pasha, 'I have neither money made honestly, nor money made dishonestly; do with me what you like.' 'Do you take me for an ordinary man?' replied the Mahdi. 'Do you not understand that I am truly the " Mahdi el Muntazer," and that the Prophet has revealed to me the hiding-place of your treasure, which you have concealed in the wall of your house? Go, Ahmed Wad Suleiman, to his house. Enter his room, and on the left side, near the door, remove the plaster from the wall, and there you will find the Turk's treasure. Bring it here.' During Wad Suleiman's absence Said Pasha sat disconsolately, close to the Mahdi, frowning deeply. He knew his treasure had been discovered, but he was too proud to admit that he had told an untruth, and he refused to join in the conversation. In a few minutes Suleiman returned, dragging behind him a large tin box, which he placed before the Mahdi, who opened it, and found it full of gold, packed up in small bags. Over £7,000 was counted out. 'Mohammed Said,' said the Mahdi, 'you have told a lie; but I will forgive you. Ahmed, take the money to the Beit el Mal, and distribute it amongst the poor and needy.' 'You, who preach renunciation, have now got my money; do what you like with it,' said Said Pasha, turning on his heel and marching off. The Mahdi, frowning darkly, muttered, 'Di ma biyenfa maana' (This man won't do for us), and soon afterwards a pretext

was found for executing this gallant officer, as well as Ahmed
Bey Dafalla, Ali Bey Sherif and Yasin.   Such was the end
of the four men who had. so bravely defended El Obeid,
and in truth they deserved a better fate!

CHAPTER VII.

VAIN EFFORTS TO STEM THE TIDE OF MAHDISM
IN DARFUR.

I advance on Shakka—The Battle of Om Waragat—Besieged in the
    Zariba—My Retreat on Dara through the Enemy's Country—The
    Illness and Death of Gottfried Rott—I despatch Secret Emissaries
    to Kordofan—The Revolt of the Mima Arabs—I learn of the Fall
    of El Obeid—The Death of Sheikh Afifi—My Campaign against
    the Mima and Khawabir Arabs—Discovery of a Plot amongst the
    Troops in Dara—My Officers and Men ascribe our Defeats to the
    fact that I am a Christian—I decide to nominally adopt the
    Mohammedan Religion—I decide to send Zogal Bey to El Obeid—
    My Campaign against the Beni Helba—Beshari Bey seeks Death
    and finds it—Gravity of the Situation in Darfur.

HAVING reached Hashaba, I now did my utmost to organize
a force capable of operating successfully against Madibbo.
The tribes I had summoned to aid the Government had
arrived, and my troops consisted approximately of the
following :

Regulars, armed with Remingtons	550
Gellabas	200
Armed Bazingers under Sharaf ed Din, amongst whom, as leaders, were Abder Rasul, Sheikhs Khudr, Um-batti, Mungid Madani, Hassan Wad Sattarat, Sultan Begu, Suleiman Wad Farah, Muslem Wad Kab-bashi, and others	1,300
Various	100
Total guns (of which about 600 were Remington rifles)	2,150

Also a muzzle-loading mountain-gun and thirteen artillerymen.

The friendly tribes consisted of contingents from the
Begu, Berket, Zagawa (of southern Darfur), Messeria,

Tagu, and some of the Maalia who were hostile to Sheikh Abu Salama, numbering in all some seven thousand spearmen and four hundred horses.

The garrison I had left behind at Dara consisted of four hundred regulars, seven guns and the gunners required for their service, thirty horses, and two hundred and fifty Bazingers, all under the command of Zogal Bey, who was carrying on the duties of Acting-Governor in Emiliani's place. With him I had also left a certain Gottfried Rott, a Swiss, who had been sent to the Soudan in connection with the suppression of the slave trade. He was a good Arabic scholar, and in a very confidential talk I had with him I confided to him my suspicions about Zogal, and asked him to find out all he could from his relatives, and keep me fully informed.

At the end of October I moved south from Hashaba with my entire force. The Rizighat country, through which we advanced, was covered with dense bush and forests ; and, being constantly exposed to attack, I had to march in such a way as to avoid confusion in the event of an ambush or surprise.

The Bazingers on the flanks were well provided with buglers, in order to give timely warning of an alarm. The rear guard I made stronger than the flank guards, because the Arabs generally attack from the rear, and I considered that, in case of a flank attack, I should have ample time to reinforce from the main body in case of necessity. The rear guard had, of course, the most troublesome duty to perform, as they had to look after any camels that broke down, and keep a careful look-out for men who fell out or attempted to desert. I therefore gave orders that it should be relieved daily by the flank guards in rotation from the left ; thus the left flank guard would become rear guard, the relieved rear guard would become the right flank guard, and the latter would become the left flank guard. I also relieved the three hundred Bazingers and sixty regulars daily from the main body.

In this manner I hoped to reach Shakka without any serious loss; and on arriving there it was my intention to build a fort, where I should mount the gun, and, leaving a small garrison there, make expeditions in light marching order to the various disturbed districts, where my Arab spearmen, if fortunate, would have ample opportunities of capturing any quantities of Rizighat cattle.

On arrival at Deain, we found quantities of corn stored in the new village just built by Madibbo. This was distributed amongst the men, and they had now sufficient supplies to last them some days. We halted here for three days, in order to obtain correct information as to the water on the road, and then continued the march towards Shakka.

As I was suffering from a heavy bout of fever, I handed over the command of the troops temporarily to Sharaf ed Din, my second in command, but ordered him to remain close to me. The following day, having left the village of Kindiri on our flank, and having made a short halt, there was an alarm that horsemen were advancing to attack us. Immediately everyone was in his place, and, in spite of my fever, I joined the rear guard, whence the alarm had come, and from this position I could see numbers of horsemen; there might have been some hundreds, but, owing to the intervening trees, it was impossible to estimate accurately. Signalling to the flank guards to join me, I advanced with the cavalry and Arab horsemen, and a skirmish ensued amongst the trees, in which the enemy were driven back with some loss, and we captured six horses. Our own losses were seven horses killed, two men missing, and several wounded. Having pursued for some distance, we returned, and as it was still early, the march was continued till nightfall, when we encamped at a place called Om Waragat.

Still suffering from fever, I told Sharaf ed Din to make exactly similar dispositions (see plan); and starting off the following morning, after a march of two hours, we reached some more or less open but boggy moorland, at the south-

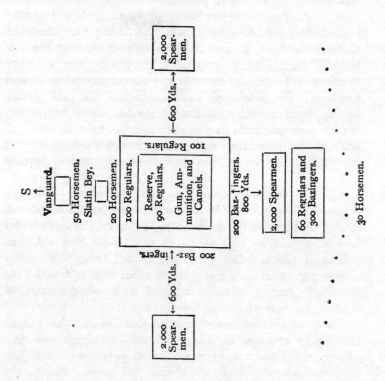

BATTLE OF OM WARAGAT.
Disposition of Troops on the March to Shakka.

east end of which were visible a few huts, such as are
erected by the Rizighat slaves who work in the fields.
The vanguard had already cleared the soft ground—I had
gone forward with it to examine the huts whilst the men in
the square were occupied in trying to help out the animals
whose feet had sunk into the mire—when suddenly from the
rear guard the alarm was sounded twice, followed almost
immediately by some rifle-shots. Ordering the vanguard
to hold the huts, I immediately galloped towards the left
flank of the square, and, sounding for the reserve of ninety
regulars, I proceeded towards the rear guard; but it was
too late. The Bazingers and regulars of the rear guard,
having fired a volley, had no time to reload before the
enemy was on them; and, overpowered by thousands of
half-naked Arabs, they were being forced back on to the
rear face of the square, the men composing which, fearing
to fire on friend and foe alike, did nothing to stop the rush,
and already several of the enemy had penetrated. Without
a moment's hesitation, I ordered my bugler to sound 'lie
down' for those in the square, and, firing on the Arabs who
had broken in, as well as on those still pushing on from
behind, I checked the rush, and caused them to split up
into two parties, who, trending off right and left, made for
the flank guards, already engaged with other parties of
Arabs who were attacking them in front.

The confusion was now indescribable; within the square
the Arabs who had already penetrated, although suffering
heavily from the fire from my small party, were creating
frightful havoc amongst the almost defenceless Bazingers,
who, armed only with muzzle-loaders, could do nothing,
whilst the regulars—so sudden had been the rush—had not
even time to draw their bayonets; eventually, however,
those who had entered were all killed. The flank guards,
taken in front and rear, suffered even more heavily than
the square, and, breaking up entirely, they fled in all
directions, hundreds being killed by the Rizighat horsemen
concealed in the forest.

The action had lasted only twenty minutes, but in that short space of time our losses were terrible. Fortunately, on the dispersion of the flanking parties the enemy had pursued them hotly. My fire, it is true, had driven them away from the square, but at what sacrifice! Amongst the regulars who had obeyed my signal to lie down the losses had not been so severe; but the untrained Bazingers had suffered terribly, and many of our camels had also been killed.

In the midst of the confusion, I saw one of the enemy, who passed close to us, carrying off a red bag containing the fuses for the gun. He evidently thought he had some very special loot; and so indeed it was, as without the fuses our gun was useless. 'Kir,' said I to my young black attendant, who seldom left me, 'let me see if you are as brave as you always say you are; go and fetch the red bag —here is my horse;' and, jumping off, I gave it to him. He mounted, and taking only a spear in his hand, dashed off, returning in a few minutes with the red bag and a still redder spear.

The last horseman had disappeared in the distance, and I now sounded the 'assembly.' Only a few hundred responded to the call, and dividing these up into parties, I detailed half as guards, while the others were employed in collecting together the ammunition and arms of those who had fallen, packing them on the camels and depositing them in the little village, which, standing on a small sandy plain, afforded us a fairly clear field of view; then, collecting a quantity of thorn-bushes, we constructed a zariba as quickly as possible, fearing that at any moment the enemy might return. This done, our next thought was for the wounded; those only slightly hurt had already crawled to the zariba, and the severely wounded we now carried in, and did what was possible to alleviate their sufferings.

As far as the eye could reach the ground was strewn with dead bodies, and what numbers, too, lay in the forest out of view! Curiously enough, this disaster had taken place on the actual spot where, years before, Adam Tarbush, the Vizir of Sultan Hussein, had suffered a similar defeat and lost his life.

Now came the terribly sad duty of calling the roll. Of my fourteen infantry officers, ten had fallen, and one was wounded. The Gellaba chiefs, Sheikh Khidr, Mangel Medani, Hassan Wad Sattarat, and Suleiman Wad Fatah had been killed, as well as Fiki Ahmed, Hassib, and Shekelub. Of the thirteen artillerymen, one only remained alive. The Greek Alexander, too, who had previously been wounded at Deain, and who had not yet recovered, had been killed. Sorrowfully we collected the dead, to pay them the last honours. Amongst a heap of bodies we found Sharaf ed Din, stabbed to the heart. In the soft damp ground we hurriedly dug rough graves, and officers and chiefs we buried in twos and threes—a terribly sad task.

As for the poor wounded, there was little we could do for them. Those only slightly hurt were already dressing their own wounds; but for the severe cases we had no means of dressing them, and a few comforting words was all the small help we could give them. It was indeed painful to see such suffering, and feel how utterly incapable one was of alleviating it. Catching sight of one of my boys, who was carrying my satchel with a few bandages in it, I took it from him and began dressing one or two cases, when it suddenly occurred to me that I had not seen my other boy, Morgan Hosan, who was leading one of my horses. He was a fine, intelligent young fellow, scarcely sixteen years old, honest, quiet, and brave. 'Isa,' said I, to the boy carrying the satchel, 'where is Morgan, who was lead- ing my horse Mabarak [on which were my note-books and sketches in the saddle-bags] ; he is an active fellow, and perhaps mounted the horse, and has managed to escape.' Sad and broken-hearted, poor Isa shook his head, and, his eyes filling with tears, he handed me a bit of my horse's bridle. 'What is this?' I asked. 'Master,' said he, 'I did

not want to make you more sorry than you are. I found
him not far from here, lying on the ground, with a spear-
wound in his chest. When he saw me he smiled and
whispered, " I knew you would come and look for me. Say
good-bye to my master, and tell him I was not a coward.
I did not let go his horse, and it was only when I fell down
stabbed in the chest that they cut the bridle to which I
clung, and took him; show my master the bit of the bridle
that is still in my hand, and tell him that Morgan was faithful. Take the knife out of my pocket—it belongs to my
master ; give it to him, and say many salams to him from
me." ' Isa, his voice choked with sobbing, handed me the
knife, and I, too, now quite broke down. Poor Morgan, so
young and so true! Poor master, to have lost so faithful
a servant and so true a friend! ' Tell me, Isa, what was
the end ?' I said. ' He was thirsty,' he replied, 'and I took
his head in my hands, and in a few seconds he was dead.
I then got up and left him ; I had other things to do, and
there was no time to cry.'

Ordering the zariba to be strengthened, and trenches to
be dug inside, I then had the drums beaten, bugles blown,
and some rifle shots fired, so that any who might still be
fleeing, or stopped by the swampy ground slightly wounded,
might know that a place of refuge was at hand. During
the day a considerable number came in, and, calling over
the roll in the evening, I found we mustered in all nine
hundred men, including regulars and Bazingers—a sad and
broken remnant out of a force of eighty-five hundred men,
but still something for which to be thankful. Of our horsemen and cavalry, thirty only were left—the enemy had
probably captured a large number, and some had perhaps
escaped and returned to Dara, or to their own homes ; but
of arms and ammunition of those who had fallen we had
abundance.

At sunset the Rizighat Arabs returned from the pursuit,
and, to their astonishment, found us in an entrenched position, ready to fight them. Madibbo now sent forward his

Bazingers to attack us; but after a short struggle we drove
them back, and darkness coming on, all firing ceased.
Whilst sitting talking to my officers, Sheikhs Abder Rasul,
Muslim Wad Kabbashi, and Sultan Begu approached, and
asked whether it would not be better to retreat from our
present position under cover of night, as, after our heavy
defeat and losses, we had no chance now against the enemy.
'Well,' said I, 'you wish to retreat during the night; but what
will you do with all our wounded comrades and brothers?
Do you want to leave them to the tender mercies of our
enemies?' Shamefaced, they were silent, and did not reply.
'No,' said I, 'your proposal is not a good one; I have been
talking over the matter with my officers, and we have
resolved to remain where we are for a few days. We have
now nothing to fear but hunger; the wounded and tired
camels can be killed for food for the soldiers. Besides, we
can exist somehow or other for a few days. We shall most
certainly be attacked, as we have already been, but we
shall equally surely drive off the enemy. In this way the
men will regain confidence after the terrible shock we have
all suffered. I know the Rizighat; they will not stay here
and watch us. I feel confident we shall settle accounts
with Madibbo, his Bazingers, and Sheikh Jango, who fled
once before to the Bahr el Ghazal. Our wounded comrades
will have time to recover their strength a little; those only
suffering slightly will be able to march in a few days, and
the others we can mount on our horses. I think my proposal is a much better one than yours.'

Whilst I had been talking I had overheard Sultan Abakr
making remarks of approval, and by the time I had finished
all had agreed to stay.

Speaking generally to all present, I said to them, 'Can
any of you understand how it was we were defeated to-
day?' 'No,' they all answered. 'Well, I will tell you,' I
replied. 'This evening I saw amongst the wounded the
assistant of Hassan Wad Sattarat, commander of the rear
guard. He said, "Sharaf ed Din did not carry out your

instructions to relieve the rear guard, as on the previous days; the regulars were annoyed, and joined their companies without permission, and no fresh men were sent in their places. At the same time the friendly Arabs joined the flank guards, and when we were attacked Hassan Wad Sattarat had at his disposal only about two hundred and fifty Bazingers armed with old percussion-guns." Sharaf ed Din has paid for his negligence with his life, and we have all suffered as well. It is too late for recrimination now; let us think of something else. Go and cheer up your men; get some sleep, so that you may be fit for what to-morrow may bring. But you, Said Agha Fula, as you are wounded, will probably not be able to sleep; so we will put an angareb for you to lie down on at the gate of the zariba, and, should anyone attempt to go out without my permission, you have my orders to shoot him.'

Now that I was alone, I had time to think over the situation. It was very probable we should succeed in retiring on Dara; we had over eight hundred rifles and guns. But I bitterly deplored the losses; all my best officers and advisers were killed, and I dreaded lest the news of our disaster should reach Dara before I could communicate, as, in the event of this, the effect might be most serious, both on the garrison and amongst the inhabitants. I therefore woke up my clerk, and ordered him to write two short notes —one to Zogal, and the other to the commandant, Adjutant-Major Mohammed Farag—informing them that, in spite of heavy losses, we were well, and that we hoped to return to Dara in about a fortnight; but should fugitives come in and spread false and alarming news about our situation, they were to be arrested and kept under guard till I returned. I myself wrote a few lines to Gottfried Rott, describing the situation, and informing him that I hoped to return to Dara before long with the remainder of the troops; that he must not be down-hearted, but should do his utmost to keep up the spirits of all. I enclosed also a note to my mother, brothers, and sisters, bidding them farewell, as it was im-

possible to foresee what would be the end of all this trouble.
In case I should fall, I begged Rott to send these on to my
dear ones at home.

Taking the letters in my hand, I now went to Abdulla
Om Dramo, Sheikh of the Messeria Arabs, who resided
near Dara, and, waking him up, I said, 'Where is your
brother Salama?' ' There he is,' said he, pointing to the
man lying beside him, and waking him up also. ' Salama,'
said I, ' you can render me a great service, which will also
be of much advantage to yourself. You see these letters :
you must take them to Dara and hand them over to the
European Rott, whom you have often seen with me ; I
shall give you my own horse, which you always say is such
a good one, for this mission. You must leave at once, and
when you get near the line of the enemy encircling us, ride
sharply through, for they are all asleep, and you will have
disappeared in the dark before they can get their horses
ready ; once through their lines you will be safe, and in two
days you should be in Dara. As a reward, I will give you
my black mare, which is in my stable.' Whilst I was talking, Salama had tightened up the cloth round his chest and
loins, and merely said, ' Where are the letters ?' I gave
them to him, and, taking them, he said, ' Please God, and
with the help of the Almighty, I shall take these letters to
their destination. But I prefer to ride my own horse ; he
may not be so swift as yours, but he is quite strong enough
to take me home on his back. I know my horse, and he
knows me. Mutual acquaintances are always an advantage
on such expeditions.' Whilst he was girthing up his saddle,
I scribbled a line to Rott, telling him to give the bearer of
these letters my black mare, and, handing it to him, I told
him what I had written ; then, leading his horse to the gate,
we came to Said Agha Fula, who was lying restlessly and
in pain on his angareb : he was wounded in the right leg
and left arm. I told him about Salama's mission, and he
then ordered the gate to be opened. In a moment Salama
had mounted, and, holding in his right hand his long spear,

and in his left his bundle of small spears, he started off. 'I commit you to God's keeping,' I cried. 'I trust in God,' was his reply. Going slowly at first, he approached the lines cautiously; then I heard the rapid clatter of hoofs; in a few minutes one or two rifle-shots rang out in the still night, then all was as silent again as death. 'May God go with him!' we all ejaculated, and then re-entered the zariba. Exhausted nature now claimed me, and, utterly tired out, I was soon fast asleep.

When I woke up at early dawn I found the men already at work strengthening the breastworks, and, as I had anticipated, the enemy renewed their attack at sunrise. For some time a very brisk fire was kept up on both sides, but, owing to our dominating position, the Arabs were at length forced to retire, after suffering considerable loss. On our side there were a few killed and wounded, amongst the former being Ali Wad Hegaz, a Jaali, and one of the best and bravest of his tribe. As it was our intention to remain here four or five days, the men busied themselves in strengthening the zariba, and we also buried the bodies of friends and foes in the immediate vicinity, as already the air was contaminated with the fetid smell of decaying corpses.

We passed five days in the zariba, attacked once, if not twice, every day. During the action fought on the third day Koreina Nur, the commander of Madibbo's gun-bearers, and the bravest and boldest of his Arabs, was killed; and henceforth the enemy's attacks diminished greatly in vigour.

But now we had a new enemy to contend against— famine. Almost everything eatable in the camp had been consumed; the camel meat, which had amply sufficed for the men, was now finished; there was not a grain of dhurra left; my officers and I had lived for some time on some old crusts of dhurra bread, which we had cooked with the leaves of a plant called kawal, and stirred up into a sort of tasteless porridge. We had no prospect of being relieved; to stay longer where we were was impossible, and already we were weakened by want of food; I therefore assembled the entire force—consisting of nine hundred men, almost all of whom were armed with rifles and guns, except a few Arabs, who, being ignorant of fire-arms, preferred to trust to their lances—and, addressing them in a few words, I told them that the blood of their dead officers and chiefs cried to them for vengeance, that their wives and children anxiously awaited their return, but that it was impossible to reach them without enduring troubles with patience, and facing difficulties with courage and endurance; and I closed my harangue by saying that those in whose hearts was fear had left us in the day of battle, but those now before me had bravely stood their ground against overwhelming odds, and that I had no doubt they would do so again, and that God would crown our efforts by victory.

A shout, and the shaking of rifles and guns over their heads, which is their usual method of signifying their obedience and courage, was their reply; and I then dismissed them, with orders to prepare to march the following day. I now took out the hammers from the percussion-guns belonging to the killed, which lay heaped up in the middle of the zariba, and threw them into a rain-pool; but of the stocks I made a bonfire. The filled shells for the gun I threw into the water, and as much ammunition as possible was distributed amongst the soldiers, each man carrying from sixteen to eighteen dozen rounds; but all the percussion-gun ammunition I was obliged to destroy, in case it should fall into the hands of the enemy; the lead in the cartridges was removed, and some of the very severely wounded having just died, I placed it in the open graves, over which we laid the bodies of our poor comrades, as guardians of our precious metal.

It was on a Saturday, the seventh day after our disaster, and just after sunrise, that we marched out of the zariba, and, forming up in square with flank and rear guards, we began our retreat. The only two camels remaining drew the gun in the middle of the square, and I sent out two

Arab horsemen as far as possible on each side to scout.
We had one hundred and sixty wounded inside the square,
and as many of them as could march did so; but the most
severe cases we mounted on the few remaining horses, each
horse carrying two or three men. I myself was prepared to
walk, but, at the urgent request of my officers, I mounted,
so as to obtain a better view over the country. We all knew
that when we had marched some distance from the zariba
we should most certainly be attacked; I therefore had the
gun loaded, and we resolved to sell our lives dearly. We
well understood the Arab mode of fighting, and were confident that if we succeeded in driving back the first two or
three attacks, we should not be further molested. It was
decided the line of direction should be north-east, as the
ground was more open; but we were ignorant of the rain-
pools, as our guides were either killed or had deserted.

Before we had been on the march an hour, we were
attacked in the rear by horsemen, and I knew the decisive
moment had come. Halting instantly, I called in the flank
guards closer to the square, and, accompanied by my own
escort of fifty men, proceeded to the rear guard, distant
about two hundred yards. The gun was run out to the rear
face of the square, and several of the slightly wounded held
the cartridges and shell ready to reload without delay.
Before the enemy's footmen were in sight we could hear the
sound of their advance, and when they did appear, a few
well-directed volleys from the rear guard had the effect of
slightly checking them; but, encouraged by those coming
up behind, they rushed towards us, waving their great
lances in their right hands, and carrying in their left bundles
of small throwing spears. They succeeded in coming so
close that several of our men were wounded by thrown
spears; but our fire created havoc among their ranks, and
the gun played on them freely from the square. Their
spearmen now gave way to Madibbo's and Jangho's
Bazingers, and a very brisk fire was maintained on both
sides; but, getting reinforcements from the square, we

succeeded, after twenty minutes' hard struggle, in driving back the attack. On the first shots being fired, I had at once jumped off my horse, which is always understood in the Sudan to mean that, abandoning his chance of flight in case of a reverse, the commander has determined to conquer or die with his troops; and now that the action was over, the men came round me, and we had a great mutual hand-shaking over this our first success.

Whilst we had been engaged in combating the attack on the rear, the left flank guard had also become engaged, and, though the enemy had been driven off, nevertheless it had suffered somewhat, and my best remaining officer, Zeidan Agha, was dangerously wounded. He was a Nubian by birth, and during the Darfur campaign had shown conspicuous gallantry in recapturing, at the head of only twelve men, a gun which had been taken by the enemy. For this service he had been promoted to the rank of an officer, and now he lay with a bullet through his right lung. I asked him how he was, and, giving me his hand, he murmured, ' Now that we have conquered, we are all right '; and, pressing my hand, in a few minutes he was dead. Besides him, we had lost twenty men killed, and several wounded. Our dead we buried roughly, as there was no time to dig graves; but we covered them sufficiently to avoid the reproach that we had left our dead unburied, and then continued our march with the same precautions, but with considerably increased confidence.

About three o'clock another attack on the rear was signalled; but this time it was not pressed home, and we drove off the enemy without suffering any loss ourselves. We now halted and formed a zariba, momentarily expecting another attack. But to our surprise we passed the night undisturbed, and the next morning at sunrise, having finished all our water, we resumed our march. Again we were subjected to an attack, but on this occasion it was even weaker than that of the previous afternoon, and was driven off without any trouble. We continued our march till mid-day without finding any water, but got a little rest under the shady trees, and found a quantity of 'fayo,' a sort of native radish, and very juicy. Three small leaves springing from the ground denote its presence, and it was sucked with avidity by our parched troops, and in some measure assuaged our thirst; but, still, it was absolutely necessary to find water. After a short halt we pushed on again, and by good fortune accidentally came across a Rizighat shepherd, driving before him a flock of sheep. In an instant the men had seized the sheep, while the unfortunate shepherd, taken completely by surprise, did not attempt to escape, and would certainly have been killed had I not rushed forward and prevented the men from harming him. I now had all the sheep driven inside the square, and meanwhile, my boys, having tied the Arab's hands behind his back, brought him before me. But before interrogating him, I gave orders for the sheep, of which there were over two hundred, to be distributed amongst the famished men, to every five men one sheep, and we kept a few for ourselves. What a godsend to us was this food! Turning now to the Arab, I told him that his life would be spared if he would guide us to a rain pool; and that if he proved faithful I should give him a good reward, and let him go to his own home. He agreed, but said that there were only a few small pools in this neighbourhood, and that if we went on some distance and then halted he would guarantee to bring us to the 'fula el beida' (the white rain-pool) early the next morning, where there was sufficient water to last us for months. I was somewhat suspicious of him, and therefore ordered a non-commissioned officer and eight men to keep guard over him, and not to allow him to go far from me. We then resumed the march, halted at sunset, and made our zariba as usual. We came across a few pools, but they were quite insufficient; and as we were still suffering considerably from thirst, I started on again at earliest dawn, having passed a miserable and sleepless night. About mid-day the guide pointed out some large trees, under which he said the pool lay. Halting, therefore, at once, I ordered the gun to be dismounted and loaded, and all preparations made to resist. It seemed to me very probable that the enemy, knowing that we should be suffering from thirst, would be in concealment somewhere near the water, and would charge us as we were approaching. I now called on the men to strictly obey all orders, and on no account to become undisciplined. But as soon as the water came in view the poor thirsty troops could contain themselves no longer, and rushed pell-mell towards it. I managed to restrain the forty men I had as escort, and there were about the same number with the rear guard; and although I sounded the 'assembly' again and again, the men were now completely out of hand, plunging up to their waists in the water, in their frenzy of delight. But, as I had anticipated, the enemy were concealed behind the trees—fortunately at some distance off— and, seeing our disorder, they now made a general attack from all sides. Galloping to the front, followed by the escort, we opened fire; while Mohammed Suleiman did the same as regards the rear. Our demoralized men, seeing the situation, at once fell in, and after some heavy firing we drove off the enemy, losing in this mêlée only one horse. We now selected a suitable position near the water, and set to work to make a zariba; and that finished, the men killed their sheep; fires were lighted, and in an hour they were enjoying the first solid meal they had had for many a day. As we were all sadly in need of a rest, I decided to remain in this position till the following day.

That evening a report came in from the outposts that a man was seen waving a piece of white calico, and asking to be allowed to see me. I did not wish him to enter the zariba and see all our wounded; I therefore went out, and found that he was one of Madibbo's slaves, bearing a letter for me from his master. In this letter Madibbo called on me to surrender and hand over my arms. He further wrote that the Mahdi was now encamped before El Obeid, which he expected to capture shortly. He promised to treat me

with all respect, and to send me under safe escort to the
Mahdi. I now ordered this letter to be read aloud to the
men, who greeted it with jeers, and asked the slave if his
master was mad, to which the terror-stricken man replied
that he did not really know. I then turned to him seriously,
and, speaking loud enough for all to hear, I said, 'Tell
Madibbo it was God's will we should have suffered losses,
but we are not defeated. We are wandering about in his
country, and if he does not like us to do so he must accept
the situation, as he has neither the power nor the courage
to stop us. If he is really an adherent of the Mahdi, and
desires to enjoy the pleasures of Paradise promised him,
then let him come here to-morrow morning. We shall wait
for him, and for his sake we shall not march to-morrow.'

Most of the men had now gathered round us, and were
listening to this speech and laughing; and when I bade the
messenger good-bye, some of the wits begged him to give
Madibbo their compliments, and tell him they hoped soon
to have the pleasure of his personal acquaintance. The
men were now in the highest spirits; they really did wish
to make Madibbo's acquaintance, and wipe out, if possible,
the defeat they had suffered at Om Waragat.

That evening I presented our guide with a piece of red
cloth, a pair of silver bangles, and a few dollars, which I
borrowed from the surviving merchants, and he quitted the
zariba full of gratitude. At the same time I told him that
should he come to Dara I would repay him the value of his
sheep.

The next morning we ascertained in various ways that
Madibbo was not far off, and after our boasting it behoved
us to be very cautious. However, we were not attacked.
The next morning I gave orders to march, and on the
following day we reached Bir Dilwei, and thence we continued our march without interruption to Dara.

On the road letters reached me saying that Salama,
whom I had sent off from Om Waragat, had arrived safely;
they reported rumours that the Mima intended to revolt;

and Rott, in a letter of which the handwriting was scarcely legible, told me that he had been taken ill the previous Saturday, and was very anxious to see me. I also received a report from Omar Wad Darho, stating that he had heard El Obeid was besieged, and that he did not think the Homr Arabs would dare to attack Om Shanga again, after their constant defeats. The reports of the Mudir of El Fasher were in general satisfactory, except as regards the Mima Arabs. News from Kebkebia and Kulkul was also good.

It behoved me now to look after my own bruises. In the various fights I had been wounded three times. A bullet had shattered the ring-finger of my right hand, which had to be amputated almost to the root; the fingers on either side were also damaged. Another bullet had struck me in the upper part of my leg, and, flattening against the bone, made it protrude. A thrown lance had also struck me in the right knee. In spite of these wounds, I had been able to go through the campaign without much suffering; but I felt weak and overdone, and was very glad of a few days' rest.

I found poor Gottfried Rott very seriously ill. He wanted to move to Fasher for change of air; so I sent him, in charge of an officer, who was ordered to take him to my house in El Fasher, and at the same time I wrote to a Greek merchant named Dimitri Zigada, and asked him to do all he could for the patient.

The news from Kordofan being very contradictory—though at the same time the general tenor was unsatisfactory—I set to work to try and procure some reliable information. I therefore sent Khaled Wad Imam and Mohammed Wad Asi—the latter a most faithful man—to that province, with instructions either to send me news with the least possible delay, or return with it themselves. Khaled Wad Imam had been brought up with Zogal, and although they were not related to each other, they were generally looked upon as brothers. My reason for sending him with Asi was that he should protect him in El Obeid, and the plan succeeded admirably; for Khaled was naturally anxious to do nothing which would jeopardize Zogal, who, of course, remained with me at Dara. At the same time I cautioned Asi to remain on as friendly terms as possible with Khaled, and to try and find out if Zogal was in communication with the Mahdi, and, under any circumstances, to return to me as quickly as possible.

In twelve days the caravan which I had sent with Gottfried Rott to procure ammunition returned from El Fasher with the fifty camels, a hundred boxes of Remington ammunition, and ten kantars of lead. Said Bey made the usual excuses, that he could hire no camels from the employés, and Adam Amer wrote that, owing to the disturbed aspect of affairs in the Fasher district, it was impossible to send me the reinforcements I had ordered.

I now thoroughly understood the situation. The officers were undoubtedly hostile to me. They had talked amongst themselves, and had spread rumours all through the country that Ahmed Pasha Arabi had turned his master, the Khedive, out of Egypt, because he was friendly to Christians, and admitted them into his service ; that Arabi was now master of the country, and had turned out all who were not Egyptians, such as Turks and Circassians, and had confiscated their property, which had been turned over to the Government. They had further declared that I had been discharged from my position, but that, owing to the roads being cut, the authority for my dismissal had not come to hand. Of course the more sensible people placed no credence in these idle tales; but there was no doubt my authority was distinctly impaired, and this state of things was taken full advantage of by those who owed me a grudge. Hitherto there had been no overt act of disobedience to my orders; but excuses were being continually made, so there was evident inclination not to comply with them. However, such was the situation, and I had to put up with it, and be as cheerful as I could under the circumstances. I was reminded of the Arab proverb, ' El kalb yenbah wa el gamal mashi ' (' The dog barks, whilst the came' *unheeding* passes

by ') ; in other words, I thought it better to take no notice
of all this cackling.

The next post brought me news of poor Gottfried Rott's
death.   In spite of most careful nursing and attention he
gradually sank, and was buried at El Fasher, beside Dr.
Pfund and Friedrich Rosset, who had died there some years
before.

The Mima were now in a state of open revolt.   I therefore sent instructions to Omar Wad Darho to proceed
with two hundred regulars and two hundred horsemen
into their country, to chastise them ; and at the same time
I decided to operate against the Khawabir, who were acting
in conjunction with the Mima.   Darho started off, and had
a successful little campaign, defeating the Mima at Fafa
and Woda, whilst I proceeded, with a hundred and fifty
regulars and fifty horsemen, *viâ* Shieria, to Bir Om Lawai,
where the Khawabir, apprised of my approach, were waiting
to attack me.   After a short fight they were defeated and
dispersed, and we captured a considerable number of sheep
and oxen.

When these operations were over, I instructed Darho to
join me at Bir Om Lawai with the remainder of his men.
In a few days he arrived, and gave me a full account of all
his doings, and further details of the Mahdi's successes in
Kordofan, which to me were excessively disquieting.

On the evening in which I was writing out his instructions for his expedition against the Khawabir, a certain
Abderrahman Wad Sherif came and urgently begged to
speak to me.   He was a well-known Dara merchant, and
had previously travelled to Khartum.   He began by saying
that as I had always treated him with kindness, he thought
it his duty to inform me that El Obeid had capitulated,
adding that the early news of this sad event might enable
me to take the measures I considered necessary.   This was
a terrible blow, but I thanked him for his melancholy news,
and he then described to me in detail what had taken place.
He was present at the time of the surrender, and had left

three days afterwards to visit his family in Dara, but hearing at Toweisha that I was at Bir Om Lawai, he had come straight to me, as he was most anxious that this news should reach me first through a friend.

As I knew it was useless to try and keep this secret, I summoned Darho and Suleiman Basyuni, and told them what I had heard, and we talked over the steps which we should now take. It was very evident that this news would prove an immense incentive to those hostilely inclined to the Government, and there was no doubt my presence in Dara was un urgent necessity. As the Mima and Khawabir had been chastised, the next thing in order of importance was to send an expedition to Toweisha, and on the following day I wrote to Said Bey Guma that Om Shanga should be evacuated, and that the garrison, merchants, and any who wished should withdraw to El Fasher. I explained that as El Obeid had fallen, it was more than probable the Arabs would now turn on Om Shanga, and if invested, it would be quite impossible to send relief; and that, under any circumstances, it was imperative that the principal fighting forces in the province should be concentrated at Fasher. I also ordered him to establish a strong post at Fafa and Woda, in the Mima country, in order to keep open communication between Fasher and Dara. Omar Wad Darho and his men I instructed to return forthwith to El Fasher, adding that any booty taken from the Mima should be distributed amongst his men and the Fasher garrison, whilst that taken from the Khawabir should go to the Dara troops. On the following day we separated—Darho to Fasher, and I back to Dara.

In a few days the news of the fall of El Obeid had spread far and wide, and the effect on the Arab tribes became immediately apparent ; meetings were held in all parts of the country, and it was decided almost unanimously to rise against the Government.

The day I arrived at Dara I ordered all the dhurra I could find to be bought up ; we had a considerable amount now in store, but more would certainly be advantageous. Sheikh Afifi now sent me news that his tribe had revolted, and had joined the Rizighat, but he himself, true to his promise, was leaving his own country with his family and relatives, and was coming to me *viâ* Dar Helba, and that he had sent his brother Ali with a message to Beshari Bey Wad Bekir, the head Sheikh of the Beni Helba, with whom solemn oaths had been exchanged, agreeing to his safe conduct through his country, and therefore he hoped to be with me in a few days.

I was awaiting his arrival when the sad news came that he had been killed. In him I lost my most faithful Arab Sheikh. It transpired that the Beni Helba, who had been ordered by their Sheikh to let him through, wanted to take from him his numerous sheep and oxen, and having refused, a fight had ensued ; he had performed prodigies of valour, but had been slain by some spearmen concealed amongst the trees, when in pursuit of the mounted Arabs, whom he had twice successfully driven off.

Mohammed Wad Asi, whom I had sent with Khaled Wad Imam, now returned from Kordofan, and gave me the fullest particulars regarding the situation there. He brought me the good news that Government was collecting a large force in Khartum for the re-conquest of Kordofan, but that no doubt a considerable time must elapse before the expedition could start. I told him to spread this news in all directions, and then inquired as to Zogal's relations with the Mahdi. He replied that, in spite of the most careful investigation, he could not ascertain definitely if any direct correspondence took place between them, but he had no doubt that Zogal received verbal messages from the Mahdi, brought by itinerant merchants ; he, however, shared my views, that Zogal, being a man of position and education, must be well aware of the actual motives of the revolt, and would not be likely to embark on any foolish undertaking. No doubt the capitulation of El Obeid had greatly weakened our position, and with the whole of Kordofan in the hands of the enemy, it behoved us to act with the greatest caution and circumspection. Wad Asi's news about the expedition preparing in Khartum would probably have the effect on the Mahdi of making him keep his forces together so as to offer a united resistance; it was not, therefore, likely he would turn to us just at present. We must give all our attention to the revolt of the Arab tribes, who, now thoroughly inflamed by the news of the capitulation of El Obeid, and stirred up by fanatical proclamations, were ready to proceed to any extremity. As the operations of the intended expedition to Kordofan would not probably be finished till the winter, it was imperative that we should try and hold out by some means till then.

In spite of the formation of the military post at Fafa and Woda, the Bir Om Lawai Khawabir Arabs had again collected, and, joined by a number of Mima who had been irritated by the roads to their country being cut, and stimulated by the fall of El Obeid, were now stirring up the entire country between Fasher and Dara, whilst the troops at Fafa were not in sufficient force to attack them. I therefore decided on another expedition against them, as I was resolved to show them that the fall of El Obeid had not discouraged us. Selecting two hundred and fifty old soldiers, well inured to war, I had them trained in bayonet exercise for a few days preparatory to my departure, the date of which I kept strictly secret.

Taking with me all the horses I could muster at the time, some seventy in number, and instructing Wad Asi to keep me informed of events in Dara during my absence, I advanced rapidly, and in two days reached the neighbourhood of Bir Om Lawai, where both the Mima and Khawabir were collected. We took with us only our arms and ammunition, as our intention was to attack them and then return. The instant, therefore, the enemy came in view, I gave the order to 'fix bayonets,' and, in spite of the Bazingers and their guns, after a sharp fight of twenty minutes we drove them off and dispersed them. A few of the Mima Arabs had got amongst my men, but had all been bayoneted. I

now ordered the horsemen to take up behind them the
regulars and pursue, and do their utmost to discover where
the water-melons were stored, as they would undoubtedly
make for them to quench their thirst. This order was well
carried out, the water-melons were destroyed, and a number
of women and children captured, whilst the tribesmen were
scattered over the country in search of water, and many
died of thirst. The next day the enemy's camp was burnt,
and the women and children, who would otherwise have
perished, I ordered to be brought to Bir Om Lawai, which
I now attacked. The enemy here made a most determined
defence, and I lost sixteen men killed, and twenty wounded.
This loss brought home the fact to me that I had very few
good regulars left, whilst the enemy, even if defeated, were
daily increasing in number.

Being the solitary European in a foreign country, and in
the midst of an intriguing and unfriendly population, I had
to resort to all sorts of means to discover the plots and
designs of those by whom I was surrounded ; and sometimes, by money, or by gifts distributed in secret, I was able
to learn beforehand what was likely to occur, and take
measures accordingly. Through the help of my servants I
utilised the services of some of the profligate women of the
town, who, as was the custom of the country, prepared the
native beer, or marissa, which is consumed in large quantities by the lower classes in the brothels. These houses
were the rendezvous for every description of loafer, grumbler,
and tattler who wished to let his tongue wag without restraint,
under the influence of drink. My servants had told me that
during these drinking-bouts they frequently talked of the
great religious rising of the Mahdi, for which, it may be
readily imagined, those present had not much sympathy.
It was, however, generally agreed that the Government
having placed so many Christians and unbelievers in high
positions, in which they were employed in combating this
religious reformer, the result must be bad. The soldiers
who frequented these houses of ill-fame often remarked, I

was told, that although they liked me, they attributed the losses we had suffered in action to the fact of my being a Christian. I was perfectly well aware that these views were not the outcome of the brain of the Black soldier, who, as a rule, cares little about religion, but were instigated by those who were doing their utmost to upset and nullify my authority, and make me unpopular with the men.

Now, on my return from Bir Om Lawai, still more serious news awaited me. My servants told me that in one of the brothels belonging to a woman in my secret pay, daily meetings were held, in which the soldiers discussed the project of wholesale desertion. On inquiry I found that the principal instigators of these seditious meetings were non-commissioned officers and men of the Fur tribe, who were reported to be tired of this constant fighting, and who declared that the days of Turkish authority were numbered. Their plan was to desert to Sultan Dud Benga, the successor of Sultan Harun, who resided on the western slopes of Jebel Marra. As the Fur section was the most numerous and powerful in the battalion, the matter was a most serious one; I therefore sent for the battalion commander, Adjutant-Major Mohammed Effendi Farag, and told him what I had heard. He appeared greatly surprised, and assured me he knew nothing of the matter, and that he should not fail to unearth the plot, and bring the ringleaders to justice. I ordered him to maintain the strictest secrecy, and do nothing which would raise the slightest suspicion. Whilst he was with me I sent for my servant and handed him a bag full of money, telling him to take it to the woman and instruct her to invite the various persons concerned to her house the next day, and give them an exceptionally good entertainment at her own expense; at the same time I told my servant to induce her to let him hide somewhere in the house where he could overhear what was said, and that if she could carry out these directions to my satisfaction I should reward her handsomely. Soon after my servant returned, telling me he had arranged everything.

The day following the entertainment I again sent for the
adjutant-major, and was now able to communicate to him
the names of six of the ringleaders, whom I ordered him
to instantly arrest; moreover, I was able to give him the
details of the design and the actual date of its intended
execution. In half an hour he returned with the six prisoners, whose hands were tied behind their backs. They
comprised one sergeant, three corporals, and two lance-
corporals—all of the Fur tribe. They were accompanied
by a crowd of kavasses and spectators, whom I sent off, and
then, in the presence of their commanding officer, I asked
them what instigated them to revolt against the Government. They absolutely denied having any such intention,
and assured me of their innocence. 'But,' said I, 'I know
perfectly well you have been holding meetings in the house
of your compatriot Khadiga. I gave you plenty of time to
come to reason, but you grew daily more rebellious. Yesterday you were all with Khadiga, drinking marissa, and
you agreed that the day after to-morrow you would execute
your plan. Your object was to join with your friends in the
third, fourth, and fifth companies, take your arms, open the
western gate of the fort, and desert to Sultan Abdullahi,
and, if necessary, to have recourse to force to carry out your
design. Did you not assert yesterday, Sergeant Mohammed,
that you had almost two hundred men at your disposal?
You see now I know everything, and it is useless to deny it.'
They listened in silence; they knew they had been discovered, and now they freely confessed, and asked for my
pardon. 'That is out of my hands,' I replied. 'Go now
with your commandant and confess openly that you are
guilty in the presence of the other officers of the battalion;
the law shall decide.' I then instructed the commandant
to assemble a court-martial, and to arrange that all the non-
commissioned officers should be present whilst the evidence
was being taken; but at the same time I warned him to let
it be understood by all (as I was afraid that some of the
men might desert through fear) that other men implicated

in the case should not be punished, as I held the non-commissioned officers alone responsible.   The same afternoon
the proceedings of the case, with the full confessions, were
brought to me, but without the sentence.   I therefore returned them to the court to give sentence, and soon afterwards the commandant returned.   The court had sentenced
them to death, but recommended them to mercy.   In my
opinion an example was absolutely necessary, and though it
was pain and grief to me, I confirmed the sentence of death,
which was ordered to be carried out at once.

The regulars and irregulars were marched to an open
space outside the zariba ; six graves were dug, and the condemned men, who showed no signs of fear, after saying two
rakas (short prayers), were led to the brinks of the graves,
and there shot dead by the six detachments.   I spoke to the
assembled men, warning them that anyone again found
guilty of mutinous or seditious conduct would undoubtedly
suffer the same penalty, and I sincerely trusted this would
be the first and last case of the kind that should ever be
brought to my notice.   I hoped we should all be better
friends in the future, and that times would improve.   I then
ordered the garrison to march back to the fort.

I was upset and sad.   I thought of the number of good
men lost in our fights, and now I was forced to take the
most extreme measures to maintain discipline.   On all sides
intriguers were doing their utmost to impair my authority,
quite ignoring the fact that should they succeed they would
be no better off—indeed, times were to come when they
would be only too glad to obey the orders of the European
they now so detested.   That evening I sent for Mohammed
Effendi Farag, and questioned him about the day's proceedings, and whether the men had been impressed by the execution, remarking, at the same time, that the soldiers must
thoroughly understand their non-commissioned officers fully
deserved the punishment they received, and, moreover, that
it was an act of great leniency on my part not to take action
against the other men implicated in the plot.   'Now, Farag

Effendi,' said I, ' I want you to be thoroughly true and straightforward with me. I know that you are friendly-minded towards me, otherwise I should not certainly have asked you to come and speak with me alone. Tell me, how am I regarded personally by the men and the officers, excepting, of course, those who are selfishly seeking their own interests ?' 'Although not accustomed to such severe discipline,' he answered, ' they are fond of you, and you are beloved by the men because you pay them regularly, which was not formerly the case. Besides, they much appreciate your custom of distributing the plunder amongst them. But this year we have had very heavy losses, and the men are getting tired of continual fighting.'

' But,' said I, ' we have to fight. I do not go out on expeditions to make conquests or gain honour and glory ; personally, I would much prefer rest and peace.' ' Of course I quite understand that,' said Farag Effendi ; ' still, these losses, which might have been avoided, have greatly affected the men. One man has lost his father ; another his brother ; many have lost friends and relatives ; and if this goes on they will become disinclined to fight.'

' I also quite understand that,' I replied. ' Although I have not lost a father or brother, still I have lost friends ; and I risk my precious life equally with my officers and men. I am always with them, and am just as liable to be struck by bullets and spears as they are.' ' They are well aware of that,' he answered, ' and you should give them credit for their obedience to foreigners, with whom they are always ready to risk their lives.' ' Certainly I am a foreigner and a European,' I said ; ' and I have no reason to make a secret of it, or be ashamed of it. Is this what they object to ? Now, tell me truly.'

Mohammed Farag was one of my best-educated officers. He had studied in various schools in Cairo, but had been taken as a conscript ; he was one of those rare men who acknowledge others' merits, and was always ready to learn from those he thought better educated than himself. He was neither fanatical nor religious, but he was a grumbler, and rather hot-tempered. These were, I think, his only bad qualities, and they had led him to commit some crime, for which he had been banished to the Sudan.

When I now called upon him to tell me the truth he threw up his head and looked straight at me, and said, ' Well, you wish me to tell you the truth, then here it is : they do not object to you on account of your nationality, but on account of your faith.' At last I had drawn out of him what I was so anxious to know.

' Why on account of my faith ?' I asked. ' During all these years that I have been in Darfur they knew that I was a Christian, and yet no one ever said a word to me.' ' Ah !' said he, ' the times were very different then, and much better ; but now that this rascally Dongolawi has made a cloak of religion, he has adherents everywhere who purposely incite the people so as to attain their own evil ends. The idea has got about in the battalion (I do not know who started it) that in this religious war you will never be able to gain a victory, and that in every battle you fight you will suffer great losses, till at length you yourself will be killed. You can perfectly understand how an ignorant soldier would credit all this, and how he would impute it to the fact of your being a Christian. Our men are far too stupid to realize that our losses are due to the vastly superior strength of the rebels, and that as we have no chance of being relieved, so we must go on suffering defeat.'

' Suppose that I now turned Mohammedan,' said I, ' would my men believe in me and hope for victory ? and would that give them more confidence in me ?' ' Of course the men would believe you,' said he—' at least the majority of them ; have you not taken every opportunity of showing respect to our religion, and even caused it to be respected by others ? They will trust you implicitly ; but will you change your faith from conviction ?' he asked, smiling.

' Mohammed Effendi,' said I, ' you are an intelligent and well-educated man ; here conviction has nothing to do with

the case. In this life one has often to do things which are
contrary to one's persuasions, either by compulsion or from
some other cause. I shall be quite content if the soldiers
believe me and abandon their silly superstitions. Whether
others believe me or not is a matter of indifference to me.
I thank you most sincerely; keep our conversation entirely
to yourself. Good night!'

Mohammed Effendi Farag now left, and after a few
minutes' deliberation I resolved to present myself to the
troops the following morning as a Mohammedan. I was
perfectly well aware that in taking this step I should be
placing myself in a curious position, which could not fail to
be condemned by some. However, I made up my mind to
do it, knowing that I should thereby cut the ground from
under the feet of these intriguers, and should have a better
chance of preserving the province with which the Government had intrusted me. In my early youth my religious
ideas were somewhat lax; but at the same time I believed
myself to be, by conviction as well as by education, a good
Christian, though I was always inclined to let people take
their own way to salvation. The simple fact was that I
had not been sent to the Sudan as a missionary, but as an
official of the Egyptian Government.

At sunrise the next morning I sent for the adjutant-major,
and ordered him to have all the troops paraded, and to wait
for me; I then sent word to Zogal to summon before me
the Kadi, Ahmed Wad Beshir, and the chief merchant,
Mohammed Ahmed. When they came I talked to them on
general matters, and then told them to come on parade with
me inside the fort, only a few hundred paces from my door.
Taking command of the parade, I ordered the troops to
form square, and, mounted on horseback, I then entered
it, accompanied by the officers, attendants, and officials.
'Soldiers!' said I, 'we have passed through many hard
times together; the presence of danger shows what a man
is made of. You have fought and endured bravely, and I
am certain you will continue to do so. We fight for our

master the Khedive, the ruler of this country, and for our lives. I have shared with you your joys and your sorrows. Where danger was to be faced I was there with you, and that shall ever be my place. Although I am your chief, my life at such times is of no more value than yours.' 'Allah yetawel umrak ! Allah yekhallik !' (' May God give you long life ! May God preserve you !') shouted most of the men. I then continued : ' I hear that I am considered a foreigner and an unbeliever. You also all belong to different tribes ; my birthplace is far away, it is true, but I am not a foreigner. I am not an unbeliever ; I am as much a believer as you. Ashadu inna la ilaha illallah wa inna Mohammed rasul Allah !' (' I bear witness that there is no God but God, and Mohammed is His Prophet '). On my uttering these words the soldiers raised their rifles, shook their lances, and shouted out congratulations to me, whilst the officers and officials advanced and shook hands with me. When order was restored, I told them that I should openly attend prayers with them, and, ordering the men to re-form, Farag Effendi gave the ' present arms,' and the men then marched off to their quarters.

When everything was over, I invited Zogal Bey, my former companion, and the officers, to remain and partake of food and coffee with me ; they then bade me good-bye, assuring me of their delight, fidelity, and obedience. They made as if they credited me with my convictions, and I gave them equally to understand that I believed in the reality of their feelings and sentiments (though I well knew how little they were really worth). When they left I told Farag Effendi to select twenty of the best oxen from our stock and distribute them amongst the men as ' karama ' (sacrificial offerings), as well as one ox for each officer, at my own expense.

The effect on the men of the step I had now taken was much greater than I expected ; there was no longer any reluctance to be sent on expeditions, although our enemies were increasing daily in number and strength.

Merchants whom I paid to send me news from Kordofan informed me that reinforcements were daily arriving at Khartum from Cairo, and that the Government was hurrying on preparations for the despatch of the expedition, under European officers, to retake Kordofan; whilst the entire population, without exception, had joined the Mahdi, and were determined to offer a powerful resistance.

In Darfur all the southern tribes were now in open revolt; but thanks to our military posts, and to the fact that the northern tribes had been in contact with Egypt, from which they had derived considerable benefit through the caravan routes, they had hitherto shown no hostility. Of course it had been for long impossible to gather taxes in any part of the country; I had, therefore, paid the troops out of our reserve stores.

The Mahdi's continual victories were at last beginning to tell openly on Zogal Bey, and I noticed a distinct change in his conduct, though he still appeared loyal and submissive. It was abundantly clear to me that in his heart he wished all success to his cousin, the Mahdi, because he knew that, in that eventuality, he would be one of the first to reap tangible benefits. He was a man much liked by the officials under him, fairly well educated for a Sudanese; he was ever ready to do a favour when his own pocket was not thereby touched, and he got the character of being liberal. He was very wealthy, and kept up an enormous household in great state. He kept open table, and his popularity amongst the officials was, I think, in a large measure due to the fact that, as Acting-Governor, he had freely pardoned past offences, and took no steps to prevent them enriching themselves in all sorts of illicit ways. Through his influence most of his relatives had secured good positions and become wealthy. He was, therefore, a man with whom I had to reckon somewhat circumspectly. His popularity, coupled with the fact that he generally concurred in and executed my orders, rendered an open split with him undesirable, and would have certainly led to a diminution

of my authority; I was therefore inclined to let him alone
for the present. 'Ebed en nar an el kotn wa enta tertah'
('Keep fire away from cotton, and you will be at ease'),
as the Arabs say, seemed to me to thoroughly apply in this
case, and to that principle I adhered.

Summoning Farag Effendi, Wad Asi, and Kadi el Beshir,
all of whom were loyal to Government, and prayed from
their hearts for its success, I communicated my plans to
them, in the strictest secrecy, and obtained their full concurrence. When they had left me I summoned Zogal, and
now conversed with him quite alone. 'Zogal,' I began,
'you and I are perfectly alone here, and God is our witness.
For years we have eaten bread and salt together, and
although from the day I arrived I have been your superior,
our relations with each other have been rather those of a
friendly than of an official nature. I now ask you to do
two things for me—trust me and render me a service.'

'Well, Mudir Umum' (Governor-General), he replied,
'you are my superior; tell me what you want and I shall
obey.' 'Your cousin the Mahdi,' said I, 'has now conquered Kordofan, El Obeid has fallen, and the entire
population has joined him. The country between us and
Government is in his hands. His extraordinary success
has inclined your heart to him. Have you forgotten all the
favours you have reaped from Government? Are you
unmindful of the distinction bestowed upon you by the
Khedive, in the shape of a decoration and rank obtained for
you through the good offices of the Government? Have
you forgotten the duties required of you from your position?
Speak, is it not so?' 'It is so,' replied Zogal quickly;
'the Mahdi is my cousin, and I cannot deny that our blood-
relationship has inclined me to him. Still, hitherto I have
faithfully performed my duties, and I trust I shall continue
to do so in the future.'

'Speaking generally,' I replied, 'you have performed
your duties well; but I am told you are in communication
with the Mahdi. Why should you hide this from me?'

'I do not communicate directly,' replied Zogal quickly, 'but merchants coming from Kordofan give me verbal messages from him, and I have sworn to the bearers of these messages that I would not tell you; that is why I kept it secret. But I assure you that they only referred to news from Kordofan, and no attempt has been made to win me to his cause.'

'Well, let it be,' said I, 'I do not want you to justify yourself; but, tell me, what have you heard about this expedition which the Government is preparing to send to retake Kordofan?' 'I have heard,' replied he, 'that a large expedition has arrived at Khartum, and that they are going to try and reconquer the country.' 'Not only will they try, but they will effect the reconquest of the country,' I answered. 'Now, Zogal, you are a man of sense and intelligence. It must be perfectly clear to you that, if compelled by circumstances, I am still sufficiently powerful to make you harmless; but I do not think this would be an advantageous step to take, and it would pain me deeply to take action against a man like yourself, who has served the Government loyally for many years, and has always befriended me. I will therefore discharge you for the present, and you may now go to Kordofan with my full consent. Religious movements, such as that now going on, have a certain amount of glamour from a distance, and induce sympathy; but when examined more closely they are neither so seductive nor so alarming. I shall intrust you with letters to the Government, which I want you to send secretly to Khartum, and which will inform them of the nature of your mission. As the expedition will probably start for Kordofan next month, I want you to do your utmost to prevent the Mahdi sending a force into Darfur or despatching proclamations to the tribes inciting them to revolt. If you can arrange this, it will be of advantage both to him and to you. Should the expedition succeed, I will take all responsibility for your conduct on my shoulders, and you need have no fear: but if the Mahdi is successful

—which God forbid—then we shall be entirely cut off from all hope of relief, and shall probably be compelled to submit, in which case it will be of advantage to him to have the country handed over in fairly good condition. As a guarantee for the loyal conduct of your undertaking, I shall keep your wives, children, and households in the fort here. The Mahdi will respect this, and for your sake will not run the risk of endangering their lives.'

'I shall carry out your instructions,' said Zogal, 'and prove to you that I am loyal. Are you going to write a letter to the Mahdi?'

'No,' I replied, 'because I do not want to have any dealings with him. I know perfectly well that you will repeat the whole of this conversation to him. Your cousin is very cunning, and, privately, will give me credit for having spoken the truth, and he will no doubt make as much capital as he can out of your mission; but as long as you hold loyally to your promise, I shall take every care of your family, and although you are nominally discharged, I shall continue to issue your pay in full, but should you fail to keep to the conditions of this arrangement, the guarantee will no longer hold good. I should like you to start as soon as possible, and in three days I shall expect you to be ready; I think that should be sufficient time.'

'I would prefer to stay here with my own people,' said Zogal; 'but as you wish me to perform this mission, and to put my loyalty to the test, I shall carry it out, but with a sorrowful heart.'

Sending now for Farag Effendi, Wad Asi, and the Kadi, in Zogal's presence I told them of the arrangement we had made. They showed much apparent surprise and excitement, and summoned Zogal to swear a solemn oath of loyalty. He swore on the Kuran by the oath of divorce* that he would adhere truly and faithfully to the agreement made between us.

* One of the most solemn forms of administering an oath is for the person taking the oath to say, 'I impose upon myself divorcement

I now wrote the necessary letters to the Government, giving a brief account of the situation in Darfur; and three days later Zogal, accompanied by three servants, left Dara for El Obeid, *viâ* Toweisha. It was well known he was a relative of the Mahdi; he had therefore nothing to fear, and I subsequently learnt he was received everywhere with open arms.

I now set to work to build fresh batteries at the angles of the fort, and collected all the corn I could find; but this short period of tranquillity did not last long. Beshari Bey Wad Bekir, chief of the Beni Helba Arabs, instigated by his father-in-law, Sheikh Taher et Tegawi, planned a raid on Dara.   In spite of my threatening letter, he had attacked the Tagu and Messeria Arabs, killing a number of them, and capturing many women and children. In consequence I placed two hundred and fifty regulars and one hundred Bazingers under the command of Mattar, one of Zogal's relatives; but I could only take twenty-five horses, as most of them had been attacked by some sort of disease, and with this force I quitted Dara.

After three days' march we arrived at Amaké, where I was attacked by the Beni Helba, under Beshari Bey, with whom was my old friend Gabralla.   They were in considerable force, but had few fire-arms, and we succeeded in beating them off and dispersing them without much difficulty. The next day they attacked us again at Kalambasi, a march of a day and a half from Amaké : but here again we put them to flight with equal ease.   Our insignificant losses on both occasions were ascribed by my men to the efficacy of my Friday prayers with them, and not to the small number of fire-arms possessed by our enemies. We now advanced on Hashaba, which was the head sheikh's village, turned him out, and then offered to conclude peace with him; but our efforts failed, and I proceeded thence to Guru, about half a day's march further on. On the way the twelve mounted scouts in advance were suddenly attacked by Beshari Bey alone, who broke through their line, wounded

one of them slightly, and then, turning to the left, he drew
his horse up between the scouts and my main body, at the
edge of the forest, and about eight hundred yards from us.
Advancing some three hundred paces closer, I recognised
him, but purposely did not shoot : instead, I sent one of my
boys unarmed to him, saying, ' Isa, give my compliments
to Beshari Bey, and tell him that if he wants to show his
wife how brave he is, he should set about it in a different
way; if he repeats this manœuvre he will certainly be
killed.' The road was fairly open, with trees only here
and there, and as we marched on, I could see my servant
standing for a few seconds before Beshari Bey, and then
returning towards us. On reaching us, he said : ' Beshari
Bey sends you his compliments. He says he has no wish
to live any longer, and seeks death.' Deluded man ! he
soon found it.

Arriving at Guru, we constructed a zariba, and feeling
sure that Beshari's ill-considered dash would make him
attack, I ordered the troops to move out about three hundred
paces, whilst I posted the cavalry on the flank and sent forward about twenty horsemen to try and decoy the Arabs
out of the wood. The latter had barely started when I saw
two mounted Arabs dashing at them full speed, with lances
lowered ; they were Beshari Bey and his attendant. Before
he reached my men his horse stumbled and fell, and while
his companion was holding his horse to enable him to mount,
my horsemen seized the occasion to attack him, and a thrown
spear striking him full in the eye, he fell, whilst his attendant
was struck by a spear in the back and killed. Meanwhile
I had galloped up to the spot, and there I found Beshari
Bey lying dead : my men had twice plunged a huge spear
into his body. His son Abo, who had dashed out to his aid,
was also wounded, but succeeded in escaping, though two
other Sheikhs who had accompanied him—Shartia Habiballa
and Et Tom—were killed. Seizing their horses, I now
called out to the regulars to advance, and on their arrival I
ordered each of the horsemen to take up an infantryman

behind him and pursue the Arabs, who I felt sure would not attempt to stand after the death of their leaders.   After a gallop of about two miles we came up with the flying Arabs, and ordering the regulars to dismount and fire, I turned the horsemen against the mounted Beni Helbas.   No quarter was given, as my men were determined to avenge the death of Sheikh Afifi, who had been killed near here.

After a few hours the rout was complete, and we now returned to the zariba.   On our way back we stumbled across Beshari's body.   My officers at once asked to be allowed to cut off his head and send it to Dara, but out of respect to his nephew, who had pleaded yesterday for peace, I prevented them from doing this, giving over the body to him, with a piece of calico in which to enshroud it, and I myself attended the burial of my old friend who had fought against us—contrary to his own convictions—and who, seeking death, had now found it.   In this engagement we lost two killed and several wounded, amongst whom was the faithful Salama, who had taken my letter from Om Waragat to Dara, and who was ever foremost in pursuit.

I now returned to Guru.   The disease of *filaria medinensis* (guinea-worm) had broken out in the upper part of my leg and in both feet, and caused me such excruciating pain that I could scarcely remain in the saddle.   Having crushed the Beni Helbas, it was useless for me to remain out any longer; I therefore returned to Dara.

CHAPTER VIII.

HICKS PASHA'S EXPEDITION.

Spread of belief in the Mahdi's Divinity—Sheikh Sennusi is offered, but refuses, the Position of Mahdi's Khalifa—The Mahdi begins to organize his Government—The spread of the Revolt in the Gezira —Criticisms on the Attitude of the Egyptian Government—The Despatch of Osman Digna to the Eastern Sudan—Hicks Pasha's Expedition enters Kordofan—Incidents on the March—Gallantry of Colonel Farquhar—The Diaries of Farquhar and Vizetelly— The Desertion of Gustav Klootz—The Mahdists harass the Expedition—The final Attack on the doomed Square—Extract from O'Donovan's Diary—The Mahdi's trumphal Entry into El Obeid.

AFTER the capture of El Obeid the Mahdi turned all his attention to increasing his power. His adherents on the river kept him very fully informed of all that passed. He was aware that Abdel Kader had applied to Cairo for reinforcements, which had arrived, and he did not doubt the Government would do all in its power to reconquer its lost provinces; that was his reason for so constantly preaching the Jehad, and reminding his followers that a great war was impending, in which they would be victorious.

Giegler Pasha had been successful at Duem in November, 1882, and at the end of January, 1883, Abdel Kader Pasha had scored a signal success at Maatuk. But the Mahdi paid little attention to these defeats; he was principally concerned with the news that an expedition was being prepared in Khartum, under European officers, for the reconquest of Kordofan. He therefore lost no time in at once despatching proclamations ordering the tribes to leave their districts and join him. To these assembled multitudes he now preached more fervently than ever, urging them to renounce the pleasures of this life, and think only of the life to come. 'Ana akhreb ed dunya wa ammer el akhera' ('I destroy this world, and I construct the world to come'), was his endless theme. To those who were obedient he promised pleasures in Para-

dise beyond all the heart could conceive; but the disobedient
he threatened with condign punishment and hell-fire. Cir-
culars written in this sense were despatched far and wide,
and the Emirs were enjoined to allow only those to remain
in their districts whose services were absolutely necessary
for the cultivation of the lands, but that all others must
forthwith immigrate to him and range themselves under
his banners.

Men, women, and children now flocked in hundreds of
thousands to El Obeid to see this holy man and catch even
a word of his inspired doctrine ; and the ignorant multitudes
saw in his face and person what they believed to be truly 'a
man sent from God.'

Dressed only in a jibba and sirual (drawers), with a belt
of gus, or straw, round his waist, and wearing a Mecca takia
(skull-cap), round which was bound a muslin turban, he
stood with all humility before his followers, preaching of
love to God and the cause, and of the necessity of renouncing
the vanities of this world. But once in his house it was
quite another matter ; here he lived in a state of grandeur
and luxury, and became a slave to those passions for food
and women to which the Sudanese are so addicted. Should
any women, young girls, and slaves be captured, they were
brought before him, and all the prettiest and the best found
a home in his harem ; whilst the maid-servants, who were
versed in all the arts of the most approved Sudan cooking,
were relegated to his kitchen.

After the siege of El Obeid, he considered whom he
should appoint as his fourth Khalifa, and decided that
Mohammed es Sennusi, the most influential religious sheikh
in North Africa, should be nominated. He therefore
despatched Taher Wad Ishak, of the Zaghawa tribe, with
a letter to him to that effect ; but Sennusi treated the offer
with scorn, and left the letter unanswered.

The Mahdi now set to work to regulate his government.
His administration was based on very simple lines. First
of all he established the Beit el Mal, or treasury, over which

he placed his faithful friend, Ahmed Wad Suleiman. In this treasury were deposited the tithes (ushr) and the fitra and zeka (alms for the poor, two and a half per cent.) on all booty taken in war as well as confiscated property, and fines for theft, drinking, and smoking. There was no system to regulate the revenue and expenditure. Ahmed Wad Suleiman was therefore free to give what he liked to whom he pleased.

Jurisdiction was placed in the hands of the Kadi, who was called by the Mahdi ' Kadi el Islam,' and several assistants. Ahmed Wad Ali, who had formerly been Kadi at Shakka under me, and who had been one of the foremost in the storming of El Obeid, was the first to hold this high position. Of course, the Mahdi and his Khalifas reserved to themselves the right to punish all crime—more especially anything connected with doubt or suspicion as to the Divine nature of the Mahdi—with death. As such judgments were in entire opposition to the sharia (or Moslem religious law) as taught, the Mahdi strictly forbade the study of theology, and ordered all books of this description to be burnt, the Kuran alone being allowed to be read, though even this he did not permit to be openly expounded.

Communication between the Mahdi and the inhabitants of the Gezira, who now looked upon themselves as his most devoted adherents, was, of course, frequent and detailed. He learnt of Abdel Kader's departure for Kawa and Sennar with a large force in February. That town had been besieged by Ahmed el Makashef, but the Pasha inflicted a defeat on him at Meshra ed Dai, and had raised the siege. Saleh Bey had pursued the rebels as far as Jebel Sekhedi, and had driven them into the waterless plain between that place and Kawa, where numbers perished from thirst. This district is still called by the local people, ' Tibki wa teskut ' (' You cry and are silent ').

These defeats, however, in no way diminished the Mahdi's popularity. They relieved the situation for the soldiers and officials, it is true, but they only put off the evil day which was surely to come. Had attention been paid to Abdel Kader Pasha's advice the whole situation in the Sudan might have been changed. He was against the despatch of a large expedition to reconquer Kordofan, but recommended the reinforcements coming from Cairo should be garrisoned in strong defensive positions along the White Nile, and that for the time being the rebels should be left to themselves. The military forces at his disposal were quite sufficient to stamp out the revolt in the Gezira (Island) between the Blue and White Niles, and to check the advance of the Mahdists from the west. Had this plan been adopted, and the rebels been left to themselves, it is more than probable the complete absence of any regulated system of administration would have soon resulted in discord breaking out, and gradually, at a later period, Government would have been able to recover the ground it had lost. I certainly could not have preserved authority in Darfur until that time; but even if that province were lost, it would undoubtedly have been the lesser of two evils. However, those at the head of the Government in Cairo thought otherwise. The edict went forth that the prestige of the Government was to be restored at all costs, and this was to be effected by an army despatched under the English General Hicks, assisted by other European officers. Abdel Kader Pasha was recalled, and relieved by Ala ed Din Pasha, formerly Governor-General of the Eastern Sudan. All these facts were known almost at once to the Mahdi, and he took good account of them.

Meanwhile Zogal had arrived at El Obeid, where he had received an enthusiastic reception. One hundred guns were ordered to be fired in his honour, and it was reported far and wide that Darfur had surrendered to the ever-victorious Mahdi. Zogal's return to Darfur was considered quite a sufficient guarantee for the preservation of the province as a possession of the new ruler, consequently no force was despatched, and the Mahdi now directed all his attention to events on the Nile.

General Hicks shortly after his arrival proceeded with a portion of his force to Kawa, inflicted a defeat on the rebels at Marabia (29 April, 1883), and killed Ahmed el Makashef.

Amongst the various emissaries despatched to different parts of the country was Osman Digna, the former Suakin slave-dealer, who was enjoined to raise the Jehad in the neighbourhood of his own town. The Mahdi showed much astuteness in selecting this man, who subsequently became so celebrated ; and he rightly judged that a local revolt in the Eastern Sudan would in all probability seriously embarrass the Khartum Government, and delay, or perhaps put off altogether, the expedition about to be sent to Kordofan. The details of the various encounters between this redoubtable Emir and the Government troops are too well known to require more than a mere passing reference here ; suffice it to say that the operations in the eastern districts, although successful to the Mahdists, did not have the effect of causing the Government to alter their intention in regard to the Kordofan expedition, and early in September, 1833, the ill-fated Hicks left Khartum for Duem, on the White Nile, where he joined Ala ed Din Pasha, who had been instructed to accompany the expedition.

Surely the situation in Kordofan must have been misunderstood by the Cairo authorities if they imagined that, by the despatch of this expedition, they would succeed in overturning the Mahdi, who was then supreme ruler of these western districts in which every man was his most devoted adherent. Did they not realize that the annihilation of Rashed, Shellali, and Lutfi, as well as the fall of Bara, El Obeid, and a host of other towns had placed the Mahdi in possession of a far larger number of rifles than those disposed of amongst Hicks' force of ten thousand men ? Were they not aware that these rifles were now in the hands of men who thoroughly understood how to use them—men who had been owners of Bazingers, who were

elephant and ostrich hunters, and had now at their command contingents of reliable fighting material? Besides,
were there not now enrolled under the Mahdi's banners
thousands of regulars and irregulars who had been formerly
in the Government service? Did they imagine for a moment
that all these men, when the chance came, intended to desert
and join Hicks? No; they seemed to realize nothing of
this, and, on completely wrong presumptions, they risked
the lives of thousands. Surely there were those amongst
the Government advisers who had sufficient knowledge of
the Sudan to realize how fully the negro proverb applied
in this matter : ' Illi beyakhud ummi hua abuya ' (' He who
marries my mother is my father'). The Mahdi had conquered the country, and had thus metaphorically married
their mother. Him, therefore, they had fully accepted as
their lord and master. What do those people care about
good actions and kindnesses previously done to them? I
do not, of course, deny that to this general rule there are
exceptions, yet unquestionably my remarks, severe as they
are, apply to the majority.

Ten thousand men in square formation, with six thousand
camels in their midst, were to march through districts overgrown with vegetation and grass taller than a man's height;
at most they could not see more than two hundred or three
hundred yards to their front, in the little open patches where
the sparse population had cultivated small clearings. They
must be ready at any moment for the attack of an enemy
far more numerous and as well armed as themselves, besides
being infinitely better fighters, and who to this day pride
themselves on their bravery and headlong dash. Along
almost the entire route by which the army was to march
there were scarcely any wells, though plenty of stagnant
rain-pools ; and when they had drunk up the water in them,
what were they then to do?

Had they adopted the northern road, *via* Gebra and Bara,
they would at least have had the advantage of open ground
and a good supply of water at certain places, which, if in-

sufficient, could, with modern appliances, have been made amply sufficient for the whole force. At the same time the support of the powerful Kababish tribe against the Mahdists would have been assured, and the enormous train accompanying the force could thus have been greatly diminished.

Six thousand camels, huddled together in the centre of a square, presented a perfect forest of heads and necks; it was impossible for a bullet fired by one of the enemy from behind a tree to altogether miss this gigantic target : if it failed to strike in front, it would most certainly have its billet in the centre or rear. Then, again, an advance might have been made by detachments, and the great baggage train left under strong guard at either Duem or Shatt, the men merely advancing in light marching order, clearing the road north, south, and west, and establishing a military post whenever they had subdued a district. Of course this plan would have taken some time—perhaps a year—to execute ; but there was no hurry. Then internal dissensions were rife— Hicks and his European officers on the one side; Ala ed Din Pasha, his officials, and most of the Egyptian officers on the other.

And were not the troops composed mostly of the disbanded rabble of Arabi Pasha's army, which had just been defeated by the British? General Hicks no doubt fully understood matters, and replying to a question put to him by one of his friends at Duem as to what he thought of the situation, he replied quietly, ' I am like Jesus Christ in the midst of the Jews.' Still he marched off ; perhaps he thought that if he refused to advance, his honour might be impugned.

Slowly moved the great mass of men and animals onward ; the few inhabitants who lived in this part of the country had long since fled. Now and then in the far distance Arabs were seen watching the advance, and then disappearing from view. On one occasion Hicks, looking through his glasses, observed some horsemen amongst the trees ; halting the square, he ordered a division of irregular cavalry to advance and attack them. A few minutes later they returned in hopeless confusion; they had lost some killed and many wounded, and reported they had been attacked by a greatly superior force. Hicks then despatched Colonel Farquhar with half a battalion of regulars to examine the spot where the skirmish had taken place. He reported that he found six cavalrymen lying dead, shot in the back; they had been completely stripped, but nothing was to be seen of the 'powerful enemy'; there were the hoofmarks of at most ten horses, and no doubt by these the cavalry division had been put to flight.

The following day three horsemen again appeared in sight, when Colonel Farquhar, accompanied only by his servants, galloped at them, killing two, and bringing in the third a prisoner. I was told of both these episodes by the survivors of the expedition, and they related how the huge square crawled forward like a tortoise. Under the circumstances it was impossible to send out the camels to graze; they had to eat anything they could pick up in the square, and that was very little; of course they died in quantities. They used to eat even the straw pads of their saddles, and consequently the hard wood came down on their haunches and galled them till they became in a truly pitiable condition; still they dragged along, carrying not only their own loads, but those of their broken-down companions in misery.

No doubt Colonel Farquhar, Baron Seckendorff, Major Herlth, the other European, and some of the principal Egyptian officers did all they could to help General Hicks in this critical situation, but the bulk of the army appeared to be utterly regardless of the impending catastrophe. Poor Vizetelly made his sketches, and O'Donovan wrote his diary; but who was to send them home to those who were so anxiously awaiting them?

No sooner did the Mahdi learn that the expedition had started than he again sent proclamations to call the tribes, summoning them instantly to the Jehad, with the usual promises of reward to those who obeyed, and of punishment to those who hung back. Quitting El Obeid himself, he encamped under an enormous Adansonia-tree near the town, and there he awaited the approach of the Egyptians ; his Khalifas and Emirs followed his example, and soon a gigantic camp of tukuls (straw huts) was formed. Reviews were held daily, war-drums beaten, guns fired, and men and horses trained in all sorts of exercises, in preparation for the great battle. The Emirs Haggi Mohammed Abu Girga, Omar Wad Elias Pasha, and Abdel Halim Mussaid had already been sent to Duem to watch the enemy's advance and cut their communications ; but they were strictly forbidden to attack the main body of the army. Before leaving, the real condition of the advancing force was known, and they begged the Mahdi's permission to attack it, but it was refused.

Shortly before the expedition reached Rahad, Gustav Klootz, a German non-commissioned officer, formerly Baron Seckendorff's, and latterly Mr. O'Donovan's, servant, foreseeing the almost certain annihilation of the force, deserted, with the intention of joining the Mahdi. Ignorant of the country, he wandered about, and the next morning was found by a small party of Mahdists, who were about to kill him, but he endeavoured to make them understand, in his broken Arabic, that he wanted to be taken to the Mahdi, and after robbing him of all he possessed, he was sent under escort to El Obeid, three days distant. Although clothed only as a servant, thousands of people crowded round to see this English general who had come to ask for terms of peace. He was brought before the Mahdi, and through the other Europeans present was questioned about the state of the expedition. Gustav did not hesitate to say that it could not be worse, and that neither courage nor harmony existed amongst its ranks. Naturally this news greatly pleased the Mahdi, but Gustav added that the army would not submit without a fight, and that in all probability it would be annihilated. Immensely cheered by this information, the Mahdi now summoned Gustav to be converted to Islam, in which he of course readily acquiesced, and he was then handed over for further care to Osman Wad el Haj Khaled.

So confident of victory had the Mahdi become after Gustav's statement, that he had hundreds of summonses written out and distributed along the road, calling on Hicks and his officers to surrender. Of course they were left un-answered, but at the same time they had their effect on many who were concerned about their own safety. Others, on the contrary, used these papers in a manner which so irritated the Mahdi that for long he visited his wrath on the unfortunate survivors who had dared to put to such con-temptuous uses documents in which divinely inspired words were written.

Prior to his departure from Duem, Hicks had been in-formed by the Government that he would be joined *en route* by six thousand men from Jebel Tagalla, as well as some hundreds of Habbania Arabs, and he daily expected to meet these, and thus revive the flagging courage of his demoralized men. But he waited in vain—not a man came to him, nor did he ascertain a word of news. On quitting Rahad he advanced to Aluba in Dar Ghodayat, in the hope of obtain-ing an abundant supply of water there; and on the 3rd November he reached Kashgeil, some thirty miles south-east of El Obeid.

Meanwhile the Mahdi had worked up his fanatical fol-lowers to a pitch of the wildest enthusiasm, and had told them the Prophet had announced to him that on the day of battle they would be accompanied by twenty thousand angels, who would attack the unbelievers. On the 1st of November he quitted El Obeid for Birket, where his fol-lowers, uniting with the force previously despatched to watch the square, now worried the tired and thirsty Egyp-tians incessantly. On the 3rd November Abu Anga and his Black Jehadia, concealed in the thick forest and broken ground, poured a continuous fire on the square, which was forced to halt and zariba; and here human beings and animals, huddled together, offered a target which none could fail to hit. Every moment a weary man, horse, camel, or mule would fall to the bullet of an invisible enemy; and for hours this decimation continued, whilst the wretched troops suffered agonies from thirst, and were unable to move in any direction. It was not till the afternoon that the enemy drew off, just out of rifle range, and from this position kept careful watch on the square, as a cat would play with a mouse. Their losses had been insignificant; one or two Emirs, amongst them the son of Elias Pasha, had fallen— and no wonder! his fanaticism had induced him to dash up, almost alone, to within a yard of the zariba. How terrible must have been the feelings of poor Hicks! Instead of water, his wretched men received a hail of lead—yet only a mile off there was a large pool of rain-water; but none in that doomed square knew the country, and even had they known, it was now too late to reach it. Abu Anga and his men, under cover of darkness, crept close up to the zariba, and all night long poured an incessant fire into this seething mass of men and animals. Utterly demoralized, poor Hicks's troops moaned, ' Masr fein, ya Sitti Zenab dilwakti waktek!' (' Where is Egypt! Oh, our Lady Zenab, now is your time to help us!') while the hardy Blacks, lying flat on the ground within a few yards of the zariba, unharmed by the shower of bullets which passed overhead, would answer back, ' Di el Mahdi el muntazer ' (' This is the expected Mahdi').

The next morning (November 4) Hicks continued the advance, leaving behind him a heap of dead and dying and a few guns, the teams of which had been killed; but ere he had proceeded a mile he was attacked by at least one hundred thousand wild fanatics concealed amongst the trees. In a moment the square was broken, and a whole-sale massacre took place. The European officers, with a few Turkish cavalry, alone attempted to make a stand under the wide-spreading branches of a large Adansonia tree; but, attacked on all sides, they were eventually killed almost to a man. The heads of Baron Seckendorff (who wore a full light-coloured beard) and General Hicks were cut off and sent to the Mahdi, who at once summoned Klootz (now known as Mustafa) to identify them; but this seemed hardly necessary, as it was well known they had been killed.

After this immense victory, the Mahdi and his Khalifas now returned with their troops to Birket, literally drunk with success.

Several Emirs and their men had been left on the battle-field to collect the plunder and bring it to the Beit el Mal. The thousands upon thousands of dead bodies, which lay piled up in heaps, were divested of every stitch of clothing. Some time later the note-books of Colonel Farquhar and Mr. O'Donovan were sent to me. I read all they contained most carefully, and terribly sad reading it was! They both wrote much about the discord that existed, and of the quarrel between General Hicks and Ala ed Din Pasha. Farquhar attacked his chief somewhat severely for his military mistakes. Both had foreseen what had now occurred, and Farquhar reproached him bitterly for having ever started with a force whose condition and *morale* were such as to warrant certain disaster. The European officers got little assistance; apparently one of the few Egyptian officers who helped them was a certain Abbas Bey. One passage in Colonel Farquhar's diary I well remember; he wrote: 'I spoke to Mr. O'Donovan to-day, and asked him where he thought we should be eight days hence. "In Kingdom-Come," was his reply.' O'Donovan's journal was also written in much the same strain; he was greatly annoyed about Klootz's flight, and quoted it as an instance of the general feeling existing in the force. 'What must be the condition of an army,' he remarked, 'when even a European servant deserts to the enemy?' In another passage he wrote: 'I make my notes and write my reports, but who is going to take them home?'

Some fifteen days afterwards, when all the plunder had been deposited in the Beit el Mal, the Mahdi returned to El Obeid. Besides the guns, machine-guns, and rifles, a considerable sum of money had been found; but quantities

of loot were carried off by the Arabs, in spite of the barbarous punishments for theft enacted by Ahmed Wad
Suleiman : it was no uncommon thing for a thief to have
both his right hand and left foot cut off. The cunning
Blacks had secreted quantities of arms and ammunition in
the forests and in their own camps, which at a later period
proved very useful to them.

Nothing could have exceeded the savage grandeur of the
Mahdi's triumphal entry into El Obeid after the battle.
As he passed along, the people threw themselves on the
ground and literally worshipped him. There is not the
slightest doubt that by his victory at Shekan the Mahdi
had now the entire Sudan at his feet. From the Nile to
the Red Sea, from Kordofan to the frontiers of Wadai, all
looked to this holy man who had performed such wonders,
and they eagerly awaited his next move. Those who had
been already convinced of his Divine mission were now of
course more than ever his ardent supporters, and spread
his fame far and wide ; those who had doubted, doubted
no longer ; and the few who in their hearts understood
the imposture decided amongst themselves that if Government was not strong enough to send a force sufficient to
uphold its authority even in the Nile districts, they must,
against their own convictions, side with the stronger.

Several Europeans and some Egyptians living in the
large cities and towns now realized the seriousness of the
situation, and lost no time in making the best of their way
out of the doomed country, or, at any rate, despatched
north as much as they could of their portable property, well
knowing that it was impossible to stay any longer in the
Sudan, across which the Mahdi's hands now stretched from
east to west.

CHAPTER IX.

THE FALL OF DARFUR.

Dara Besieged — A Strange Expedient for concealing Letters — An
Armistice proposed and accepted between Myself and the Besiegers
—I resort to Stratagem to gain Time—Zogal writes from El Obeid,
and describes the Annihilation of the Relief Expedition—I review
the Situation and decide to Surrender—The Mahdists enter Dara—
Madibbo and his War-drums—Horrible Tortures inflicted on the
Inhabitants who had concealed Money—The Siege and Fall of El
Fasher—Letters from Egypt—The dreadful Fate of Major Hamada
—The Fall of Bahr el Ghazal—I leave for El Obeid.

By this time I had recovered from my disease (*filaria
medinensis*), and felt strong enough to undertake another
expedition; but the number of my trusted followers had
sadly diminished, and our stock of rifle ammunition was
getting very low. Said Bey Guma still affirmed that it
was impossible for him to send me any from Fasher, owing
to the fact that the Zayedia and Maheria Arabs had begun
to show signs of defection, and had been raiding cattle in
the neighbourhood of the town, which they had refused to
restore.

All my hopes were now centred in the success of the
Hicks expedition. Fortunately at that time I knew nothing
of the route they had chosen, nor of the demoralized condition of the force. For almost a year I had received no
news direct from Khartum, and latterly, in order to keep
up the spirits of the men, I had to have recourse to stratagem, by asserting that I had received news of great victories
for the Government forces. These scraps of news I of
course concocted myself, and wrote out in the form of
messages, which when received were read out with great
éclat before the assembled troops, and were greeted by the
salute of guns and general rejoicings. As a matter of fact,
about this time I did receive a little slip of paper from Ala
ed Din Pasha, informing me that His Highness the Khedive

had officially appointed me commandant of the troops in
Darfur, and that it was the intention of the Government to
send a strong force to chastise the rebels and re-establish
authority. I despatched copies of this note to Fasher and
Kebkebia, with orders that it should be read publicly and
salutes fired. I gave the bearer of the letter a public
reception, and loaded him with presents; he announced
that when he left Khartum the expedition was being prepared, and described the force as certain to be victorious.
Those who really knew hesitated to credit the glowing
accounts of the appearance of the troops; but at the same
time their hearts were full of glad expectation.

A few days later Khaled Wad Imam, whom I had sent
to Kordofan to collect news, returned, and gave me a verbal
message from Zogal; he also confirmed the news just
received as to the intention of the Government to despatch
an expedition against the Mahdi; but a few days afterwards
a man was intercepted wandering off to Shakka, bearing a
letter from Khaled to Madibbo, in which he told him to be
prepared to meet him shortly, in order to aid him in his
enterprise, and I had now no doubt that Khaled was really
Zogal's secret and confidential agent.

I now ordered Khaled to be seized and brought before
me. He admitted he had received Zogal's orders to take
his wives away to some safe refuge beyond my jurisdiction,
and his two special ones he had ordered to be brought to
him in Kordofan. It was on this account he had written to
Madibbo.

In consequence I had Zogal's family arrested, placed
Khaled in chains, and had his and Zogal's property confiscated and removed to the Beit el Mal, while that of the
other persons arrested was sequestrated.

My difficulties were now increasing daily, one might
almost say hourly. Zogal's disloyalty did not disturb me
very much, as I had long suspected it: but I was greatly
put about by the unsatisfactory news of the state of the
expeditionary force.

My time was fully taken up hurrying hither and thither combating the various local revolts, which sprang up with amazing rapidity. One day I was attacking Madibbo, another day some other chief, and then came the news that Darho's expedition against the Mima had been annihilated. My proposal to evacuate Dara and concentrate on El Fasher had been vetoed by my officers. Added to all this, dissensions now began to spring up amongst those whom I had hitherto looked upon as loyal adherents. Hassan Wad Saad Nur, whose pardon, it will be remembered, I had procured in Khartum, and whom I had brought with me on my own guarantee to Dara, to whom I had given a house just outside the fort, and when his horse died of disease I had given him another, and whom, being a native of the place, I had intrusted with procuring news, now sadly disappointed me. Unmindful of all the benefits I had bestowed on him, under the pretence of visiting a relative, he mounted the horse I had given him, and rode straight to El Obeid, where he became one of the Mahdi's faithful followers.

For a long time past communication with Khartum had become impossible: the Mahdists were fully on the alert, and any men I attempted to send with letters were invariably intercepted. On one occasion, when fighting against the Beni Helba Arabs, I managed to send a letter to Egypt by a caravan marching along the Arbaïn road to Assiut. But now the various methods of concealment which I had successfully employed—such as fixing letters between the soles of shoes or sandals, soldering them into the inside of ablution water-bottles, or placing them in hollow spear staves —had all been discovered. One morning, whilst inspecting the fort, I noticed some soldiers giving a donkey medical treatment. It was lame in the fore-leg, and, having thrown it on the ground, they proceeded to make an incision in the shoulder, in which they placed a small piece of wood, so as to tighten the skin, across which they made several transverse slits, and then, taking out the stick, poured in powdered natron. The idea at once struck me that I might conceal a letter in this way under the skin. I therefore procured a good-sized donkey, and in the privacy of my own house, I repeated the operation I had just seen performed, inserting in the first cut a small note, describing the situation, which I enclosed in a goat's bladder. The entire size of the communication in its cover did not exceed that of a postage stamp. I then sewed up the wound with silk thread, and the donkey walked without the smallest difficulty. The man to whom I intrusted this mission subsequently told me that he had delivered the packet to Ala ed Din Pasha at Shatt a day or two before the expedition started for El Obeid, and the latter had told the messenger a reply was unnecessary, but that he should accompany the force to El Obeid, whence he would despatch him to me with a letter.

I was now, however, in a sorry plight as regards ammunition. The total in charge of the men and in the magazines amounted to twelve packets per rifle, and if I had attempted to risk a fight, at least half would have been at once expended. Relief I knew was still far off, and the question was how to hold out till then with this slender quantity of cartridges. In order to gain time, I now had recourse to a stratagem. Through the intermediary of a loyal Arab chief, I informed the rebels, who were now collected in considerable strength close to Dara, that I was prepared to capitulate, but I would not agree to my life or that of my soldiers being intrusted to the hands of Arabs against whom I had been continuously fighting for more than a year. I said, however, that should the Mahdi despatch a special delegate to me, I was ready to make the necessary conditions of peace. The plan succeeded, and with the concurrence of the hostile chiefs, I wrote to the Mahdi, requesting him to send one of his own relatives, to whom I could hand over the government of the province.

The days which now passed were for me full of anxious expectancy. I knew that by this time Hicks' force must have almost reached El Obeid, and that the decisive battle, on the result of which hung all our hopes and fears, was about to be fought. I used to frequent the market, and chat with the people on all the topics of the day. Everyone was aware that a large army was advancing on El Obeid, but none yet knew how it was progressing.

At length, towards the end of November, to my unutterable grief, rumours began to circulate that the army had been defeated, and although they sounded suspiciously near the truth, still we could not absolutely credit them; but a day or two later definite news was received that the expedition had been annihilated. Gloom settled down on us all. After so many hardships and such constant trouble to at length fall into the hands of the enemy, without the smallest chance of escape! Yet could it be possible the news was grossly exaggerated? A flicker of hope still remained, only to disappear finally when information was received that Zogal had arrived at Om Shanga, and that the garrison had surrendered to him as Mudir Umum el Gharb (Governor-General of the West), appointed by the Mahdi.

On the 20th of December, 1883, the messenger whom I had sent to the Mahdi arrived at the gate of the fort dressed in a jibba, and was brought in to me. He related to me in full detail the heart-rending news of the complete overthrow of the expedition, of which he himself had been a witness; he also brought me a letter from Zogal, calling on me to surrender, and to prove the disaster which had overtaken the Egyptians, he sent me several of the principal officers' commissions, a number of reports on the situation, and the journals of Colonel Farquhar and Mr. O'Donovan.

That evening Farag Effendi and Ali Effendi Tobgi, the commandant of the artillery, told me that the officers had decided to surrender to the Mahdi, but not to Zogal Bey. They stated their reasons for coming to this decision very simply: everyone, from the highest to the lowest, was now absolutely convinced that we had not the smallest chance of relief; the total force of regulars in Dara amounted to five hundred and ten men, of whom a large number were quite useless; the spirit of the troops was such as to render all idea of eventual success quite out of the question; the ammunition was scarcely sufficient to last out one fight, if we were attacked or if we took the offensive. Both the officers pointed out that I should never succeed in getting the men to fight any longer; they had made up their minds to surrender, and they urged that there was now no other course open. I told them I would carefully consider the matter, and would give them an answer the following morning.

That night I did not close my eyes. To think that, after all the dangers and difficulties through which we had passed, there was no other course now open but to submit! And after that what was to be our fate?

I reviewed the situation from beginning to end during those sleepless hours. For four years I had struggled alone to uphold the Government's authority in the province which had been intrusted to my care—first against the local revolts, which I had suppressed; and, latterly, against the great fanatical movement which had attacked the very roots of my administration, and whose canker-worm had spread into the branches, till at length, the leaves withering one by one, the tree was all but dead.

In short, this strange fanaticism had thoroughly taken possession of my officers and men; they had openly held out against it as long as it was possible for me to dangle before their eyes the prospect of an immediate reassertion of Government authority, through the anticipated success of the Egyptian expedition under Hicks, and the consequent advantages which would accrue to one and all of those who had loyally served the Government. By every means in my power I had striven to prove to my officers and men that the Government must eventually succeed; but at length the crash had come, and all prospect of relief was absolutely and entirely gone. I had struggled against intrigues from within and without, with what success the reader can judge.

With the small amount of ammunition that remained, I might have made a vain struggle for a few hours; but would my officers and men have obeyed my orders? They had no wish and no heart to fight; they knew as well as I did the futility of it; and why should I call on them to sacrifice themselves, and perhaps their wives and children, to a cause to which they were no longer attached?

Looking at the matter entirely from a general point of view, I had no doubt in my own mind that capitulation was not only the right course, but was practically inevitable. Having arrived at this conclusion, I had now to turn to the personal aspect; and the solution of this problem was to me beset with the greatest difficulties. As an officer, the idea of surrender to such an enemy was repulsive in the extreme. I had no fear of my own life; I had risked it sufficiently during the past four years to effectually dispose of any notion that my surrender was occasioned by any want of personal courage—on that point I felt sure that, if spared, I could without the smallest difficulty vindicate my action to my military superiors; but the very word 'surrender' was repulsive to me, and doubly so when I thought over the consequences which must follow to me— a European and a Christian—alone amongst thousands and thousands of fanatical Sudanese and others, the meanest among whom would consider himself superior to me. It is true I had nominally adopted the religion of the country; but this I had done merely as a means of stifling the injurious opinions which I knew existed in the minds of officers and men that the cause of my defeat lay in my being a Christian. My ruse had succeeded to a greater extent than I had expected, but the proceeding had been a distasteful one to me. I had no pretensions to holding very strict religious views on the expediency or otherwise of the step I had taken; nevertheless, at heart I was, I believe, as good a Christian as the majority of young men of my acquaintance; and, that being so, a continuance of the life of religious deception I was then living was by no means a prospect which I appreciated. Moreover, I was well aware that my surrender would place me absolutely and entirely in the hands of this mock-religious reformer, and that not only should I have to show myself to be a Moslem in the ordinary sense of the term, but to carry out the rôle surrender would entail on me, I must be prepared to pursue this religious deception to its fullest extent—I must become a devotee, and henceforth I must show myself heart and soul a Mahdist!

Can anyone imagine that this was a pleasing prospect? Nevertheless, I confess that the religious considerations involved in the step I contemplated—although they weighed with me to no small extent—did not occupy my mind so fully as the considerations in regard to my duty. Generally speaking, I felt it to be my duty to surrender, and make no further sacrifice of life in a cause which could not now, by any possibility, succeed. There was no particular reason, however, why I should voluntarily submit to the indignities and practical slavery which must follow on my personal surrender; to be accessory to my own death occurred to me more than once, but my nature revolted against this thought. I was young, my life during the past four years had been one of anxious responsibility, but of stirring adventure as well, and I had no particular desire to bring it to a close, even with the dark prospect in front of me. God in His mercy had spared me almost miraculously in this constant fighting, and perhaps He would still spare me to be of use to the Government I had tried to serve most loyally.

These were the thoughts which were uppermost in my mind when the dark hours of anxious meditation gave place to the first streaks of the dawn of perhaps the most memorable day of my life. Yes, I concluded, there is nothing for it now but submission; I must become, so to speak, the slave of those whom I have governed; I must be obedient to those who are in every respect my inferiors, and I must, above all, be patient. If by a careful practice of these I

should succeed in saving my life and eventually recovering
my liberty, no doubt the experience which I should gain
would be valuable to the Government in whose service I
still was. With this determination and resolution I rose,
and dressed for the last time for many a long year in the
uniform the honour of which I had done my utmost to
uphold, now to be discarded for the Mahdist garb, in which
I was to play an entirely new part in life; but beneath it
would beat a heart as truly loyal as ever to Government,
and filled with a determination that, come what might, if it
were God's will I should be eventually restored to liberty,
the strange experiences which it would now be my fate to
undergo might be turned to useful account. It was now to
be a case of my wits against those of my new masters—who
would win? I did not shrink from the contest, though I
should have had no little excuse for doing so, could I have
scanned the future, and seen before me the long years of
servitude, and the double life which I should be compelled
to lead, in order to carry through the resolution at which I
had now arrived.

The next morning the two officers arrived; I showed them
Zogal's letter calling on me to surrender peacefully, and to
meet him on the 23rd of December at Hilla Shieria, where
he would personally hand me the Mahdi's letter; he further
wrote that, in accordance with his present instructions, my
life and those of all the men, women, and children in the
fort should be spared, and we should be afforded all protection.

It was absolutely clear to me that further resistance was
impossible. I therefore sent for my clerk and dictated to
him a letter to Zogal, giving in my submission and that of
the garrison, and agreeing to meet him at Hilla Shieria on
the 23rd of December; this I handed to a messenger, with
instructions to take it to Zogal, who was now to be called
Sayed Mohammed Ibn Khaled.

The following day, in the afternoon, I assembled all the
officers, and told them that, as further resistance was not

possible, I had concurred in their proposals; that I was leaving Dara that evening in order to meet Zogal the next day at Hilla Shieria, and that I would take the Kadi with me, but would leave the officers to look after the garrison during my absence. In a few words, which seemed to stick in my throat, I thanked them for their loyalty, their readiness to sacrifice their lives in the service of the Government, and their adherence to me; then, warmly shaking each of them by the hand, and taking a general leave of the civil officials, I departed.

At midnight, accompanied by my kavasses, and a few Arab chiefs who remained faithful to the last, I quitted Dara. During my service in Darfur I had had many disagreeable experiences, but this journey was quite the hardest. Not a word passed. We were all fully occupied with our miserable thoughts. At sunset we made a short halt, but the food put before us by the servants remained untouched. Our appetites had gone, so we rode on. As we approached Hilla Shieria, I sent an orderly ahead to see if Zogal had arrived, and he soon returned, stating he had been there since yesterday, and was waiting for me. In a few moments we reached the spot where he was standing, and, jumping off my horse, I advanced to salute him; he pressed me to his heart, and assured me of his entire friendliness, begged me to be seated, and then handed me the Mahdi's letter. It merely stated that he had appointed Sayed Mohammed Khaled as Emir of the West, had granted me pardon, that he had commissioned his nephew to treat me with the respect to which my rank entitled me, and to act with leniency and forbearance to all those who were formerly Government officials. After I had finished reading the letter, Zogal informed me that it was entirely owing to his good offices on my behalf that the Mahdi had pardoned me, and that he would, of course, do his utmost to help me. I thanked him for his kind sympathy. The Emirs were then introduced to me; Elias, Tayeb, and Hassan Nejumi I had met before. After partaking of food, Zogal discussed his intended journey

to Dara. Whilst we were talking, one of my officers, Mohammed Agha Suleiman, arrived, and without taking the smallest
notice of me, went up and greeted Zogal most effusively. I
at once recognised him as one of the three officers whom I
had been told were ' Black Zogal's' (as he was called)
secret agents.   Mohammed Khaled, as I must call him in
future, now took me aside, and spoke to me about his relatives and his family.   I told him that I had left them
all well, and that the former were still in arrest.   He at
once said he quite concurred in the steps I had taken, which
of course were in the interests of self-preservation, and best
for us both.   We then started off, and encamped the same
evening near Dara.   Several of the inhabitants and officials
came out to greet the new Governor, already dressed in their
Dervish clothes.

That night I again passed almost without closing my
eyes.   It was Christmas Eve.   I thought of home and of
the beautiful Church festival which was being celebrated
there, whilst I, alone and defeated, was handing over my
men and arms to the enemy.   In those still hours—they
were the saddest in my life—I passed in review all that had
happened.   More fortunate by far were those who had fallen
on the field of honour !

The next morning Zogal officially received all those who
had come out to pay homage to him.   The fort was now
garrisoned by Dervish troops, and this completed his
occupation of the country.   The inhabitants flocked to
him to give their oaths of allegiance to the Mahdi, and
later in the day the troops were paraded by his orders to
go through the same ceremony.

Madibbo, who had joined Abd es Samad at Bringel, and
had come to Dara with him, followed me home.   We shook
hands, and I begged him to be seated.   He then began :
' You seem to be annoyed with me, and accuse me of
having broken faith with you, but now listen to me.   I
was discharged from my position of Head Sheikh by
Emiliani, and proceeded to the Bahr el Arab, where the

Mahdi's summons reached me. I am a good Moslem, and therefore I followed him. I beheld the Mahdi's Divine nature, and listened to his doctrines : I was also present at the marvellous destruction of Yusef Shellali. I therefore believed in him, and am still a believer. You, of course, trusted in your strength, and did not wish to submit without fighting. We both fought, each seeking his own advantage. I fought against the Government, but not against you personally. God knows I have never forgotten that you were friendly-minded to me, therefore let anger depart from your heart, and be a brother to me.'

'I am not at all angry at what you have done,' I answered. 'You are but one among many, and should I have been annoyed with you, your words have quite reconciled me.' 'I thank you,' said Madibbo. 'May God strengthen you, and as He has protected you hitherto, may He continue to protect you !' 'In truth,' I replied, 'I put my trust in Him. Still, it is hard to have to bear all that has now happened ; but I suppose it must be.' 'Not so,' he answered ; 'I am only an Arab, but listen to me. Be obedient and patient ; practise this virtue, for it is written, "Allah ma es saberin" ["God is with the patient"]. However, I have come to ask you something, and my request is this : If you are really a brother to me, then, in token of our friendship, I wish you to accept my favourite horse. You knew him before ; he is the Sakr ed Dijaj [the Chicken Hawk].' Before I could reply he had got up and gone outside, and in a few minutes returned, leading his horse, which was the finest and most handsome animal owned by the tribe. He then handed me the leading-rope. 'I do not wish to insult you,' I replied, 'by refusing to accept your present, but I do not require it ; I shall not want to ride much now.' 'Who knows ?' said the Sheikh. "'Illi umru tawil bishuf ketir" ["He who lives long sees much"]. You are still young, and may often ride yet—if not on this horse, then on another.' 'You may be right, Madibbo, but now do you accept from me this token of friendship,' said I,

pointing to his precious war-drums, which my servants took
up and handed to him. These drums, it will be remembered, I had taken in the night attack on Kershu. On the
drums I also laid a sword which I had taken down from the
wall. 'To-day,' said I, 'these are mine, and I can offer
them to you ; to-morrow they may be another's.' 'I thank
you, and accept them gladly,' said the Sheikh. 'Only a
short time ago your men captured my war-drums, but, as
the Arabs say, " Er rigal sharrada urrada' ["A man runs
away and comes back again "],* and I may truly say I have
fought many times in my life, and sometimes I have run
away ; then I have returned, and have succeeded.' Madibbo
now ordered his men to carry off his drums, and departed in
great delight. His conversation had affected me considerably. So I was now to be 'obedient and patient, for he
who lives long sees much.'

The next morning the new Governor ordered all inhabitants out of their houses, which were ransacked, and their
contents carried off to the Beit el Mal. People suspected
of concealing money were flogged mercilessly, or tied by
their legs, head downwards, in wells until they became
unconscious. In vain I expostulated, for Khaled was
obdurate.

The male and female servants of the former officials
were now distributed amongst the Mahdists, but all the
good-looking young girls were put aside for the Mahdi
himself.

Seven days after our surrender Khaled informed me that
Said Bey Guma had sent the principal officials, with Omar
Wad Dario, to make their submission. He therefore
decided to go to Fasher himself, but on his arrival near that
town the inhabitants, having heard of Khaled's bad treatment of the Dara people, decided not to surrender, and in
consequence the Dervishes invested the place. Several
heroic sorties were made, but after a siege of fifteen days

* More familiarly, 'He who fights and runs away lives to fight
another day.'

the town capitulated, and Khaled entered the ancient capital of his new kingdom. The horrible scenes at Dara were now re-enacted with even greater severity, and numbers of people were tortured in the most merciless manner.

Amongst the latter was a certain Major Hamada Effendi, who, in spite of every effort to make him confess, persisted in declaring that he had no money. One of his female slaves, however, told his persecutors that he had a quantity of gold and silver, but she did not know where he had concealed it. Consequently, he was brought before Khaled, who called him an unbelieving dog. Hamada Effendi, losing control of himself, retorted that he was a wretched Dongolawi ; and Khaled, furious at this insult, ordered the unfortunate man to be flogged until he confessed the hiding-place of his treasure. For three days in succession he received a thousand lashes a day, but it was all in vain ; had he been a block of wood or stone he could not have stood this awful flogging more doggedly. To the repeated questions of his tormentors as to where his money was he merely answered, ' Yes, I have concealed money, but it will remain buried in the ground with me.' Khaled now ordered the flogging to be stopped, and the poor mangled man was handed over to the Mima Arabs, who were told to guard him ; and even they were struck with the resolution of this officer, from whom no amount of torture could wring a confession. Ibrahim Tegalawi, who had been called a ' slave ' by one of the Emirs, deliberately shot dead his own wife, his brother, and then himself. Said Agha Fula also preferred to commit suicide rather than undergo torture. After these occurrences Khaled gave orders to stop the flogging, and banished the Egyptian officers to various places in the neighbourhood.

Shortly after the fall of Fasher, I received a summons from Khaled to join him, and I arrived there early in February. He gave me Said Bey Guma's house to live in, and told me that I might send to Dara for my horses and servants, but as regards the house furniture, that must

be passed into the Beit el Mal as an 'act of renunciation.'
I carried out these instructions, and handed over all the
property in my house in Fasher to the treasurer of the Beit
el Mal, Gaber Wad et Taib, only retaining such things as
were absolutely necessary for daily life. I had heard on my
arrival here of Hamada's heroism, and sought out the poor
old Major, whom I found in a truly terrible state. The
gaping wounds from his shoulders to his knees were morti-
fying rapidly, and his tormentors used to pour over them
daily a strong solution of salt and water, well seasoned with
Sudan pepper, thus hoping to wring a confession from him
during the awful pain which ensued. But it was useless;
he absolutely refused to utter a word. In desperation I
went to Khaled, told him of the poor man's horrible condition, and begged him to allow me to take him to my own
house, and treat him there. 'He is dishonest,' said Khaled;
'he has concealed money, and has publicly insulted me.
For this he must die a miserable death.' 'For the sake of
our old friendship,' said I, 'I beg and pray you will forgive
him, and hand him over to me.' 'Well,' said he at last, 'I
will if you will prostrate yourself before me.' In the Sudan
this is considered a terrible humiliation. The blood rushed
to my face. To save my own life I would never do such a
thing, but if by this self-sacrifice I could rescue the poor
wretched man from his awful sufferings, I ought surely to
do so. For a moment I hesitated; then, with a fearful
effort of self-control, I knelt down, and laid my hands on
his bare feet. He drew them back, raised me up, and,
apparently ashamed of having asked such a sacrifice of me,
said: 'It is only for your sake that I shall liberate
Hamada; but you must promise that, should you find out
where his treasure is, you will let me know.' I promised
to do so, and he then sent a man with me to Hamada.
Calling up my servants, I had him carried on an
angareb, as tenderly as I could, to my house, and washed
his wounds, spreading over them fresh butter to deaden the
pain. It was quite impossible he could live much longer.

I gave him a little soup, and in a low voice he called down all the curses of heaven on his enemies. He lay in my house four days, and then, calling me to his bedside, he motioned to the servants to leave us. He now whispered, in words which were scarcely audible, ' My hour has come. May the Lord reward you for all your kindness to me ! I cannot do so, but I will show you that I am grateful. I have buried my money——' ' Stop !' said I. ' Are you going to tell me where you have hidden your treasure ?' ' Yes,' he murmured ; ' it may be of some use to you.' ' No,' I answered, ' I will not and cannot use it. I secured your release from your tormentors on the one condition that, should I learn where your money was hidden, I should tell Khaled, your enemy. You have suffered greatly, and are paying with your life for your determination not to let your treasure fall into your enemy's hands. Let it lie unknown in the ground ; it will keep silence.' Whilst I was talking, Hamada held my hand. With a supreme effort he murmured, ' I thank you ; may you become fortunate without my money. Allah Karim ' [' God is merciful !']. Then, stretching out his limbs, and raising his forefinger, he slowly muttered, ' La ilaha illallah, Mohammed Rasul Allah,' closed his eyes, and died.

As I gazed at this poor mangled corpse my eyes filled with tears. How much was I still to suffer before it came to my turn to enter into everlasting rest ? Calling my servants, I bade them bring in two good men to wash the body, and wrap it in some linen I had procured ; meanwhile, I went to Khaled to inform him of his death. ' Did he not tell you where his money was buried ?' said he sharply. ' No,' said I, ' the man was too stubborn to betray his secret.' ' Then, may God curse him !' said the Emir, turning to me. ' However, as he died in your house, you may bury him ; he really deserves to be thrown out, like a dog, on the dunghill.' Quitting him, I went home and buried poor Hamada, with the usual form of prayer, just in front of my house.

Khaled was a very cunning man, excessively strict with

the former Government officials, and unnecessarily lenient
in his transactions with the local population. He filled all
important positions by his own relatives, and although he
strove by every means in his power to squeeze all he could
out of the country, he was specially careful to avoid the risk
of incurring popular discontent. He appropriated to himself the greater part of the revenues, and every now and
then he sent as presents to the Mahdi and his Khalifas a
batch of pretty girls, some good horses, or some exceptionally fine camels, so as to retain his good reputation in the
household of his lord and master. He kept up great state,
and surrounded himself with an enormous household. He
married Mariam Isa Basi, the sister of the Sultan of Darfur,
although she was over fifty years old. This good lady had
hundreds of male and female slaves, and kept up her state
in true Sudanese fashion. It did not seem to occur to Khaled
that any self-abnegation, as required by the Mahdi creed,
should be demanded of him. Every evening he caused a
hundred dishes, plates, and twisted mats, full of every variety
of food, to be distributed amongst his followers, who, seated
at their ease under the palm-trees, would sing the praises of
the Mahdi, coupling every now and then his name with that
of their benefactor and Emir, Khaled.

At about this time a long letter, sent from Cairo to me,
through the Mudir of Dongola, by the hands of a trusty
Arab, arrived. In it I was ordered to concentrate the troops
at Fasher, hand over the province to Abd es Shakur bin
Abderrahman Shattut, a descendant of the Darfur Sultans,
and move with all troops and war *matériel* to Dongola. The
king's son in question was, however, still in Dongola, unable
to find means to come to Darfur ; and I greatly doubt if his
arrival would have made the smallest difference in the situation. Concentration at Fasher would have been rendered
impossible by the defection of the officers and men ; and had
I been able to collect sufficient troops ready to obey my
orders, and had I been able to march out with them and the
war *matériel* unmolested, I could equally well have been able

to stay in the country and maintain my position, in which case the Egyptian Government would have had in me a vassal of equivalent, if not greater, fidelity than the powerless Abd es Shakur. Khaled showed me these letters, and also gave me permission to write a few lines to my family at home, which he allowed the Arab who brought the letters to take back; but I do not think my letter ever reached its destination.

During all this time I remained quietly at my house, awaiting the instructions of the Mahdi as to my movements. About the middle of May, Khaled informed me that, owing to scarcity of water, the Mahdi had quitted El Obeid and marched to Rahad, that he wished to know me personally, and that, therefore, I should make preparations to start at once.

News now reached us of the fall of Bahr el Ghazal, under Lupton Bey, and of the despatch of the Emir Karamalla as Mahdist Governor of the Province. Deserted by all his people, Lupton had no other course open than to capitulate, which he did, without fighting, on 28th April, 1884. Had it not been for the defection of his own men and officials, Lupton, by a judicious management of the Negro tribes, could have held his province against all comers for years; but deserted by all, and by them sold over to the Mahdists, he could not do otherwise than surrender.

Khaled wished Said Bey Guma to accompany me as well; he was still living at Kobbé, and, in spite of his former intrigues against me, I agreed to the proposal; also a certain Greek merchant named Dimitri Zigada asked to accompany me, and Khaled gave him permission to do so.

About the middle of June Zigada and I quitted Fasher under an escort of ten men, and after an unpleasant journey reached El Obeid, where the Mahdist Governor Sayed Mahmud received us with scant courtesy, and ordered us to proceed the following day to Rahad, where the Mahdi was encamped.

CHAPTER X.

THE SIEGE AND FALL OF KHARTUM.

Gordon returns to the Sudan—The Siege of Khartum—I join the
Mahdi at Rahad—Interviews and First Impressions of the Mahdi—
The Oath of Allegiance—Description of the Khalifa—The Arrival
of Hussein Pasha—Criticisms on Gordon's Mission—The Abandonment of the Sudan Proclaimed—Incidents in Various Parts of the
Sudan—The Arrival of Olivier Pain—His Mission, Illness, and
Death—Arrival outside Khartum—I write to Gordon—I am
Arrested and thrown into Chains—Incidents during my Imprison-
ment—The Surrender of Omdurman—The Delay of the British
Expedition—Khartum is Attacked and Taken—Gordon's Head is
brought to me—Account of the last Days of Khartum—Massacres
and Atrocities after the Fall—The Retreat of the British Expedition—The Rigours of my Imprisonment increased—My Comrade
in Captivity, Frank Lupton—We are both released—I enter the
Khalifa's Body-guard—Illness and Death of the Mahdi—Khalifa
Abdullahi succeeds him—The Rules and Ordinances of the Mahdi.

AFTER the destruction of Hicks Pasha's expedition, the
Mahdi well knew that the whole Sudan was at his feet : to
take possession of it was only a question of time. His first
step was the despatch of his cousin Khaled to Darfur, where
he knew no resistance was possible. Through the influence
of Karamalla he was able to acquire possession of the Bahr
el Ghazal, the employés having merely transferred their
allegiance from the Khedive to the Mahdi. Already Mek
Adam of Tagalla had submitted, and had come to El Obeid
with his family. Mahdism had seized a firm hold of the
Eastern Sudan, and found a ready home amongst the brave
Arabs of those regions; Egyptian troops had been anni-
hilated at Sinkat and Tamanib; General Baker's disaster at
Teb had given the tribes great confidence; and Mustafa
Hadal was besieging Kassala. In the Gezira, between the
Blue and White Niles, the Mahdi's brother-in-law, Wad el
Basir, of the Halawin tribe, had scored successes against the
Government, and such was briefly the condition of the

country when Gordon reached Berber, on 11th February, 1884.

The Egyptian Government, in accord with the British Government, thought that by the despatch of Gordon, who had a special knowledge of the Sudan, the agitation would be stopped; but neither these Governments, nor Gordon himself, seemed to realize how serious the situation really was. Did they imagine for a moment that Gordon, who had had occasion to show considerable personal bravery, who had gained a name for charity and benevolence amongst the lower classes of the Darfur population, and had suppressed a number of revolts in the Equatorial Negro lands, was capable of checking the blazing flames of fanaticism? The Jaalin between Berber and Khartum, and throughout the Gezira, had become restive and dissatisfied; and was the personal influence of Gordon going to pacify them? On the contrary, these same tribes had every reason to remember with little satisfaction the name of the Governor-General who had issued the ejection edict against the Gellabas of the southern districts, during the Suleiman Zubeir war against the Arabs. In the events which followed on this drastic measure, and which I have described elsewhere, many of these people had lost fathers, brothers, and sons, and had been reduced to beggary: were they likely to forgive Gordon this?

On the 18th of February he reached Khartum, and received a warm welcome from the officials and inhabitants. Those who were in immediate contact with him, and anticipating for themselves much personal benefit, were convinced that the Government would never leave a man like Gordon in the lurch. Almost his first step was to issue a proclamation appointing the Mahdi Sultan of Kordofan, permitting the slave-trade, and proposing to enter into relations with him; in his letter he also asked for the release of the prisoners, and sent the Mahdi some very fine clothes. Gordon's letter would have been all very well if he had had a force at his back with which to march into Kordofan; but

the Mahdi had been told that he had arrived at Khartum
with merely a small body-guard. Naturally he thought it
an extraordinary proceeding for Gordon to give him what
he had already taken by force of arms, and which it was
most improbable any troops at Gordon's disposal could have
wrenched from him ; and it was in this frame of mind that
the Mahdi couched his reply advising Gordon to surrender
and save his life.

In all matters, Khalifa Abdullahi was the Mahdi's principal adviser, and consequently he was detested by the immediate relatives of the Prophet, who did all in their power
to frustrate his designs and intrigue against him.   He was,
however, well aware that the Mahdi could not get on without
him ; he therefore retaliated by complaining against these
intrigues, and asked the Mahdi to take an occasion to openly
acknowledge his services.   This led to the issue of a proclamation which to this day is referred to whenever any
exceptionally severe measure or important change is contemplated by his successor.

This proclamation enjoined on all the followers to implicitly obey Khalifa Abdullahi, and to treat him in all
respects as the Mahdi's agent in carrying out the will of the
Prophet.

As the water was daily becoming more scarce, the Mahdi
resolved to move his entire camp to Rahad, about one day's
journey from El Obeid ; and about the middle of April
the transfer of this immense mass of men, women, and
children to the new position was completed.

The camp at Rahad soon became a perfect sea of straw
huts, or tokuls, stretching as far as the eye could reach ;
and all day long the Mahdi occupied himself in his religious
duties, preaching and praying incessantly.   Mohammed Abu
Girga he nominated Emir of the Gezira, and despatched
him, with a considerable following, to the Nile, with
instructions to head the revolt in these districts, and besiege
Khartum.

Such was the state of affairs when Said Bey Guma,

Dimitri Zigada and I approached Rahad. I now sent on
one of my servants to apprise the much-feared Khalifa of
our approach; but, as he delayed returning, we rode on
along the broad road leading to the market-place, and soon
heard the dismal sound of the ombeya, which was the
signal that the Khalifa had gone out on his horse. By
chance, I came across a Darfuri who, when I asked him
what the ombeya was being sounded for, replied, 'Very
probably Khalifa Abdullahi is giving orders for someone's
head to be cut off, and this is a summons to the people to
witness the execution.' Had I been superstitious, I should
certainly have taken this as a bad omen—an execution the
moment I entered the camp! However, we rode on, and
soon came in sight of a large open place where we saw my
servant and another man hastening towards us. 'Stay
where you are,' cried he, 'and come no further; the Khalifa,
with his escort, has gone out to meet you; he thought you
were still outside the camp.' We halted while the other
man returned to let the Khalifa know we had arrived. A
few minutes later we saw hundreds of horsemen surrounded
by numbers of armed footmen approaching us, and marching to the sound of the ombeya. At the farther end of the
open space was the Khalifa himself; he had halted, and
several horsemen, ranging up to his right and left, stood
awaiting his instructions. He now ordered them to begin
their horse exercise, which consisted of batches of four men
abreast, with poised lances, galloping at full speed towards
some point, then suddenly pulling up, turning round and
galloping back again; this useless sort of drill continued
until men and horses became utterly exhausted. Sometimes
I was the objective of their charge, and, as they galloped
up, they shook their spears close to my face, shouting, ' Fi
shan Allah wa Rasulahu' (' For God and His Prophet ')
and then galloped back again. After repeating this operation for upwards of half an hour, one of the Khalifa's
servants at length approached me on foot, and told me that
the Khalifa wished me also to gallop towards him. I did

so, shook my lance in his face, shouted, ' Fi shan Allah wa
Rasulahu !' and then returned to my place. He now sent
word to me to ride behind him, and in a few minutes we
reached his quarters. He was assisted to dismount by a
special attendant, the remainder keeping at a respectful
distance, and he disappeared behind the fence. In a few
moments he sent out a message to us to come in, and we
were conducted to a spot fenced off from the rest of the
enclosure, which is designated the rekuba ; it was merely a
small square apartment with straw walls and a thatch roof.
In it were several angarebs and palm-mats ; we were told to
seat ourselves on these, and were served with a mixture of
honey and water in a pumpkin gourd, and some dates. Having
partaken of this, we patiently awaited the appearance of our
hospitable host and master. He soon came in, and we at
once rose ; seizing my hand, he pressed me to his heart,
saying, ' God be praised, we are at last united ! How do
you feel after your long and tiring journey ?' ' Yes, indeed,'
I replied, ' God be praised for having granted me to live to
see this day ! When I beheld your countenance, my fatigue
at once left me !' I well knew that to win his favour I
must flatter him as much as possible ; he now gave his
hand to Said Bey and Dimitri to kiss, and asked how they
were. I scrutinised him very carefully ; he had a light-
brown complexion, a sympathetic Arab face, on which the
marks of small-pox were still traceable, an aquiline nose, a
well-shaped mouth, slight moustache, and a fringe of hair
on his cheeks, but rather thicker on his chin ; he was about
middle height, neither thin nor stout, was wearing a jibba
covered with small square patches of different colours, and
a Mecca takia, or skull cap, round which was bound a
cotton turban; he generally spoke with a smile, and showed
a row of glistening white teeth. Having greeted us, he told
us to be seated ; and we at once sat on the palm-mats on
the ground, whilst he sat, cross-legged, on an angareb. Once
more he inquired after our health, and expressed his great
delight that we had at last reached the Mahdi. On a sign

to one of his servants, a dish of asida, and another of meat, were laid before us, and, sitting beside us, he told us to help ourselves; he himself ate heartily, seeming to thoroughly enjoy his food, and during the meal he asked several questions. 'Why,' said he, smiling, 'did you not wait for me outside the camp, instead of entering without permission? You know you are not supposed to enter a friend's house without his permission.' 'Pardon,' said I, 'my servant kept us waiting so long, and none of us thought you would take the trouble to come out and meet us; then, as we reached the entrance of the camp, we heard the beating of war-drums and the sound of your ombeya, and when we inquired what that meant we were told that you had ridden out to witness the execution of a criminal; we therefore intended following the sound of your ombeya, when your order reached us.' 'Am I then known as a tyrant amongst the people,' said he, 'that the sound of my ombeya should always mean the death of someone?' 'No, indeed, sir,' said I; 'you are generally known to be strict, but just.' 'Yes, I am strict,' he replied; 'but this must be so, and you will understand the reasons as you prolong your stay with me.'

A few people whom I had previously known were now permitted by the Khalifa to come in and greet me, but they had no chance of conversation with me, only Abderrahman ben Naga, who had been one of the Hicks expedition, said, in a low, quick tone, 'Be very careful; hold your tongue, and trust no one.' I took his warning to heart.

The Khalifa then departed, and at about two o'clock in the afternoon sent us a message to perform our ablutions and prepare to go to the Mesjed (place of worship); a few minutes later he arrived himself, and told us to follow him. He was on foot, as the mosque, which was close to the Mahdi's hut, was only about three hundred yards off. On arrival, we found the place crowded with devotees, ranged in closely packed lines; and when the Khalifa entered, they made way for him with great respect. A sheepskin was spread on the ground for us, and he directed us to take our places beside him. The Mahdi's quarters, consisting of several large straw huts fenced off by a thorn zariba, were situated at the south-west end of the mosque. A gigantic tree afforded shade to a number of the worshippers, but those beyond had no protection from the burning sun. A few paces from the front line, and to the right, lay a small hut which was reserved for those with whom the Mahdi wished to converse in private. The Khalifa now rose and entered this hut, probably to inform his master of our arrival; for in a few moments he returned, again seated himself beside me, and almost immediately the Mahdi himself came out. The Khalifa at once arose, and with him Said Bey, Dimitri, and I, who were just behind him, whilst the others quietly remained in their places. The Mahdi being the Imam, or leader of prayers, his sheepskin was spread out in front, and he then stepped towards us. I had advanced slightly, and he greeted me with ' Salam aleikum,' which we at once returned by ' Aleikum es salam.' He then presented his hand for me to kiss, which I did several times, and Said Bey and Dimitri followed my example. Motioning us to be seated, he welcomed us, and turning to me said, ' Are you satisfied?' ' Indeed I am,' I replied readily ; ' on coming so near to you I am most happy.' ' God bless you and your brethren!' (meaning Said Bey and Dimitri) said he ; ' when news reached us of your battles against my followers, I used to pray to God for your conversion. God and His Prophet have heard my prayers, and as you have faithfully served your former master for perishable money, so now you should serve me ; for he who serves me, and hears my words, serves God and His religion, and shall have happiness in this world and joy in the world to come.' We of course all made professions of fidelity, and as I had been previously warned to ask him to give me the ' beia,' or oath of allegiance, I now besought this honour. Calling us up beside him, he bade us kneel on the edge of his sheepskin, and placing our hands in his, he told us to repeat after him as follows :

' Bism Illahi er Rahman er Rahim, bayana Allaha wa
Rasulahu wa bayanaka ala tauhid Illahi, wala nushrek
billahi shayan, wala nasrek, wala nazni, wala nati bi buhtan,
wala nasak fil maruf, bayanaka ala tark ed dunya wal akhera,
wala naferru min el jehad ' (' In the name of God the most
compassionate and merciful, in the name of the unity of
God, we pay God, His Prophet, and you our allegiance ;
(we swear) that we shall not associate anything else with
God, that we shall not steal, nor commit adultery, nor lead
anyone into deception, nor disobey you in your goodness ;
we swear to renounce this world and (look only) to the
world to come, and that we shall not flee from the religious
war ').

This over, we kissed his hand, and were now enrolled
amongst his most devoted adherents ; but at the same time
we were liable to suffer their punishments. The muazzen
(prayer caller) now gave the first signal to begin prayers,
and we repeated the usual formulæ after the Mahdi. When
they were over, all those present raised their hands to heaven
and besought God to grant victory to the faithful. The
Mahdi now began his sermon. An immense circle was
formed around him, and he spoke of the vanity and nothing-
ness of this life, urging all to renounce the world, and to
think only of their religious duties, and of the Jehad ; he
painted, in most glowing terms, the delights of Paradise,
and the heavenly joys which awaited those who paid heed
to his doctrine. Every now and then he was interrupted
by the shouts of some fanatic in an ecstasy ; and, indeed, I
am convinced everyone present, except ourselves, really
believed in him. The Khalifa, having something to do, had
left the mosque, but had ordered his mulazemia (body-guard),
who remained, to tell us to stay with the Mahdi till sunset.
I had now a good opportunity of making a careful survey of
Mohammed Ahmed ; he was a tall, broad-shouldered man
of light-brown colour, and powerfully built ; he had a large
head and sparkling black eyes ; he wore a black beard, and
had the usual three slits on each cheek ; his nose and mouth

were well shaped, and he had the habit of always smiling, showing his white teeth and exposing the V-shaped aperture between the two front ones, which is always considered a sign of good luck in the Sudan, and is known as 'falja.' This was one of the principal causes which made the Mahdi so popular with the fair sex, by whom he was dubbed 'Abu falja' (the man with the separated teeth). He wore a short quilted jibba, beautifully washed, and perfumed with sandal-wood, musk, and attar of roses; this perfume was celebrated amongst his disciples as 'Rihet el Mahdi' (the odour of the Mahdi), and was supposed to equal, if not surpass, that of the dwellers in Paradise.

We remained exactly on the same spot, with our legs tucked away behind, until the time for evening prayers came. Meanwhile the Mahdi had frequently gone to and fro between his house and the mosque; and, prayers over, I begged leave to depart, as the Khalifa had told me to return to him at that hour. He gave me permission, and took the opportunity of saying that I must adhere closely to the Khalifa, and devote myself entirely to his service. Of course I promised to obey him to the letter, and Dimitri, Said Bey, and I, covering the Mahdi's hand with kisses, quitted the mosque. My legs were so cramped by the posture in which I had been sitting for hours together that I could scarcely walk; but, in spite of the pain, I was obliged to keep as cheerful a face as possible in the Mahdi's presence. Said Bey was more used to it, and did not seem to suffer so much; but poor Dimitri limped behind, muttering Greek in an undertone, which I have no doubt conveyed the most frightful imprecations—at any rate, I can vouch that they were not songs of praise of the Mahdi. A mula-zem returned with us to the Khalifa's house, where he was waiting for us to sit down to supper with him.

He told us that since he had seen us in the morning Hussein Khalifa, formerly Mudir of Berber, had arrived. So it was true Berber had fallen; we had heard rumours to this effect, on the Darfur frontier, but met no one whom we

could ask confidentially about it. The town must have
fallen through the Jaalin ; and now communication with
Egypt must be entirely cut off. This was terribly bad news.
I anxiously looked out for Hussein Khalifa's arrival ; he
would be able to give us all the facts.

The Khalifa now left us for the night, and, utterly tired
out, we stretched out our weary limbs on the angarebs and
gave ourselves up to our own thoughts.

Early the next morning, after partaking of a breakfast of
asida and milk, the blowing of the ombeya, and the beating
of drums, announced that the Khalifa was about to ride ;
and horses were at once saddled. Directing my servants to
get two horses ready—one for myself and the other for
Said Bey—we mounted and soon caught up the Khalifa,
who had gone on ahead. He was riding for pleasure round
the camp, accompanied by some twenty footmen ; on his
right walked an enormous Black of the Dinka tribe, and on
his left a very tall Arab named Abu Tsheka, whose duty it
was to help the Khalifa in and out of the saddle. When he
came again to the open space, he directed the horsemen to
repeat yesterday's exercise ; and, after watching this for
some time, we rode on to the end of the camp, where he
showed me the remains of an immense zariba and small
tumbled-in trench, which he told me had been one of
Hicks's last halting places before his annihilation, and
where he had awaited reinforcements from Tagalla. The
trench had been made for his Krupp guns. The sight of
this awakened very sad memories ; to think of the thousands
who but a short time before had been camped in this great
zariba having been killed almost to a man, and that this
disaster was the cause of my being where I now was !

On our way back the Khalifa took me to pay a visit to
nis brother Yakub, whose huts were close to his own, the
fences being merely separated by a narrow passage. Yakub
received me very kindly, and appeared as pleased to see me
as Abdullahi had been ; he warned me to serve him faithfully, which I of course promised to do. Yakub is a some-

what shorter man than the Khalifa, broad-shouldered, with
a round face deeply pitted with small-pox ; he has a small
turned-up nose, and slight moustache and beard; he is
distinctly more ugly than handsome, but has the art of
talking in a curiously sympathetic way. He, too, like the
Mahdi and the Khalifa, smiled continually ; and what wonder, when their affairs were progressing so very satisfactorily ! Yakub reads and writes, and knows the Kuran by
heart, whilst Abdullahi is comparatively very ignorant.
He is some years the Khalifa's junior, and is his trusted
and most powerful adviser. Woe to the unfortunate man
who differs in opinion with Yakub, or who is suspected of
intriguing against him : he is infallibly lost !

Partaking of some of the dates he offered me, I took leave
of him and returned to the rekuba, whence, in accordance
with the Khalifa's order, we proceeded to the mosque, and
stayed till sunset, as we did the previous day. Again the
Mahdi preached renunciation, urging his hearers to be ready
for the Jehad, so as to enter into the future joys of Paradise.
Again and again the faithful devotees, half intoxicated with
fanaticism, shouted his praises ; whilst we poor wretches,
enduring agonies in our cramped position, imprecated in
our hearts Mahdi, Khalifa, and his whole crew of base
hypocrites.

The next day the Khalifa summoned us, and asked if we
wished to return to Darfur. I knew the question had only
been put to us as a test ; and we at once answered with one
voice, that we should deeply regret leaving the Mahdi. I
saw that he anticipated this answer, and, smiling, he commended us for our wise decision. The Khalifa now, of his
own accord, suggested that a longer stay in the rekuba was
probably distasteful to us; he therefore sent Dimitri with
a mulazem to the house of his future Emir, who was
a Greek, and he also gave instructions to Ahmed Wad
Suleiman to issue twenty dollars to him. After he had
gone, he turned to Said Bey, saying, ' Said Guma, you
are an Egyptian, and everyone likes his own compatriots

best; we have with us several Egyptians, many of proved fidelity. You are brave, and I know I can count on you; you will therefore join the Emir of all the Egyptians, Hassan Hussein, and he will give you a house, and see to your requirements. I shall also do what is necessary on my side.' Said Bey was of course much pleased with the arrangement. Then, turning to me, he said, 'Abdel Kader, you are a stranger here, and have no one else but me. You know well the Arabs of Southern Darfur; therefore, in accordance with the Mahdi's orders, you are to remain with me as a mulazem.' 'That is the very wish of my heart,' I answered readily; 'I call myself fortunate to be able to serve you, and you can rely on my obedience and fidelity.' 'I knew that,' said he; 'may God protect you and strengthen your faith; you will no doubt be of much use to both the Mahdi and myself.'

Once more I was alone with the Khalifa, and again he repeated how gratified he was to have me in his service, and always beside him; at the same time he warned me not to associate with his near relatives, whose jealous feelings might lead to an estrangement between us. He also gave orders for some straw huts to be erected in the zariba next his own, belonging to Abu Anga, who was now absent, fighting against the Nubas; meanwhile he said I was to stay in the rekuba, and without fail attend the Mahdi's noon-day and evening prayers. Thanking him profusely for all these favours, I promised to do my utmost to please him and continue in his good graces.

The next day Hussein Pasha Khalifa was brought in, and Abdullahi began the conversation by inquiring after the health of the late Governor of Berber. Receiving the usual replies, he then turned to the situation on the river, and Hussein described the whole country between Berber and Fashoda as being entirely with the Mahdi, and communication between Egypt and the Sudan quite interrupted, whilst Khartum, which was defended by Gordon, was invested by the Gezira tribes. He naturally coloured the situation in the way which he knew would be most acceptable to the Mahdi, and that he was favourably impressing the Khalifa was evident from the expressions of satisfaction which escaped the latter as the narrative proceeded. Abdullahi promised that at noon-day prayers he would present Hussein Khalifa to the Mahdi, of whose forgiveness he might rest assured. In the meantime he was to rest in the rekuba.

I subsequently accompanied him to the mosque, where the usual form of presentation was gone through, and on our return I was greatly relieved to hear that he was ordered to remain that night in the rekuba. As usual we supped with the Khalifa, but when he and the servants had retired, we took this long-looked-for occasion to greet each other most heartily, and to mutually bemoan the sad fate which brought us together in this wretched position. 'Hussein Pasha,' said I, 'I trust you and yours may rest assured of my silence. Tell me what is the present condition of Khartum, and what are the population doing?' 'Alas!' he replied, 'it is exactly as I have described it to the Khalifa. Gordon's reading at Metemmeh of the proclamation abandoning the Sudan upset the situation entirely, and was indirectly the cause of the fall of Berber. No doubt it would have been lost later on, but this action of Gordon's greatly precipitated it. At Berber I stopped him from taking this fatal step, and I cannot think what induced him to disregard my advice almost immediately afterwards.' We talked so long about the situation and the various events that Hussein Pasha, who was old and tired, fell asleep; but this conversation had banished all sleep from my eyes. So this is to be the end, I thought, of all Gordon's efforts to settle the country, and is all the blood and treasure expended in past years to go for nothing? Now the Government wanted to abandon this great country, which, though hitherto it had not proved a financial benefit to Egypt, was a land of great prospects, and could at least produce thousands of splendid black recruits with whom to fill the ranks of its army. So the Government was to leave this country to its own people, and yet to remain on friendly terms with it; it was to withdraw the garrisons and war *matériel*, and to establish a form of local government, when a form of such government had already sprung into existence by the most violent of means, namely, by the wholesale overturning of every vestige of the authority which it was to replace, and the massacre or capture of almost every individual representative of the ousted ruling power.

To carry out this plan they had sent Gordon, in the hope that his personal influence with the people, and their regard for him—which he was inclined to estimate somewhat highly—would enable him to succeed in this herculean task. Gordon, it is true, was popular with some of the western and equatorial tribes, whom he had won over by his munificence and his benevolent nature. During his stay in these districts he had constantly travelled about, and his noted courage and fearlessness in action had won him the sympathy of those tribes whose greatest pride it is to possess such qualities. Yes, there is no doubt he had been popular with the western Arabs, but they had now a Mahdi whom they adored; they had almost forgotten Gordon. The Sudanese, it must be remembered, are not Europeans; they are Arabs and Blacks, and are little given over to sentimental feelings. But in this particular case of the reading of the proclamation the people concerned were river tribes, and, of all others, the Jaalin were perhaps the most hostile to Gordon, for they had not forgotten the eviction of the Gellabas.

The mere fact that Gordon had come to Khartum without a force at his back proved to these people that he depended on his personal influence to carry out his task; but, to those who understood the situation, it was abundantly clear that personal influence at this stage was as a drop in the ocean. Then what could have induced him to read that fatal notice, proclaiming far and wide that the Government intended to abandon the Sudan? At Hussein Pasha's advice he had not read it at Berber, but at Metemmeh he had proclaimed it before all the people. Had Gordon never been informed of the Mahdi's proclamations sent to all the tribes after the fall of El Obeid? Was he not aware that these proclamations enjoined all the people to unite in a religious war against the Government authority, and that those who disobeyed the summons, and were found giving assistance to the hated Turk, were guilty of betraying the faith, and as such would not only lose their money and property, but their wives and children would become the slaves of the Mahdi and his followers? Gordon's idea was to obtain the assistance of these tribes, in order to facilitate the withdrawal of the garrisons, and he would have come to terms with them to effect this object; but how could he expect them to help him when, in the words of that fatal proclamation, it was decreed they were to be abandoned to their fate? And what would, in this eventuality, have been their fate? Could they have opposed the Mahdi, his forty thousand rifles, and his hosts of wild fanatics, panting for blood and plunder? No, indeed; these tribes were sensible enough to understand that assistance given to Gordon to retreat meant the annihilation of themselves and the enslavement of their families. Why should they commit this self-sacrifice? How could Gordon's personal influence avail him for an instant against the personal interests of every man, woman, and child in the now abandoned Sudan?

If for political or other reasons it was impossible for the Government to maintain the Sudan, or to reconquer it by degrees, it was an equally useless step to have sent Gordon there to sacrifice him. It did not require a person of any special military capacity to remove the garrisons and war *matériel* by the steamers to Berber, under pretext of relieving that town, and thus the whole or a considerable portion of the Sudan garrisons might have been successfully withdrawn, though it would have been necessary to do this

without delay, and it could not have been feasible after the
fall of Berber ; but Berber, it must be remembered, did not
fall till the 19th of May, three months after Gordon's arrival
in Khartum.   However, under any circumstances the reading of that fatal proclamation precipitated matters to an
alarming extent.   The intention of the Government was
openly declared to the Sudanese, and they naturally from
that moment looked to their own immediate interests, which
were now directly opposed to those of the Government, so
hopelessly overturned by their victorious compatriot, the
Mahdi.

How could Gordon's qualities of personal bravery and
energy, great as they undoubtedly were, arrest the progress
of events after that most grave political error ?

Perplexed and worried with such thoughts as these, I was
tossing about on my angareb, whilst Hussein Khalifa was
snoring.   There was no small advantage in being a fatalist,
but as yet I was too European to have arrived at this
stage, though gradually I learnt to look at such matters
with more equanimity, and my experiences in the Sudan
have undoubtedly taught me to practise that great virtue—
patience.

A few days afterwards a rumour was spread through the
camp that Abu Girga had been attacked by Gordon, and
had been wounded ; his forces, which were then investing
Khartum, were reported to have been repulsed, and the
siege raised.   This news filled my heart with delight, though
openly I was obliged to appear quite unconcerned.

Saleh Wad el Mek now arrived in the camp ; he had been
obliged to submit at Fedasi, and had been sent on by Abu
Girga.   He received the pardon of the Khalifa and Mahdi,
and confirmed the above news ; he also privately gave me
much interesting information about Gordon.   That evening
the Khalifa summoned me to supper with him, and no
sooner had we set to work to tear the huge piece of meat
before us than he asked, ' Have you heard the news to-day
about Hajji Mohammed Abu Girga ?'   ' No,' I replied

hypocritically, 'I did not leave your door the whole day, and have met no one.'

'Gordon,' continued the Khalifa, 'made a sudden attack on Hajji Mohammed from both the river and the land, when the Blue Nile was in flood; and he has built structures on the steamers which stop the bullets of our faithful Ansar. The unbeliever is a cunning man, but he will reap God's punishment. Hajji Mohammed's men, who have suffered, have been obliged to retire before superior force. Gordon is now rejoicing in his victory; but he is deceived. God will grant victory only to those who believe in Him, and in a few days God's vengeance will fall on him suddenly. Hajji Mohammed is not man enough to conquer the country; the Mahdi is therefore sending Abderrahman Wad en Nejumi to besiege Khartum.'

'I hope,' said I, 'that Hajji Mohammed has not suffered serious loss?' meaning in my heart exactly the reverse.

'Battles cannot be fought without loss,' said the Khalifa, with some truth; 'but I have not heard the full details yet.' He was anything but affable to-day. Gordon's victory had thoroughly upset him, and he evidently anticipated that the effect would be serious. When I returned to my hut, I sent my servant to ask Saleh Wad el Mek if he could come and see me secretly; he was only a few huts off, and arrived some minutes afterwards. I told him the Khalifa's corroboration of the news, but he had already heard it from his relatives, and we continued talking over past and present till a late hour. This victory had raised my spirits enormously, and I found myself chatting quite hopefully of the future; but Saleh looked on the success as only temporary, and his reasons for this view were, I felt, fully justifiable.

He explained that, very soon after Gordon's arrival at Khartum, the effect of the fatal proclamation began to be felt, and his difficulties increased. The Jaalin had begun to collect, and had chosen as their chief Haj Ali Wad Saad, who soon had at his disposal a considerable force, but for personal reasons he was secretly inclined to the Govern-

ment, and therefore delayed actually fighting as long as
possible. The Consuls of the various nationalities at Khartum,
seeing the situation getting worse, had applied to Gordon
to send them to Berber ; but it was doubtful if it would have
been safe to let them go, and at Gordon's suggestion they
decided to remain. The inhabitants of Khartum had themselves begun to look with mistrust on Gordon, for they
realized, from the proclamation of which they had heard,
that Gordon had only come to withdraw the garrison, though
later on they thoroughly understood that Gordon himself
had come to conquer with them or to die. The Sheikh El
Obeid, one of the great religious Sheikhs of the Sudan,
had collected together his followers at Halfaya to besiege
Khartum. Gordon had sent troops under Hassan Pasha
and Said Pasha Hussein, who had been formerly Governor
of Shakka, to drive the rebels out of their position, and
watching the operations through a telescope from the top of
the Palace, he had seen his trusted officers endeavouring to
make over his troops to the enemy, whilst they themselves
were retreating to Khartum. He had tried these traitorous
officers by general court-martial, and had had them shot.
In spite of this disaster, he had succeeded in relieving the
Shaigias, who were loyal to Government, and had brought
them, under their commander Sanjak Abdel Hamid Wad
Mohammed, to Khartum.

Saleh Wad el Mek, himself invested by the rebels at
Fedasi, had begged Gordon to relieve him ; but it was impossible to do so, and he had been obliged to surrender with
one thousand four hundred irregulars and cavalry, with all
their arms. In consequence of this success, Hajji Mohammed Abu Girga had collected all the inhabitants of the
Gezira to besiege Khartum. Whilst these events were
happening in the neighbourhood of that town, the Mahdi's
former teacher, Sheikh Mohammed el Kheir (formerly
Mohammed el Diker), had come to the river, and had been
appointed by his early pupil Emir of Berber ; he had placed
all the tribes in the province under his orders, and the latter,

collecting adherents from his own tribe, the Jaalin, and reinforced by the Barabra, Bisharia, and other Arabs, had laid siege to Berber, which had fallen in a few days.

The province of Dongola had hitherto held out, owing principally to its crafty Mudir, Mustafa Bey Yawer, who had twice written to the Mahdi, offering him his submission, but the latter, fearing to trust one of the hated Turks, had sent his relative, Sayed Mahmud Ali, to join the Shaigia Emir Sheikh el Heddai, who had already headed a disturbance in the province, to take possession. But Mustafa Bey, secretly learning that he was not acceptable, had fallen suddenly on Heddai at Debba, and, encouraged by the presence of a British officer* in his province, had followed up this success by inflicting a crushing defeat on the Mahdists at Korti, in which both the Emirs Mahmud and Heddai were killed.

At Sennar matters were not so satisfactory; it was closely invested, but had large reserve supplies of corn. Communication with the outside was, however, completely stopped, though Nur Bey, the brave commander, had made a successful sortie which had driven off the rebels to some distance, and enabled the town to breathe again.

Appeals now reached the Mahdi from all parts to come down to the river, but he was in no particular hurry, for he knew that the country was securely in his hands, and that it would require a large Egyptian or foreign army to reconquer it from him. Every Friday he held a review of his troops, at which he himself was always present. His force was divided into three portions, each under the command of a Khalifa, though, in addition, Khalifa Abdullahi was entitled 'Reis el Gesh' (Commander-in-Chief of the Army). His own special division was known as the Raya ez Zarga, or blue flag, and his brother Yakub represented him as its commander. The Raya el Khadra, or green flag, was under the command of the Khalifa Ali Wad Helu; while the red

* Major Kitchener, now Sir Herbert Kitchener, the Sirdar of the Egyptian army.

flag, the Raya el Ashraf (flag of the nobles), was placed under Khalifa Mohammed Sherif. Under each principal flag were grouped the flags of the various Emirs.

When the reviews took place, the Emirs of the Raya ez Zarga deployed into line with their banners facing east; those of the green flag were drawn up opposite to them, facing west; and connecting these two lines, and facing north, were the Emirs and flags of the Ashraf. The numbers of the Mahdi's followers being now enormous, an immense square was thus formed, open on one side, and the Mahdi and his staff, advancing to the centre, would receive the salute, and would then ride along the lines, welcoming his faithful adherents with the words, ' Allah yebarek fikum !' (' May God bless you !').

During these Friday reviews, called Arda or Tarr, extraordinary occurrences were said to take place. One would assert that he saw the Prophet riding beside the Mahdi, and talking with him; others would say they heard voices from Heaven, shouting blessings on the Ansar, and promises of victory. They would even affirm that a passing cloud was formed by angels' wings in order to give shade and refreshment to the faithful.

About three days after the news had been received of Abu Girga's defeat, an Italian named Joseph Cuzzi arrived at Rahad from Khartum; he had been residing in Berber at the time of its fall, having been left behind by A. Marquet, the agent of Debourg and Company, to wind up some of their affairs. Mohammed el Kheir had sent him, as a prisoner, to Abu Girga, and he had despatched him with a letter to Gordon; but the latter had refused to see him, and had sent him back to the enemy's post, on the east bank of the Blue Nile, opposite Khartum. The Mahdi now sent Cuzzi back in company with a Greek named George Calamatino, with letters to Gordon summoning him to submit. By the hands of this Greek I also sent secretly a few lines to Gordon Pasha. The Greek was permitted to enter the lines; but Cuzzi was kept at a place some distance off, as, on the first occasion on which he had come, he was reported by the officers to have personally summoned them to surrender.

When the fast of Ramadan was over, Abu Anga and his entire fighting force were recalled from Jebel Daïr ; and the Mahdi then publicly announced that the Prophet had directed him to proceed to Khartum and lay siege to it. Every Emir was enjoined to collect his men, and order them to prepare for the march ; whilst any who remained behind were declared lawful prey, and liable to total confiscation of all they possessed. However, there was no hanging back on the part of the people, whose fanaticism knew no bounds, and who were well aware that treasure and plunder generally fell to the share of the faithful followers. The consequence was that the Mahdi's summons brought about a wholesale immigration of the entire population, such as had never before been seen in the Sudan.

We left Rahad on August 22, the Mahdist forces marching by three separate roads : the northern one, *viâ* Khursi, Helba, and Tura el Hadra, was selected by the camel-owning tribes ; the central road, *viâ* Tayara, Sherkela, Shatt, and Duem, was taken by the Mahdi, Khalifas, and the majority of the Emirs ; whilst the Baggaras and cattle-owning tribes adopted the southern route, which was well supplied with water, owing to the frequent rain pools which served as drinking places for the cattle. I, of course, in my capacity as mulazem of the Khalifa, followed my master ; but, as a rule, when halted in camp, I used to send my horses and servants to Saleh Wad el Mek, who had joined the Mahdi's suite. The Khalifa, however, for some unknown reason, had a particular aversion to him, and ordered me in future to remain with my servants near him, and charged his cousin, Osman Wad Adam, to look after me. Nevertheless, every now and then I used to see Saleh Wad el Mek, who was kept informed of all that was happening in the Nile districts.

Just before arriving at Sherkéla, strange rumours were

spread about that an Egyptian who was a Christian had
arrived at El Obeid, and was now on his way to overtake
the Mahdi. Some believed him to be the Emperor of
France; others affirmed that he was closely related to the
Queen of England. However, there was no doubt a
European was coming, and I was naturally most anxious
to know who he could be. That evening the Khalifa told
me a Frenchman had arrived at El Obeid, and that he had
sent orders for him to be brought to the Mahdi. ' Do you
belong to the French race?' said he to me; 'or are there
different tribes in your country, as there are here with us in
the Sudan?'—he had not, of course, the slightest knowledge
of Europe and the European nations, and I enlightened him
as far as I thought necessary. ' But what should a Frenchman want with us, that he should come all that long
distance?' asked the Khalifa inquiringly; 'possibly God
has converted him, and has led him to the right way.'
' Perhaps,' said I, ' he is seeking your and the Mahdi's
friendship.' The Khalifa looked at me incredulously, and
said curtly, ' We shall see.'

At length we reached Sherkéla; and scarcely had we
halted when my master sent for me, and said, ' Abdel
Kader, the French traveller has arrived; I have now
ordered him to be brought before me. You had better wait
and listen to what he has to say; I may want you.'—
Almost immediately afterwards Hussein Pasha came in,
and he too had evidently been summoned by the Khalifa.
After waiting some little time longer, a mulazem announced
that the stranger was waiting outside the hut; and he was
at once admitted. He was a tall, young-looking man—about
thirty years of age, I should say—and his face was much
bronzed by the sun; he had a fair beard and moustache,
and wore a jibba and turban. He greeted the Khalifa with
' Salam aleikum '; and the latter, who did not rise from his
angareb, merely motioned him to be seated. ' Why have
you come here; and what do you want from us?' were the
Khalifa's first words to him; he replied, in such broken

Arabic that it was difficult to understand, that he was a Frenchman, and had come from France. 'Speak in your own language with Abdel Kader,' interrupted the Khalifa, 'and he will explain to me what you want.' The stranger now turned and looked at me distrustfully, saying, in English, 'Good-day, sir.' 'Do you speak French?' said I; 'my name is Slatin. Stick to business entirely now, and, later on, we can speak privately.' 'What are you talking about together?' muttered the Khalifa, in an annoyed tone; 'I wish to know what he wants.'

'I only told him my name,' said I, 'and urged him to speak openly to you, as both you and the Mahdi are men to whom God has granted the power to read the thoughts of others.' Hussein Khalifa, who was sitting beside me, now broke in, 'That is true, indeed! May God prolong the Khalifa's life!' and then, turning to me, he said, 'You did well to call this stranger's attention to the fact.' The Khalifa, appeased and flattered, now said, 'Well, try and find out the truth.'

'My name is Olivier Pain,' said the stranger, whom I had now told to talk in French, 'and I am a Frenchman. Since I was quite a boy I was interested in the Sudan, and sympathized with its people; it is not only I, but all my compatriots, who feel the same. In Europe there are nations with whom we are at feud; one of these is the English nation which has now settled in Egypt, and one of whose generals (Gordon) is now commander in Khartum. I have therefore come to offer you my assistance, and that of my nation.'

'What assistance?' interrupted the Khalifa, to whom I was translating word for word Olivier Pain's statement.

'I can only offer you advice,' said Pain, 'but my nation, which is anxious to gain your friendship, is ready to help you practically with arms and money, under certain conditions.'

'Are you a Mohammedan?' asked the Khalifa, as if he had not heard what he had said.

'Yes, certainly,' said he ; 'I have been of this faith for a long time, and at El Obeid I openly acknowledged it.'

'Well,' said the Khalifa, 'you and Hussein can stay here with the Frenchman whilst I go and let the Mahdi know, and I shall then come back to you.'

When the Khalifa had gone I shook hands with Olivier Pain, and introduced him to Hussein Khalifa ; but I confess to feeling considerably prejudiced against him by his offer to assist our enemies. However, I urged him to be most careful, and to say that he had been induced to come here rather out of love for religion than for political motives. Even Hussein Pasha, who was evidently very much annoyed, said in Arabic to me : 'Is that what you call politics, to offer money and arms to people whose only object is to kill others, rob them of their property, and enslave their wives and daughters ? Yet if one of us, no matter how poor he may be, buys a Black slave who is really little better than an animal, except that he can till the ground, you call it wicked and cruel, and punish us most severely.'

'Mailaish' ('Never mind'), said I ; 'he who lives long sees much.'

We were now occupied with our own thoughts whilst waiting for the Khalifa's return ; and at length he arrived, ordered us to make our ablutions, and prepare to attend the Mahdi's prayers. Having done so, the Khalifa leading, we went to the place of worship, where there was an immense concourse of people, who, having heard of Olivier Pain's arrival, were indulging in the wildest speculations about him. After we had taken our places, Pain was directed to the second row, and the Mahdi now arrived. He was dressed in his speckless and beautifully-perfumed jibba ; his turban was more carefully folded than usual, and his eyes were well painted with antimony, which gave them a more fiery expression. He had evidently done his utmost to appear to the greatest possible advantage. No doubt he was pleased and flattered that a man should have come

from so far to offer him assistance. He now sat himself
down on his prayer-carpet, and, calling up Olivier Pain
before him, greeted him with a very beaming smile, but did
not shake hands with him, and, using me as an interpreter,
asked him to explain why he had come here.

Pain reiterated the same story as before, which the Mahdi
told me to repeat in a sufficiently loud voice for everyone to
hear ; and when I had finished he said, in an equally loud
tone : 'I have heard your intentions, and have understood
them ; but I do not count on human support ; I rely on God
and His Prophet. Your nation are unbelievers, and I shall
never ally myself with them. With God's help I shall
defeat my enemies through my brave Ansar and the hosts
of angels sent to me by the Prophet.' Shouts of acclama-
tion from thousands upon thousands of throats greeted this
speech, and when order had been restored the Mahdi said
to Pain : 'You affirm that you love our faith, and acknowledge that it is the true one. Are you a Mohammedan ?'

'Certainly,' answered he, repeating the creed, 'La ilaha
illallah, Mohammed Rasul Allah,' in a loud voice. The
Mahdi after this gave him his hand to kiss, but did not
administer the oath of allegiance.

We now took up our positions in the ranks of the faithful,
and repeated prayers with the Mahdi ; and, that over, the
Divine Master gave us one of his usual sermons on salvation and renunciation. We then departed with the Khalifa,
who directed me to take Olivier Pain to my tent, and there
await further instructions.

Once alone with Pain in my tent, I could talk to him
without fear of interruption. I had the strongest aversion
to his mission, but I pitied the man who, if he thought to
succeed in such an enterprise in this country, was the
victim of so absurd a delusion. I again greeted him
heartily, saying, 'Now, my dear Mr. Olivier Pain, we
shall be quite undisturbed for a few minutes ; let us speak
frankly. Although I do not agree with your mission, I
assure you, on my word as an officer, I will do all in my

power to secure your personal safety. I have now been for years an exile from the civilized world. Tell me something about outside affairs.'

'I trust you thoroughly,' he replied. 'I know you well by name, and have often heard of you, and I thank my good fortune which has brought me to you. There is a great deal to tell you, but for the present I will confine myself to Egypt, which must interest us most.'

'Tell me, then,' said I, 'all about the revolt of Ahmed Arabi Pasha, about the massacres, about the intervention of the Powers, and about England, which has just occupied Egypt.'

'I,' said he, 'am working for the *Indépendence*, with Rochefort, of whom you must have heard. England and France are politically antagonistic, and we do what we can to put as many difficulties as possible in England's way. I have not come here as a representative of my nation, but as a private individual, with, however, the knowledge and concurrence of my nation. The English authorities, discovering my intentions, issued a warrant of arrest against me, and I was sent back from Wadi Halfa; but on my way down the river, at Esna, I agreed secretly with some Alighat Arabs to bring me here by the road running west of Dongola, through El Kaab, to El Obeid. To-day the Mahdi has received me most kindly, and I hope for the best.'

'Do you think that your proposal will be accepted?' said I.

'Should my proposal be refused,' he answered, 'I still hope the Mahdi will be induced to enter into friendly relations with France; for the present that will be quite sufficient, and, as I have come here of my own free will, I trust the Mahdi will not make my return impossible.'

'That is very questionable,' said I; 'but have you left a family at home?'

'Oh, yes,' answered Pain, 'I have left my wife and two children in Paris; I often think of them, and hope to see them soon again. But tell me, sir, frankly—why should I be detained?

'My dear sir,' I replied, 'as far as I know these people, I do not think you need at present have any fear for your own safety; but when and how you are going to get away from them, it is beyond my power to say. What I sincerely hope is, that your proposals, which may be advantageous to the enemy—and I admit these Mahdists are my most bitter enemies—will not be accepted, and I also hope they will allow you to return unmolested to your wife and children, who must be anxiously awaiting you.'

Meanwhile, I had told my servants to get us something to eat; and I had sent for Gustav Klootz, O'Donovan's former servant, to share our meal with us. We had scarcely begun, when two of the Khalifa's mulazemin entered, and told Olivier Pain to follow them. He was much taken aback at being called off alone, and, in a whisper, commended himself to me. It also struck me as curious, for Pain's Arabic was quite unintelligible. I was talking about this to Mustafa (Klootz), when I also received a summons, and, on entering the Khalifa's hut, I found him quite alone; he motioned to me to be seated, and I sat on the ground beside him.

'Abdel Kader,' said he confidentially, 'I look on you as one of us; tell me, what do you think of this Frenchman?'

'I believe he is sincere, and means well,' said I; 'but he did not know the Mahdi, nor you; he did not understand that you trusted only in God, and sought no support from other powers, and that this is the cause of your continual victories, because God is with those who put their trust in Him.'

'You heard the Mahdi's words,' continued the Khalifa, 'when he said to the Frenchman that he wished to have nothing to do with unbelievers, and that he could defeat his enemies without their help?'

'Most certainly I did,' I replied; 'and therefore the man is useless here, and may as well return to his nation, and tell them about the victories of the Mahdi and his commander-in-chief, the Khalifa.'

'Perhaps, later,' said the Khalifa; 'for the present, I have ordered him to stay with Zeki Tummal, who will take all care of him, and attend to his wants.'

'But it will be very difficult for him to make himself understood in Arabic,' I pleaded; 'he is by no means a good Arabic scholar yet.'

'He has been able to get here without an interpreter,' answered the Khalifa; 'however, you have my permission to visit him.' He then talked about other things, and showed me the horses Zogal had sent him from Darfur, some of which I knew very well. After leaving my master, I went in search of Pain, whom I found sitting under the shade of a very battered old tent, his head resting on his hands, and evidently in deep thought; when he saw me, he at once rose, saying, 'I don't know what to think about it all. I have been ordered to stay here; my baggage has been brought, and I am told that a certain Zeki has been ordered to look after me. Why don't they let me stay with you?'

'It is the Mahdi's nature; and the Khalifa is even worse in working his will in contrariety to every human being under the sun. You are going through a course of what they call " putting one to the test in patience, submission, and faith,"' said I, by way of sympathy; 'but you need have no fear. The Khalifa suspects us both, and is anxious to keep us apart, so that we should not criticize his actions. Here comes Zeki Tummal. He was with me in many a fight; I will strongly commend you to him.' I had now advanced to meet Zeki, who shook hands with me, and asked how I was. 'My friend,' said I to him, 'this is a stranger, and your guest. I recommend him to your kind care; be forbearing with him for old acquaintance' sake.'

'I shall let him want for nothing as far as it is in my power to do so,' he replied; and then, more slowly, he said, 'But the Khalifa has told me not to let him have any intercourse with others, and I therefore beg you will come here only very occasionally.'

'These orders do not apply to me,' said I; 'just this moment I left our master's hut, and he has given me special permission to visit your guest. So again I beg you to treat this poor man with all consideration.'

I then returned to Pain, and tried to cheer him up, telling him that the Khalifa had given orders he was not to be allowed to see other people; but this, I said, was no disadvantage, for they would probably have used the occasion to intrigue against him, and so put him in danger. As regards myself, however, I said I would come to see him as often as possible.

The next morning, the Khalifa's great war-drum, called 'El Mansura' (the victorious), was beaten; this was the signal for the march to begin again, and off we started. We generally marched from early morning till noon only, and thus our progress was not rapid. When we halted at mid-day, I went to look for Pain, and found him sitting under his tent as before: he appeared in good health, but complained about the bad food. Zeki, who was present whilst we were speaking, said that he had twice sent him some asida, but he would not touch it. I explained that he was not, of course, accustomed to native food yet, and that therefore I proposed getting my servant to prepare some food specially for him; and, returning at once, I ordered him to make some soup and boil some rice, and take it to Olivier Pain. That evening the Khalifa asked me if I had seen him. I told him I had; but that, as he was not accustomed yet to native food, I had ordered my servant to prepare something else. I explained that if he were forced to eat the native food he might get ill; and that therefore, with his permission, I proposed sending him, every now and then, something special. The Khalifa assented. 'But,' said he, 'you eat of our food; it would therefore be better he should get used to it as soon as possible. By-the-bye, where is Muotafa? I have not seen him since we left Rahad.'

'He is staying with me, and helps my servants to look after the horses and camels,' said I.

'Then send for him,' said the Khalifa. I did so; and in a few minutes he entered and stood before us. 'Where have you been? I have not seen you for weeks,' said the Khalifa angrily. 'Have you forgotten that I am your master?'

'With your permission I went to Abdel Kader, whom I help in his work. You do not care for me now, and have left me alone,' replied Klootz, in an annoyed tone.

'Then I will take good care of you in the future,' cried the Khalifa, still more angrily; and, calling in a mulazem, he ordered him to take Mustafa to his clerk, Ben Naga, who should put him in chains. Mustafa, without uttering a word, followed his guard.

'Mustafa and you,' continued the Khalifa, 'have servants enough, and you can quite well do without him. I took him for myself, but he left me without any cause. I then ordered that he should serve my brother Yakub, but he complained and left him too; and now that he is with you he thinks he can dispense with us altogether.'

'Pardon him,' said I; 'he is merciful who forgives. Let him stay with your brother; perhaps he will improve.'

'He must remain a few days in chains,' he answered, 'so that he may know I am his master; he is not the same as you, who come every day to my door;' this he evidently said to quiet me, as he thought I was getting annoyed. He then ordered supper to be brought in, and I ate more than usual, so that he should not imagine I was doing anything contrary to his orders. He talked very little during the meal, and seemed out of spirits. After supper he made an attempt to say something kind, but I felt that his words belied him. We then separated, and as I returned to my tent I thought over the situation. I had resolved to remain on as good terms as I could with the Khalifa until the hour of my deliverance should come; but his imperious character, want of consideration, and immense self-conceit, made my task a most difficult one.

After five days' march, we reached Shatt, where most of

the wells were filled up, and had to be reopened, and several straw huts erected, for the Mahdi had decided to halt here for some days. During the march I frequently visited Pain, who daily grew more and more disheartened about the situation. He knew very little Arabic, and was not permitted to talk to anyone but the slaves charged with looking after him. In a few days the object of his mission had vanished from his mind, and he thought now only of his wife and children. I urged him to look more hopefully on the future, and not to give way to depressing thoughts, which would only make him more miserable. The Khalifa seemed to have almost forgotten his existence, and scarcely ever asked for him.

The day after our arrival at Shatt, the Mahdi's former Sheikh, Mohammed Sherif, who had been expected for so long, at length arrived. He also had been forced by his friends, and by fear, to come to the Mahdi as a penitent; but the latter received him most honourably, and himself led him to the tents he had specially pitched for him, and also presented him with two exceptionally pretty Abyssinian girls, horses, etc. By this generous treatment the Mahdi attracted to himself almost all Mohammed Sherif's secret adherents.

Just at the time we left Sherkéla news arrived that Gordon's troops had suffered a severe reverse, and now in Shatt we received the detailed accounts of the overthrow of Mohammed Ali Pasha at Om Debban by the Sheikh El Obeid.

This success had encouraged the rebels to press the siege more closely, and now, reinforced as they were by Wad en Nejumi and his hosts, Gordon found himself not strong enough to make a successful attack on the Mahdists.

From Shatt we now advanced to Duem, where the Mahdi held an enormous review; and, pointing to the Nile, he said, 'God has created this river; He will give you its waters to drink, and you shall become the possessors of all the lands along the banks.' This speech was greeted with

shouts of joy by these wild fanatics, who at once believed
that the wonderful land of Egypt was to be their prey.

From Duem we proceeded to Tura el Hadra, where we
spent the Feast of Great Bairam ; Olivier Pain was suffering from fever, and was growing more and more depressed.
' I have tried many ventures in my life,' said he, ' without thinking much beforehand of the consequences, but my
coming here was a fatal mistake.   It would have been very
much better for me if the English had succeeded in preventing me from carrying out my design.'   I did my best
to comfort him, but he only shook his head.

At the Feast of Bairam the Mahdi repeated prayers in an
unusually loud voice, and when he read the ' Khutba ' he
wept long and bitterly.   We unbelievers well knew that
this weeping was hypocrisy, and boded no good ; but it had
the desired effect on the fanatical crowds who had flocked
to his banners from the river tribes, and who were roused
by this touching sermon to the highest pitch of enthusiasm.

After a halt of two days, we again moved on, creeping
forward like a great tortoise, so swelled were we by the
thousands upon thousands who were now joining daily from
every part of the Sudan.   Poor Olivier had grown considerably worse ; his fever had turned to typhus.   He begged
me to induce the Mahdi to let him have some money, as he
was so pestered by the begging appeals of his attendants.   I
went to him and explained Pain's condition, and the Mahdi
at once sent to the Beit el Mal for £5, and wished the sick
man a speedy recovery.   I had also told the Khalifa of
Pain's serious illness, and that the Mahdi had given him
£5 ; but he blamed me for having asked for it without his
permission, adding, ' If he dies here, he is a happy man.
God in His goodness and omnipotence has converted him
from an unbeliever to a believer.'

Early in the morning, at the end of the first week in
October, I was sent for by Pain, and found him so weak
that he could not stand up.   For two days he had not
touched the food I had sent him, and, placing his hand in

mine, he said, ' My last hour has come ; I thank you for your great kindness and care of me. The last favour I have to ask of you is this : when you escape from the hands of these barbarous people, and you happen to go to Paris, tell my unfortunate wife and children my dying thoughts were for them.' As he said these words, tears rolled down the poor man's hollow and sunken cheeks. Again I tried to comfort him, saying that it was too soon to give up hope ; and as the war-drum was beating for the advance, I had to hurry away and leave him. It was the last time I saw him alive. I left behind with him one of my servants named ' Atrun ' (Natron), and during the march I told the Khalifa of Pain's condition, urging him to leave the poor man behind at some village where he might have a few days' rest ; he told me to remind him of it that evening. The evening came, but no sick man arrived ; Atrun came alone. ' Where is Yusef ?' (this was Pain's Mohammedan name), said I, for the boy seemed much agitated. ' My master is dead,' he answered, ' and that is the reason we are so late.' ' Dead !' said I. ' Yes, dead and buried,' replied Atrun.

' Tell me at once what has happened,' I asked. ' My master Yusef was so weak,' said he, ' that he could not ride ; but we had to go on marching. Every now and then he lost consciousness ; then he would come to again and talk words we could not understand. So we tied an angareb on to the saddle, and laid him on it ; but he was too weak to hold on, and he fell down suddenly and very heavily. After this he did not come to again, and he was soon dead, so we wrapped him up in his farda [cotton shawl], and buried him, and all his effects were taken to Zeki by his slaves.'

Olivier Pain was undoubtedly very seriously ill, but the fall was probably the immediate cause of his sudden death. Poor man ! with what a high-sounding mission he had come ; and now this was the end of it all ! I immediately went to the Khalifa, and reported his death to him. ' He is a happy man,' was his curt remark ; he then despatched a mulazem to warn Zeki to have all his effects carefully kept, and he sent me to the Mahdi to apprise him of his end. The latter took it to heart much more than the Khalifa, said several sympathetic words, and repeated the prayers for the dead.

After three days we reached the neighbourhood of Khartum, and halted at a place about one day's journey from the city. On our way we had seen Gordon's steamers in the distance; they had come up evidently to watch our movements, and had returned again without firing.

It was evening, and we had just finished pitching camp, when a mulazem of the Mahdi arrived, and directed me to follow him; I went at once, and found him sitting with Abdel Kader Wad Om Mariam, formerly Kadi of Kalakla, and a man who exercised a great influence on the people of the White Nile. Hussein Khalifa was also there, and I formed the fourth of the party.

' I have sent for you,' said the Mahdi, ' to tell you to write to Gordon to save himself from certain defeat. Tell him that I am the true Mahdi, and that he ought to surrender with his garrison, and thus save himself and his soul. Tell him, also, that if he refuses to obey, we shall everyone of us fight against him. Say that you yourself will fight against him with your own hands. Say that victory will be ours, and that you merely tell him this in order to avoid useless bloodshed.'

I remained silent till Hussein Khalifa called on me to answer. ' O Mahdi!' said I, ' listen, I beg of you, to my words. I will be honest and faithful; and I pray you to forgive me if what I say is not pleasing to you. If I write to Gordon that you are the true Mahdi, he will not believe me; and if I threaten to fight against him with my own hands, he will not be afraid of that. Now, as you desire under any circumstances to avoid shedding blood, I shall simply summon him to surrender. I shall say that he is not strong enough to attempt to fight against you who are ever-victorious, as he has no hope of help from outside ; and, finally, I shall say that I will be the intermediary between you and him.'

'I accept your sincere proposal,' said the Mahdi; 'go now and write the letters, and to-morrow they shall be despatched to Gordon.'

I now returned to my quarters. My tent, owing to the difficulties of transport, had been torn to shreds, and I had made a present of the rags to someone; I had in place of it stretched some strips of cloth on sticks, and thus provided a slight shade for myself during the daytime, whilst at night I slept in the open. Searching about for a lantern, I wrote the letters seated on an angareb under the open sky. First I wrote a few lines to Gordon in French, explaining that I was writing to him fully in German because my French Dictionary having been burnt by the Mahdists, who thought it was a Prayer-Book, I did not feel capable of expressing myself as I wished in that language. I said that I hoped I should soon have an opportunity of joining him; and I prayed God that he might be successful. I also mentioned that some of the Shaigias who had recently joined the Mahdi did so to save their wives and children, and not because they entertained any feelings of hostility towards Gordon.

I then wrote a long letter to him in German, saying that I had learnt through George Calamatino that he was annoyed at my capitulation, and that therefore I took the liberty of placing the facts of the case before him, begging him to form his opinion accordingly. I began by recalling my campaigns against Sultan Harun and Dud Benga, and explaining how, on the outbreak of the Mahdi revolt, the few officers left, believing that Arabi Pasha had succeeded in driving the Europeans out of the country, had spread reports that my recent defeats lay in the fact that I was a Christian; how I had stifled the injurious effects of these intrigues by giving out that I was a Mohammedan; and how I had, by this means, been subsequently successful until the annihilation of Hicks' army had cut off all hope of relief. I told him how my constant fights had reduced my available force to some seven hundred men; that my stock of ammunition was well-nigh exhausted ; that both officers and men desired capitulation ; and what, therefore, could I do—a European and alone—but submit. I told him how this surrender had been one of the hardest acts of my life ; but that as an Austrian officer I felt that I had not acted in a dishonourable manner. I then went on to say that by obedient and submissive behaviour I had in some measure gained the confidence of the Mahdi and the Khalifa, and had obtained their permission to write to him, on the pretext that I was asking him to surrender ; but that, instead, I availed myself of this opportunity to offer him my services in order to assure him that I was ready to conquer, or die with him, if God willed, an honourable death. Should he agree to be an accessory to my escape to Khartum, I begged him to write me a few lines in French to that effect ; but, in order to carry out the ruse, I suggested that he should also write me a few lines in Arabic, asking me to obtain the Mahdi's permission to come to Omdurman, in order to discuss with him the conditions of surrender. I went on to tell him that Saleh Bey and several of the Sheikhs wished to express their loyalty and devotion to him ; but that, under the circumstances, it was impossible for them to come to him, as by so doing they would necessarily sacrifice their wives and children.

I now wrote a third letter, in German, to Consul Hansal, asking him to do his utmost to arrange that I should re-enter Khartum, as, being thoroughly cognisant of the Mahdi's plans, intentions, strength, etc., I believed I could be of great service to General Gordon ; but, at the same time, as rumours had been in circulation in the Mahdi's camp that, if relief should not soon come, Gordon intended to surrender the town, and as at that time I was quite ignorant of Gordon's prospects of relief, I begged Consul Hansal to inform me of this, as, in the event of the town being surrendered subsequent to my having entered Khartum, I should naturally be the Mahdi's lawful victim on which to vent all his anger at my escape and my efforts to aid his enemies.

It seemed to me that it was quite reasonable on my part to seek some such assurance. At the same time, rumours being current in the camp that the Khartum garrison were much out of heart and wished to surrender, I strongly urged Hansal in my letter not to feel discouraged, pointing out that the Mahdi's forces were not so numerous as he imagined, and that it only required energy and perseverance on the part of the Egyptian troops to be eventually successful, and I urged that they should wait at least six weeks, or two months, longer before submitting, so as to give the relief expedition a chance of saving them.*

I also told him there was a rumour in camp that the small steamer which had been sent to Dongola had been wrecked at Wadi Gamr; but that I was not at present in a position to say whether it was true or not.

Early the next morning, October 15, I took these letters to the Mahdi, and he told me to send them by one of my boys to Omdurman. I at once went and fetched Morgan Fur, a boy of about fifteen years of age, and handed him the letters in the Mahdi's presence; and the latter ordered Wad Suleiman to give him a donkey and some money. Before sending him off, I gave him the most strict injunctions to speak to no one in Khartum except to Gordon Pasha and Consul Hansal, and to assure them that I wished to come to them.

At mid-day some horsemen arrived from Berber, confirming the news of the wreck of the steamer, and of the murder of Colonel Stewart and those with him. The men brought with them all the papers and documents found on board; and I was ordered by the Khalifa to examine those written in European languages in Ahmed Wad Suleiman's office. Amongst them I found several private letters from people in Khartum, as well as official documents and records. The most important of these was, of course, the military report

* On my return to Cairo in 1895, I learnt that the full text of the letters to which I have referred had reached the British authorities, and had been published in General Gordon's Journal.

describing the daily occurrences in Khartum; it was un
signed, but I had no doubt it was General Gordon's. A
portion only of the correspondence, etc., was shown to me;
and before I had had time to peruse it fully, I was again
summoned before the Mahdi, who asked me what the
contents were. I replied, that most of them were private
letters, and that there was a military report, which I did
not understand. Unfortunately, amongst the captured
correspondence were numbers of Arabic letters and reports,
from which the Mahdi and the Khalifa were able to
thoroughly grasp the situation in Khartum. There was
also a half-ciphered Arabic telegram from General Gordon
to His Highness the Khedive, which Abdel Halim Effendi,
formerly head clerk in Kordofan, was able to decipher.
Amongst the consular reports, I found a notice of the
death, in Khartum, of my old friend Ernst Marno, who had
succumbed to fever.

The Mahdi now discussed in my presence what papers
should be sent to Gordon, in order to convince him that
the steamer had been wrecked, and Colonel Stewart and
the others killed, thinking that this would force Gordon to
surrender. I pointed out that the only document likely to
convince Gordon was his military report, which I suggested
should be returned; and, after a long discussion, it was
decided to send it.

The next evening my boy Morgan returned from his
mission, but brought no reply. When I inquired how this
was, he said he had reached Omdurman fort, had delivered
his letters, and, after waiting for a short time, the commandant had told him to return, as there was no answer.
I at once took the boy to the Mahdi, to whom he repeated
what had occurred; and afterwards I went and informed
the Khalifa. The same evening the Mahdi again summoned
me, and ordered me to write another letter, which he said
Gordon would be sure to answer, when he heard of the loss
of the steamer. I at once expressed myself ready to carry
out his wishes; and he directed that my boy Morgan should

again act as messenger. Once more I betook myself to my angareb, and, by the flickering light of an old lantern, scribbled another letter, reporting the loss of the steamer, the death of Stewart, and repeating much of what I had said in my first letters, adding that if in his opinion I had done anything contrary to the honour of an officer, and if that had hindered him from writing to me, I begged he would give me a chance of defending myself, and thus give himself an opportunity of coming to a correct judgment.

Early the next morning I went again with Morgan to the Mahdi; the latter ordered Ahmed Wad Suleiman to supply him with a donkey, and, taking my letter, he went off, returning the following morning with a reply from Consul Hansal, written in German, with an Arabic translation; it ran as follows:

' Dear Friend Slatin Bey,
    ' Your letters have been duly received, and I request you will come to Tabia Ragheb Bey [Omdurman fort]. I wish to speak to you about the steps to be taken for our rescue; you may then return unmolested to your friend.
                        ' Yours very truly,
                            ' (Signed)   Hansal.'

This letter puzzled me somewhat; I could not be sure if it was written with the object merely of deceiving the Mahdi, in which case the Arabic was amply sufficient for the purpose; but I thought he might have written more clearly in German, though perhaps he conceived there might have been someone else with the Mahdi who under-stood that language, and I might have been thereby endangered. Then, taking the letter literally, he seemed to hint at joining us himself—indeed, we had already heard rumours that he, becoming alarmed at the probable fall of the town, wished to submit, with the other Austrian sub-jects, to the Mahdi; but it was, of course, quite impossible to say if he meant this or not. Then, again, as regards

my joining Gordon in Khartum, could he really mean that
the latter had refused to listen to my request, or was his
expression that I 'may then return unmolested to my
friend' merely meant as a blind to the Mahdi?   I confess
I was utterly perplexed; my suspense, however, was not
of long duration.

I at once took the letter to the Mahdi, and explained to
him that the Arabic text exactly corresponded with the
German original.   When he had finished reading it, he
asked me if I wished to go, and I replied that I was ready
to comply with his orders, and that my services were always
at his disposal.

'I am rather afraid,' said he, 'that if you go to Omdurman
to speak to your Consul, Gordon may arrest or kill you.   Why
did he not write to you himself, if he thinks well of you?'

'I do not know why he is so silent,' said I; 'perhaps it
is contrary to his orders to enter into communication with
us; however, when I meet Hansal I may be able to arrange
matters.   You say you are afraid Gordon might arrest me;
but I am not, and even if he did I am quite sure you could
release me; but as to his killing me, that is altogether out
of the question.'

'Well,' said the Mahdi, 'get yourself ready to go, and
I will let you know.'

On my way to the Mahdi's hut I had heard of Lupton
Bey's arrival from Bahr el Ghazal; and now, on my way
back, I went in search of him, and found him outside the
Khalifa's door waiting to be received.   Although it was
against rules to speak to anyone before he had received the
Mahdi's pardon, I could not resist greeting him heartily,
and in a few words told him about the letters, and he said
he earnestly hoped I might be allowed to go to Khartum.
He told me he had left his servants and the rest of his
people at some hours' distance, and he asked me to obtain
the Khalifa's permission for them to come in.   A few
minutes afterwards he was summoned before the Khalifa,
obtained his pardon, was told that he might go and bring in

his people, and that he would be presented to the Mahdi on
his return.

Meanwhile, I went back to my quarters, and lay on my
angareb impatiently awaiting my orders to be allowed to go
to Omdurman; or had the Mahdi, perhaps, changed his
mind, and decided not to let me go? At length one of my
boys came and told me that a mulazem of the Khalifa's
wished to see me, and, getting up, he told me to follow him
to Yakub's camp, where his master was waiting for me.
Without a moment's delay I bound my turban round my
head, put on my hizam (belt), and followed. At Yakub's
camp we were told that the Khalifa had gone on to Abu
Anga's zariba, where he was waiting for us. I was beginning to get suspicious; all this wandering about at night
was very unusual. I knew how deceitful these people were,
and I was therefore prepared for any eventuality. Arrived
at Abu Anga's zariba, we were admitted by the sentry. It
was an immense enclosure, filled with little shelters made of
strips of cotton fixed on poles, and separated from each
other by small dhurra-stalk fences. We were directed to
one of these shelters, and there, by the dim light of a
lantern, I saw Yakub, Abu Anga, Fadl el Maula, Zeki
Tummal, and Hajji Zubeir seated round in a circle talking
earnestly; behind them stood several armed men, but no
trace was to be seen of the Khalifa, who, I had been told,
had sent for me. I was now almost certain in my own
mind that foul play was intended. The mulazem advanced
and spoke to Yakub, and I was then summoned to enter,
and to place myself between Hajji Zubeir and Fadl el
Maula, while opposite to me sat Abu Anga.

'Abdel Kader,' began Abu Anga, 'you have promised to
be faithful to the Mahdi, and it is your duty to keep your
word; it is also your duty to obey orders, even should you
suffer thereby. Is not this so?'

'Certainly,' said I; 'and you, Abu Anga, if you give me
any orders from the Mahdi or the Khalifa, you will see that
I know how to obey them.'

'I received orders to make you a prisoner, but I do not know the reason,' said he. And as he spoke, Hajji Zubeir snatched away my sword, which, as was customary, I had laid across my knees whilst speaking, and, handing it to Zeki Tummal, he seized my right arm with both hands.

'I did not come here to fight,' said I to Hajji Zubeir. 'Why should you seize my arm? But you, Abu Anga, of course you must do as you are bidden.'

What I had often inflicted on others I was now about to undergo myself. Abu Anga then stood up, and also Hajji Zubeir and myself, when the latter let go my arm.

'Go to that tent,' said Abu Anga, pointing to a shelter which in the dark I could scarcely see; 'and you, Hajji Zubeir, and the rest, go with him.'

Accompanied by my gaoler and some eight others, I went to the tent, where I was directed to sit on the ground, and chains were now brought out. Two large iron rings, bound together by a thick iron bar, were slipped over my feet, and then hammered close. An iron ring was placed round my neck, and to this was attached a long iron chain with the links so arranged that I had the greatest difficulty in moving my head. I endured all this in perfect silence. Hajji Zubeir then left, and I was told by the two soldiers who were guarding me to lie down on the palm-mat close by.

Left to myself, I had now time to collect my thoughts; and, first of all, I bitterly regretted not having attempted to escape on my horse to Khartum; but who could tell if Gordon would have received me? Now, in accordance with the Mahdi's orders, I was out of harm's way; but what was to be my fate? Was it to be that of Mohammed Pasha Said and Ali Bey Sherif? I was not in the habit of worrying about my personal concerns, and making life miserable. What had Madibbo told me?—'Be obedient and patient, for he who lives long sees much.' I had been obedient; it was now my turn to practise patience, and as for a long life, that was entirely in God's hands.

About an hour later, during which, as may be imagined,

I had not slept, I saw several mulazemin approaching,
carrying lanterns, and as they neared the tent I made out
Khalifa Abdullahi walking in the middle. I stood up and
waited for him.

'Abdel Kader,' said he, when he saw me standing in front
of him, 'are you submitting with resignation to your
fate?'

'Since my childhood,' I replied quietly, 'I have been
accustomed to be obedient; now I must be obedient
whether I like it or no.'

' Your friendship with Saleh Wad el Mek,' said he, 'and
your correspondence with Gordon, have cast suspicion on
you, and we doubt if your heart is still inclined to us. That
is the reason I have ordered you to be forcibly directed in
the right way.'

' I made no secret of my friendship with Saleh Wad el
Mek,' said I; 'he is a friend of mine, and I believe he is
loyal to you. As regards my correspondence with Gordon,
the Mahdi ordered me to write the letters.'

'Did he also order you to write what you did?' interrupted the Khalifa.

'I think I wrote what the Mahdi required,' I replied,
' and no one knows the contents except myself and the person
who received the letters. All I require, sire, is justice, and
I beg that you will pay no heed to lying intriguers.'

I was again alone, and tried to sleep, but was too excited.
All sorts of strange thoughts and ideas coursed through my
brain; the iron round my feet and neck, too, pained me
considerably, and I could get no rest. I scarcely got a
wink of sleep that night, and at sunrise Abu Anga came,
followed by servants carrying some dishes of food. Seating
himself beside me on the palm-mat, the food was placed
before us. It was quite a feast, composed of meal, chickens,
rice and milk, honey, roast meat, and asida. But when I
told him I had absolutely no appetite, he said, 'I think,
Abdel Kader, you are afraid, and that is why you do
not eat.'

'No,' I replied, 'it is not fear, but want of appetite. However, to please you, I will try and eat something;' and I managed to swallow a few mouthfuls, whilst Abu Anga did all he could to show that I was his honoured guest.

'The Khalifa,' said he, 'was rather disappointed yesterday when he saw you were not humbled, and remarked you were strong-headed, and that, he supposed, was the reason you were not afraid.'

'How could I throw myself at his feet,' said I, 'and crave his pardon for a crime I never committed? I am in his hands, and he can do as he likes with me.'

'To-morrow we shall advance,' said Abu Anga, 'and draw nearer to Khartum; we shall press the siege more closely, and then make a sudden attack. I shall ask the Khalifa to let you stay with me; that will be less hard for you than going to the common prison.'

I thanked him for his kindness, and he then left.

All that day I was quite alone, but went through my prayers most carefully in the sight of the bystanders, holding in my hand the rosary which all good Mohammedans carry; but in reality I was repeating over and over again the Lord's Prayer. In the far distance, near Abu Anga's tent, I caught sight of my servants and horses, and the little baggage I had. One of my boys also came and told me he had been ordered to attach himself to Abu Anga.

Early the next morning the great war-drum sounded the advance; tents were struck, baggage packed and loaded on camels, and the whole camp was in movement. The weight of iron on my feet prevented me from walking, so they brought me a donkey; the long neck-chain—the number of figure-of-eight links of which I had amused myself in counting, and which amounted to eighty-three, each about a span long—I wrapped round and round my body, and in this iron casing I was lifted on to the donkey, and held in position by a man on each side, otherwise my weight would have made me overbalance and fall. On the march several of my old friends passed, but dared do nothing but pity me in

silence. We halted on some rising ground in the afternoon,
and from here I could see the palm-trees in Khartum ; how
I longed to join in its defence as one of its garrison !

The order was now given to make a temporary camp in
this position, under Khalifa Abdullahi, whilst the principal
Emirs went forward to select the site for a permanent camp.
By this time the pangs of hunger had seized me, and I
longed for some of the food which Abu Anga had offered
me yesterday ; but the latter was now with the Khalifa, and
had evidently forgotten all about us. However, the wife of
one of my guards found him out, and brought him some
stale dhurra-bread, which he shared with me. Next morning
we were again ordered to advance, and halted about an hour
further on, at the spot selected for the main camp. As Abu
Anga had promised, it was now arranged that I should
definitely remain under his charge ; a tattered old tent was
pitched for me, and around it, close to the tent ropes, a thorn
zariba was made. I was put in here, and the entrance, which
was guarded by soldiers, was blocked by a large thorn-bush.

The Mahdi now ordered the siege to be vigorously pressed ;
that evening several Emirs were sent over to the east bank
of the White Nile to reinforce Wad en Nejumi and Abu
Girga, and all the local people were summoned to join in
the investment. Abu Anga and Fadl el Maula were told
off to besiege Omdurman Fort, which was situated about
five hundred yards from the river, on the west bank, and
was defended by Faragalla Pasha—a Sudanese officer, who,
in the space of one year, had been promoted from the rank
of captain to that of general officer by Gordon. Abu Anga
succeeded in establishing himself between the fort and the
river, and, by digging deep trenches, he obtained sufficient
shelter to hold this advanced position, in spite of the heavy
fire from both the fort and the steamers ; one of the latter
he succeeded in sinking by shells fired from a gun he had
placed in position, but the crew managed to escape to
Khartum.*

* The steamer *Husseinyeh*.

During the siege I was quite neglected; my guards were changed every day, and my welfare entirely depended on their treatment of me. If they happened to be slaves who had been captured, I was most carefully watched, and permitted to have no intercourse with anyone; but if they happened to be old soldiers who knew me, I was not so closely restrained, and they often did me little services, though they prevented me from speaking to anyone. My food was of the very worst description, and, Abu Anga being always occupied in the siege, I was left to the tender mercies of his wives, to whom he had given orders to feed me.

On one occasion one of my former soldiers happened to be on guard over me, and I sent him with a message to Abu Anga's chief wife, complaining that I had been kept without food for two days, and I got back the answer, ' Well, does Abdel Kader think we are going to fatten him up here, whilst his uncle, Gordon Pasha, does nothing but fire shells all day at our master, whose life is always in danger through his fault ? If he had made his uncle submit, he would not now be in chains.' From her own standpoint, the woman's views were perfectly justifiable.

Occasionally some of the Greeks were allowed to come and see me, and they used to tell me the news.

On the day we arrived here, poor Lupton Bey was also thrown into chains, as he was suspected of attempting to join Gordon; besides, when his effects were searched, a document was found, signed by all the officers of his regular troops, stating that he had been forced to surrender his province. His wife and little daughter of five years old were sent to live at the Beit el Mal. The former had been brought up as a Black servant girl in the house of Rosset, formerly German Consul at Khartum, and, on his being appointed Governor of Darfur, she had accompanied him there; on his death at El Fasher, she went with Lupton to Equatoria and Bahr el Ghazal. By the Khalifa's orders, all Lupton's property was confiscated; but he allowed his wife and child the services of a Black female slave to help them in their daily work.

One day, George Calamatino brought me the news that the English army, under Lord Wolseley, was advancing slowly, and had reached Dongola; but they had delayed too long in Upper Egypt, and now that Khartum was in the greatest danger, their advanced guard was no further south than Dongola: under these circumstances, when could their main body arrive?

Some time after the proclamation of the abandonment of the Sudan had been made known, Gordon had given the Khartum people to understand that the English army was coming up to relieve them; and he had thus inspired the garrison and inhabitants with hope and courage. They had been, so to speak, given a new lease of life, and all eyes were anxiously turned to the north, from whence the expected help was to come. Would it come in time?—that was the question.

These days passed in my tattered tent were full of hopes and fears. It was not that I was concerned about my own safety, but I could not help anticipating coming events with the greatest anxiety; how would it all end, and what was to be my future?

One day some of the Khalifa's mulazemin came and forged on to my ankles another set of iron rings and a bar—to humble me, I suppose; but as the weight I already bore prevented me from standing upright, and I was obliged to remain lying down day and night, an iron more or less did not make much difference.

The next few days passed without anything noteworthy occurring. Occasionally I heard the crack of the rifles and the booming of the guns of besieger and besieged; but the Greeks were not allowed to come and see me now, and I was in complete ignorance of what was going on.

One night, about four hours after sunset, when blessed sleep, which makes one forget all one's troubles, was gradually stealing over me, I was suddenly aroused by the

sentry, and ordered to get up at once; as I did so, I saw
one of the Khalifa's mulazemin, who announced that his
master was just coming; and, as he spoke, I saw men
approaching carrying lanterns. What could the Khalifa
want of me at such an hour? I asked myself in great
perplexity.

'Abdel Kader,' said he, in a kindly tone, as he approached,
'sit down;' and, his servants having stretched out his
sheepskin, he sat on it beside me. 'I have here,' he continued, 'a piece of paper, and I want you to tell me what
is written on it, and so prove to me your fidelity.'

'Certainly, if I can do so,' said I, taking the paper. It
was about half the size of a cigarette paper, and there was
plain writing in black ink on both sides of it. I at once
recognised Gordon's handwriting and signature. I held
the paper close to the lantern, and saw the following words
written in French:

'I have about 10,000 men; can hold Khartum at the
outside till the end of January. Elias Pasha wrote to me;
he was forced to do so. He is old and incapable; I forgive
him. Try Hajji Mohammed Abu Girga, or sing another
song.

'GORDON.'

There was nothing to show for whom it was intended.
I was certain there was no one in the camp who knew
French, and that was the reason the Khalifa had come
to me.

'Now, then,' said the Khalifa impatiently, 'have you
made out what it means?'

'The note is from Gordon,' said I, 'and it is written with
his own hand, in French cipher language, which I cannot
understand.'

'What do you say?' said the Khalifa, now evidently
much agitated; 'explain yourself better.'

'There are some words written here the sense of which
I cannot make out,' said I; 'every word has its own

special meaning, and can only be understood by those
accustomed to the use of ciphers; if you ask any of the
old officials, they will confirm what I say.'

'I was told that the names of Elias Pasha and Hajji
Mohammed Abu Girga are mentioned; is this so?' roared
the Khalifa, now thoroughly angry.

'The man who said that told you the truth, and I also
can read their names; but it is impossible for me to understand the reference. Perhaps the man who told you their
names were there can make out the rest of the letter,' said
I, somewhat ironically; 'besides, I can also make out 10,000
in figures; but whether it means soldiers, or something
else, it is quite impossible for me to say.'

He now seized the paper from my hand, and stood up.

'Pardon me,' said I, 'I would with pleasure have proved
my fidelity to you, and have thus regained your gracious
favour; but it is out of my power. I think your clerks
understand about ciphers better than I do.'

'Even if I do not know what this paper contains,' said
the Khalifa, 'still Gordon shall fall, and Khartum will be
ours;' and then he departed, leaving me alone with my
guards.

Gordon had said in his little note that he could hold
Khartum at the outside till the end of January; we were
now nearly at the end of December. Could the rescuing
army possibly arrive in time? But why should I worry
myself with such thoughts? Here am I in chains, and
utterly useless to anyone, and nothing I can do can change
the course of things.

We soon reached the beginning of January, and Gordon
had said he could hold out till the end of the month; so
the decisive moment was drawing closer and closer.

During the next few days there was very heavy firing
between the Dervishes and Omdurman Fort. Faragalla
Pasha was doing his utmost, and in spite of the small number
of his men, he attempted a sortie, but was driven back.
The supplies in the fort were finished, and negotiations were

now going on for its surrender. Faragalla had signalled to Gordon for instructions, but the latter, being unable to support him, had told him to capitulate. The entire garrison received the Mahdi's pardon. The men had nothing but the clothes in which they stood, and their wives and children were all in Khartum. As they marched out, the Mahdists marched in, but were almost immediately driven out again by the artillery fire from Khartum; in the fort itself there were two breech-loading guns, but their range did not extend as far as the town. The surrender took place on the 15th of January, 1885.

Although Omdurman had now fallen, the Mahdi did not send any reinforcements to the besiegers south and east of Khartum; he well knew that the number of his followers collected there was quite sufficient for the purpose. Both he and the garrison of Khartum now looked with the most intense anxiety towards the north, from whence the final decision must be awaited.

Gordon Pasha had sent five steamers to Metemmeh some time ago, under Khashm el Mus and Abdel Hamid Wad Mohammed, in order to await the arrival of the English, and bring some of them, with the necessary supplies, to Khartum as soon as possible. No doubt he was expecting their arrival with the greatest anxiety. He had staked everything on this, and no one knew what had become of them.

At the beginning of the month Gordon had allowed several of the families to leave Khartum. Up to that time he could not bear to forcibly drive them out of the town, and in consequence he had been obliged to make a daily distribution of hundreds of okes of biscuit and dhurra amongst these destitute people; and for that he had, no doubt, God's reward, but he thereby ruined himself and his valuable men. Everyone was crying out for bread, and the stores were almost empty. He now did all he could to induce the people to leave the town. Had he only done so two or three months earlier there would have been ample supplies to last the troops a long time; but Gordon, thinking that help was coming so soon to him, to the troops, and to the inhabitants, did not provide for possible detentions. Did he think that it was out of the question for an English expedition to be delayed?

Six days after the fall of Omdurman, loud weeping and wailing filled our camp; since I had left Darfur I had not heard anything like it. The Mahdi's doctrine forbade the display of sorrow and grief for those who died, or were killed, because they had entered into the joys of Paradise. Something very unusual must therefore have happened to make the people dare to transgress the Mahdi's regulations. My guards, who were old soldiers, were so curious to know the cause that they left me to make inquiries, and in a few minutes brought back the startling news that the English advanced guard had met the combined force of Barabra, Jaalin, Degheim, and Kenana, under Musa Wad Helu, at Abu Teleh (Abu Klea), and had utterly defeated them; thousands had fallen, and the few who had survived had returned, many of them wounded. The Degheim and Kenana had been almost annihilated; Musa Wad Helu, and most of the Emirs, had fallen.

What news!—my heart was literally thumping with joyous excitement. After all these long years a crowning victory at last! The Mahdi and Khalifa at once gave orders that all this noise should cease; but for hours the weeping and wailing of the women continued. Instructions were now given to Nur Angara to start off with troops towards Metemmeh. But what good would this do? Even if he had had the will—which he had not—what could he do with a few troops when thousands and thousands of wild fanatics had failed? Within the next two or three days came the news of other defeats at Abu Kru and Kubba (Gubat), and of the erection of a fort on the Nile close to Metemmeh. The Mahdi and his principal Emirs now held a consultation. All the wonderful victories they had gained up to the present were at stake, for those besieging Khartum were terrified and had retired. It was now the question of a few days only, and the Mahdi was done. They must risk everything. Consequently, orders were sent out to the besiegers to collect and make all preparations. Why did the long-expected steamers with the English troops not come? Did their commanders not know Khartum, and the lives of all in it, were hanging by a thread? In vain did I, and thousands of others, wait for the shrill whistle of the steamer, and for the booming of the guns announcing that the English had arrived, and were passing the entrenchments made by the Dervishes to oppose them. Yes, in vain! The delay was inexplicable; what could it mean? Had new difficulties arisen?

It was now Sunday, the 25th of January—a day I shall never forget as long as I live. That evening, when it was dark, the Mahdi and his Khalifas crossed over in a boat to where their warriors were all collected ready for the fight. It was known during the day that Khartum would be attacked the next morning, and the Mahdi had now gone to brace up his followers for the fray by preaching to them the glories of Jehad, and urging them to fight till death. Pray Heaven Gordon may have got the news, and made his preparations to resist in time!

On this occasion the Mahdi and his Khalifas had most strictly enjoined their followers to restrain their feelings, and receive the last injunctions in silence, instead of with the usual shouts and acclamations, which might awaken the suspicions of the exhausted and hungry garrison. His solemn harangue over, the Mahdi recrossed, and returned to the camp at dawn, leaving with the storming party only Khalifa Sherif, who had begged to be allowed to join in the holy battle.

That night was for me the most excitingly anxious one in my life. If only the attack were repulsed Khartum would be saved, otherwise all would be lost. Utterly exhausted, I was just dropping off to sleep at early dawn when I was startled by the deafening discharge of thousands of rifles and guns; this lasted for a few minutes, then only occasional rifle-shots were heard, and now all was quiet again. It was scarcely light, and I could barely distinguish objects. Could this possibly be the great attack on Khartum ? A wild discharge of firearms and cannon, and in a few minutes complete stillness ?

The sun was now rising red over the horizon; what would this day bring forth ? Excited and agitated, I awaited the result with intense impatience. Soon shouts of rejoicing and victory were heard in the distance, and my guards ran off to find out the news. In a few minutes they were back again, excitingly relating how Khartum had been taken by storm, and was now in the hands of the Mahdists. Was it possible the news was false ? I crawled out of my tent and scanned the camp; a great crowd had collected before the quarters of the Mahdi and Khalifa, which were not far off; then there was a movement in the direction of my tent, and I could see plainly they were coming towards me. In front marched three Black soldiers; one named Shatta, formerly belonging to Ahmed Bey Dafalla's slave bodyguard, carried in his hands a bloody cloth in which something was wrapped up, and behind him followed a crowd of people weeping. The slaves had now approached my tent, and stood before me with insulting gestures; Shatta undid the cloth and showed me the head of General Gordon !

The blood rushed to my head, and my heart seemed to stop beating; but with a tremendous effort of self-control I gazed silently at this ghastly spectacle. His blue eyes were half-opened; the mouth was perfectly natural; the hair of his head and his short whiskers were almost quite white.

'Is not this the head of your uncle, the unbeliever?' said Shatta, holding the head up before me.

'What of it?' said I quietly. 'A brave soldier, who fell at his post. Happy is he to have fallen; his sufferings are over.'

'Ha, ha!' said Shatta, 'so you still praise the unbeliever; but you will soon see the result;' and, leaving me, he went off to the Mahdi, bearing his terrible token of victory; behind him followed the crowd, still weeping.

I re-entered my tent. I was now utterly broken-hearted: Khartum fallen, and Gordon dead! And this was the end of the brave soldier who had fallen at his post—the end of a man whose courage and utter disregard of fear were remarkable, and whose personal characteristics had given him a celebrity in the world which was quite exceptional.

Of what use was the English army now? How fatal had been the delay at Metemmeh! The English advanced guard had reached Gubat on the Nile on the 20th of January, at 10 a.m., on the 21st Gordon's four steamers had arrived. Then, why did they not send some Englishmen on board, no matter how few, and despatch them instantly to Khartum? If they could only have been seen in the town, the garrison would have taken fresh hope, and would have fought tooth and nail against the enemy; whilst the inhabitants, who had lost all confidence in Gordon's promises, would have joined most heartily in resisting the Dervish attack, knowing that the relief expedition was now certain to reach them. Gordon, of course, had done his utmost to hold the town: he had announced that an English army was coming; he had made a paper currency; had distributed decorations and honours almost daily, in order to keep up the hearts of the garrison; and, as the position had become more desperate, he had made almost superhuman efforts to induce the troops to hold out; but despair had taken possession of them. What was the use of all these decorations now? what good were all their ranks and honours? And as for the paper money, perhaps there were one or two still hopeful people who would buy a pound note for a couple of piastres,* on the chance that, by some stroke of luck, the Government might yet be victorious; but gradually even these slender hopes disappeared. Gordon's promises were no longer credited. If but one steamer with a few English officers had reached the

---

* One Egyptian piastre = 2½d.

town, to bring the news that they had won a victory, and
had reached the Nile, the troops and inhabitants would
have doubted no longer, and they would have been convinced that Gordon's words were true. An English officer
would at once have noticed that part of the lines which had
been damaged by the overflow of the White Nile, and
would have ordered its repair. But what could Gordon do
single-handed, and without the assistance of any European
officers? It was impossible for him to look to everything,
nor had he the means of seeing that his orders were carried
out to his satisfaction. How was it possible for a commander who could not give his troops food to expect these
starving men to carry out with precision and energy the
instructions he issued?

On the unfortunate night of the 25th of January Gordon
was told that the Mahdists had decided to make an attack,
and he had issued his orders accordingly. Perhaps he
himself doubted if they would attack so early in the morning. At the time the Mahdi was crossing the river,
Gordon, to stimulate his followers, had made a display of
fireworks in the town ; various coloured rockets were fired,
and the band played, with the object of reviving the
flagging spirits of the famished garrison. The display was
over, the music had ceased, and Khartum was asleep,
whilst the enemy crept cautiously and silently forward to
the attack. They knew all the weak and strong points of
the lines of defence ; they knew also that the regulars were
stationed at the strong points, and that the broken-down
parapet and tumbled-in ditch near the White Nile were
weakly defended by the feeble inhabitants. This particular
part of the lines was sadly out of repair ; it had never been
actually completed, and when damaged by the water no
steps had been taken to re-make it. Every day the Nile
became lower, and every day exposed a broader strip of
undefended wet mud, which the hungry and hopeless people
merely made a show of defending. It was opposite to this
open space that, at early dawn, the bulk of the attacking

force had collected, whilst the other portion of the Mahdist army faced the main position. At a given signal the attack began. Those holding the White Nile flank, after firing a few shots, fled precipitately; and, while the troops were occupied in repelling the storming parties in their immediate front, thousands and thousands of wild Arabs, dashing through mud and water which was only up to their knees, poured into the town, and, to their dismay, the defenders on the lines found themselves attacked from the rear. Very slight resistance was made, and most of the troops laid down their arms. Numbers of the Egyptians were massacred, but of the Blacks few were killed, whilst the enemy's losses within the lines did not exceed eighty to one hundred men. Soon afterwards the gates were opened by the Dervishes, and the troops were permitted to march out to the Mahdist camp.

Once the line of the White Nile was crossed, the great mass of the enemy rushed towards the town. ' Lil Saraya ! lil Kenisa !' (' To the Palace ! to the Church !') was the cry; for it was here they expected to find the treasure and Gordon, who had so long defended the city against them, and had up to that day defied all their efforts. Amongst the leaders in the attack on the Palace were the followers of Makin Wad en Nur, who was afterwards killed at the battle of Toski, and belonged to the Arakin tribe. Makin's brother, Abdalla Wad en Nur, their beloved leader, had been killed during the siege, and they were now seeking to avenge his death. Many of Abu Girga's men were also forward in the rush to the Palace; they wanted to wipe out the defeat they had suffered when Gordon had driven them out of Burri. The Palace servants who lived in the basement were instantly massacred, and Gordon himself, standing on the top of the steps leading to the divan, awaited the approach of the Arabs. Taking no notice of his question, ' Where is your master, the Mahdi ?' the first man up the steps plunged his huge spear into his body; he fell forward on his face without uttering a word. His murderers dragged him down the steps to the Palace entrance, and here his head was cut off, and at once sent over to the Mahdi at Omdurman, whilst his body was left to the mercy of those wild fanatics. Thousands of these inhuman creatures pressed forward merely to stain their swords and spears with his blood, and soon all that remained was a heap of mangled flesh. For a long time stains of blood marked the spot where this atrocity took place, and the steps, from top to bottom, for weeks bore the same sad traces, until they were at last washed off when the Khalifa decided to make the Palace an abode for his former and his future wives.

When Gordon's head was brought to the Mahdi, he remarked he would have been better pleased had they taken him alive; for it was his intention to convert him, and then hand him over to the English Government in exchange for Ahmed Arabi Pasha, as he had hoped that the latter would have been of assistance to him in helping him to conquer Egypt. My own opinion, however, is that this regret on the part of the Mahdi was merely assumed; for had he expressed any wish that Gordon's life should be spared, no one would have dared to disobey his orders.

Gordon had done his utmost to save the lives of the Europeans who were with him. Colonel Stewart, with some of the Consuls and many of the Europeans, he had allowed to go to Dongola; but unfortunately the incapable and disaffected crew of their steamer, the *Abbas*, had run her on to a rock in the cataracts, and had thus given up him and his companions to the treacherous death which had been prepared for them. On the pretext that the Greeks were good men on boats, Gordon had offered them a steamer, on which it was arranged they should make a visit of inspection on the White Nile, thus intending to give them an opportunity to escape south to join Emin Pasha; but they had refused to accept. Being much concerned as to their safety, Gordon now made another proposal: he ordered all roads leading towards the Blue Nile to be placed out of bounds after ten o'clock at night, and he charged the Greeks with watching them, so that they might have a chance of escaping to a steamer moored close by, in which it was arranged they should escape ; but, owing to a disagreement between themselves as to the details of the plan, it fell through. I have little doubt in my own mind that these Greeks did not really wish to leave the town. In their own homes and in Egypt most of them had been very poor, and had held merely subordinate positions ; but here in the Sudan many had made their fortunes, and were therefore by no means anxious to quit a country from which they had reaped such great advantages.

Gordon seemed anxious about the safety of everyone but himself. Why did he neglect to make a redoubt, or keep within the fortifications, the central point of which might well have been the Palace ? From a military point of view, I think this is a fair criticism ; but probably Gordon did not do so, lest he should be suspected of being concerned for his own safety, and it was probably a similar idea which influenced him in his decision not to have a strong guard at the Palace. He might well have employed a company of soldiers for this purpose ; and who would have thought of questioning the advantage of protecting himself? With a guard of this strength, he could easily have reached the steamer *Ismailia*, which was lying close to the Palace, scarcely three hundred yards from the gate. Fagarli, the captain, saw the enemy rushing to the Palace. In vain he waited for Gordon ; and it was only when the latter was killed, and he saw the Dervishes making for his boat, that he steamed off into midstream, and moved backwards and forwards along the front of the town until he received a message from the Mahdi offering him pardon. As his wife and family and some of his crew were in the city, he accepted the offer and landed ; but how sadly had he been deluded ! Rushing to his home, he found his son—a boy of ten years old—lying dead on the doorstep, whilst his wife, in her agony, had thrown herself on her child's body, and lay pierced with several lances.

The cruelties and atrocities perpetrated in the terrible massacre which followed Gordon's death are beyond description. Male and female slaves, and young, good-looking women of the free tribes, alone were spared; and if some others succeeded in escaping, they had only to thank a lucky chance which saved them from the merciless bloodshed of that awful day. Not a few resolved to put an end to their own lives; amongst these was Mohammed Pasha Hussein, the head of the Finance, who, standing beside the dead bodies of his only daughter and her husband, was urged by some friends to fly with them, and let them save him; but he refused. They tried to take him by force; but, in a loud voice, he heaped curses on the Mahdi and his followers, and some fanatics passing by soon despatched him. Several people were killed by their former servants and slaves, who, having previously joined the enemy, now acted as guides to the wild hordes thirsting for blood, plunder, and rapine.

One could fill a volume with the details of the terrible atrocities committed on that memorable day; yet I doubt if the fate of the survivors was very much better. When all the houses were occupied, the search for treasure began, and no excuse or denial was accepted; whoever was suspected of having concealed money—and the majority of the inhabitants had done so—was tortured until the secret was disclosed, or until he succeeded in convincing his tormentors that he had nothing. There was no sparing of the lash; the unfortunate people were flogged until their flesh hung down in shreds from their bodies. Another torture was to tie men up by their thumbs to a beam, and leave them dangling in the air till they became unconscious; or two small pliant slips of bamboo were tied horizontally to their temples, and the two ends, before and behind, being joined together and twisted as tightly as possible, were struck with vibrating sticks which produced agony inexpressible. Even women of an advanced age were tormented in this way, and the most sensitive parts of their bodies were subjected to a species of torture which it is impossible for me to describe here. Suffice it to say that the most appalling methods were resorted to in order to discover hidden treasure. Young women and girls only were exempted from these abominable tortures, for no other reason than that such atrocities might interfere in some manner with the object for which they had been reserved. All such were put aside for the harem of the Mahdi, who, on the actual day of the conquest, made his selections, and turned over the rejected ones to his Khalifas and principal Emirs. This picking and choosing continued for weeks together, until the households of these libidinous and inhuman scoundrels were stocked to overflowing with all the unfortunate youth and beauty of the fallen city.

The next day a general amnesty was given to all, with the exception of the Shaigia, who were still considered outlaws; but, in spite of this, murders and atrocities continued for many days subsequent to the fall of Khartum.

The plunder taken in Khartum was carried off to the Beit el Mal; but, of course, large quantities were made away with. The principal houses were distributed amongst the Emirs; and, on the day after the town fell, the Mahdi and Khalifa Abdullahi crossed over from Omdurman in the steamer *Ismailia* to view the scene of their bloody victory and massacre. Without a sign of pity or regret they occupied the houses selected for them, and, addressing their followers, described the disaster which had overtaken Khartum as the just judgment of Heaven on the godless inhabitants of the city, who had repeatedly rejected the Mahdi's summons to them to surrender and become his faithful followers in the true religion.

The first few days were spent in the wildest debauchery and excesses, and it was not until the Mahdi and his followers had to some extent satiated their vicious passions that they turned their attention to the dangers which

threatened them from without. To oppose the English
expedition, the renowned Emir Abderrahman Wad Nejumi
was ordered to collect a large force and proceed forthwith to
Metemmeh, to drive out the infidels, who were known to
have reached the Nile near this town.

On Wednesday morning, two days after Khartum had
fallen, at about eleven o'clock, the thunder of guns and the
sharp crack of rifles were heard in the direction of the north
end of Tuti Island; and soon two steamers came in view—
these were the *Telahawia* and *Bordein*—carrying Sir Charles
Wilson and some English officers and men who had come
up to assist General Gordon. Sanjak Kashm el Mus and
Abdel Hamid Mohammed, whom Gordon had despatched
in command of the Shaigias, were also on board; they had
already heard of Gordon's death, and of the cruel fate which
had overtaken the town and its inhabitants. Although
those on the steamer had little doubt of the accuracy of the
sad news, they wished to see with their own eyes, and
reached a point midway between Tuti Island and the left
bank of the White Nile. Here they were heavily fired on
by the Dervishes from an entrenched position, situated
north-east of Omdurman Fort, and having seen Khartum in
the distance, and been convinced, they turned about and
steamed away.

I subsequently heard from some of the crew of these
steamers, that both they and the Englishmen on board
were deeply affected by the fall of the city; they now knew
that the entire Sudan was in the Mahdi's hands. It was
the talk on board, they said, that the English expedition
had only come up to save Gordon; and, now that he was
killed, the object of the expedition had failed, and they
naturally concluded that it would retire to Dongola, and
that they would be called upon to accompany it. Consequently the chief pilot of the *Telahawia* and the captain,
Abdel Hamid, agreed together to run the steamer on to a
rock, and then escape during the night. This plan was
successfully carried out, and the steamer stuck so hard and

fast that the cargo had to be at once transferred to the *Bordein.* During the confusion these two conspirators escaped, and, through the intermediation of their friends, they succeeded in securing the Mahdi's pardon, and returned subsequently to Khartum. Here they were well received and publicly commended by the Mahdi for having inflicted loss on their enemies, the British. Abdel Hamid, in spite of being a hated Shaigia, and a relative of Saleh Wad el Mek, was presented by the Mahdi with his own jibba, as a mark of honour, and, moreover, several of his female relatives who, after the sack of the town, had been distributed amongst the Emirs, were given back to him.

Meanwhile, the *Bordein,* on its return journey towards Metemmeh, struck on a sand-bank, and, being heavily laden, could not be floated off. Sir Charles Wilson's position was now very critical. With his small force he could not have attempted to land on the west bank and attack the enemy, which was entrenched at Wad Habeshi, between him and the British camp at Gubat. It is true that the courage of this body of Dervishes had been considerably shaken by the defeat at Abu Klea, but the fall of Khartum, and the knowledge that Wad en Nejumi with a large force was advancing north to their support, now transformed them into a formidable enemy. A third steamer, the *Safia,* was still at Gubat. Sir Charles Wilson therefore sent an officer down stream in a small boat to ask for help. The appeal was promptly responded to, the *Safia* starting, without delay, to the relief of the *Bordein.* The enemy, hearing of this, at once threw up entrenchments to oppose its progress, and on its approach poured on the unfortunate steamer a perfect hail of rifle and cannon shot; but those on board, determined to relieve their comrades in distress, fought most bravely until a shot, penetrating the boiler, disabled the steamer and placed it in the greatest danger. Undismayed, however, the commander set to work, under a heavy fire, to repair the damage. The work was continued during the night, and early the next morning the *Safia* was able to continue her running fight with the Dervishes, eventually succeeding in silencing the guns, and killing the principal Emir, Ahmed Wad Faid, and a considerable number of subordinate Emirs and men. The passage was forced, and Sir Charles Wilson and his men relieved.

This daring exploit, which resulted in the rescue of the little band of Englishmen who had ventured to Khartum, also had a very important, though indirect, effect on the subsequent fate of the small British column near Metemmeh. The advance of Nejumi, which, under any circumstances, was not rapid, owing to the difficulty of collecting the men, was still further delayed by the news of the death of Ahmed Wad Faid, and the defeat of the strong body of Dervishes at Wad Habeshi by one steamer. I was informed that, on hearing of the success of the *Safia* (whose able commander I learnt on my return to Egypt was Lord Charles Beresford), Nejumi addressed his men, and pointed out to them that, if the English advanced with the intention of taking the Sudan, they must, of course, oppose them; but if, on the other hand, they retired towards Dongola, then he and his men would be able to occupy the country they had abandoned without the risk of further fighting, and it was this latter course which he eventually took. Delaying his advance, he reached Metemmeh only after the British had retired from Gubat; and although he pursued them as far as Abu Klea, he hesitated somewhat to attack unless quite assured of success.

It was only when the Mahdi learnt of the final retirement of the British advance guard that he was convinced the Sudan had at last been completely won. And now his delight knew no bounds. He announced the news in the mosque, and drew a striking picture of the flight of the unbelievers, embellishing it further by a revelation from the Prophet to the effect that their water-skins had all been pierced, through Divine intervention, and that all those who had taken part in the expedition had died of thirst.

On the fifth day after the fall of Khartum a small band

of soldiers suddenly appeared in my tattered tent, and placing me, still shackled and bound, on a donkey, they carried me off to the general prison, where they hammered on to my ankles a third and exceptionally heavy iron bar and rings (nicknamed the Hajji Fatma); it weighed about eighteen pounds, and was only put on those who were considered exceptionally obstinate or dangerous prisoners. I was quite ignorant of the reasons which caused me to fall still lower in the Khalifa's disfavour, but I found out later that Gordon, when he had ascertained from my letters to him that the Mahdist force advancing on Khartum was not a strong one, that many of the Mahdi's adherents were discontented, and that there was considerable scarcity of ammunition, had written to this effect to several of the principal officers on the lines. One of his letters containing this information was discovered in the loot handed over to Ahmed Wad Suleiman in the Beit el Mal, by whom it had been passed to the Mahdi and Khalifa. Thus were their suspicions regarding my behaviour confirmed, and my schemes to escape and join Gordon laid bare.

I was deposited in one corner of the immense zariba, where I was ordered to stay, and to hold no converse with anyone without permission, on pain of instant flogging. At sunset I, a number of slaves who were under sentence for having murdered their masters, and other gentlemen of this description, were bound together by a long chain passing round our feet, and fastened to the trunk of a tree, and at sunrise the next morning we were unfastened, and I was sent back to my corner again. I could just see Lupton in the distance in another corner of the enclosure. He had been in here for some time, and had become used to it. He had permission to speak to others, but was under strict orders of the saier, or gaoler, not on any account to speak to me. On the day that I had been brought to the prison Saleh Wad el Mek had been discharged; his brother, sons, and almost all his relatives had been killed, and he was now allowed to go and search for the survivors. As regards

food, I now fared considerably worse; I had, in this respect,
fallen out of the frying-pan into the fire. I used to complain of being occasionally hungry, but now I received only
uncooked dhurra, getting the same share as the slaves, and
a very small share it was. Fortunately, the wife of one of
my warders—a Darfur woman—took pity upon me, and
used to take the corn away, boil it, and bring it back to me;
but she was not allowed to bring me any other food, as her
husband feared the principal gaoler might find out, and he,
in his turn, was afraid of incurring the Khalifa's displeasure.
I lay on the bare ground, with a stone for my pillow, the
hardness of which gave me a continual headache; but one
day, whilst we were being driven to the river one hundred
and fifty yards distant to wash, I picked up the lining of
a donkey saddle, which the owner had evidently thrown
away as old and useless; and, hiding it under my arm, I
bore it off in triumph, and that night I slept like a king on
his pillow of down.

Gradually my position improved somewhat. The principal
gaoler, who was not really disinclined towards me, allowed
me to converse occasionally with the other prisoners, and removed my lightest foot-irons; but the Hajji Fatma and her
sister still remained, and I cannot say this pair of worthies
conduced much to my personal comfort during those long
and weary months of imprisonment.

A few days later there was considerable commotion
amongst the warders, and the saier told me privately that
the Khalifa was coming to visit the prison. I asked him to
advise me how I should behave, and he recommended me to
answer all questions promptly, on no account to make any
complaints, and to remain submissively in my corner. About
mid-day the Khalifa arrived, accompanied by his brothers
and mulazemin, and began to walk round and view these
victims of his justice. It seemed that the saier had given
the same advice to all the prisoners that he had given to me,
for they all behaved quietly. Some were ordered to have
their chains removed, and to be discharged. At length the

Khalifa approached my corner, and, with a friendly nod, said, ' Abdel Kader, enta tayeb ?' (' Abdel Kader, are you well ?'). To which I replied, ' Ana tayeb, Sidi ' (' I am well, sire '). And with that he moved on. Yunes Wad Dekeim, the present Emir of Dongola, and a near relative of the Khalifa, pressed my hand and whispered, ' Keep up your spirits ; don't be downhearted ; everything will come right.'

From that day my condition distinctly improved, but the time passed very slowly. Small-pox had broken out in Omdurman, and every day the disease swept off hundreds—indeed, whole families disappeared, and I believe that the loss from this disease was greater than that suffered in many battles. Curiously enough, almost all the nomad Arabs were attacked, and several of our own warders went down, and not a few of them died. We prisoners, however, entirely escaped, and during the whole period of my imprisonment I do not recollect having seen one of us unfortunates attacked, though most of us were much alarmed. Perhaps God in His mercy thought our punishment already more than we could bear, and spared us a further visitation.

I had now many opportunities of talking to Lupton, who daily grew more and more impatient ; indeed, so furious was he at times, I used to get alarmed, for he would complain most bitterly, and in a loud tone, of our miserable treatment. I did all in my power to pacify him, but the wretched life we were living had affected him to such a degree that I seriously feared for his health. Through constantly speaking to him, I succeeded to some extent in quieting him ; but, although scarcely thirty years of age, the hair of his head and beard had during our imprisonment grown almost white.

One day it was rumoured that the Khalifa was coming. I had carefully prepared a speech, and Lupton had done the same ; but it was more than likely he would speak to me first. At length the critical moment came : the Khalifa, entering the prisoners' yard, instead of, as was his usual custom, sending for the prisoners one by one, ordered an angareb to be brought and placed in the shade; he then directed all the prisoners to be led out, and to sit down before him in a semicircle. He spoke to several, set a few free who had been imprisoned by his own personal orders, and promised others, who complained against the sentences pronounced by the Kadi, to inquire into their cases; of Lupton and myself, however, he appeared to have taken no notice. Lupton glanced at me, and shook his head; but I put my finger to my lips to warn him against doing anything foolish. ' Have I anything else to do ?' asked the Khalifa of the saier, who was standing behind his angareb. ' Sire ! I am at your service,' replied the head gaoler; and the Khalifa sat down again. He now turned his eyes on me, and repeated the same words he had used on the previous occasion. ' Abdel Kader,' said he, ' are you well ?' ' Sire,' said I, ' if you will allow me to speak, I shall tell you of my condition.' He was then sitting at his ease, and he gave me the required permission.

' Master,' I began, ' I belong to a foreign tribe; I came to you seeking protection, and you gave it me. It is natural for men to err, and to sin against God and against each other. I have sinned, but now I repent, and regret all my misdeeds. I repent before God and His Prophet. Behold me in irons before you! See, I am naked and hungry, and I lie here patiently on the bare ground waiting for the time to come when I may receive pardon. Master, should you think it well to let me continue in this sad plight, then I pray God for strength to enable me to bear His will; but now I beg of you to give me my freedom.'

I had studied this speech very carefully, and had delivered it as effectively as I could; and I saw that it had made a favourable impression on the Khalifa. Turning then to Lupton, he said, ' And you, Abdullahi ?' ' I can add nothing to what Abdel Kader has said,' replied Lupton. ' Pardon me, and grant me liberty.'

The Khalifa now turned to me and said, 'Well, from the day you came from Darfur, I have done everything I possibly could for you; but your heart has been far from us : you wanted to join Gordon, the infidel, and fight against us. As you are a foreigner, I spared your life; otherwise you would not be alive now. However, if your repentance is real and true, I will pardon both you and Abdullahi. Saier, take off their irons.'

We were then removed by the warders, who, after long and hard work, and by making use of ropes, at last succeeded in opening my foot-irons. We were then again brought before the Khalifa, who was patiently sitting on his angareb waiting for us. He ordered the saier to bring the Kuran, which he laid on a furwa (sheepskin), and called on us to swear eternal allegiance to him. Placing our hands on the Kuran, we swore to serve him honestly in the future. He then rose and directed us to follow him; and we, almost beside ourselves with delight at our release after this long imprisonment, joyfully followed in his footsteps.

The Khalifa, having been assisted on to his donkey by his servants, ordered us to walk by his side; but we could scarcely keep up with him, for our eight months' imprisonment in chains had so cramped our legs and feet that we found we had lost the habit of stepping out. When we reached his house, he directed us to wait in a rekuba in one of the outside enclosures, and left us. He returned again a few minutes later, and, seating himself beside us, warned us most seriously to adhere to all his orders. He then went on to say that he had received letters from the Commander of the army in Egypt, stating that he had seized and imprisoned all the Mahdi's relatives in Dongola, and that he demanded in exchange all the captives who had formerly been Christians. ' We have decided to reply,' said he, ' that you are now all Mohammedans, that you are one with us, and that you are not willing to be exchanged for people who, though the relatives of the Mahdi, are far from us in thought and deed; and that they can do as they like with their captives; or,' added he, ' perhaps you would like to go back to the Christians?' With these words he ended his speech.

Lupton and I assured him that we should never leave him of our own free-will; that all the pleasures of the world would never tear us from his side; and that it was only by being constantly in his presence that we learnt to act in such a way as would lead to our salvation. Thoroughly taken in by our mendacity, he promised to present us to the Mahdi, who had arranged to come to the Khalifa's house that afternoon, and then he left us.

The rekuba being in one of the outer enclosures, into which people were admitted, several friends who had heard of our release came to congratulate us, amongst them Dimitri Zigada, but this time without his usual quid of tobacco. One of my friends, Esh Sheikh, also came, and when I told him that we were to be presented to the Mahdi, he again gave me the benefit of his good advice, and instructed me how to behave when the momentous occasion arrived. It was almost evening when the Khalifa came, and, directing us to follow him, he led us to an inner enclosure, where we saw the Mahdi sitting on an angareb. He had become so stout that I scarcely knew him. Kneeling down, we repeatedly kissed the hand he held out to us. He now assured us that his only wish was for our good, that when men are placed in chains it exercises a lasting and beneficial influence on them; by this he meant to say that when a man is timid this punishment makes him avoid committing offences in the future. He then turned the conversation to his relatives who had been captured by the British, and about the exchange they had proposed, but which he had refused, adding, with a hypocritical smile, ' I love you better than my own brethren, and therefore I refused to exchange.' In reply, I assured him of our love and sincerity to him, saying, ' Sire, the man who does not love you more than himself, how can his love

proceed truly from his heart?' (This was a paraphrase of
the Prophet's own words, which my friend the Sheikh had
suggested I should repeat.) 'Say that again,' said the
Mahdi, and, turning to the Khalifa, he said, 'Listen.'
When I repeated the words, he took my hand in his and
said, 'You have spoken the truth; love me more than
yourself.' Summoning Lupton as well, he took his hand,
and made us repeat the oath of allegiance, saying, that as
we had proved unfaithful to our first oath it must be renewed. This over, the Khalifa signed to us to retire, and,
again kissing the Mahdi's hand, we thanked him for his
beneficence, and returned to our rekuba to await his further
instructions.

It was some time before the Khalifa returned; and when
he did he permitted Lupton, without further ado, to join
his family, who were still located in a tent in the Beit el
Mal, and, sending with him a mulazem to show the way,
assured him that he would take every care of him. I was
now alone with the Khalifa. 'And you,' said he, 'where
do you wish to go; have you any one to take care of you?'
And I felt him gazing at me, whilst I cast my eyes to the
ground, knowing that was what he wished me to do.
'Besides God and yourself,' I replied, 'I have no one, sire;
deal with me as you think best for my future.'

'I had hoped and expected this answer from you,' said
the Khalifa; 'from this day you may consider yourself a
member of my household. I shall care for you, and shall
never allow you to want for anything; and you will have
the benefit of being brought up under my eye, on condition
that, from this day forth, you absolutely sever your connection with all your former friends and acquaintances, and
associate only with my relatives and servants; you must,
moreover, obey implicitly every order you receive from me.
During the day, your duty will be to stay with the mulazemin employed on my personal service at the door of my
house; and at night, when I retire, you will be permitted
to go to the house which I shall assign to you. When I

go out you must always accompany me; if I ride, you must walk beside me, until the time comes when, should I see fit, I will provide you with an animal to ride. Do you agree to these conditions, and do you promise to put them into full effect ?'

'Master,' I replied, 'I agree with pleasure to your conditions. In me you will find a willing and obedient servant; and I hope I may have strength to enter upon my new duties.'

'God will strengthen you,' he replied, 'and bring you to all good.' He then rose, and added, 'Sleep here to-night; may God protect you till I see you again to-morrow.'

I was now quite alone. So I had gone from one prison to another! I fully grasped the Khalifa's intentions; he had no real wish for my services, for he had not the slightest confidence in me; nor did he wish to utilise me against the Government and against the civilised world. He merely wanted to keep me always under control; probably it flattered his vanity to know he could point to me, his slave, once a high official of the Government, who had commanded his own tribe, which was now the foundation on which his power rested, and show them and other Western tribes that I was now his humble servant. Nevertheless, said I to myself, I shall take good care not to displease him, or give him a chance of putting his evil purposes into effect. I thoroughly understood my master; his smiles and friendly looks were not worth a jot; indeed, one day he had told me as much himself. 'Abdel Kader,' he had said to me in the course of conversation, 'a man who wants to command must neither betray his purpose by gesture nor by his countenance; otherwise his enemies or his subjects will discover some means of frustrating his designs.'

The next morning he came to me, and summoning his brother Yakub, he directed him to show me some spot in the neighbourhood where I might build my huts, adding that it must be as near his house as possible. As, however, most of the vacant spots in the vicinity had been already occupied by the Khalifa's relatives, a piece of ground about six hundred yards from the Khalifa's house, and not far from Yakub's residence, was given to me.

The Khalifa now summoned his secretary, and showed me a document addressed to the Commander of the English army, to the effect that all the European prisoners had of their own free will become Mohammedans, and that they had no wish to return to their countries. This document he desired me to sign.

He then asked me abruptly: 'Are you not a Mohammedan?—where, then, did you leave your wives?' This was indeed an ugly question. 'Master,' said I, 'I have only one, and I left her in Darfur; and I am told that she was arrested, with all my other servants, by Said Mahmud, and is now in the Beit el Mal at El Obeid.'

'Is your wife of your own race?' asked the Khalifa inquiringly. 'No,' I replied; 'she is a Darfurian; and her parents and relatives were killed in the battle with Sultan Harun. She and several others had been captured by my men; and I gave most of them to my servants and soldiers to marry. This orphan alone was left; and she is now my wife.'

'Have you any children?' asked he; and when I replied in the negative he said, 'A man without offspring is like a thorn-tree without fruit; as you now belong to my household, I shall give you some wives, so that you may live happily.'

I thanked him for his kindness, but begged that he would postpone his present until I had at least erected my huts; because, I remarked, this exceptional mark of his favour must not be exposed to the public gaze. To recompense me for my property which had been taken by Abu Anga, the Khalifa instructed Fadl el Maula to hand over the effects of the unfortunate Olivier Pain, which were at once sent to me. They consisted of an old jibba, a well-worn Arab cloak, and a Kuran printed in the French language. Fadl el Maula had sent word to me that during the time which had elapsed his other effects had been lost. At the same time, the Khalifa directed that the money which had been taken from me when I was imprisoned, and had been deposited in the Beit el Mal, should be returned to me. It amounted to £40, a few sequins, and a few gold nose-rings which I had collected as curios; all these were handed back to me by Ahmed Wad Suleiman.

I was now able to set to work to build my huts; but whilst they were being put up I lived in the Khalifa's house. I entrusted my old servant Saadalla, the Nubawi, who was the most competent of all my attendants, with the construction of my residence, which was to consist for the present of three huts and a fence. I myself, from early morning till late at night, was always in attendance at the door of my master. Whenever he went for a short walk or a long ride, I was always obliged to accompany him, barefooted. During the first few days, as my feet got cut and bruised, he allowed me to have some light Arabic sandals made, which, though they gave me some protection against the stones, were so hard and rough that they rubbed off all the skin. Occasionally the Khalifa used to call me in to eat with him, and frequently sent what was over of his own food to be consumed by the principal mulazemin, of whom I was now reckoned as one. When he retired at night, I was at liberty to return to my huts, and there, stretching my weary limbs on an angareb, I slept till early dawn, when I was again obliged to await the Khalifa at his door, and accompany him to morning prayers.

Meanwhile the Khalifa had been informed that my huts were erected, and returning home late one night my old servant, Saadalla, informed me that a female slave, closely muffled up, had been brought to my house, and was now installed within. Directing Saadalla to light a lantern and show the way, I followed, and found the poor thing huddled up on a palm-mat. When I spoke to her about her past life, she answered, in a deep voice which did not presage well for the future, that she was a Nubawi, and had formerly

belonged to an Arab tribe in Southern Kordofan, but had
been captured, and sent to the Beit el Mal, from whence
she had just been despatched to me by Ahmed Wad Suleiman. Whilst speaking, she removed her scented white
drapery from her head, as slaves always do when talking to
their masters, and exposed her bare shoulders and part of
her bosom.

I signed to Saadalla to bring the light nearer; and
then I had to summon all my presence of mind so as
not to be terrified and fall off my angareb. Out of her ugly
black face peered two little eyes; a great flat nose, below
which were two enormous blubber-shaped lips, which when
she laughed were in danger of coming in contact with her
ears, completed one of the most unpleasant physiognomies
I had ever beheld. Her head was joined to her enormously
fat body by a bulldog-like neck; and this creature had the
audacity to call herself Maryam (Mary). I at once directed
Saadalla to remove his compatriot to another hut, and give
her an angareb.

So this was the Khalifa's first gift to me: he had not
given me a horse, a donkey, or even a little money, which
would have been of some use to me, but had presented me
with a female slave, for whom, even if she had been fair, he
knew well I should not have cared, as, let alone her disagreeable presence, her food and dress were items of expense
which I by no means relished. When he saw me the next
day, after morning prayers, he asked me if Ahmed Wad
Suleiman had satisfactorily carried out his wishes. I
replied, 'Yes; your order was most promptly carried
out,' and then gave him an exact description of my new
acquisition.

The Khalifa was furious with Ahmed Wad Suleiman,
who, he asserted, not only did not comply with his order,
but had made him unfaithful to the Mahdi's ordinances.
My candour in describing exactly the class of slave given
me reacted somewhat unpleasantly on my head, for the
following evening a young and somewhat less ugly girl,

selected by the Khalifa himself, was sent to me, and her also I handed over to the tender mercies of the faithful Saadalla.

The Mahdi, his Khalifas, and their relatives, having now no longer any fear from external enemies, began to build houses suitable to their new positions and requirements. The numbers of young women and girls who had been seized and distributed on the fall of Khartum were now hurried off into the seclusion of these new residences; and their masters, no longer disturbed by the jealous and envious looks of their friends, were able to enjoy their pleasures undisturbed.

Naturally the Mahdi, the Khalifas, and, more especially, the relatives of the former, were most anxious that it should not be known that the greater part of the loot taken in Khartum was in their own hands; it was a striking contradiction of the doctrine of the Divine master, who for ever preached renunciation and abandonment of the pleasures of life. They set to work to enlarge their habitations and enclosures, anticipating that they would fill them still further with the rich spoil which was expected from the provinces that still remained to be conquered.

But the Mahdi fell suddenly ill; for a few days he did not appear at the mosque for prayers. No particular attention, however, was paid to his absence at first, for he had asserted, over and over again, that the Prophet had revealed to him that he should conquer Mecca, Medina, and Jerusalem, and after a long and glorious life should expire at Kufa. But the Mahdi was attacked by no ordinary indisposition; the fatal typhus fever had fallen upon him, and six days after he had sickened, his relatives in attendance began to despair of saving his life. My master, the Khalifa, was, of course, watching with the most intense interest the outcome of the disease, and did not leave the Mahdi's bedside day or night, whilst I and the other members of the body-guard aimlessly waited for our master at his door.

On the evening of the sixth day, the multitudes collected before the Mahdi's house and in the mosque were commanded to join together in prayer for the recovery of the Divine patient, who was now in the greatest danger ; and this was the first occasion on which the malignant disease from which the Mahdi was suffering was announced to the public. On the morning of the seventh day he was reported to be worse, and there was little doubt that he was dying.

The disease had now reached its crisis. By the Mahdi's angareb stood the three Khalifas, his near relations, Ahmed Wad Suleiman, Mohammed Wad Beshir (one of the principal employés of the Beit el Mal in charge of the Mahdi's household), Osman Wad Ahmed, Said el Mekki (formerly one of the most renowned religious Sheikhs of Kordofan), and a few of his principal and most faithful adherents, to whom special permission had been granted to enter the sick-room. From time to time he lost consciousness, and, feeling that his end was drawing near, he said, in a low voice, to those around him, ' Khalifa Abdullahi Khalifat es Sadik has been appointed by the Prophet as my successor. He is of me and I am of him ; as you have obeyed me, and have carried out my orders, so should you deal with him. May God have mercy upon me !' Then, gathering up all his strength, with one final effort he repeated a few times the Mohammedan creed (' La Illaha illallah, Mohammed Rasul Allah '), crossed his hands over his chest, stretched out his limbs, and passed away.

Around the body, which was not yet cold, the late Mahdi's adherents swore fidelity to Khalifa Abdullahi, Said el Mekki being the first to take the Khalifa's hand, own his allegiance, and praise his name. His example was immediately followed by the two Khalifas and the remainder of those assembled. It was impossible to keep the Mahdi's death secret, and the crowds waiting outside were informed about it ; but, at the same time, strict injunctions were given that no weeping and lamentation should be made, and it was further

announced that the Khalifa (successor) of the Mahdi would
demand the oath of allegiance from the entire populace.
The Mahdi's principal wife, named Sittina Aisha Um el
Muminin (Our Lady Aisha, Mother of the Believers), who
lay huddled up and closely veiled in a corner, and who had
been a witness of the death of her master and husband,
now arose and proceeded to the Mahdi's house, bearing to
the other wives the sad news of his death. Her office was
to comfort them, and prevent them from making loud
lamentation. Most of these good women rejoiced secretly
in their hearts at the death of their husband and master,
who had brought such terrible distress upon the land, and
whom, even before he had fully enjoyed the fruits of his
success, Almighty God had summoned to appear before the
Supreme Seat of Judgment.

In spite of the strict and oft-repeated injunctions against
loud lamentation, weeping and wailing arose from almost
every house on the death of the Mahdi el Muntazer, who,
it was reported, had voluntarily departed from his earthly
abode to God, his Master whom he longed to see.

Some of those now present began to wash the body, and
then wrap it in several linen cloths ; whilst others dug the
grave in the room in which he had died, and which, after
two hours' hard work, was finished. The three Khalifas,
together with Ahmed Wad Suleiman and Wad Beshir, now
placed the body in the grave, built it over with bricks,
and then filled it up with earth, on which they poured
water. This over, lifting up their hands, they recited the
prayers for the dead ; then, leaving the room, they proceeded to pacify the impatient crowd awaiting the news
without.

We mulazemin were the first to be summoned before the
new ruler, who henceforth was called Khalifat el Mahdi
(successor of the Mahdi), and he gave us the oath of
allegiance, directing us at the same time to move the
Mahdi's pulpit to the entrance-door of the mosque, and to
inform the populace that he was about to appear before

Bedayat praying to the Sacred Tree.

Surrender of the Bedayat to Slatin.

Fight between the Rizighat and Egyptian Troops.

A Dervish Emir.

The Death of Hicks Pasha.

Bringing Gordon's Head to Slatin.

An Abyssinian Scout.

A Slave Dhow on the Nile.

The Mahdi's Tomb.

The Execution of the "Batahin."

R. Talbot Kelly

Famine Stricken.

The Khalifa inciting his troops to attack Kassala.

The Khalifa and Cadis in Council.

R.Talbot.Kelly. 1895.

Slatin Pasha flying from Omdurman.

Slatin in hiding in the hills.

A Camel Corps Scout, Wady Halfa.

them. Informed that this had been completed, he left his late master's grave, and, for the first time, ascended the pulpit as ruler. He was in a state of intense excitement. Great tears rolled down his cheeks as, with a trembling voice, he began to address the multitude. 'Friends of the Mahdi,' he shouted, 'God's will cannot be changed. The Mahdi has left us, and has entered into heaven, where ever-lasting joys await him. It is for us to obey his precepts, and to support one another, just as the stones and walls of a house go to make a building. The good things of this life are not lasting. Seize, therefore, with both hands, the good fortune which is yours of having been the friends and adherents of the Mahdi, and never deviate in the slightest degree from the path which he has shown you. You are the friends of the Mahdi, and I am his Khalifa. Swear that you will be faithful to me.'

This short address over, all those present now repeated the well-known oath of allegiance; but the Khalifa altered the first sentence of it as follows: 'Bayana Allah wa Rasulahu wa Mahdina wa bayanaka ala tauhidillahi,' etc.

As only a certain number could take the oath of allegiance at one time, those who had finished made way for others, and the crowd was so enormous that many were in danger of being trodden to death. The ceremony went on till nightfall. The Khalifa had now long since ceased weeping, and was rejoiced to see the crowds who thronged to him to swear him eternal allegiance. From continual talking he had become quite exhausted, and, descending from the pulpit, he took a draught of water to moisten his parched throat. But the thought that he was now the assured ruler of the enormous masses before him seemed to keep him up, and it was only when darkness actually supervened that some of his principal men urged him to desist, and leave the pulpit.

Before doing so, however, he summoned all the Emirs of the Black Flag, and called upon them to take a special oath of allegiance, admonishing them to adhere faithfully to him and to his brother Yakub, and calling their attention to the fact that, being strangers and foreigners, they should endeavour to live in harmony with each other as long as they were in the valley of the Nile, for they would require union in order to successfully oppose the intrigues of the local inhabitants; and once again he impressed upon them the all-important necessity of adhering most strictly to the doctrines of the Mahdi. By this time it was past midnight; but it was out of the question to think of going home. Utterly exhausted, I lay on the ground, and heard the passers-by loud in their praises of the late Mahdi, and assuring each other of their firm resolve to support his successor in carrying out their late master's precepts.

Now, what had the Mahdi done, and wherein lay his power to revive a religion which had become so debased? What was the nature of his teachings? He had preached renunciation; he had inveighed against earthly vanities and pleasures; he had broken down both social and official ranks; he had made rich and poor alike; he had selected as clothing a jibba, which became the universal dress of his adherents. As a regenerator of religion, he had united the four distinct Moslem sects: the Malaki, the Shafai, the Hanafi, and the Hambali, which differ from each other only in minor details—such as the method of performing ablution, the method of standing or kneeling down in prayers, the manner of conducting marriage ceremonies; and, by astutely making certain much-needed reforms, he had succeeded in combining these four great divisions. He had made a collection of certain specially selected verses from the Kuran, which he called the Rateb, and which he enjoined should be recited by the entire congregation after morning and afternoon prayers—a ceremony which lasted at least forty minutes. He had facilitated the method of performing prayer ablutions, and had strictly forbidden the drinking bouts which were an invariable accompaniment of marriage ceremonies in the Sudan; he had reduced the amount of the ' Mahr ' (the present usually given by the bridegroom to the bride) to ten dollars and two dresses for unmarried girls, and to five dollars and two dresses for widows. Whoever sought for more or gave more was considered to have performed an act of disobedience, and was punished by deprivation of all property. A simple meal of dates and milk took the place of the costly marriage feast. By these innovations the Mahdi had sought to facilitate the ceremony of matrimony, and had strictly enjoined parents and guardians to see that their daughters and wards were married early.

At the same time he had forbidden dancing and playing, which he classified as ' earthly pleasures ' ; and those found disobeying this order were punished by flogging and confiscation of all property. The use of bad language was punished with eighty lashes for every insulting word used, and seven days' imprisonment. The use of intoxicating drinks, as marissa or date wine, and smoking were most strictly prohibited. Offences of this description were punishable by flogging, eight days' imprisonment, and confiscation of goods. A thief suffered the severance of his right hand, and should he be convicted of a second offence, he lost his left foot also. As it was the general custom amongst the male population of the Sudan, and especially amongst the nomad Arabs, to let their hair grow, the Mahdi had directed that henceforth all heads should be shaved. Wailing for the dead and feasts for the dead were punishable by deprivation of property.

In order, however, that the strength of his army should not be decreased and endangered by desertion, owing to the severe mode of life he had prescribed, and fearful that his doctrines, which were considered unorthodox, should be made known in the various foreign countries by which he was surrounded, he practically made a cordon round the countries he had already conquered, and absolutely prohibited passage of persons through these districts for the purpose of performing a pilgrimage to Mecca. Should anyone cast the slightest doubt on the Divine nature of his mission, or should there be the slightest hesitation to comply with his orders, on the evidence of two witnesses, the delinquent was invariably punished by the loss of the right hand and left foot. On some occasions, witnesses were dispensed with—a revelation from the Prophet was even more efficacious in proving the guilt of the offender.

As, however, most of the dispositions and ordinances were entirely at variance with the Moslem law, he therefore issued the most strict injunctions that the study of theology and all public commentaries thereon should cease, and ordered, moreover, that any books or manuscripts dealing with these subjects should be instantly burnt or thrown into the river.

Such were the teachings of the expected Mahdi, and he had left no stone unturned to carry into the fullest effect the ordinances he had made. Openly, he showed himself a most strict observer of his own teachings; but, within their houses, he, his Khalifas, and their relatives, entered into the wildest excesses, drunkenness, riotous living, and debauchery of every sort, and they satisfied to their fullest extent the vicious passions which are so prevalent amongst the Sudanese.

CHAPTER XI.

EARLY RULE OF KHALIFA ABDULLAHI.

Execution of Darho—Sieges of Sennar and Kassala—My Journey to Abu Haraz—My Plans of Escape impracticable—The Khalifa presents me with a Wife—Mutiny of Black Soldiers at El Obeid—Death of the Emir Mahmud—Abu Anga seizes Khaled and throws him into Chains—Campaign in the Nuba Mountains—Lupton in Difficulties—He works in the Khartum Dockyard—Difficulties begin with Abyssinia—Death of Klootz.

LITTLE of importance had occurred in Darfur subsequent to my departure. Khaled had firmly established the Mahdi's rule throughout the province, and had sent emirs and forces in all directions to consolidate his position. My old officer, Omar Wad Darho, showed himself a warm partisan of this new régime; but when news of the Mahdi's death reached him, he made an ill-timed attempt to render himself independent, and, in consequence, fell a victim to a stratagem, carefully prepared by Khaled's orders, which resulted in his being brought into El Fasher and beheaded.

Abu Anga was now in Kordofan. This province had submitted entirely to the Mahdi, with the exception of the southern mountainous regions, the inhabitants of which were looked upon as slaves who had objected to pay tribute, and who were consequently ordered to emigrate to Omdurman.

As they had refused to comply with these demands, Abu Anga had been despatched south, with injunctions not only to enforce their subjection, but also to quarter his enormous force of Jehadia on them, and to procure plenty of slaves. After losing a considerable number of men and a quantity of ammunition, he succeeded in carrying out these orders to some extent; but a large proportion of the inhabitants still continued to defend themselves most bravely in their mountain fastnesses, and remained independent. Thus, with the exception of this small proportion of the natives, the entire Western Sudan, from the banks of the White Nile to the frontiers of Wadai, acknowledged the sway of the Mahdi.

In the eastern districts, however, the Governors of Sennar and Kassala continued to defend their posts, and the Egyptian Government, learning the critical situation of the garrisons in the Eastern Sudan, now appealed to King John of Abyssinia to co-operate in relieving the posts of Gallabat, Gira, Senhit, and Kassala, and bring their garrisons to Massawa. The Governor of Kassala, however, declared that, as the garrison of the town was composed for the most part of local people, he could not induce them to leave the country. The Mahdi now sent Idris Wad Abder Rahim and El Hussein Wad Sahra with reinforcements

to hasten the fall of the town. Meanwhile, King John
had succeeded in relieving the garrisons of Senhit, Gira,
and Gallabat, and relieving them to Massawa ; thus all
the Arab tribes lying within the Suakin-Berber-Kassa a
triangle became fanatical adherents of the Mahdi. Osm n
Digna had already been appointed Emir of this distri t,
whilst Mohammed Kheir was ordered to proceed from
Berber with instructions to occupy Dongola with the
Jaalin and Barabra, after the retirement of the Briti h
army.

Such was briefly the situation in the Sudan when Khalifa
Abdullahi became its ruler. It was not, therefore, without
reason that he summoned the western Arab tribes to unite
together, and seriously called their attention to the fact that
they were strangers and foreigners in the Nile valley. It
can be readily understood that the Aulad-Belad, or local
population, more especially the Barabra, Jaalin, and the
inhabitants of the Gezira, did not appreciate the advent of
the Khalifa and his western Arabs, from whom they entirely
differed in ideas and character. They saw with dread the
new ruler seizing the reins of government, and relying
entirely for the execution of his orders on his western
compatriots.

One of the Khalifa's first steps was to expel from his
position Ahmed Wad Suleiman, the Director of the
Beit el Mal, whom he detested, and appoint in his place
Ibrahim Wad Adlan, who was of the Kawahla tribe
located on the Blue Nile, but had spent many years of his
life as a merchant in Kordofan, and was in favour with the
Khalifa.

Adlan was now ordered to open ledgers showing the
revenue and expenditure, and to keep his books in such a
manner that at any moment, on the demand of the Khalifa,
he should be able to give an exact statement of the financial
situation. He also ordered him to keep a careful list of
those to whom money was issued, or who were in receipt of
pensions.

Almost simultaneously with the death of the Mahdi came the news of the failure of the attack on Sennar, and of the repulse of Abdel Kerim. The Khalifa, therefore, at once despatched Abderrahman en Nejumi to take supreme command, and in August, 1885, the garrison surrendered to that redoubtable warrior. As usual, the fall of the town was the signal for a series of brutal atrocities and cruelties. A number of the inhabitants were sent to the Khalifa, amongst them, all the good-looking young girls and the daughters of the former Government officials, of whom the Khalifa kept some for himself and distributed the remainder amongst his Emirs.

And now the Khalifa began to steadily make himself master of the situation. Realizing that in Abdel Kerim he had a powerful rival, he summoned him to Omdurman with his entire force, and then, by a carefully arranged plan, in which he was aided and abetted by Khalifa Ali Wad Helu, he succeeded in making both Abdel Kerim and Khalifa Sherif hand over all their Black soldiers, arms, and ammunition to his brother Yakub, thus crippling their power and rendering them practically harmless.

Whilst all these important matters were transpiring in the capital, the news arrived that Kassala had surrendered, and that Osman Digna was fighting against the Abyssinians under the leadership of Ras Alula. Although the Abyssinians had been victorious, and had driven Digna back to Kassala, they did not pursue him, but returned to their own country.

Osman Digna now accused the former Governor, Ahmed Bey Effat, of having incited the Abyssinians to take up arms against him, and of having been in communication with them. There were no grounds for this suspicion, but, nevertheless, he and six former officials of Kassala had their hands tied behind their backs like criminals and were shot dead.

Abdullahi fully realized that his action in regard to the

other Khalifas would naturally rouse the ire of the Mahdi's relatives, with whom he was already on bad terms; but this was a matter of little concern to him. He was determined, by all the means in his power, and, if necessary, by recourse to violence, to enforce his commands, whatever they might be. But, on the other hand, he did not wish to entirely alienate public opinion, nor to give grounds to the numerous Mahdists, who, owing to their love for the Mahdi, entertained a certain affection for his relatives, for bringing against him accusations of injustice or hostility; he therefore presented them with numbers of female slaves, and to Khalifa Sherif he gave some very fine horses and mules, and distributed quantities of slaves amongst his retainers. He took great care to make these gifts widely known, and the populace, in their turn, praised him for his magnanimity, and went so far as to extol his justice and liberality in songs.

It was clear to the Khalifa that to allow the outlying provinces to be governed by the late Mahdi's special adherents would jeopardize his position; he therefore lost no time in sending to Kordofan and Darfur his own relatives to take over the government. At the request of the Emir Yunes ed Dekkeim, I also was despatched with the latter to Sennar, but before my departure the Khalifa summoned me to his presence. 'I urge you,' said he, 'to serve me faithfully; I look upon you as my son, and my heart is inclined toward you. God's holy word, the Kuran, promises rewards to the faithful, but threatens the traitor with the Divine wrath. Yunes is your well-wisher, and will attend to what you may say to him. Should he attempt to undertake anything which is not likely to lead to his advantage, you should warn him, for he is your master; but I have told him that I look upon you as my son, and he will take heed of what you say.'

'I will always endeavour,' said I, 'to act in accordance with your instructions; but Yunes is my master, and will naturally do what he thinks right. Do not there-

fore attribute ill-will to me, and I beg you will not make
me responsible for anything which may happen contrary
to your wishes.'

'You are only in a position to offer an opinion,' said he,
'but you have no power to act. Should he pay heed to
you, well and good; if not, it will be his own look-out if
matters go wrong.'

He then turned the conversation to affairs in Darfur and
other parts of the Sudan.

The conversation had already lasted some time, and I
was about to ask permission to retire, when he beckoned to
one of his eunuchs who was standing close by, and whispered a few words in his ear. I knew my master well, and
had a foreboding of ill.

'I have already instructed you,' said he, 'to leave behind
all the members of your household; for, having only just
arrived from a long journey, they must be fatigued, and I
do not wish to expose them further. Yunes will give you
a servant; but I am giving you a wife, so that in case of
indisposition or illness you may have someone to attend on
you. She is pretty, and not plain, like the one Ahmed
Wad Suleiman sent you,' he said, with a smile. And now,
beckoning to the woman who had just entered to come
nearer, the latter approached and threw off her veil. I
glanced at her, and, in spite of her dark colour, she really
was very pretty. 'She was my wife,' added the Khalifa;
'she is very good and patient; but I have so many, I
therefore give her her freedom; but you may now call her
your own.'

I was much embarrassed, and all the time had been
casting over in my mind how I could refuse this gift without
offending the giver.

'Sire, allow me to speak candidly,' said I.

'Certainly,' said he; 'here you are at home. Speak!'

'I am at home where I need fear nothing,' I began
hastily; 'this woman was your wife, and has, in consequence, a right to be treated with consideration for your

sake; this, of course, is an easy matter. But, sire, how can I, your servant, take your own wife for myself? Moreover, you said yourself that you look upon me as your son.' Having said this, I dropped my head, and fixed my eyes on the ground, continuing, 'I cannot accept this gift'; and then I awaited his answer with anxiety.

'Your words are good, and I pardon you,' said he, signing to the woman, who was standing near us, to withdraw. 'Almas!' said he to the eunuch, 'bring my white jibba!' And when the servant brought it he handed it to me, saying, 'Take this jibba, which I have often worn myself, and which was specially blessed by the Mahdi for me.* Hundreds and thousands of people will envy you this; guard it carefully, for it will bring you blessings.'

I was delighted with this present, and fervently kissed his hand, which he extended to me; but inwardly I rejoiced to be rid of the woman, who would have been a useless encumbrance to me, besides an additional expense; and I thought the jibba an excellent exchange. I then begged leave to withdraw, and carried off with me my valuable present.

Yunes had fixed his departure for that day; but before leaving I was summoned once more to the Khalifa, who, in the presence of Yunes, again reminded me to be faithful and submissive.

That evening we left Omdurman on board the steamer *Bordein*, and on the third day we reached the banks of the Blue Nile, and saw Sennar in the distance.

Just north of Wad el Abbas there is a strip of high sandy ground, and this was selected as the position of the camp, because the land in the vicinity is low-lying, and unfit for habitation during the rainy season. All my thoughts were now bent on flight; but, as most of the people entirely sympathized with the Khalifa's Government, it required the greatest care on my part to select anyone in whom to place

---

* Unfortunately the jibba was too big and long for me, consequently I was unable to wear it at the time of my escape.

confidence. Very soon after our arrival at Wad el Abbas, however, I received a letter from the Khalifa, which was to the effect that news had reached him that my wife had arrived at Korosko, and was making arrangements there for my escape ; he urged me to put aside all such ideas and cling to the Faith. Yunes also received a letter on the same subject, and under the pretext of supplying the Khalifa with information of affairs in Sennar, he ordered me to return forthwith to Omdurman. So all my plans for escape fell through, and a few days later found me once more in the presence of my lord and master the Khalifa. He at once began to talk of the letter which had come from Berber. I assured him that if the letter had really come, it must have been written with an intention to do me harm, or that there was some mistake ; and, in proof of this, I told him that I had never been married, and that in conse-quence there could be no pining wife to come and look for me. Should anyone, however, come to Omdurman and try to induce me to fly, my first step would be at once to inform the Khalifa. He assured me that he did not believe the rumour, and then asked me if I preferred to stay with him or return to Yunes. Guessing his intention, I told him that nothing in the world would induce me to leave him again, and that I considered the time spent with him as the happiest in my life. Although pleased at my flattering words, he took occasion to remind me, in a very serious tone of voice, to be faithful and true, and to have nothing whatever to do with people other than his own household ; and he then ordered me to take my place as usual before the gate.

On withdrawing from his presence, and thinking the matter over, I had no doubt now that his suspicions against me had not only taken root, but had begun to grow.

At this time the force in El Obeid included about two hundred Blacks, mostly old soldiers, whose numbers had been increased by the arrival of a portion of the former garrison of Dara. Many of them were inhabitants of Jebel

Dair, who were in constant enmity with the Mahdists, and who had been captured by them, and utilized as slaves to build their huts. Indignant at this treatment, they resolved to regain freedom by force. Fortunately for them the Emir Sayed Mahmud was absent in Omdurman, and by a bold stroke the mutineers succeeded in seizing the arsenal, where they fully armed themselves, and, after a sharp struggle, marched out of the town, whence they proceeded to the Nuba mountains. On this news reaching Omdurman, Mahmud hurried back, placed himself at the head of his troops, and advanced against the rebels. His attempt to storm their stronghold completely failed, and he and a large number of his followers were killed.

Meanwhile the growing independence of Khaled in Darfur did not escape the Khalifa. Well aware that, as a member of the late Mahdi's family, he was in complete sympathy with Khalifa Sherif, Abdullahi determined to render him powerless, and under the pretext of bringing about better relations between the Mahdi's family and himself, he summoned Khaled to come with his whole force to Omdurman; but on the arrival of the latter at Bara, he suddenly found himself surrounded by the powerful following of the Emir Abu Anga, to whom the Khalifa had given instructions to take over Khaled's force, incorporate it with his own, and attack the rebels in the Nuba hills. Completely caught in this trap, Khaled had to submit, was thrown into chains, and removed to Omdurman; all his property was confiscated, and for several months he remained a close prisoner, but was eventually pardoned, while his place as Governor of Darfur was taken by the Khalifa's cousin, Osman Wad Adam.

Abu Anga's campaign against the mutineers proved completely successful; almost all the ringleaders were killed, and numbers of the unfortunate Blacks who had joined them were enslaved.

I ascertained from a merchant who had recently arrived from Kordofan that my friend, Joseph Ohrwalder, had quitted El Obeid, and would shortly arrive in Omdurman. Although I knew that I should have considerable difficulty in meeting him, I rejoiced to think that one of my old countrymen would be near me. I sat at my master's gate, ready at all times to obey his orders. Occasionally I was spoken to kindly, and commanded to dine with him; at other times, without rhyme or reason as far as I knew, I was taken no notice of for days, receiving from my master only the blackest and most disdainful looks; but this was due to the extraordinary changeability of his character, and I knew I must put up with it. I suppose this was part of my education. To my comrades I showed myself absolutely callous to everything that happened in the country, so that they should have no reason to increase the distrust felt by the Khalifa, who, I knew, frequently inquired as to my conduct. As a matter of fact, however, I watched all the occurrences as closely as my position would allow, and endeavoured to impress them on my mind, for I was, of course, prohibited from writing a single line. The Khalifa contributed very little towards the support of my household, and only occasionally gave orders for me to be supplied with a few ardebs of dhurra, or a sheep, or a cow.

Ibrahim Adlan, whom I had known in the time of the Government, used to send me monthly from ten to twenty dollars, and a few of the officials and merchants who were in better circumstances than myself used secretly to send me small sums of money. Thus, though by no means well off, I did not lack the absolute necessaries of life, and only occasionally felt the actual pinch of want. Anyhow, I was better off than my friend Lupton, whom the Khalifa had promised to assist, but paid absolutely no attention to his wants. Lupton, it is true, enjoyed a certain amount of freedom—he was allowed to wander about in Omdurman, and to talk to the people, nor was he obliged to attend the five prayers daily at the mosque; but, in spite of this, life to him was full of trouble and sorrow. I begged Ibrahim Adlan to interest himself in Lupton, and to give a kind thought to him occasionally by helping him with small sums of money, but this was not sufficient to keep him, and, though ignorant of any trade, he had perforce to earn a livelihood by mending old arms. Having been an officer in the English merchant service, I thought he might know something about machinery. Meeting him one day in the mosque, he complained bitterly of his wretched position, and I suggested to him that, if he could secure an appointment in the Khartum dockyard, it might improve his condition. He jumped at the idea, and I promised that I would do my best to help him.

A few days later it happened that the Khalifa was in a good temper, and showed a friendly disposition towards me, as Abu Anga had sent him a present of a young horse, some money, and some of Khaled's slaves. I was commanded to dine with him, and, in the course of conversation, succeeded in turning the subject to the steamers and their machinery, which up to that day had been an absolute mystery to him. ' The steamers,' said I, ' require competent men to look after them and repair damages. As most of the workmen in the dockyard were killed during the siege of Khartum, I suppose you have had some difficulty in replacing them ?'

' But what is to be done ?' said the Khalifa. ' These steamers are of the greatest value to me, and I must do all I can to preserve them.'

' Abdullahi Lupton,' said I, ' was formerly engineer on a steamer. If he received a good monthly salary from the Beit el Mal, I believe he would be really useful for this work.'

' Then will you speak to him ?' said he, apparently much pleased. ' If he undertook this work of his own free will and accord, without being forced into it, I believe he would be of some use in these matters, of which, I admit, I know absolutely nothing. I will order Ibrahim Adlan to pay him well.'

' I do not even know his whereabouts,' said I. ' I have

not seen him for a long time, but I will make inquiries. I feel confident that he will be only too glad to serve you.'

The following day I sent for Lupton, told him of the conversation, but begged him to do as little as he possibly could for our enemies.

He assured me that the steamers, of the machinery of which he had only a superficial knowledge, would, under his charge, grow worse instead of better, and that it was only his unfortunate circumstances which obliged him to accept the position. The Khalifa had also spoken to Ibrahim Adlan, and that evening Lupton sent me word that he was now appointed an employé in the arsenal, with pay at the rate of forty dollars a month, which would be just sufficient to save him from absolute want.

It was now rumoured in Omdurman that the Abyssinians intended attacking Gallabat. It was said that a certain Hajji Ali Wad Salem, of the Kawahla, who resided in Gallabat, and who had formerly had some trading transactions with the Abyssinians, was travelling in their country, had been made an Emir of a portion of his tribe, had invaded Abyssinian territory, and had destroyed the church of Gabta.

A certain Takruri named Saleh Shanga, who had resided at Gallabat, and had held a position of some importance under Government, had quitted that town on its evacuation by the Egyptian troops, and had settled down in Abyssinia; but his cousin, Ahmed Wad Arbab, had been made Dervish Emir of the district. Ras Adal, Governor of the province of Amhara, now called on Arbab to deliver up Hajji Ali, who had been disturbing the peace; and as this demand was refused, he had collected a considerable force, and had invaded Gallabat. Meanwhile, Arbab, who had received warning of Ras Adal's approach, now collected his followers, amounting to some six thousand men, and awaited his arrival outside the town. The rush of the Abyssinian force, which was ten times as strong as that of Arbab, was terrible: in a few minutes the Mahdi's forces were com-

pletely surrounded, Arbab himself killed, and almost all
his troops massacred, only a very few escaping. The Abyssinians mutilated the bodies of all except that of Arbab,
which, out of consideration for Saleh Shanga, was untouched. The Dervishes had stored their spare ammunition
in an isolated house, and had placed it in charge of an
Egyptian, who being called upon after the battle to
surrender, refused to do so; and on the Abyssinians
attempting to storm it he blew it up, thus destroying
himself and his enemies. The wives and children of those
who had been killed were now carried off into captivity by
the Abyssinians. Gallabat itself was burnt to the ground,
and for a long time its site was little else than a great open
cemetery, the abode of nothing save hyenas.

When the news of the destruction of Wad Arbab's army
reached the Khalifa, he sent a letter to King John requesting him to release the captive wives and children in exchange
for a sum of money which he asked him to fix; but at the
same time he ordered Yunes to quit Omdurman with his
entire force, and proceed to Gallabat, where he was to await
further orders. On the departure of the army of Yunes the
Khalifa himself, with a number of his followers, crossed to
the west in a steamer, and after staying with them three
days, he gave the warriors his parting blessing, and then
returned to Omdurman.

Some time since Gustav Klootz, who had failed to make
a living in Omdurman, had disappeared, and I thought he
must have escaped out of the country; but I now learnt
from some merchants who had just arrived from Gedaref
that he had reached that place, but had succumbed to the
fatigues of the journey, and had died just before the
Abyssinian invasion.

CHAPTER XII.

EVENTS IN VARIOUS PARTS OF THE SUDAN.

Madibbo's Quarrel with Karamalla—Execution of Madibbo—Capture of Charles Neufeld—My Interview with him—Arrival of Abu Anga's Army in Omdurman—Destruction of the Gehéna Tribe—Abu Anga's Campaign in Abyssinia—Sack of Gondar—Terrible Fate of the Captives—Death of Sultan Yusef—Instances of the Khalifa's Tyranny—Building of the Mahdi's Tomb—Letters from Home—Death of my Mother—Death of Lupton.

THE Emir Karamalla, who had succeeded Lupton as Mahdist Governor of Bahr el Ghazal, eventually took up his residence at Shakka, and was soon at loggerheads with my old friend Sheikh Madibbo, who, subsequent to the fall of the province, had ruled this district. A quarrel ensued, and Madibbo, after making an ineffectual resistance, fled, but was captured and sent to Abu Anga, who had an old account to settle with him. When serving under Suleiman Wad Zubeir he fell on one occasion into the hands of Madibbo, who was very hostile to him, and forced him to carry a huge box of ammunition on his head during several days' march, and, when he complained about it, mercilessly flogged and abused him. When Madibbo was brought before Abu Anga, he had little hope of his life; but he determined to try and obtain justice, affirming that he had not fought against the Mahdi, but had been forced to take up arms by Karamalla. But of what use were all his excuses and proofs of innocence, or his fidelity? The only answer he received from Abu Anga was, 'And yet I will kill you.' Madibbo, now convinced of the uselessness of his pleading, resigned himself to his fate, and, despairing of his life, said, 'It is not you who will kill me, but God. I have not asked for mercy, but for justice; however, a slave like you can never become noble. The traces of the lashes of my whip, which may still be seen on your back, were well deserved. In whatever form death may come upon me, it will always find me calm and a man. I am Madibbo, and the tribes know me.' Abu Anga ordered him to be sent back to prison, but forbore to have him flogged, and the following morning he had him executed in front of his whole army. Madibbo was true to his word. Standing in an open space with a chain round his neck, he sneered at the soldiers who galloped up to him, shaking their lances over his head. When told to kneel down to receive the death-blow, he called on the people who stood round to report faithfully after his death how he had borne himself ; a moment afterwards all was over. Thus ended Madibbo, one of the ablest Arab Sheikhs in the Sudan.

When his head was brought into Omdurman, there was general mourning amongst the Rizighat Arabs, who had years before quitted their country as pilgrims. Even the Khalifa himself regretted his death ; but as the deed had been done, he would not blame his greatest Emir. He therefore concealed his indignation ; but to me he remarked that had Abu Anga not killed him, Madibbo might have done him many a valuable service.

Yunes was now apparently quite happy. He had gone from Abu Haraz to Gedaref and Gallabat, where he had settled down, and as his authority was an extended one, and the people over whom he ruled were turbulent, he asked the Khalifa's permission to undertake a campaign against the Abyssinians, and Abdullahi, having received no answer from King John to his peaceful letters, gave his consent. His troops, under Arabi Dafalla, now attacked the villages along the frontier and destroyed several of them, killing the men and carrying off their wives and children as captives. By the rapidity of their movements, committing wholesale robberies one day, and making murderous raids twenty miles distant the next, they had become a perfect scourge to the Abyssinians ; but, in spite of all this, the latter still continued their commercial relations with Yunes, who, by his amicable treatment of them in Gallabat, had induced them to come in large numbers to sell the produce of their country, such as coffee, honey, wax, tomatoes, ostriches, etc., as well as horses, mules, and slaves. The market-place lay just beyond the town, and when one day an exceptionally large caravan of merchants, consisting of Gebertas (Abyssinian Moslems) and Makada (Abyssinian Christians) arrived at Gallabat, the rapacity of Yunes could not be controlled, and, on the pretext that they had come as spies of Ras Adal, he threw them into chains, and seized all their goods. They were then sent under escort to Omdurman, where the ignorant mob imagined them to be the spoil of a great victory; while the Khalifa, ever ready to increase his and his people's prestige, publicly dubbed Yunes ' Afrit el Mushrikin ' (The Devil of the Polytheists), and ' Mismar ed Din ' (The Nail of the Faith). Yunes had been careful to send him all the prettiest of the Abyssinian girls taken in the various raids, as well as a number of horses and mules; thus, greedy of more victories, he decided to unite the army of Yunes and Abu Anga, and attack King John, who, by not answering his letters, had mortally offended him. In the meantime Yunes was instructed to remain strictly on the defensive.

Abu Anga now received instructions to despatch fifteen hundred of his men, all armed with Remington rifles, to Osman Wad Adam, who had been appointed Emir of Kordofan and Darfur; but he himself was ordered to come to Omdurman with the remainder of his troops.

Some time previous to the events I have just described, the powerful Kababish tribe, who inhabit the northern portion of Kordofan as far as Dongola, had shown a disposition to resist the Khalifa's authority. An expedition had in consequence been despatched against them which was completely successful; quantities of cattle and slaves were taken, and the Kababish Sheikh Saleh, who had been of considerable use to the British Expedition in 1884-85, was driven to the distant wells of Om Badr, where, with only a few followers, he remained in constant fear of attack; he

now despatched to Wadi Halfa fifty of his most faithful
slaves with letters begging the support of the Egyptian
Government, and the faithful Saleh's agent obtained two
hundred Remington rifles, forty boxes of ammunition, £200
in cash, and some beautifully embossed revolvers.

At this time there resided at Assuan a German merchant
named Charles Neufeld, who had previously made the acquaintance of Dafalla Egail, a brother of Elias Pasha, who
had recently escaped from the Sudan.   From him he learnt
that in Northern Kordofan there was a large quantity of
gum which the merchants had been unable to dispose of in
consequence of the rebellion, and which could easily be
brought to Wadi Halfa with the assistance of Sheikh Saleh.
Enticed by this pleasant prospect of making money, and
filled with a love of adventure, he resolved to join Saleh's
people in order to travel with them to their Sheikh.   He
had apparently no difficulty in obtaining permission from the
Government to proceed on his journey, promising that he
would send detailed accounts of the situation in the Sudan;
and early in April, 1887, he left Wadi Halfa with the
caravan.

Nejumi, who had full information of the departure of the
caravan, now had all the roads carefully watched; and, to
add to their misfortunes, their guide lost his way, and the
caravan suffered considerably from thirst.   When at length
they approached some wells near El Kab, they found them
in possession of a party of Dervishes who were on the look-
out for them.   A fight ensued in which Saleh's people, exhausted and thirsty, were utterly defeated; most of them
were killed by rifle fire, and the remainder, Neufeld amongst
them, were captured.   At the beginning of the action
Neufeld had seized a rifle, and, with his Abyssinian female
attendant, had taken up a position a short distance from the
caravan, and here on some rising ground he had determined
to sell his life dearly; but he was not attacked.   When the
fighting was over they offered him pardon, which he accepted, and was then taken off to Nejumi in Dongola.   The

latter had all the captives beheaded, with the exception of Neufeld, who was spared in order that he might be sent to Omdurman. I had heard privately that a European captive was about to arrive, and consequently I was not surprised when, one day in May, 1887, I saw a crowd of people approaching the Khalifa's house, and in their midst, under escort, rode a European on a camel. It was generally rumoured that he was the Pasha of Wadi Halfa. At that period the buildings in Omdurman were not very far advanced, and between the wall of the Khalifa's house and the wall of the mosque was a large rekuba built of straw, which served as a house for the mulazemin; and into this Neufeld, after dismounting, was ushered. I held aloof, as I well understood the nature of my master and his spies; and I pretended to be quite indifferent to what was going on. The Khalifa, on Neufeld's arrival, had sent for the two Khalifas and the Kadis, Taher el Magzub, the Emir Bekhit, and Nur Angara, who had just arrived in Omdurman from Kordofan, where he had been fighting under Abu Anga; Yakub had also been summoned. As they entered, I whispered to Nur Angara, ' Do your utmost to save the man.' To my delight the Khalifa now summoned me, and ordered me to sit with his advisers. He informed us that the man had been brought in as an English spy; and he instructed Sheikh el Taher Magzub to question him. I at once asked to be allowed to speak to him in European language, and the request being granted, I went with Taher into the rekuba.

When my name was mentioned, Neufeld shook my hand with great delight. I at once drew his attention to the fact that he must address himself to Sheikh Taher, who was the principal personage to judge him, and that he should behave as submissively as possible. He spoke Arabic very well, and his extreme readiness to talk made a bad impression on those present, who ordered me to take him before the Khalifa, their general opinion being, ' He is a spy, and should be killed.' Once in the presence of the Khalifa, the latter said to me, 'And what is your opinion?' 'All I know is,' I replied, 'that he is a German, and consequently belongs to a nation which takes no interest in Egypt.' I could see the Khalifa watching me very carefully as he handed me some papers, and ordered me to look through them: they included a list of medicines written in German, and a letter to Neufeld in English, regarding news received in the Sudan; also a long letter from General Stephenson, in which he was granted permission to proceed to the Sudan with the caravan, and at the same time requested to give the fullest accounts of the state of affairs in the country. I translated this letter, but omitted the General's request for information. 'Sire,' I said, 'this letter shows that he has asked permission of the Government to make this journey, and that he is a merchant, as he told Sheikh Taher.' Again the Khalifa looked suspiciously at me, and then ordered us to withdraw and await his further commands outside the house. An immense crowd had by this time collected near the rekuba to see the English Pasha; and in a few moments some of the Black mulazemin, whom the Khalifa had summoned, came out, and having tied his wrists together, ordered Neufeld to leave the rekuba. The Kadi, Nur Angara, and I had climbed up on a heap of bricks, and from this position could see exactly what was going on. Neufeld, who evidently thought his last hour had come, raised his eyes to heaven and knelt down, without having received any order to do so, and was at once ordered to get up. Meanwhile, a man arrived carrying an ombeya, and began to make its melancholy notes resound over Neufeld's head; I was delighted to see that this did not appear to disturb him in the least. His poor servant, in her devotion to her master, now rushed out of the rekuba, and begged to be killed with him; but she was at once driven back. The Kadi and I quite realized that the Khalifa was playing with Neufeld, just as a cat plays with a mouse; and as sentence had not yet been given, I endeavoured to signal to him, but he did not appear to quite understand me. In a few moments we

were again summoned before the Khalifa. ' Then you
are for having the man killed ?' said the Khalifa to Sheikh
Taher, who replied in the affirmative. ' And you ?' he said,
turning to Nur Angara, who, in a few brief words, recalled
Neufeld's bravery, and begged to have him pardoned.
' And now, Abdel Kader, what have you to say ?' he said,
turning to me. ' Sire,' I replied, ' the man deserves to be
killed, and any other ruler but yourself would have had him
killed ; but, of your magnanimity and mercy, you will spare
him ; for he says he has turned Mohammedan, and your
mercy will strengthen his faith.' Kadi Ahmed was also for
pardoning him ; and now the Khalifa, who, I saw from the
first moment, had no intention of killing Neufeld, ordered
his fetters to be removed, and that he should be taken back
to the rekuba ; but that afternoon he said to the Kadi,
' Let him be shown to the crowd beneath the scaffold, and
then imprison him till further orders ; and as for you,' he
said, turning to me, ' you will have no more intercourse with
him.' We now all withdrew, but took occasion to tell
Neufeld that, although he had been pardoned, he was to be
shown to the populace that afternoon under the scaffold.
The Kadi carried out his instructions, and, to the delight of
the mob, Neufeld's head was placed in the noose by the
saier.

The following day the Khalifa summoned me before him,
and informed me that Nejumi had reported that Neufeld
had been induced by the Government to go and join Sheikh
Saleh el Kabbashi, and assist him in fighting the Mahdists.
I explained that this could not possibly be true, and that
Neufeld's papers were all in order. Moreover, I said that
the Government would never have taken upon itself to do
such a thing. For the time being, I think he credited my
explanation ; but he revenged himself by showing the most
marked mistrust and contempt for me for some time.

A few days afterwards the Khalifa held a great review,
and Neufeld, whose feet were in irons, was mounted on a
camel, and taken to see it. The Khalifa asked him what

he thought of his troops, and he replied that, although they were very numerous, they were not well trained, and that the discipline in the Egyptian army was much better. The Khalifa, who did not appreciate candid speaking, at once had him sent back to prison, and, wishing to revenge himself on Sheikh Saleh for his want of loyalty, he again despatched an expedition against him. This time the unfortunate Sheikh, deserted by most of his followers, was surrounded at one of the desert wells and killed. Thus ended the last of the Sheikhs faithful to Government.

Towards the end of June, Abu Anga, with a force of nearly twenty thousand men, arrived at Omdurman, and, after remaining some weeks, a portion of this army, under the command of Zeki Tummal, was despatched against the Gehéna tribe, whose Sheikh, Abu Rof, had refused the Khalifa's summons to come to Omdurman. In the fighting which ensued, the principal chiefs fell, and the greater part of the tribe was annihilated. The finest of the young women and children captured were selected and sent as presents to the Khalifa; but the remainder were brought to Omdurman, where they eked out a miserable existence by becoming water-carriers, or makers of straw mats. Their great herds of cattle went for almost nothing in the bazaars, and the price of an ox or a camel, which formerly varied between forty and sixty dollars, fell to two or three dollars.

After the destruction of this tribe, Abu Anga received orders to proceed from Omdurman to Gallabat, and take the command of the troops there. Collecting the forces from the southern districts at Abu Haraz, he proceeded to his destination, and on arrival at once set to work to organize his army in order to revenge the defeat of Wad Arbab. He had at his disposal the largest force which had ever been collected by Khalifa Abdullahi; according to the rolls brought in, he had upwards of fifteen thousand rifles, forty-five thousand spearmen, and eight hundred cavalry, and, quitting Gallabat with this force, he marched through the Mintik (pass) towards Ras Adal. Up to this day I have

failed to understand why the Abyssinians did not attack
their enemy whilst crossing the narrow passes and deep
valleys, in which it would have been most difficult to use
firearms with effect; if they had not succeeded in checking
the advance in this manner, they would have at least inflicted very heavy losses on the Dervishes. I can only
conceive that the Abyssinians made certain of their ultimate
success, and purposely enticed their enemies far into the
country with the object of cutting off their retreat, and
utterly annihilating them. Fighting began on the plain of
Debra Sin. Ras Adal had about two thousand rifles, and
had taken up a position threatening Abu Anga's left; but
the latter had sufficient time to clear the hills, and arrange
his troops in battle array. Attacked over and over again
by the Abyssinians, the Dervishes drove them off with
frightful loss, and Abu Anga, taking the offensive, succeeded
in gaining a complete victory. So sure were the Abyssinians
of gaining the day that they had taken up a position in front
of a river, and now many of them, in their flight, were
drowned while attempting to cross it. For a short time,
the Abyssinian cavalry was to some extent successful; but,
after suffering considerable loss, they fled with Ras Adal.
The entire Abyssinian camp, consisting of quantities of
tents, fell into the hands of Abu Anga, who captured Ras
Adal's wife and grown-up daughter, and in this victory
practically conquered the whole of the Amhara Province.
He advanced without delay on Gondar, where he expected
to find great treasures, but was disappointed; for, with the
exception of some goods belonging to the Geberta, and
some large stores of coffee, honey, and wax, which were of
no value to him, as he had no means of transport, he got
practically nothing. In the large and lofty stone building,
said to have been erected by the Portuguese, they found
one poor old Coptic priest, who was thrown out of the
highest story into the street below. Staying here only one
day, Abu Anga ordered the town to be fired, and, on his
way back, attacked and looted villages right and left, killing

the men, and seizing the women and children as captives; the Geberta, and some little boys, alone were spared and carried off as booty. In this manner thousands of Abyssinian women and girls were driven in front of the army, urged on by the lash. On arrival at Gallabat, a fifth of the loot was sent to the Khalifa, and several hundred women were despatched to the Beit el Mal in Omdurman, where they were sold to the highest bidders. The road between Gallabat and Abu Haraz was strewn with corpses, and amongst them the daughter and young son of Ras Adal.

Abu Anga, in accordance with the Khalifa's instructions, now began to put Gallabat into a state of defence; for, in spite of the success just gained, they knew that the Abyssinians would seek revenge. But he did not long survive his victory; although only fifty-two years of age, he suffered from constant illness, and was always trying to cure himself. He had grown immensely stout, owing to the good living in which he indulged, which contrasted greatly with what he had been formerly accustomed to; he suffered much from indigestion, and used to treat himself with a poisonous root which came from Dar Fertit. One day, however, he took an overdose, and in the morning was found dead in his bed. In him the Khalifa lost his best Emir, who, though by descent a slave, had, through his liberality and kindness, gained the affection of all who knew him, as well as the esteem and regard of his subjects, who admired his personal courage and sense of justice. He was mourned by his entire force—by Arabs as well as by Blacks—who recognised in him a strict though just master, and one who, though he punished very severely any offences against his orders, was ever ready to help those in need. He was buried in his red-brick house, and many of his servants and slaves worshipped him as a saint.

At the same time that Abu Anga had left Omdurman for Gallabat, Osman Wad Adam had received instructions to move with his whole force towards Darfur, as there was some fear that Sultan Yusef, who had replaced Khaled on his departure, was hatching a mutiny; for a long time he had sent no consignment of horses and slaves to the Khalifa, and was evidently beginning to feel himself sufficiently powerful to overturn the authority of the latter.

A fight took place near Wad Berag, south of Fasher ; and Osman gained an easy victory. Sultan Yusef fled, but was overtaken at Kebkebia and killed, whilst Fasher, where all his wives and relations had been collected, as well as a quantity of goods belonging to Fezzan and Wadai merchants, also numbers of women and children, fell into Osman's hands. Thus Darfur, which had been practically lost to the Mahdists, was re-taken by them in the same month (January, 1888), just at the time that Abu Anga had gained his great victory over the Abyssinians.

Whilst these momentous events were transpiring in the east and west of the Sudan Empire, the Khalifa governed the country at Omdurman in a most tyrannical and despotic manner. He mistrusted everyone. Numbers of spies were employed by his brother Yakub, and their duty was to tell him of everything that went on in the city. He was kept fully informed of the general temper of the people ; and should any persons express doubt about the truth of the Mahdi's Divine mission, they were punished with special severity. It happened one day that a sailor used some irreverent expression regarding Mahdism, and was reported to the Khalifa. The plaintiff, who was a fanatical Baggari, had, however, no witnesses, those who were present at the time admitting to the Khalifa that they were too far off to hear what passed ; but the latter determined to make an example. He therefore summoned the Kadi, and ordered him to force a confession out of the accused, at the same time advising him how to set about it. Two persons were then sent to the prisoner, to apprise him that witnesses had been found ; but that if he made a confession of his own free will, and admitted that he was sorry before the witnesses had been questioned, the Khalifa would mitigate his sentence, and would probably pardon him. The poor man failed to see the trap that had been laid for him, made a confession, and begged the Khalifa's pardon. The confession was taken down in writing, and submitted to Abdullahi, who ordered the sentence, which was execution, to be carried out in accordance with the Mahdi's code. The Khalifa, in giving sentence, said that had the insult been against his own person he would have forgiven him ; but the prisoner having sinned against the Mahdi, he would be committing a crime if he mitigated it in the slightest degree.

That afternoon the Khalifa gave orders for the ombeya to be sounded, while the dull beats of the great mansura (war-drum) boomed through the city, and he himself rode with an immense escort to the parade-ground. On his arrival his sheepskin was spread on the ground, and on this he sat, facing the east, whilst the Kadi and others stood behind him in a semicircle. He then ordered the accused to be brought before him. Already his hands had been tied behind his back; but he showed not the slightest signs of fear. When within a hundred paces of the Khalifa he was decapitated by Ahmed Dalia, the chief executioner.

In order to show his veneration for the Mahdi, the Khalifa decided to erect a monument to him, as is the custom in Egypt; but this he did rather to satisfy his own vanity than out of respect for his late master. A square building was erected, some thirty feet high, and thirty-six feet each way, and the stone for this construction, of which the walls were upwards of six feet thick, had to be brought all the way from Khartum. Above this a hexagonal wall fifteen feet high was built, from which rose a dome forty feet high. On the corners of the main building were four smaller domes. This was called Kubbet el Mahdi (Mahdi's dome). It was furnished with ten large arched windows and two doors, and in the hexagonal portion were six sky- lights. It was whitewashed all over, and surrounded by a trelliswork fence ; the windows and doors were made by the workmen in the Khartum arsenal ; while directly beneath the dome, and over the Mahdi's grave, a wooden sarcophagus was erected, covered with black cloth. On the sides of the walls condelabra were hung, while suspended by a long chain from the centre of the dome was an immense chandelier taken from the Government palace in Khartum. The sombre appearance of the inside of the building was relieved by some gaudy painting on the walls. A few yards from the building is a small cistern, built of red bricks cemented together; and this is used by the visitors for their religious ablutions. The plans for this building were devised by an old Government official who had been formerly employed as an architect; but, of course, public opinion dutifully attributed the design to the Khalifa.

The ceremony of laying the foundation-stone of this building was conducted with great unction by the Khalifa, who 'turned the first sod.' Accompanied by a crowd of upwards of thirty thousand people, he proceeded to the river bank, where the stones were heaped up, and lifting one of them on his shoulder, carried it to the spot, his example being followed by every individual person in this vast assemblage; the noise and confusion were perfectly indescribable. Numbers of accidents happened; but those injured thought it fortunate to suffer on such an occasion. The building was not completed till the following year, and entailed a considerable amount of labour, though little expense; and during its construction the Khalifa frequently asserted that angels lent their assistance. An Egyptian hearing this, and aware that many of his compatriots were masons, was constrained to remark to them, 'You are probably the Khalifa's angels, and require neither food, drink, nor payment.' Had the Khalifa heard this, he would undoubtedly have removed this wag's head.

As usual, I was always in close attendance on the Khalifa, and as a token of his goodwill he presented me with one of the Abyssinian girls sent by Abu Anga. Her mother and brother had been killed before her eyes, and the poor creature had been torn from their bodies and driven into captivity at

the end of the lash. Although not treated as a slave by
my people, who did all they could to lighten her sad lot, she
never seemed bright or happy; she continually brooded
over her losses and her home, until at length death released
her from her sufferings. Occasionally Father Ohrwalder
used to visit me secretly, but as the Khalifa did not approve
of our meeting, his visits were few and far between. We
used to talk of our home, and of our present wretched existence; but we never lost hope that, sooner or later, our
captivity would come to an end.

Abu Girga, who commanded at Kassala, was now ordered
to proceed to Osman Digna, and assist him in his fighting.
Leaving Ahmed Wad Ali as his representative at Kassala,
he was summoned to Omdurman to report to the Khalifa
on the state of the Arab tribes in the Eastern Soudan. He
arrived late one evening, and was at once received in long
private audience by the Khalifa; and, on withdrawing,
hurriedly told me that he had given him a letter from my
family in Europe. A few minutes later I was called in, and
informed that the Governor of Suakin had sent a letter to
Osman Digna, which was supposed to be from my family,
and which he had sent on. In handing me this letter the
Khalifa ordered me to open it at once, and acquaint him
with its contents. I glanced through it hurriedly, and, to
my intense grief and sorrow, saw that it was an announce-
ment from my brothers and sisters that my poor mother had
died, and that on her death-bed she had expressed an earnest
hope that we should all be reunited. The Khalifa, impatient that I took so long to read it, again asked me who
had written it, and what were its contents. ' It is from my
brothers and sisters,' I replied, ' and I will translate it to
you.' I had no reason to conceal its contents; it was
merely a few lines from distressed brothers and sisters to
their distant brother. I told him how disturbed they were
about me, and how they were ready to make any sacrifice in
order that I should regain my liberty. When I came to the
part about my mother, it required all my self-control; I told

him that, owing to my absence, her death was not so peaceful as it might have been, and that during her long illness her constant prayer to God had been that she might see me again. Her prayer, alas! had not been answered; and now this letter had brought me her last greeting, and her tender hopes for my welfare. My throat felt parched and dry, and had not the Khalifa suddenly interrupted me, I must have broken down. 'Your mother was not aware that I honour you more than anyone else,' said he, 'otherwise she certainly would not have been in such trouble about you; but I forbid you to mourn for her. She died as a Christian and an unbeliever in the Prophet and the Mahdi, and cannot therefore expect God's mercy.' The blood rushed to my head, and for a moment I could say nothing; but gradually regaining my self-control I continued to read on that my brother Henry was now married, and that Adolf and my sisters were quite well. Finally, they begged me to let them know how I could obtain my liberty, and urged me to write to them. 'Write and tell one at least of your brothers to come here,' said the Khalifa, when I had finished the letter. 'I would honour him, and he should want for nothing; but I will talk to you about this another time.' He then signed to me with his hand, and I withdrew.

My comrades, who had already heard that a letter had arrived for me, were very inquisitive, and asked me all manner of questions, but I answered them only briefly, and as soon as the Khalifa had retired to rest I went home. I flung myself down on my angareb, and my servants, much concerned, asked me what was the matter, but I told them to leave me. 'Poor mother, then it was I who made your last hours so unhappy!' My brothers and sisters had written her last words: 'I am ready to die; but I should have loved to see and embrace my Rudolf once more. The thought that he is in the hands of his enemies makes my departure from this world very difficult for me.' How well I remembered her words when I left for the Sudan: 'My son, my Rudolf, your restless spirit drives you out into the world!

You are going to distant and almost unknown lands. A time, perhaps, will come when you will long for us, and a quiet life.' How true had been her words—poor mother! How much trouble I must have given her! And then I cried and cried—not about my position, but for my dear mother, who could never be replaced.

The next morning the Khalifa sent for me, and again made me translate the letter to him ; and he ordered me to reply at once that I was perfectly happy in my present position. I did as I was told, and wrote a letter praising the Khalifa, and saying how happy I was to be near him ; but I put inverted commas against many words and sentences, and points of exclamation, and wrote at the bottom of the letter that all words and sentences thus marked should be read in exactly the opposite sense. At the same time, I asked my brothers and sisters to write a letter of thanks to the Khalifa in Arabic, and to send him a travelling bag, and to me two hundred pounds, and twelve common watches, suitable for presents, as on certain seasons of the year the Emirs attended the feasts in Omdurman, and would greatly appreciate them. I also asked them to send me a translation of the Kuran in German, and advised them not to worry for the present, but that I hoped to find some means of being reunited to them. I told them to send the things, through the Austrian Consul-General in Cairo, to the Governor of Suakin, by whom they would be forwarded to Osman Digna. I handed this letter to the Khalifa, who gave it to some postmen who were going to Osman Digna with instructions to send it to Suakin.

About a month before I received the sad news of my mother's death, I had to deplore the loss of one of my comrades in captivity, Lupton. He had been working in the dockyard at Khartum until recently ; but the feeble state of his health had obliged him to ask to be relieved from this position. He had then returned to Omdurman, and had suffered great want ; but, to his relief, Saleh Wad Haj Ali, with whom he was on very friendly terms, returned

from Cairo, and brought him some money which he had
received from Lupton's family. Haj Ali naturally tried to
make as much money out of the transaction as he could.
He had advanced a sum of a hundred dollars to Lupton as
a loan, receiving from him, in return, a bill on his brother
for two hundred pounds, which had been cashed on his
arrival in Cairo; and, returning again to Omdurman, had
paid Lupton two hundred dollars, keeping the remainder,
about eight hundred dollars, for himself. In spite of this
robbery, this small sum delighted poor Lupton, and helped
him, for a short period, to stave off the miseries of living
like a beggar. He also rejoiced that a medium of communication had been found with his relatives, whereby he
eventually hoped to regain his freedom. These hopes, alas!
were not to be realized.

He had come home one Tuesday morning from the
mosque with me, and was consulting me as to whom he
should trust with the remainder of his two hundred dollars,
so as to obtain small sums when he required them, as it
was necessary for him to be most careful not to attract
attention to himself by spending large sums, and thus endanger his communication with Egypt. We talked of home
and of our present situation, and he seemed more cheerful
than usual, but complained of pains in his back, and of a
general feeling of indisposition. I left him about mid-day,
and on the following Tuesday he sent his servant to me,
begging me to go and see him, as he felt very ill. In reply
to my question, the man told me that his master was in a
high fever, and had been in bed for three days. I promised
to come as quickly as possible, and that evening asked the
Khalifa's permission to go and see him. The next morning,
having obtained leave to spend that day with the invalid, I
at once went to his house, and found him in a dying condition. He was suffering from typhus fever, and already
the illness had reached such a stage that he scarcely recognised me, and, in a few broken words, begged me to take
care of his daughter. He then said something about his

father and mother ; but he was almost incoherent, and at times became quite unconscious. I understood, however, that he was begging me to be the bearer of his dying messages, should I ever succeed in escaping. On Wednesday, the 8th May, 1888, he passed away at mid-day without having recovered consciousness. We washed him, wrapped him in a shroud, and, according to the usual custom, carried him to the mosque, where the prayers for the dead were recited, and then we buried him in a cemetery near the Beit el Mal. Father Ohrwalder, the majority of the Greek colony, and a number of natives who had learnt to love and respect his noble and unassuming character, were present.

CHAPTER XIII.

THE ABYSSINIAN CAMPAIGN.

Battle of Gallabat—Death of King John—The Revolt of Abu Gemmaiza —Defeats of the Mahdists—Death of Abu Gemmaiza—Preparations for the Invasion of Egypt—Execution of Sixty-seven Batahin Arabs —More Letters from Home—My Family send the Khalifa a Dressing-bag from Vienna—Immigration of the Taaisha Tribe—They settle in the Nile Valley—Nejumi advances into Egypt—Battle of Toski—Incidents during the great Famine—The Fall of Ibrahim Adlan—His Execution—The Khalifa mistrusts me—I fall into serious Danger—I become the unwilling Recipient of the Khalifa's Favours.

IT was not, however, to be supposed that the Mahdist victories in the east and west would remain entirely undisputed. King John, who had been carrying on a war in the interior, now determined to avenge the attack on Gondar, and, collecting an immense army, he advanced towards Gallabat. A fierce conflict ensued between the Abyssinian and Dervish hosts, in which the latter were worsted; but, in the moment of victory, a stray bullet mortally wounded King John, and this event turned victory into defeat. The Abyssinian army, retiring in disorder, were followed up by

Zeki Tummal, who succeeded in capturing the King's body, his crown, and baggage.

Abyssinia now fell into a state of internecine warfare; there were several aspirants for the throne, and dissensions and quarrels put a stop to combined action. The Italians had been in occupation of Massawa since the beginning of 1885, and had seized some of the adjacent country. This fact reacted satisfactorily on the Dervish occupation of Gallabat; for they were well aware that the Abyssinians would be fully occupied with their European enemies, and once more they began raiding the Amhara frontier.

Whilst the garrison of Gallabat was in danger of destruction at the hands of King John, Osman Wad Adam was in considerable peril in the west. On the death of Sultan Yusef, his troops raided the country in all directions, and his Emirs were guilty of the greatest oppression and cruelty. Thousands of women and children were declared to be ghanima (booty), and dragged to Fasher by main force. The people were in despair, and the distress and anguish extended to the limits of Dar Tama. Here a youth resided who hailed from Omdurman, and probably belonged to one of the riverian tribes, but had been driven from his own home, and, under the shade of a wide-spreading Gemmaiza (wild fig) tree, sat and read the Kuran. In despair the wretched, oppressed people turned to this youth, whom they credited with supernatural powers, and dubbed 'Abu Gemmaiza'; placing himself at their head, he fell upon a small party of Dervishes and annihilated them. This success led to others, and soon a victorious army of Darfurians were marching against El Fasher; but an untoward event now occurred—Abu Gemmaiza was taken suddenly ill, and, deprived of their chief, the rebels were completely overthrown by Osman Wad Adam within a few miles of the town. This disaster resulted in Abdullahi's rule being established more firmly than ever in the western provinces of the Sudan.

Previous, however, to these occurrences, the Khalifa had

again directed his attention towards Egypt. He had ques‧
tioned several persons regarding the country, and they had
excited in him an avaricious longing for the grand palaces,
large gardens, and immense harems of white women (he
himself had black in abundance). Of course, the most
suitable man to undertake operations against Egypt was
Nejumi. He was an exceptionally brave man, and, when
a simple merchant, had travelled a great deal, knew the
country well, and, moreover, was an ardent devotee to the
cause of Mahdism, to which he had won over great numbers.
The greater part of his force consisted of tribesmen of the
Nile Valley ; many had seen Egypt, and had until recently
much intercourse with the frontier tribes of Upper Egypt.
Such were the outward and visible reasons which the Khalifa
brought forward when selecting the chief ; but, in reality,
he was well aware that a campaign against Egypt was a
serious undertaking, and on this account he was anxious
not to involve in it his own relatives, and the western tribes
who were his special adherents. Nejumi therefore, with
his Jaalin and Danagla, and a proportion of Baggaras,
formed the expedition ; but the two former, being followers
of the Khalifa Sherif, Abdullahi always looked upon as his
secret enemies. Should the campaign be successful—and
he never for a moment doubted the capacity and devotion
of its leader—then so much the better : he would have
conquered a new country ; but should the Egyptian troops
succeed in repelling the invasion, then the remnant of his
defeated forces would retire on Dongola with heavy loss,
and would be so far weakened as to be unworthy of further
consideration.

The circumstances connected with the death of Nejumi,
and the annihilation of his force at the hands of the Anglo-
Egyptian troops at Toski on 3rd August, 1889, are too well
known to need repetition here ; but, in connection with the
collection of men to accompany this expedition, I must
mention an act of brutality on the Khalifa's part which
surpassed anything I had hitherto witnessed. The Batahin

tribe had hesitated to obey the summons to come to Omdurman, and in consequence a raid was made upon them, and
upwards of sixty-seven men with their families were brought
in as prisoners. This tribe was celebrated for its bravery
during the Government days, and now the Khalifa, who
had already privately given his views on the matter to the
judges, ordered them to be summoned before the Court. It
was unanimously decided that the Batahin were mukhalefin
(disobedient). 'And what is the punishment for disobedience?' asked the Khalifa. 'Death,' was the reply of
the judges. They were sent back to prison, and the Khalifa
busied himself with carrying the sentence into execution.
In accordance with his orders, three scaffolds were immediately erected in the market-place, and, after mid-day
prayers, the ombeya was sounded, and the great war-drum
was beaten, summoning all the Khalifa's subjects to follow
him. Riding to the parade-ground, he dismounted, and
seated himself on a small angareb, whilst his followers
collected around him, some sitting and some standing. The
sixty-seven Batahin were now brought before him, with
their hands tied behind their backs, escorted by Abdel Baki's
men, whilst their unfortunate wives and children ran after
them, crying and screaming. The Khalifa gave instructions
that the women and children were to be separated from the
men, and, summoning Ahmed ed Dalia, Taher Wad el Jaali,
and Hassan Wad Khabir, consulted them in an undertone ;
the latter then went forward to the Batahin, and instructed
the escort and prisoners to follow them to the market-place.
After a delay of a quarter of an hour, the Khalifa got up,
and we all walked on behind him. Arrived at the market-
place, a terrible scene awaited us.

The unfortunate Batahin had been divided into three
parties, one of which had been hanged, a second had been
decapitated, and a third had lost their right hands and left
feet. The Khalifa himself stopped in front of the three
scaffolds, which were almost broken by the weights of the
bodies, whilst close at hand lay a heap of mutilated people,

their hands and feet lying scattered on the ground; it was a shocking spectacle. They did not utter a sound, but gazed in front of them, and tried to hide from the eyes of the crowd the terrible sufferings they were enduring. The Khalifa now summoned Osman Wad Ahmed, one of the Kadis, who was an intimate friend of Khalifa Ali, and a member of the Batahin tribe, and, pointing to the mutilated bodies, he said to Osman, 'You may now take what remains of your tribe home with you.' The poor man was too shocked and horrified to be able to answer.

After riding round the scaffolds, the Khalifa proceeded along the street leading to the mosque, and here Ahmed ed Dalia had been continuing his bloody work; twenty-three decapitated bodies lay stretched along the roadside. These unfortunates had calmly met their death, submitting to the inevitable. Several of them, as is the custom amongst the Arabs, had given proof of their courage by uttering a few sentences, such as, ' Death is ordained for everyone '; ' See ! to-day is my holy day'; ' He who has not seen a brave man die, let him come and look here.' Each one of these sixty - seven men had met his death heroically. The Khalifa's work was done; he was satisfied with it, and rode home. On his arrival there, by way of an act of clemency, he sent one of his orderlies with instructions that the women and children of the murdered men should be set free; he might just as well have distributed them as slaves.

In spite of all these horrors, I was secretly rejoicing, for I had heard that letters from home were on their way ; not only were there letters, but I had also been told, confidentially, by some merchants who had come from Berber, that there were two boxes of money for me. I scarcely dared think about it, and to wait patiently was no easy matter. One morning whilst I was sitting at the door, a camel laden with two boxes was brought up, and the man asked to be taken before the Khalifa, saying that he had arrived with letters and goods from Osman Digna. The Khalifa, being apprised of this, ordered the boxes to be sent to the Beit el Mal, and the letters to be given to his clerks. I was wild with impatience; but it was the Khalifa's pleasure not to summon me till after sunset, and then he handed me the letters. They were, as I expected, from my brothers and sisters, expressing their great delight at having at last received news direct from me. One letter was written in Arabic, and addressed to the Khalifa, and contained profuse thanks to him for his kindness to me, recommending me to him for further assurances of his goodwill, for which they sent many expressions of gratitude. This letter, which had been written by Professor Wahrmund, was composed in such flattering terms that the Khalifa had it read aloud the same evening in the mosque, and so gratified was he that he ordered the boxes to be made over to me. Meanwhile I translated to him my letters, which contained only private and personal information, and in which my brothers and sisters told me they had sent a travelling-bag for the Khalifa in token of their devotion to him, begging him to accept this trifling present, which was quite unworthy of his exalted position. He expressed his readiness to accept it, and ordered me to bring it to him the next morning. He then sent two of his people, so that the boxes might be opened in their presence, and late that night we went to the Beit el Mal, and there opened them. They contained £200, twelve ordinary watches, some razors and looking-glasses, some newspapers, a German translation of the Kuran, and the Khalifa's present. These things were all handed over to me, and, having read my letters once again, I literally devoured the newspapers. News from home!

There were only a few numbers of the *Neue Freie Presse*, but quite sufficient to afford me, who had had no news for six years, the pleasure of reading at night-time for months. I gradually got to know them by heart, from the political leader down to the last advertisement, in which an elderly maiden lady advertised that she was anxious to find a

kindred spirit with a view to matrimony.   Father Ohrwalder
came to me secretly by night to borrow the papers, and
studied them just as conscientiously as I did, only I do not
suppose that he paid quite so much attention to the last
advertisement!

Early the next morning, taking the present with me, I
went to the Khalifa; he told me to open it, and when he
saw all the little crystal boxes, silver-topped bottles, brushes,
razors, scissors, etc., etc., he was greatly surprised.   I had
to explain to him their various uses, and he then sent for
the Kadis, who, in duty bound, were obliged to express
even greater astonishment than he, though I had no doubt
that several of them had seen such things before.   Then,
without any further delay, he sent for his clerk, and ordered
him to write a letter to my brothers and sisters, in which
he himself informed them of the honourable position I held
in his service; he invited them to come to Omdurman and
visit me, and gave them the assurance that they would be
free to return.   He also ordered me to write in the same
strain, and, although I knew perfectly well that my people
would never avail themselves of such an invitation, which
was merely a spontaneous outburst of delight, I took
good care to warn them fully against thinking of it for an
instant.   The letters were then returned by the man who
had been sent by Osman Digna, and the latter was instructed by letter to forward them.   The real reason,
however, for the Khalifa's good-humour lay in the fact that
his own tribe, the Taaisha, had arrived in Omdurman.
They had marched through Kordofan to the White Nile at
Tura el Hadra.   The Khalifa had written to them that they
should come to take possession of the countries which the
Lord their God had ordained to be theirs, and on their
arrival they certainly behaved as if they were sole masters.
They appropriated everything they could lay their hands
on: camels, cows, and donkeys were forcibly carried off
from their owners; men and women who had the misfortune to cross their path were robbed of their clothing

and jewellery; and the populations of the countries through which they passed bitterly rued the day which had made a western Arab their ruler. For their convenience, the Khalifa erected immense grain depôts all along the roads by which they travelled, and on their arrival at the river, ships and steamers were ready to transport them to Omdurman. But before they reached the city, the Khalifa ordered them to halt on the right bank of the river, and, dividing them into two sections, he had all the men and women freshly clothed at the expense of the Beit el Mal; and they then were brought in detachments, at intervals of two or three days, to Omdurman. In order to make the populace thoroughly understand that the new masters of the country had arrived, Abdullahi drove out of their houses all the inhabitants of that portion of the city lying between the mosque and Omdurman Fort, and handed it over to the Taaisha as their residence. Other ground was allotted to those who had been forced to give up their houses, and they were promised assistance from the Beit el Mal in order to rebuild; but, of course, this was mere empty form, and resulted in their having to shift entirely for themselves.

In order to facilitate the maintenance of his tribe, and as grain began to rise in price, the Khalifa issued an order for all grain stored in the houses to be taken to the meshra el minarata (grain docks), under pain of confiscation; and, having obtained the services of some of his own myrmidons, he ordered them to sell this grain at the lowest possible rate to the Taaisha; and the money thus obtained he divided amongst the original owners, who, in their turn, were obliged to re-purchase at the high rates from other sources. This wholesale robbery can be better understood when I explain that the money paid by the Taaisha for ten ardebs of grain would scarcely pay for two ardebs purchased in the ordinary manner.

When the supply of grain at Omdurman was diminishing, he despatched messengers to the Gezira to confiscate what was still there; and in this manner, by publicly showing his preference for his own tribe, he completely estranged himself from his former followers. This, however, was a matter of little concern to him, as, by the advent of the Taaisha Arabs, he had acquired a reinforcement of several thousands of warriors.

But now famine fell on the land. There had been no rain, and Berber was the first province to feel this. The irrigation of this province is carried on by water-wheels at intervals along the river banks; and even in prosperous times the supply of grain is scarcely sufficient to meet the wants of the local inhabitants; several of them wandered to Omdurman, which was already over-populated; and here the situation became most critical: the price of grain rose at first to forty dollars, and subsequently to sixty dollars, the ardeb. The rich could purchase grain; but the poor died wholesale. Those were terrible months at the close of 1889; the people had become so thin that they scarcely resembled human beings—they were veritably but skin and bone. These poor wretches would eat anything, no matter how disgusting—skins of animals which had long since dried and become decayed were roasted and eaten; the strips of leather which form the angareb (native bedstead) were cut off, boiled, and made into soup. Those who had any strength left went out and robbed; like hawks they pounced down on the bakers and butchers, and cared nothing for the blows of the kurbash which invariably fell on their attenuated backs.

On one occasion I remember seeing a man who had seized a piece of tallow, and had crammed it into his mouth before its owner could stop him. The latter jumped at his throat, closed his hands round it, and pressed it till the man's eyes protruded; but he kept his mouth tightly closed until he fell down insensible. In the market-places the incessant cry was heard of 'Gayekum! Gayekum!' ('He is coming to you!') which meant that famished creatures were stealthily creeping round the places where the women had their few articles for sale, to protect which they were frequently obliged to lie upon them, and defend them with their hands and feet. The space between the Khalifa's and Yakub's houses was generally crowded at night with these wretched people, who cried aloud most piteously for bread. I dreaded going home, for I was generally followed by several of these famished beggars, who often attempted to forcibly enter my house, and at that time I had scarcely enough for my own slender wants, besides having to help my own household and my friends, who had now become wretchedly poor.

One night—it was full moon—I was going home at about twelve o'clock, when, near the Beit el Amana (ammunition and arms stores), I saw something moving on the ground, and went near to see what it was. As I approached I saw three almost naked women, with their long tangled hair hanging about their shoulders; they were squatting round a quite young donkey, which was lying on the ground, and had probably strayed from its mother, or been stolen by them. They had torn open its body with their teeth, and were devouring its intestines, whilst the poor animal was still breathing. I shuddered at this terrible sight, whilst the poor women, infuriated by hunger, gazed at me like maniacs. The beggars by whom I was followed now fell upon them, and attempted to wrest from them their prey; and I fled from this uncanny spectacle.

On another occasion I saw a poor woman who must formerly have been beautiful, but on whose emaciated face the death-struggle was visible, lying on her back in the street, whilst her little baby, scarcely a year old, was vainly trying to get some nourishment from its mother's already cold breasts. Another woman passing by took compassion on the little orphan and carried it off.

One day a woman of the Jaalin, who are perhaps the most moral tribe in the Sudan, accompanied by her only daughter, a lovely young girl, dragged herself wearily to my house; both were at death's door from starvation, and begged me to help them. I gave them what little I could, and the woman then said, ' Take this, my only daughter, as your slave; save her from death by starvation!' and, as she said this the tears streamed down her poor wan cheeks, whilst in her weak, scarcely audible voice, she continued, ' Do not fear that I shall molest you any further; only save her—do not let her perish!' I gave them all I could spare, and then asked them to leave me, telling them to return when they were in great want; but I never saw them again—perhaps some charitable person took pity on them. Another woman was actually accused of eating her own child, and was brought to the police-station for trial; but of what use was this? In two days the poor creature died a raving maniac!

Several sold their own children, both boys and girls, pretending they were their slaves; this they did not to obtain money, but simply to save their lives; and when this year of misery was over some parents bought them back again at even higher prices. The dead lay in the streets in hundreds; and none could be found to bury them. The Khalifa issued orders that people were responsible for burying those who were found dead near their houses, and that should they refuse to do so their property would be confiscated. This had some effect; but, to save themselves trouble, they used to drag the bodies near their neighbours' houses, and this gave rise to frequent quarrels and brawls. Every day the waters of the Blue and White Niles swept past Omdurman, carrying along hundreds of bodies of the wretched peasantry who had died along the banks—a terrible proof of the awful condition of the country.

In Omdurman itself the majority of those who died belonged rather to the moving population than to the actual inhabitants of the town, for the latter had managed to secrete a certain amount of grain, and the different tribes invariably assisted each other; but in other parts of the Sudan the state of affairs was considerably worse. I think the Jaalin, who are the most independent as well as the

proudest tribe in the Sudan, suffered more severely than
the rest ; several fathers of families, seeing that escape from
death was impossible, bricked up the doors of their houses,
and, united with their children, patiently awaited death.   I
have no hesitation in saying that in this way entire villages
died out.

The inhabitants of Dongola, though they suffered considerably, were somewhat better off.   But between Abu
Haraz, Gedaref, and Gallabat, the situation was worst of
all.   Zeki Tummal, at the commencement of the famine,
had given orders to some of his myrmidons to forcibly
collect all the grain in the neighbourhood, and this he
stored for his soldiers, thus saving the bulk of his force,
with the result that an immense proportion of the local
inhabitants died of starvation.   After a time no one dared
to go out into the streets without an escort, for they feared
being attacked and eaten up ; the inhabitants had become
animals—cannibals!   One of the Emirs of the Homr tribe
—who, in spite of the terrible year, still preserved a fairly
healthy appearance—notwithstanding constant warning,
insisted on going to visit a friend after sunset, but he never
reached his friend nor returned to his abode; the next
morning his head was found outside the city, and I presume
his body had already been consumed.

The Hassania, Shukria, Aggalaïn, Hammada, and other
tribes had completely died out, and the once thickly-popu-
lated country had become a desert waste.   Zeki Tummal
sent a detachment of his force to the southern districts of
the Blue Nile, towards the Tabi, Begreg, Kukeli, Kashankero, and Beni Shangul mountains, the inhabitants of which,
although they paid tribute to the Khalifa, refused to make a
pilgrimage or provide warlike contingents.   This he had
done not so much with the idea of military operations as to
provide some means of maintaining his troops ; but the
commander, Abder Rasul, succeeded in capturing a number
of slaves, as well as a quantity of money.

The situation in Darfur was little better than that in

Gedaref and Gallabat ; the western provinces, such as Dar
Gimr, Dar Tama, and Massalit, had no need of grain, but
not being in complete subjection they prevented its export
to Fasher.   Indeed, it seemed as if this famine had come as
Heaven's punishment on all districts owning subjection to
the Khalifa, whilst the neighbouring countries, which had
had sufficient rest to cultivate their fields, had acquired
enough grain for their maintenance.   A few Omdurman
merchants hired some vessels and proceeded to Fashoda,
where they exchanged beads, copper rods, and money for
dhurra ; the undertaking succeeded, and now crowds of
others followed their example, proceeding sometimes as far
as the Sobat, whence they imported quantities of grain, thus
enriching themselves, and saving their fellow-countrymen
from terrible want.   Had the King of Fashoda, who was
not then subject to the Khalifa, forbidden the export, half
Omdurman would have perished.   At length the rain fell ;
the thirsty land was refreshed ; the crops sprang up ; harvest
was near ; and the whole country once more rejoiced at the
prospect of help and deliverance.   But now the atmosphere
became obscure with swarms of locusts of an unusual size,
and the prospect of a rich harvest vanished ; everything,
however, was not destroyed by this plague, which, from that
date, has become one of annual occurrence.   The Khalifa,
anxious for the welfare of his own tribe, now forced the
natives to sell the little grain they had collected at an ab-
surdly low price to his agents ; but small as this was, in
comparison with the price he ought to have paid, he determined to still further economise, and consequently ordered
Ibrahim Adlan to proceed personally to the Gezira, and
induce the inhabitants to give up their dhurra of their own
free-will, and without payment.   Adlan, who thoroughly
disapproved of this measure, had, by his thoroughness and
sagacity, risen high in the Khalifa's favour ; but Abdullahi
discussed State affairs with his brother Yakub only, whose
animosity Adlan had incurred, though Yakub was too clever
to show it.

As natives go, Adlan's character was good: he did not care to lend himself to evil designs, and far from oppressing people, was often the means of lightening the burdens of others; but he was suspected, and not without reason, of having made an immense fortune, and of this the Khalifa was not ignorant; consequently, during his absence, Yakub and several of his confidants informed the Khalifa that Adlan's influence in the country was almost as great as his own, and that he had frequently spoken disparagingly of his master and his system of government; they even went as far as to say that Adlan had attributed the famine entirely to the Khalifa's treatment of his own tribe. This intrigue resulted in the unfortunate Adlan being brought before a mock tribunal, by whom he was sentenced to mutilation or death for 'disobedience.' He was allowed to make his choice, and selected the latter. With his hands tied across his chest, and to the strains of the melancholy ombeya, he was led forth to the market-place, accompanied by an immense crowd. Calmly mounting the angareb beneath the scaffold, he himself placed his head in the noose, and refusing to drink the water offered to him, told the hangman to complete his work; the rope was pulled taut, the angareb was removed, and there Ibrahim swung like a marble statue until his soul left his body, the outstretched index finger alone indicating that he died in the true faith of Islam. In spite of the interdiction, wails of sorrow filled the city, but the Khalifa rejoiced that he had rid himself of so dangerous an enemy, and refrained from punishing this disobedience to his orders. He sent his brother Yakub to the funeral, as if to show to the world that Adlan had merely been punished in accordance with the law, and that the well-known animosity between the two had nothing to do with the matter.

His successor as Emin Beit el Mal was a certain Nur Wad Ibrahim, whose grandfather was a Takruri. He did not, therefore, belong to the tribes of the Nile valley, and thus had a greater claim on the Khalifa's confidence and consideration.

As regards myself, the Khalifa seemed to grow daily more suspicious. Previous to Ibrahim Adlan's departure for the Gezira, the answer to my letter which had been sent to my family through Osman Digna had arrived. It contained only news of a private nature, and expressed the great delight of my family that they had succeeded in at last getting into communication with me. At the same time, they wrote to the Khalifa in submissive words, expressing their gratitude for the kind and honourable treatment which I received at his hands. They also assured him of their great devotion to him, and thanked him for the high honour he had conferred upon them by inviting them to come to Omdurman ; but my brother regretted his inability to accept, as he was at that time a secretary in the office of the High Chamberlain of His Majesty the Emperor of Austria, whilst the other brother was a lawyer and lieutenant in the Artillery Reserve ; they were therefore both unable, in virtue of their positions, to undertake so long a journey. My master had called me up, and on handing me the letters had ordered me to translate them to him ; then, considering for a few moments, he said to me, ' It was my intention to induce one of your brothers to come here and see me ; and I did what I had never done before—wrote a letter to them. As they make excuses and refuse to come, and as they now know that you are well, I forbid you to have any more correspondence with them. Further communication would only make you unhappy. Do you understand what I mean?' ' Certainly,' I replied, ' your orders shall be obeyed ; and I also think that further communication with my relatives is not necessary.' ' Where is the Gospel that has been sent to you ?' asked he, looking at me fixedly. ' I am a Moslem,' I answered, for I was now on my guard, 'and I have no Gospel in my house. They sent me a translation of the Kuran, the Holy Book, which your secretary saw when the box was opened, and which is still in my possession.' ' Then bring it to me to-morrow,' he said, and signed to me to withdraw.

It was perfectly clear to me that he no longer trusted me, and I knew that, after Nejumi's defeat, he had several times spoken in this sense to the Kadis. I had already spent almost all the money I had received in gifts amongst my comrades, and now some of these began to murmur, and were disappointed that the sum was so small, and I knew that they were intriguing against me. Who could have induced him to believe that the Kuran which had been sent to me was the Gospel? The next day I gave it to him. The translation was by Ullman. He examined it carefully, and then said : ' You say that this is the Kuran ; it is in the language of unbelievers, and perhaps they have made alterations.' ' It is a literal translation into my own language,' I replied calmly, ' and its object is to make me understand the Holy Book which has come from God, and was made known to mankind by the Prophet in the Arabic language. If you wish, you can send it to Neufeld, who is in captivity in the prison, and with whom I have no intercourse, and you can ascertain from him if my assertion is correct.' ' I do not mistrust you, and I believe what you say,' he replied, in a somewhat more amiable tone ; ' but people have spoken to me about it, and you had better destroy the book.' When I had told him that I was perfectly willing to do this, he continued, ' Also, I wish you to return the present your brothers and sisters sent me ; I can make no use of it, and it will be a proof to them that I place no value on worldly possessions.'

He now had his secretary summoned, and ordered him to write a letter in my name to my family, to the effect that it was not necessary to correspond any more ; and, after I had signed it, it was sent, together with the travelling-bag, to the Beit el Mal, to be despatched to Suakin. From that day I was more careful than ever to do nothing to increase the mistrust which I saw had sprung up in Abdullahi's mind. After Adlan's death, however, he thought it necessary to warn me again, and cautioned me most seriously against becoming mixed up in any sort of conspiracy.

Assembling all his mulazemin, he asserted, in the most
forcible language, that I was suspected of being a spy; that
he had been told I invariably questioned the camel postmen
who arrived about the situation; that I received visitors in
my house at night who were known to be out of favour with
him; and that I had gone so far as to inquire in what part
of his house his bedroom was situated. ' I am afraid,' he
continued, ' that if you do not change your line of conduct,
you will follow in the footsteps of my old enemy Adlan.'

This was rather a blow to me; but I knew that now,
more than ever, I had need of being calm and collected.
' Sire,' said I, in a loud voice, ' I cannot defend myself
against unknown enemies; but I am perfectly innocent of
all they have told you. I leave my detractors in the hands
of God. For more than six years, in sunshine and rain, I
have stood at your door, ever ready to receive and carry out
your orders. At your command I have given up all my
old friends, and have no communication with anyone. I
have even given up all connection with my relatives, and
that without the slightest remonstrance. Such a thing as
conspiracy has never even entered my heart. During all
these long years I have never made a complaint. Sire,
what have I done? All that I do is not done out of fear
of you, but out of love for you; and I cannot do more.
Should God still have further trials in store for me, I shall
calmly and willingly submit to my fate; but I have full
reliance in your sense of justice.'

' What have you to say to his words?' he said to the
assembled mulazemin, after a moment's silence. All, without exception, admitted that they had never noticed anything in my behaviour which could give rise to such a
suspicion; my enemies also—and I well knew who they
were, and who were responsible for getting me into this
dangerous position—were obliged to admit this. ' I forgive
you,' said he; ' but avoid for the future giving further cause
for complaint;' and, holding out his hand for me to kiss, he
signed to me to withdraw. He must have felt that he had

wronged me; for the next day he summoned me, spoke to me kindly, and warned me against my enemies, who, he said, were as a thorn in my flesh. I professed affection and confidence in him; and he then said, in quite a confidential tone, 'Do not make enemies, for you know that Mahdia is conducted in accordance with the Moslem law: should you be accused before the Kadi of treason, and two witnesses make good the accusation, you are lost; for I cannot go against the law to save you.'

What an existence in a country where one's very life hung on the evidence of two witnesses! Thanking him for his advice, I promised to follow it, and said I would, of course, do all in my power to deserve his confidence. When I returned home at midnight, tired and worn out by this constant strain, my devoted Saadalla informed me, to my great annoyance, that only a few minutes before one of the Khalifa's eunuchs had brought a closely-veiled female, who was now in my house.

I ought to have been greatly pleased about this, for it was a proof that the Khalifa had forgiven me; but my first thought was how to rid myself of this present without creating suspicion. Saadalla and I now entered the house, and, to my horror, I found that underneath the veil was an Egyptian, who had been born at Khartum, and who was consequently, from a Sudanese point of view, a lady of a comparatively fair complexion. She was seated on the carpet, and, after we had exchanged greetings, she replied to my query as to her nationality with such rapidity of speech that I, who spoke Arabic fairly well, had the greatest difficulty in following the romantic history of her life.

She was the daughter, she said, of an Egyptian officer, who, I afterwards learnt, had only been a private soldier, and who had fallen in the fight against the Shilluks, under Yusef Bey. As this had taken place upwards of twenty years before, I could, without any great effort of calculation, estimate fairly accurately that this good lady was well out of her teens; and as she admitted that her first husband had been killed during the capture of Khartum, that her mother was an Abyssinian who had been educated in Khartum, and was still alive, and that she had an enormous number of relatives, I really believe that, had my head not been clean-shaven, my hair would veritably have stood on end. This far-travelled and widely-experienced lady informed me that she had been one of the many hundreds of Abu Anga's wives, and I had now been chosen as the happy successor of this old slave. After his death she had been captured, with several of her rivals, by the Abyssinians when King John attacked Gallabat, but had been subsequently liberated by Zeki Tummal; and she knew so many details of all the fights in this neighbourhood that, had my memory been only capable of retaining them, they would have now been of great interest to my readers. A short time ago the Khalifa had ordered Abu Anga's remaining widows to be brought to Omdurman for distribution amongst his followers; she then went on to say that the Khalifa himself had especially selected her as my wife, and she added, in a subdued tone, that she rejoiced to have fallen into the hands of a fellow-countryman. I explained to her that I was not an Egyptian, but a European. As, however, my skin was somewhat tanned, and the circumstances in which I lived gave her a pretext for claiming me as a compatriot, I was obliged to say that I would provide as far as possible for her maintenance and comfort, and as night was well advanced, I bade her follow my servant Saadalla, who would make arrangements for her.

Such were the Khalifa's presents: instead of allocating a small sum of money from the Beit el Mal, by means of which I could have procured for myself a few comforts, he kept on sending me wives, who were not only a source of considerable expense to me, but also a cause of much anxiety and worry, inasmuch as I was continually struggling to free myself from their unwelcome presence. The next morning the Khalifa laughingly asked me if I had received his present, and if I liked it. With the lesson of two days ago still fresh in my mind, I assured him that I was only too happy to receive this fresh proof of his affection, and that, please God, I should always live in the enjoyment of his favour. When I returned to my house before mid-day prayer, I found it full of females, who, notwithstanding the remonstrances of Saadalla, and jeering at his wrath, had entered by main force, and now introduced themselves as the nearest relatives of Fatma el Beida (The White Fatma), as the Khalifa's present was called.

A decrepit old Abyssinian lady introduced herself as my future mother-in-law; from her loquacity I should instantly have recognised her as the mother of Fatma el Beida, and I could not help wondering how so small and fragile a body could contain so noisy and voluble a tongue. She assured me of her pleasure that her daughter had been confided to my care, adding that she was convinced that I would accord to her her rightful position in my household. Here was I, the slave of a tyrant, and obliged to submit to the most wretched of circumstances, and now she talked to me of the position due to her daughter! I assured her that I would of course treat her daughter well, and, apologizing that my time was so fully occupied, I fled. Before leaving, however, I ordered Saadalla to entertain them as well as he could, according to the custom of the country, and then to turn them all out, neck and crop, and, if necessary, to call the other servants to his assistance.

A few days afterwards the Khalifa again inquired about Fatma, and as I knew that he was most anxious that I should lead as quiet and secluded a life as possible, I told him that for the present I had no objection to her person; but as her numerous relatives might possibly come in contact with people whose acquaintance neither he, my master, nor I should consider desirable, and that as in my efforts to prevent this I frequently came into collision with both sides, it was naturally my earnest wish to prevent such disturbances. And I then went on to say that should she not submit to my arrangements, I proposed surrender-

ing Fatma entirely to her relatives, and with this proposition
the Khalifa appeared perfectly satisfied.

There was, however, no truth in this statement, for since
Saadalla had entertained and turned out his visitors I
had seen no one. Fearing to betray my intentions to the
Khalifa, I waited some time longer, and then sent Fatma
el Beida to her mother, whose whereabouts Saadalla had
at length discovered, and I instructed the lady to stay with
her mother until I should send for her. A few days afterwards I sent a few clothes to mother and daughter and a
small sum of money, with a message that she was free and
no longer under any obligations to me. Of course I told
the Khalifa what I had done, reiterating that I was most
anxious to have nothing to do with people who were
strangers to him and to me, and in this he saw an additional
proof of my anxiety to obey his orders. About a month
later the mother came to see me, and asked my permission
to marry her daughter to one of her relatives. I agreed to
this proposition with the greatest alacrity, and I left Fatma
el Beida the mother of a happy family in Omdurman.

CHAPTER XIV

DISSENSION AND DISCORD.

The Revolt of the Ashraf—Flight of Father Ohrwalder and the two
Sisters—The Khalifa revenges himself on the Ashraf—The Seizure
and Execution of the Mahdi's Uncles—Zeki Tummal's Return to
Omdurman laden with Booty—Khalifa Sherif arrested—' When
there is no Fire there is no Smoke '—I change my Quarters—Sad
News from Austria—The Khalifa falls ill—The Story of the Bird-
messenger—The Fall of Zeki Tummal—The Battle of Agordat—
The Capture of Kassala—The Congo Free State in Equatoria and
Bahr el Ghazal—I refuse to marry the Khalifa's Cousin.

MEANWHILE my old enemy Khaled, who had been kept in
prison for several months, had been released and sent to
Dongola as governor in place of Yunes, but he had not been

there long before he fell a victim to the intrigues of two of the Khalifa's cousins, who had been sent to watch his actions. Khaled was again recalled to Omdurman, and once more found himself in chains. This act served to still further irritate the relations and partisans of the late Mahdi, and in consequence the Khalifa Mohammed Sherif, in conjunction with two of the Mahdi's sons, who were scarcely twenty years of age, and many of his relatives, now agreed amongst themselves to shake off the hated yoke of Khalifa Abdullahi, and seize the reins of government. They secretly elaborated their plans in Omdurman, and gradually took into their confidence several of their friends and fellow-tribesmen. They also despatched letters to the Danagla living in the Gezira, whom they invited to come to Omdurman and join them; but one of the Jaalin Emirs betrayed them. He had been bound over by an oath to tell only his brother or best friends, and he at once informed the Khalifa, saying that he considered him his best friend. Apprised of this conspiracy, Abdullahi at once made counter arrangements; but the Ashraf, warned by their spies of the Khalifa's secret orders and doings, realized that their plot had been discovered, and immediately collected in that part of the town just north of the Khalifa's house, prepared for the fray.

Personally I longed for the fight, for I had only my life to lose, and that was in daily peril. I had before me the example of Ibrahim Adlan, and I knew that Abdullahi had no regard for the lives of his best and truest friends. Internal fighting must result in the weakening of my enemies, and that alone would have been a source of satisfaction to me; moreover, in the confusion which must arise, I might find an occasion to regain my liberty, and possibly I might be able to exercise some influence over the former Government troops, who I knew were much dissatisfied with their present treatment. Under such abnormal circumstances it was impossible to frame any distinct plan of action. My desire was that a fight should take place, and that I should make as much capital out of it as I could for my own personal benefit.

Some of the most excited of the mutineers now began firing, and some of those on our side, contrary to orders, replied; but it was by no means a fight, merely a few stray shots. The insurgents did not seem to know what they wanted; their party was undecided, their weapons were bad and out of repair, and so also was the courage of the Ashraf and their followers. After a short time the firing ceased, and on our side the total loss was five killed. The Khalifa sent out a proclamation, which was borne by Khalifa Ali Wad Helu, and to this summons the reply was favourable. They wished to know, they said, the conditions of reconciliation, and they were then told to name their proposals. The negotiations continued all that day and far into the night. They began again the following day, and, to my great regret, a clear understanding was arrived at, and agreed to by the Khalifa under a solemn oath. He promised complete forgiveness to all who had taken part in the insurrection ; to give to Khalifa Mohammed Sherif a position worthy of his dignity, and a seat in council; to allow him to again take possession of the standards which, after Nejumi's death, had been laid aside, and to collect volunteers under them ; and promised pecuniary support from the Beit el Mal to the Mahdi's relatives, in accordance with Sherif's proposals. In return for these concessions the insurgents agreed to give up all their arms, and submit unconditionally to the Khalifa's orders. The agreement was now ratified, and the terms of peace concluded by the delegates on both sides ; but somehow no one seemed in any hurry to execute them. On the following Friday morring the leaders of the insurgents came themselves before the Khalifa, and obtained a renewal of the promises he had made, in return for which they gave fresh attestations of loyalty ; and on the same afternoon Khalifa Sherif and the Mahdi's sons approached Abdullahi. Peace was now fully concluded, and the cavalry and infantry, which had been with us day and night since the disturbances began, were permitted to leave the mosque and return to their quarters ; but as the arms had not yet been handed over, the jehadia and mulazemin were ordered to remain at their posts.

On Sunday afternoon I had sent one of my servants to the missionary father, Joseph Ohrwalder, to inquire after him, and he had found his door closed. I had thoughtlessly made inquiries about him of his neighbours, the Greeks, and some of the former merchants, who, as my servant told me, had made a most careful search for him, but had been unable to trace him or the Missionary Sisters who had been with him. It at once flashed through my mind that possibly, during the disturbances, he might have found some trusty persons who had undertaken to effect his escape, and so it eventually transpired. Before evening prayer the Emir of the Muslemania (Europeans who had been forcibly made to adopt Mohammedanism), and the Syrian, George Stambuli, anxiously came and asked to be taken before the Khalifa, as they had something of considerable importance to tell him. The Khalifa, fully occupied with matters which he considered of great importance, ordered them to wait at the mosque, and after night prayers he asked them what they wanted. With trembling voices they informed him that Yusef el Gasis (Joseph the Priest) was missing since yesterday, also the women who were with him. Very much annoyed, the Khalifa at once summoned Nur el Gereifawi, the Emin Beit el Mal, and Mohammed Wahbi, the Prefect of the Police, and commanded them to do all in their power to overtake the fugitives, and bring them back to Omdurman, dead or alive. It was fortunate for the poor Greeks that the Khalifa was so much occupied with other matters, or he would (as Ohrwalder had lived amongst them) have arrested many and confiscated their property. Luckily, however, on the day of the outbreak, all the camels had been sent into the districts in order to bring in the troops,

and Gareifawi and Wahbi could only procure three camels
for the pursuit of Ohrwalder, who knew that the success of
his flight depended on its rapidity.   From the depth of my
heart I hoped he might succeed.   He had suffered a great
deal, and had borne it with Christian fortitude and patience.
I now felt completely deserted.   He was the only man with
whom I was intellectually on a par, and with whom I could,
though very rarely, talk a few words in my mother tongue.

The following day I was summoned before the Khalifa,
who angrily reproached me for Ohrwalder's flight.   'He is
one of your own race, and is in communication with you.
Why did you not draw my attention to its possibility, so
that I might have taken precautions ?   I am positive you
knew of his intention to escape,' said he.   'Sire, pardon
me,' said I.   'How could I know of his intention to
escape, and how could I tell you that he had done so ?
Since the outbreak of the revolt attempted by your God-
forsaken enemies, and which, thanks to the Almighty, you
have now defeated by your wisdom, I have not moved day
or night from my post.   Had I known that he was a traitor
I should have at once told you of it.'   To this he angrily
replied : 'No doubt your Consul arranged for him to be
taken away from here.'

Amongst the last letters which I had received was one
written in Arabic from the Austro-Hungarian Consul-
General, Von Rosty, to the Khalifa, in which he thanked
him for the kind treatment of the members of the former
Catholic Mission, and at the same time asked his permission
to send them a messenger, for whom he begged a free pass,
as they were under Austrian protection, and as His Majesty
the Emperor had a special regard for them.   The Khalifa
had shown me the letter, which he had left unanswered ;
but from that day he had looked upon the members of the
Mission as my compatriots, and was now convinced that
they had been assisted to escape by the aid of the Consul-
General.   I now remarked to the Khalifa that possibly merchants belonging to the frontier tribes, and who often came

to Omdurman, might have taken advantage of the disturbances in order to help Ohrwalder and the Sisters to escape,
so as to obtain some pecuniary reward for themselves.
Abdullahi, who was still much preoccupied with the revolt,
came round to my opinion, and after admonishing me to
remain perfectly loyal, he dismissed me.

In spite of all Abdullahi's promises to the Ashraf, he soon
found a pretext for seizing thirteen of the ringleaders, as
well as the two uncles of the Mahdi, and these he shipped
off in a boat to Fashoda, consigned to his faithful Emir
Zeki Tummal, who had been previously sent there to quell
a revolt of the Shilluks. On their arrival Zeki Tummal
had them closely confined for eight days in a zariba with
scarcely any food or water, giving them only just sufficient
to keep them alive; then, in accordance with the secret
instructions he had received, he had them beaten to death
with freshly-cut sticks from thorny trees. The execution
took place in front of the whole army, and before this cruel
operation began, their clothing was ruthlessly torn from
their emaciated bodies.

Zeki Tummal now returned to Omdurman laden with
booty; he brought with him thousands of female slaves,
and immense herds of cattle, the sale of which brought in a
large sum of ready money. Most of Zeki's Emirs indig-
nantly complained of his tyranny, and even asserted to the
Khalifa that, if he could obtain sufficient followers, he would
not hesitate to make himself independent; but the latter,
by making rich presents of female slaves, money, and cattle
to the Khalifa and his brother, succeeded in remaining in
their good graces.

Whilst Zeki Tummal was in Omdurman, the Khalifa
carried out a series of manœuvres between his forces and
those quartered in Omdurman, and personally took the
command, but as he had absolutely no idea of military
science, and as the thirty thousand troops of whom he disposed were entirely without discipline, the manœuvres resulted in the most hopeless confusion and disorder, and the

blame for this invariably fell on my devoted head, for the Khalifa employed me as a sort of aide-de-camp, and when he became inextricably muddled up he hurled abuse at me, and said I had purposely perverted his orders to make mischief. Of course I did not dare remonstrate with him, and quietly continued to carry out his orders. At length he declared the exercises over, ordered Zeki Tummal off to Gallabat, and, as was usually the case, commended me for my services, and presented me with two Black young ladies as a proof of his good-will.

Meanwhile, Khalifa Sherif had heard of the murder of his two relatives, and openly protested against this tyrannical proceeding, thus giving Abdullahi an opportunity of taking the revenge for which he had so patiently waited. He declared him to be guilty of disobedience to the instructions which the Mahdi had so strictly enforced, and of inattention to the Divine inspiration of the Prophet. He therefore ordered Khalifa Ali and the Kadis to take him to task for the manner in which he had expressed himself, and to point out to him that the entirely false impression he had of his own rights as Khalifa had brought about the death of his own relatives and followers. Promptly assembling all the Kadis and principal Emirs, they decided that Khalifa Sherif should be immediately arrested. On the following day the mulazemin being formed up in square on the open space between Abdullahi's house and the Mahdi's tomb, they went in a body to him, informed him that he was to be arrested, counselled submission, and advised him to come with them of his own free-will. Too late, he now realized what he had brought upon himself by his careless and ill-considered talking. Going outside, he was received by the mulazemin under the command of Arabi Dafalla ; when he asked for his shoes, they refused him ; and, on coming out of the mosque, he was driven and pushed along at such a rate that he twice fell to the ground from pure exhaustion, arriving at length at the Saier in a deplorable condition. Here six irons were hammered on to his legs, so that he could scarcely

move, and a small straw hut was allotted to him as his
abode. Cut off from all intercourse with his fellow-creatures,
and with only the bare ground to lie upon, he had ample
time to realize that the sacred promises given by a Khalifa
were of no avail when it was a question of upholding his
authority, or satisfying his thirst for vengeance. The Mahdi's
two young sons were sent to their grandfather, Ahmed Sharfi,
who was ordered to keep them closely locked up in his
house, and allow no one to see them. This Ahmed was an
old man, and had made an immense fortune by robbery;
fearing to lose it, he was as submissive as a slave to the
Khalifa, and had thus to some extent gained his affection.

Soon after this occurrence I passed through a period of
considerable excitement. Yunes had sent on a man from
Dongola to the Khalifa; he had come from Cairo, and was
charged with important information from the Government.
He was received personally by the Khalifa in the presence
of all the Kadis. I had a foreboding that the man's arrival
was somehow connected with me, and I endeavoured to discover from one of the Kadis, who was a friend of mine, what
had happened. He hurriedly told me that I had nothing to
fear, and advised me not to show the slightest interest in
the matter, lest I might be suspected. After prayers the
Kadis and the messenger were again summoned before the
Khalifa, and, to my great relief, I saw the man soon afterwards tied hand and foot and carried off to prison. My
comrades were quarrelling amongst themselves as to the
cause of the man's imprisonment, but mindful of the advice
I had received, I was careful to abstain from any interference.
The following day, when I had gone to my house for a short
time, I was suddenly summoned by the Khalifa, and found
several of the Kadis with him. In compliance with his
orders I seated myself down with them, and he began to
speak. Turning to the assembly, he informed them that he
had continually urged me to be loyal, that he cared for me
as a father cared for his son, and that he had steadily refused
to believe the numerous accusations which were from time

to time brought up against me; and then, turning to me, he completed his speech with the Arabic proverb, ' Where there is no fire, there is no smoke,' adding, ' but with you there is a great deal of smoke. The messenger said yesterday that you are a Government spy, and that your monthly salary is paid to your representative in Cairo, who forwards it to you here. He affirms that he has seen your signature in the Government office in Egypt, and that you assisted Yusef el Gasis to escape; he adds, moreover, that you are pledged to the English, in the event of an attack on Omdurman, to seize the powder and ammunition stores, which they know are situated opposite to your house. We have at once had the man imprisoned, for he formerly escaped from here. What have you to say in your defence?'

'Sire!' I replied, ' God is merciful, and you are just. I am no spy. I have never had any communication with the Government; and it is absolutely untrue that I receive a salary which is forwarded to me here. My brothers, your mulazemin, who go in and out of my house, know that I am often in the greatest want, and it is only my deep respect for you which prevents me from complaining; but if he states that he has seen my signature, then he is guilty of a second lie, for I am certain that he is quite unable to read any European language. I will, if you wish, write on a paper several names, and amongst them my own; if he can discover it, then it will be a proof that he can read our language; but that will not necessarily prove that I am a spy.' ' And what else have you against the man?' asked the Khalifa. ' What service has the man rendered to Government,' I continued, ' that, supposing I am a spy, I should trust this fugitive with my secrets? As far as Yusef el Gasis is concerned, you, my master, well know that he escaped at a time when it was absolutely impossible for me to have any communication with him. I, who am always near you, have no intercourse with people who assist others to fly; and even supposing I had, and that I were a traitor, it would certainly be much more natural that I should have

escaped myself. It is quite possible the English may know
that my house is opposite to the powder magazine; for the
man who, with your kind permission, brought me the letters
from my brothers and sisters, knew it, and in all probability
told them about it. It is also possible that my relatives,
with whom, at your express command, I have ceased to
have any communication, should make inquiries about my
welfare through the Government clerks and merchants who
sometimes go from here to Cairo, and who probably know
the position of my house; but the assertion that, in case of
war, I had engaged myself to seize your ammunition stores,
is quite ridiculous. As far as I can judge, the Government
would never dare to attack you, who are the ever-victorious
and unconquerable Khalifa, in your own country. And if
this well-nigh impossible event should take place, how do I
know that I shall be in my present house at that time?
Moreover, at such a critical period, my hope and desire is
to stand in the front rank of your victorious troops, and there
seek an opportunity of proving my loyalty and devotion by
shedding my blood in your cause. Sire, I rely upon your
justice, which is well known to all. Will you sacrifice one
who has been for so many years your devoted servant, to
the whim of a Dongolawi, who is one of your enemies?'
' How do you know that the man who has given evidence
against you is a Dongolawi?' asked the Khalifa quickly.
' Some time ago I saw the man at your gate with Abderrahman Wad en Nejumi esh Shahid '* (' the martyr,' as he
was called after his death), ' and owing to his forwardness
and impudence I had to call on your mulazemin to remove
him by main force. No doubt he now wishes to revenge
himself, and at the same time curry favour with you, by
casting suspicion on me. You, to whom God has given
wisdom to govern your subjects, will also judge me right-
eously and fairly.'
' I have summoned you here,' said the Khalifa, after a

By mere chance I had heard that the man's name was Taib Wad
Haj Ali, and that he had once been in Omdurman with Nejumi.

ong pause, ' not to judge you, but to show you that, in spite
of the frequent attempts to cast suspicion on you, I have in
no way withdrawn my confidence in you. Had I believed
what the man said, I should not have imprisoned him; no
doubt you have enemies here, and there are probably envious
people who are jealous of your being near me. But beware!'
where there is no fire, there is no smoke.' He then signed
to me to withdraw, and soon afterwards the assembly
broke up.

That night I asked one of my comrades whom I knew I
could trust to tell me what the Khalifa had said after I had
left. He told me that Abdullahi admitted the man was a
liar, but that there might be some truth in his statement;
he had also said I might possibly have enemies in Cairo
who were intriguing against me. This had also occurred
to me whilst I was speaking, but I did not mention it, as I
hesitated to throw down all my cards; now that he had
thought of it himself, my silence had stood me in good stead,
for I could bring forward this argument in my defence,
should some fresh accusation be brought against me. But
how long was I to continue in this wretched position? How
long was I to keep up this constant strain of always standing
on the defensive? how much longer could my present relations with the Khalifa last? I knew he was only waiting
or an opportunity to make me harmless, for he was perfectly
well aware that I was at heart his enemy; but, in truth, I
thanked God most fervently that he treated me with greater
leniency than he did the rest. How difficult it was to carry
out Madibbo's advice! but how true it was that he who lives
long sees much!

The following morning, after prayers, as I was on my
way home, I was overtaken by Gereifawi, who had succeeded
Adlan, and was on friendly terms with me. ' You are a rare
visitor,' said I, shaking hands with him; ' please God you
have good reasons for it!' ' Yes,' said he; ' but I am come
to disturb you. I require your house, and I must ask you
to leave it to-day. I will give you one in place of it which

lies to the south-east of the mosque, and in which the Khalifa's guests are usually housed ; it is somewhat smaller than your own, but you have only the road between it and the mosque, and this will thoroughly suit a pious man like you !' 'All right,' said I ; 'but tell me privately who sent you here—the Khalifa or Yakub ?' 'Ah, that is a secret !' said he, laughing ; 'but, after your conversation yesterday with the Khalifa, you can surely understand the reason ; probably,' he continued ironically, 'our master, out of his great love for you, wishes to have you in close proximity to himself ; your house is scarcely two hundred paces from his own. When may I come and take over your old house ?' 'I shall have finished moving by the evening,' said I ; 'it will take me some little time to remove the fodder for my horse and mule. Is the house I am to have uninhabited ?' 'Of course it is. I have given orders for it to be cleaned, and will now return to make the necessary arrangements ; but you had better begin moving at once, and I hope your new house will bring better luck than your old one,' said Gareifawi, leaving me.

Undoubtedly, this was a very clear case of want of confidence in me on the Khalifa's part. He was anxious to remove me from the neighbourhood of the ammunition stores and powder magazine, which, in case of war, I was supposed to seize. I now called together my household, and told them to begin moving at once. They cursed the Khalifa freely, and called down all the punishments of Heaven on his head. Little by little, year by year, they had gone on building. They had dug wells fifty feet deep, and planted lemon and pomegranate trees, which were just about to bear fruit, and had, so to speak, made themselves comfortable. For me the move was quite immaterial. How I had prayed to leave this house, though not in this way ! However, as Gereifawi had said, perhaps the new house would bring me better luck, and I was by no means the only man who had been turned out of his abode at short notice. The whole portion of the city lying north of the

Khalifa's house had been vacated at a moment's notice by the Ashraf and their relatives, and they had not even been allowed to remove their furniture, nor had they received the smallest compensation. They had been given a patch of stony ground to the west of the town, where they had been ordered to build fresh houses. After all, I was better off than they. Recent events had depressed me considerably, and I saw that the situation was now becoming almost unbearable ; but more trouble was in store for me which was to throw completely into the background that of which I now complained.

One of my acquaintances, a Darfur merchant who had frequently travelled backwards and forwards to Egypt, Alexandria, and Syria, and who had gradually understood the various nationalities, realized that I was an Austrian. He had surmised correctly that, although a captive for many years, and shut off from all communication with my own people, I still took an intense interest in all that concerned my native land. He spoke to me in the mosque, told me hurriedly about affairs in Egypt, and then handed me an Egyptian newspaper of old date which, he said, had accidentally come into his hands in Alexandria, and which contained an article about Austrian affairs. Hurrying home, I opened the paper, and found, to my dismay, the news of the death of our Crown Prince Rudolf. I cannot describe the distress which this news caused me. I had served in his regiment, and I had never given up hope that some day I should return home, and have the pleasure of assuring him that, under all the strange and sad circumstances of my eventful life, I had always endeavoured to uphold the honour of an officer belonging to the Imperial regiment. But what were the trials and troubles of one obscure individual in comparison with this great national calamity ? Nothing !

Again and again my mind turned to the grief of our beloved Emperor, to whom we Austrians look up as to a father. What must he have felt and suffered !

Here, in the midst of this unsympathetic crowd, my mind

was filled with these sad thoughts ; but I did not dare show
that I was affected. It required all my self-control to hide
from the rude gaze of the Mahdists the expressions of distress
which came over my face when I thought of my beloved
home, and, in the internal struggle which was going on
almost continuously, I sometimes longed for the time when
an end should be put to my wretched existence. To-day
all the old sores had broken out afresh. The man would
have done me a far greater service had he kept back the
newspaper. It had only brought fresh trouble upon me,
and depressed me more than ever. My comrades at the
Khalifa's door—ignorant of the real cause of my sorrow—
advised me to appear as cheerful as possible, and to show
no displeasure about my enforced removal to another house,
as the Khalifa was sure to have instructed his spies to watch
me carefully, and see how I took his unwelcome order. I
therefore tried to look as unconcerned as possible, and, to
account for my depression, I pretended to be unwell. What
a life of dissimulation ! Some time previous to the events
I have just described, Tokar had been retaken by the
Egyptian army, and the Khalifa, fearing a further advance,
recalled Abu Girga, who was a Dongolawi, and replaced
him by his relative, Mussaid. He now despatched Abu
Girga with two steamers to Equatoria to relieve Omar
Saleh, who, it will be remembered, had been sent there after
Karamalla's withdrawal, and had established the Dervish
headquarters at Reggaf on the departure of Emin and
Stanley.

A few days after the steamers had left the Khalifa fell
seriously ill with an attack of typhus fever. All Omdurman
watched the course of the illness with the most intense
anxiety, for his death would have been the signal for a
complete change in the administration of the country.
Khalifa Ali Wad Helu, who, according to Mahdist law,
should be the successor, watched the illness with almost
breathless interest, and his followers and tribe showed such
deep concern that they fell under the suspicion of wishing

to seize the reins of government. The Khalifa's powerful constitution, however, got the better of the malady, and it seemed as if the wretched inhabitants of the Sudan had not been sufficiently punished, and that God did not yet intend to remove from them this terrible scourge. After an illness of about three weeks Abdullahi took the first possible opportunity of appearing before his followers, who greeted him with frantic acclamations, the outcome in the majority of cases of a desire merely to make a noise. Only his own relatives and some of the western Arabs really rejoiced at his recovery. But the Khalifa had no delusions about the imaginary sentiment to which his followers had given vent during his illness. He knew perfectly well that in showing the preference to his own tribe he had given umbrage to many of the western Arabs, who, being strangers to the land, it was most necessary to retain on his side. The inhabitants of the Nile Valley and of the Gezira, the majority of whom were Jaalin and Danagla, were his enemies ; but, disarmed and their property confiscated, he had made them powerless, and every now and then he sent considerable detachments of them to reinforce Darfur, Gallabat, and Reggaf. He did not hide from himself that Khalifa Ali and his followers were anxious to step into his shoes ; but he knew that they would never be foolish enough to attempt to carry out their plans by main force, as the Ashraf had done.

Now that I had my abode close to him he was more suspicious than ever of me. He continually inquired of my comrades if this strict supervision did not make me indignant, and he did all he could to find fault with my conduct ; but, fortunately, the mulazemin were on friendly terms with me, and always reported favourably of me. At the same time they secretly warned me that the Khalifa's dislike of me was increasing, and that I must be most careful.

One day, in the month of December, 1892, when I had just left the Khalifa's door to take a short rest, one of the

mulazemin summoned me to the Khalifa's presence. I
found him in the reception-room, surrounded by his Kadis,
and the threats and reprimands which I had received on the
occasion of Taib Haj Ali's calumny were still fresh in my
mind. I was therefore considerably dismayed when the
Khalifa, without returning my salute, ordered me to take
my seat amongst the judges. 'Take this thing,' said he,
after a short pause, and in a very severe tone, 'and see what
it contains.' I at once arose and took in both hands the
object he gave me, and then sat down again. It consisted
of a brass ring of about four centimetres in diameter,
attached to which was a small metal case about the size
and shape of a revolver cartridge. An attempt had been
made to open it, and I could plainly see that it contained a
paper. This was indeed an anxious moment for me. Could
it be a letter from my relations, or from the Egyptian
Government, and had the messenger who brought it been
captured? Whilst I was engaged in opening the case with
the knife which had been given me, I turned over in my
mind how I should act, and what I should say; and, as
good luck would have it, I had not on this occasion to
have recourse to dissimulation. Pulling out two small
papers and opening them, I found inscribed on them, in
minute but legible handwriting, in the German, French,
English, and Russian languages, the following:

'This crane has been bred and brought up on my estate
at Ascania Nova, in the Province of Tauride, in South
Russia. Whoever catches or kills this bird is requested to
communicate with me, and inform me where it occurred.

'(Signed)   F. R. FALZ-FEIN.

'*September*, 1892.'

I now raised my head, which hitherto I had kept closely
bent down; and the Khalifa asked, 'Well, what do the
papers contain?' 'Sire,' I replied, 'this case must have
been fastened to the neck of a bird which has been killed.

Its owner, who lives in Europe, has requested that anyone
who finds the bird should let him know where it was caught
or killed.' 'You have spoken the truth,' said the Khalifa,
in a somewhat more amiable tone; 'the bird was killed by
a Shaigi near Dongola, and the cartridge case was found
attached to its neck. He took it to the Emir Yunes,
whose secretary was unable to decipher the writing of the
Christian, and he therefore forwarded it to me. Tell me
now what is written on the paper?' I translated the
message, word for word, and, at the Khalifa's command,
also tried to describe the geographical position of the
country from which the bird had come, and the distance it
had travelled before it was killed. 'This is one of the
many devilries of those unbelievers,' he said, at last, 'who
waste their time in such useless nonsense. A Mohammedan
would never have attempted to do such a thing.'

He then ordered me to hand over the case to his
secretary, and signed to me to withdraw; but I managed
to take one more hurried glance at the paper: Ascania
Nova, Tauride, South Russia, I repeated over and over
again to imprint it on my memory. The mulazemin at the
door anxiously awaited my return, and when I came out
from the presence of my tyrannical master with a placid
countenance they seemed greatly pleased. On my way to
my house I continued to repeat to myself the name of
the writer and his residence, and determined that should
Providence ever grant me my freedom I should not fail to
let him know what had happened to his bird.

In accordance with orders, Mahmud Ahmed, who, on the
death of Osman Wad Adam, had succeeded him, now returned to Omdurman with all his available troops (about
five thousand) from Darfur, leaving there only sufficient
men for the garrison. He pitched his camp at Dem Yunes
on the south of the city.

Once more I underwent a period of considerable trial.
The Khalifa again instituted a series of military manœuvres
for all the troops in Omdurman, and, as usual, they re-

sulted in the wildest confusion. I had to perform the duties of aide-de-camp, and invariably had to bear the blame for everything that went wrong; but all things come to an end, and at last Mahmud Ahmed was ordered back to El Fasher after his troops had renewed their oath of allegiance, in return for which they received some new jibbas.

The Khalifa now turned his attention to the Equatorial regions, and despatched two other steamers with three hundred men, under the command of his relative Arabi Dafalla, to Reggaf with instructions to depose Abu Girga, and throw him into chains. It was abundantly clear that the latter had only been sent to Reggaf to get him out of the way. Dafalla's departure was also taken advantage of to exile Khaled, who had been lying heavily chained in the Saier.

Next came the turn of Zeki Tummal to fall into disfavour, and once more the jealousy and pernicious influence of Yakub prevailed. Zeki, summoned suddenly from Gedaref, was, on his arrival in Omdurman, hurried off to the general prison, where his body was covered with as much weight of iron as it could possibly bear. He was then removed to a small detached stone hut, deprived of all communication with others, and not even allowed sufficient bread and water to sustain life, and consequently, after an imprisonment of twenty days, he succumbed to hunger and thirst.

Ahmed Wad Ali now succeeded Zeki in the supreme command, and, anxious to refute any idea of timidity, he sought to gain military renown. He obtained the Khalifa's permission to undertake operations against the Arab tribes living between Kassala and the Red Sea, who were subject to the Italians; but he received distinct orders not to attack any troops quartered in forts. He was allowed to utilize the services of the Kassala garrison under Mussaid Gaidum, and now made all preparations for a campaign. Leaving Gedaref with his army early in November, 1893, he joined

the Kassala force, and advancing east towards Agordat he
came up with the Italian troops, who were in an entrenched
position.   As they were in such small numbers he resolved,
in spite of the Khalifa's instructions, to attack them; but
he was heavily defeated, and himself killed, together with
his two principal leaders.

The Khalifa now nominated his cousin Ahmed Fedil as
commander of the Gedaref army, and gave him strict injunctions to remain entirely on the defensive.   He proceeded
to his post by way of Kassala, in order to collect the
scattered troops, who, after the defeat at Agordat, had
forced themselves on the villagers, and were harrying the
country for food.   Once again the Khalifa's equanimity was
upset by a rumour that the Italians now intended advancing
on Kassala; but this news was followed soon afterwards by
a contradiction, and he became pacified.   Indeed, he had
publicly announced his intention of avenging Ahmed Wad
Ali's defeat, though in reality he had not the slightest idea
of doing so; but, in his ignorance, he believed that these
false threats would prevent his enemies from assuming the
offensive.   He also sent small detachments of horse and
spear-men to Gedaref.

A few months had elapsed since this catastrophe, when
one day, just after morning prayers, three men presented
themselves at the door of the Khalifa's house, and urgently
demanded to be taken before him.   I at once recognised
them as Baggara Emirs, who had been stationed at Kassala,
and from the expression of their faces I could see that the
news they brought would not be welcome to the Khalifa.
In a few minutes they were admitted, and soon afterwards
a considerable disturbance took place round the Khalifa's
door.   Khalifa Ali Wad Helu, Yakub, as well as all the
Kadis, received a sudden summons to attend at a council.
The Khalifa's suspicions had been verified, and Kassala,
after a short fight, had been captured by the Italians.

It was impossible to withhold this news from the public.
The ombeya was sounded, the great war-drums were beaten,

the horses were saddled, and the Khalifa, accompanied by all his mulazemin, and an immense number of horse and spear-men, solemnly rode down to the banks of the Nile. Arrived here, he forced his horse into the river till the water reached its knees, and, drawing out his sword, and pointing towards the east, he shouted out in a loud voice, ' Allahu akbar! Allahu akbar!' ('God is most great!') Each time the cry was taken up by the immense crowd; but the majority were inwardly rejoicing at the Khalifa's discomfiture. They longed for him to receive fresh humiliation, thinking thereby to lighten the terrible yoke they bore. After this display the Khalifa turned his horse about, came back to the river bank, dismounted, and sat down on his sheepskin. A great crowd now collected round him, and he informed them of the fall of Kassala, declaring that his followers had been taken unawares by enormous numbers of the enemy, just after morning prayers, and had been forced to retire. He stated, however, that all the war material, women, and children had been saved, that the losses had been insignificant, whilst the enemy had suffered so heavily that they now bitterly regretted having taken the town. Even his most devoted adherents well knew that these words were a mere pretext for covering a disgraceful defeat.

The Khalifa knew perfectly well the difficulties of re-capturing Kassala, but in order to make a show of doing something, he sent instructions to Osman Digna, who was at Adarama on the Atbara, some three days' march from Berber, to join Mussaid at Goz Regeb with all his available forces. At the same time he ordered Ahmed Fedil to make a military post of a thousand rifles at El Fasher on the Atbara, about one and a half days' journey from Kassala. He also sent detachments of troops from Omdurman to Asubri on the Atbara, midway between El Fasher and Goz Regeb. He continued to assert most resolutely that he intended shortly to advance on Kassala; but all these arrangements were made entirely with a view to establishing a series of defensive posts along the line of the Atbara,

304

whilst the troops he was constantly collecting were intended to oppose the advance of the enemy towards Omdurman.

In the midst of all this disturbance and excitement two steamers arrived from Reggaf, bringing large cargoes of ivory and slaves, besides quantities of loot captured from Fadl el Maula, one of Emin's old officers, who, on the latter's departure, had with some followers nominally entered the service of the Congo Free State. Amongst the trophies he sent to Omdurman were four Congo Free State flags made of blue bunting, with a five-pointed yellow star in the centre, also two suits of black uniform with buttons, on which the words 'Travail et Progrès' were engraved. This was the first time I had seen the badge of the Congo Free State, of the existence of which I had heard; but I had no notion of its size or the extent of its boundaries. Several European letters had also been found in Fadl el Maula's camp; but the Khalifa did not show them to me. He preferred to remain in ignorance of their contents rather than that I should gain some insight into affairs in those regions.

Soon afterwards came further disquieting news from Darfur. Mahmud Ahmed now reported that Christians had entered the Bahr el Ghazal districts, and were attempting to win over the native tribes, with whom they had already made treaties. They had arrived, he said, at Hofret en Nahas (the copper-mines near Kalaka, on the south-western Darfur frontier). This news was of the greatest importance, and the Khalifa had every reason to feel alarmed and uneasy.

When Egypt governed the Sudan, it was from the Bahr el Ghazal provinces that they recruited the men for the Sudanese battalions, who had come either of their own free will or had been forcibly impressed. Owing to the climate and plenteous rainfall the country is more highly cultivated than any portion of the Nile Valley lying between Kowa and Reggaf. Besides, the majority of the tribes who inhabit these districts are, owing to internal dissensions, incapable of uniting, and would thus rather facilitate than retard the advance of any foreign power wishing to make itself master of the province. For the Khalifa, however, the possession of this country is of vital importance. Its ruler, he knows, virtually holds the Sudan in his hands. These various Black tribes have no love for the Arab slave-hunters, and would aid any power which would guarantee their protection. The recruitment of four or five thousand local levies possessing fighting qualities of a high order would, for such a power, be a matter of no difficulty; and in the space of four or five years an army of from fifteen to twenty thousand men might be raised, by which not only Darfur and Kordofan, but indeed the whole Sudan, could be conquered.

Abdullahi therefore was not slow to realize the situation, and he at once gave orders to Mahmud Ahmed to despatch a force from Southern Darfur into these districts, and drive out the strangers who had dared to penetrate the Bahr el Ghazal province.

In compliance with these instructions the Emir Khatem Musa, with a considerable force, was sent south from Shakka into the northern Bahr el Ghazal districts, and the Faroghé, Kâra, Bongo, and other frontier tribes with whom the Europeans had made treaties, being left without support, at once submitted to the Mahdists who occupied their countries.

One day I was summoned before the Khalifa, who handed to me several documents written in French, which he ordered me to translate. They included two letters from Lieutenant de la Kéthulle to his assistants, containing various orders and instructions. They had been originally in the hands of the Sheikh of Faroghé, who had handed them over to Khatem Musa. In addition to these the Khalifa showed me a treaty which had been drawn up between Sultan Hamed Wad Musa of the Faroghé and the representative of the Congo Free State. It was signed in August, 1894, by Hamed Wad Musa and the representative of the Congo Free State, and was witnessed by Sultan Zemio and the Sultan of Tiga, the names of the two latter being written in European characters.

I hurriedly translated these papers verbally to the Khalifa, and was much interested in seeing how, on this occasion, his curiosity got the better of his suspicions, though he did all he could to prevent me from noticing this.

'I did not summon you,' he said, 'merely to translate these letters, which, after all, are of not the smallest importance to me, though I have instructed Mahmud Ahmed to drive out these Christians, who are only travellers, and in small numbers, from the Bahr el Ghazal province; but I have also a proposal to make to you. I look upon you as one of us—as my friend and faithful adherent—and I have decided to publicly make known this fact by giving to you as a wife one of my cousins—one of my next of kin. What have you to say to this?' This offer did not greatly surprise me, for he had several times hinted as much. I was perfectly well aware that his object was not to publicly show appreciation of me, but to have me carefully watched in my own house. He wished to place me under surveillance in order to discover if I had any secret relations with outside countries. Through trusty friends I had ascertained that he earnestly sought some plausible grounds for making me, as he called it, 'harmless'; but in doing so he wished to justify his action before the public, by showing me more consideration as a foreigner than I had been a native. I knew too well, however, that if a man of his unscrupulous determination, who had not spared his best friends, such as Ibrahim Adlan and Kadi Ahmed, would not hesitate to take full advantage of the slightest proof of my disloyalty in order to rid himself of me.

'Sire,' I replied, 'may God bless you and give you victory over all your enemies. I feel highly honoured by your magnanimous offer; but hear of me, I pray you, the truth. Your relative is not merely descended from royalty, but from the Prophet himself. She therefore deserves to

be treated with every consideration. Unfortunately I have
a very quick temper, and at times have great difficulty in
controlling myself. Domestic quarrels would undoubtedly
arise, which might be the cause of estrangement between
you, my master, and myself. My only desire is to remain
in your greatest favour. I pray God this may ever be so,
for I dread the occurrence of anything which might cause
me to fall into disfavour.'

'I have known you now intimately for ten years,' said
the Khalifa, 'and I have never known you to be thoughtless or quick-tempered. I have often presented you with
wives, and they have never complained to me of domestic
quarrels. It is true, however, that I have heard you have
either made presents of them to your servants, or have
given them their liberty. It seems to me that, although
you pretend to be one of us, you really wish to adhere to
the manners and customs of your tribe. [He did not refer
to religion, as I suppose he thought that might hurt my
feelings.] I mean that you wish to have only one wife.'

'Sire,' I replied, 'you have often honoured me with
presents of slaves; but you surely do not wish me to be
their slave. If I have married them to my servants or
sent them away, it is because they have been disobedient,
or have behaved badly. You have been misinformed if you
think that I wish to adhere to the custom of my country
to have only one wife, for I have already three.'

'Very well, he said, 'I believe you; and so you refuse
to marry my cousin?'

'Sire,' I replied, 'I do not refuse; but I merely inform
you of my uncertain temper, so that I may prevent un-
pleasantness in the future. Indeed, I am highly honoured
by your kind offer, and I beg you to try and see if I am
worthy of it.' He understood perfectly well that what I
had said was tantamount to a refusal, and he closed the
conversation by making a sign to me to withdraw. This
offer had placed me in a most difficult position. I thoroughly
understood the Khalifa. By not joyfully accepting his offer

I had hurt his pride; and now I longed more than ever for liberty. Some months before I had sent a Sudanese merchant to Cairo, and had begged the Austrian Consul-General to place, through him, the necessary means at my disposal to effect my escape. But how often had I attempted negotiations of this sort through merchants and others, and how often had I been doomed to disappointment and failure!

CHAPTER XV.

MISCELLANEOUS REMARKS.

The Person and Characteristics of Khalifa Abdullahi—The Fate of the Mahdist Chronicler—The Princesses of Darfur—The Khalifa's Family Life—His Harem—The Organization of his Body-guard—Enforced Attendance at the Mosque—The Postal System—Military Parades—Elevation of the Western Arabs and Oppression of the River Tribes—The Military Situation and Strength—Guns and Ammunition—Revenue and Expenditure—Courage.

I WILL now say a few words regarding the Khalifa's person and his characteristics.

Sayed Abdullahi Ibn Sayed Mohammed belongs to the Taaisha section of the Baggaras (as all cattle-owning nomad Arabs are called). This section inhabits the country in the south-western portion of Darfur, and the Khalifa himself is descended from the Aulad Om Sura of the Jubarat family. I have already referred to Abdullahi's early life, and how he had established a connection with the slave-hunting Arabs when still quite a youth. He joined the Mahdi at the age of thirty-five, and was then a slim and active, though powerfully built man; but latterly he has become very stout, and his lightness of gait has long since disappeared. He is now forty-nine years of age, but looks considerably older, and the hair of his beard is almost white. At times the expression of his face is one of charming amiability, but more generally it is one of dark sternness, in which tyranny and unscrupulous resolution are unmistakably visible. He is rash and quick-tempered, acting often without a moment's consideration, and when in this mood even his own brother dares not approach him. His nature is suspicious to a degree to everyone, his nearest relatives and members of his household included. He admits that loyalty and fidelity are rare qualities, and that those who have to deal with him invariably conceal their real feelings in order to gain their own ends. He is most susceptible to flattery, and consequently receives an inordinate amount from everyone. No one dares to speak to him without referring, in the most fulsome terms, to his wisdom, power, justice, courage, generosity, and truthfulness. He accepts this absurd adulation with the greatest pleasure and satisfaction; but woe to him who in the slightest degree offends his dignity!

The following episode will give the reader a fair idea of his arbitrary nature:

A certain Kadi named Ismail Wad Abdel Kader, who had been well educated in Cairo, had gained great favour with the Mahdi by having written a laudatory account of his early victories. This had so fully gratified the great religious reformer that he instructed Abdel Kader to continue to chronicle the various important events as they happened, and further instructed his principal Emirs to forward to him detailed histories of all that occurred within their respective commands. In time these chronicles grew into an elaborate historical and inflated statement of Mahdist rule in the Sudan; and, after the Mahdi's death, the Khalifa, who had installed Abdel Kader as state chronicler, ordered the continuance of the work. One day, however, during a pleasure-party, the historian had been overheard to say that present affairs in the Sudan, as compared with those in Egypt, might be described by the following simile: The Khalifa might be considered as the Khedive Ismail Pasha, whilst, in the same proportion, he, Abdel Kader, might be likened to Ismail Pasha el Mofettish, who had been the Viceroy's principal adviser and friend. This thoughtless statement was immediately reported to Abdullahi, who, furious at such a comparison, at once ordered the judges to assemble and make a full inquiry into the matter, and, if Abdel Kader had actually made such a statement, he should be at once condemned. To the Kadis he argued thus: ' The Mahdi is the representative of the Prophet Mohammed, and I am his successor. Who, therefore, in the whole world holds so high a position as I? Who can be nobler than the direct descendant of the Prophet?' The inquiry proved the guilt of Abdel Kader, who, at the Khalifa's command, was thrown into chains, and transported to Reggaf. ' What business has he to compare affairs here with those of Egypt?' said the pompous Khalifa. ' If he wishes to compare himself to a Pasha, then I, the descendant of the Prophet, will never demean myself to be put on a par with the Khedive—a mere Turk.' I suppose by these assertions he thought to impress the populace. The stupid man, too, in his offended dignity, did not stop here. He at once ordered all the chronicles (of which several copies had been made) to be instantly burnt ; but I heard privately that his secretary, who was being frequently referred to by the Khalifa on the subject of the early events of his reign, secreted one copy for private reference ; and if these strange chronicles could only be procured and translated into European languages, they would expose to the civilized world the methods of Mahdism in all its barefaced mendacity.

Abdullahi's pride and confidence in his own powers are indescribable. He firmly believes that he is capable of doing anything and everything, and, as he pretends to act under Divine inspiration, he never hesitates to appropriate the merits of others as his own. For example, he stated that the Mahdi's tomb, which had been built with immense labour and trouble by the former Government architect Ismail, had been designed by himself entirely in accordance with Divinely inspired plans. He ascribed Osman Wad Adam's victory over Abu Gemmaiza, as well as Zeki Tummal's over King John of Abyssinia, to the inspired orders which he pretended he had issued. His character is a strange mixture of malice and cruelty. He delights to annoy and cause disappointment, and he is never happier than when he has brought people to complete destitution by confiscating their property, throwing them into chains, robbing families wholesale, seizing and executing all persons of tribal influence and authority, and reducing entire races to a condition of powerless impotence.

During the Mahdi's lifetime he was entirely responsible for the severity of the proceedings enacted in his name, and for the merciless manner in which he treated his defeated enemies. It was Abdullahi who gave the order for no quarter at the storming of Khartum, and it was he who subsequently authorized the wholesale massacre of the men, women, and children. After the fall of that city, it was he who, for the period of four days, declared the whole Shaigia tribe to be outlaws. When distributing the captured women and children, he was utterly regardless of their feelings. To separate children from their mothers, and to make their reunion practically impossible by scattering them amongst different tribes, was his principal delight. When Osman Wad Adam sent to Omdurman the sisters of the late Sultan of Darfur, the Princesses Miriam Isa Basi and Miriam Bakhita, he gave them their liberty, but took most of their female relatives into his own harem, and distributed the remainder amongst his followers; and, hearing that some Darfur people who were residing in Omdurman had called on the Princesses, and offered them presents, he had the latter arrested, and made over as slaves to his two Emirs, Hassib and Kanuna, who were on the point of starting for Reggaf. In vain poor Bakhita's blind mother implored to be allowed to accompany her daughter; but she was forcibly prevented by the Khalifa's special orders, and died a few days later of a broken heart. Her daughter threw herself into the river as the boat started. She was saved, but subsequently died on the journey from fatigue and misery. Ahmed Gurab, an Egyptian born in Khartum, who had quitted the city as a merchant before the destruction of Hicks Pasha's army, had left behind him his wife, who was a Sudanese, and his daughter. He eventually returned to see them, and, on the day he arrived in Omdurman, he was brought before the Khalifa, to whom he explained the reasons of his return, and expressed a wish to enter his service. 'I accept your offer,' said the Khalifa. 'You will at once proceed to Reggaf, and fight in the Holy Cause against the heathen.' In vain the unfortunate man begged and implored to remain with his wife and daughter, or, at least, to be allowed to see them; but the Khalifa ordered his mulazemin to take him at once on board the steamer, and guard him carefully, and on no account permit him to see his family. With a smile of fiendish delight, he said: 'His fellow-passengers are Isa Basi and Bakhita. He may enjoy their society as much as he likes, if their masters will allow him.'

Without the smallest rhyme or reason, he has caused the death of thousands of innocent people. He had the right hand and left foot of a certain Omar publicly cut off in the market-place because he had failed to make lead, which he had said he could do, and for which purpose he had received a small sum of money in advance. During the horrible execution and mutilation of the Batahin he had been present, and had looked with pleasure on the slaughter of his victims. I have described how his best friends and most faithful servants were victimized through his caprice, and how he had ruthlessly seized for himself their wives and daughters. Then what could be more cruel than his punishment of the Ashraf? No doubt they were guilty of mutiny, but he might have exiled or imprisoned them instead of killing them with clubs and axes as if they had been dogs, and yet these were the near relatives of his former lord and master, the Mahdi.

In all intercourse with him he demands the most complete humility and submission. Persons entering his presence stand in front of him with their hands crossed

over their breasts and their eyes lowered to the ground,
awaiting his permission to be seated. In his audience
chamber he is generally seated on an angareb, over which
a palm-mat is spread and his sheepskin stretched out on it,
whilst he leans against a large roll of cotton cloth which
forms a pillow. When those brought before him are
allowed to be seated, they take up a position as in prayers,
with their eyes fixed on the ground; and in this posture
they answer the questions put to them, and dare not move
until permission is given them to withdraw.

Even in the mosque, when prayers are over, and he
converses on general subjects, those in close proximity to
him invariably maintain this attitude. He is most particular that all persons brought before him should keep
their eyes downcast, whilst he himself scrutinizes them
most carefully. Some years ago a Syrian named
Mohammed Said, who had the misfortune to have only
one eye, happened to be near him when he was delivering
a religious lecture, and unintentionally cast his blind eye in
the direction of the Khalifa. The latter at once called me
up, and told me to tell the Syrian never to come n ar him
again, and if he did, never to dare to look at him. At the
same time he told me that everyone should be most careful
to guard themselves against the evil eye, 'For,' said he,
'nothing can resist the human eye. Illness and misfortunes
are generally caused by the evil eye.'

In spite of his tyrannical nature, the Khalifa shows to
greater advantage in his private life. He is devoted to his
eldest son Osman, who is now twenty-one years of age, and
who has been instructed in all the commentaries of the
Kuran by able Mohammedan teachers; but his father never
hesitated to change the teachers as often as his son wished,
and when Osman affirmed to his father that he was sufficiently instructed, the latter at once withdrew his teachers.
When he reached his seventeenth year he was married to
his cousin, the daughter of his uncle Yakub; and on this
occasion the Khalifa departed from the strict observances

as regards marriage enjoined by the Mahdi, and arranged a
series of banquets extending over a period of eight days, to
which almost every inhabitant in Omdurman was invited.
He had a large red brick house built for his son in the
space lying opposite to Yakub's residence, and had it
furnished with all the comfort available in the Sudan.   An
attempt was even made to lay out a garden on the stony
ground within the enclosure.   Shortly afterwards he gave
his son two more of his female relatives in marriage and
innumerable concubines, which he himself selected; but
he declared in the most emphatic manner that he would
never permit him to marry a woman from any of the Nile
Valley tribes.   He watches over his son's intercourse with
strangers with the greatest jealousy, and considers it a most
dangerous proceeding; and when he heard that, in the
perversity of youth, his son entirely disregarded his injunctions, and held nightly orgies in his house, he had a
new residence built for him within the Omdurman wall
close to his own, so as to exercise greater supervision, and
handed over his old house to Yakub.

He married his own daughter to the Mahdi's son
Mohammed, to whom he bore no goodwill, whilst the
latter was anxious to marry one of his own relations, and
had no love for the Khalifa's daughter.   Abdullahi, however, as father-in-law, guardian, and master, absolutely
forbade him to enter into any such alliance, and tried to
insist on his affection for his daughter, with the result that
a complete estrangement was brought about between man
and wife, ending in a divorce; but the Khalifa was so
annoyed that, out of pure fear, Mohammed had to take
her back, and swear entire devotion to her for the rest of
his life.

The Khalifa thought it incumbent on his position to maintain a large establishment; and as this was also entirely in
conformity with his own inclinations, he gradually became
possessor of a harem of over four hundred wives.   In accordance with the Mohammedan law, he has four legal wives,

who belong to free tribes ; but, being a lover of change, he never hesitates to divorce them at will, and take others in their places. The other women of the household consist for the most part of young girls, many of whom belong to tribes which have been forced to accept Mahdism, and whose husbands and fathers fought against him. They are therefore regarded as booty, and have only the rights and claims of concubines, or, in some cases, of slaves. This large assortment of ladies varies in colour from light-brown to the deepest black, and comprises almost every tribe in the Sudan. They are divided into groups of from fifteen to twenty, presided over by a superior ; and two or three of these groups are placed under the orders of a free woman, who is generally a concubine specially selected by the Khalifa. A certain amount of grain and money is granted monthly to these superiors for the maintenance of their charges ; and they also receive means to purchase the necessary cosmetics, consisting of various sorts of oils, grease, and scent. The value of their clothing is regulated entirely by the comparative beauty, position, and character of the wearers, and consists for the most part of native-woven cotton cloth with parti-coloured borders, or of bright silk or woollen shawls, imported from Egypt. These are always distributed by the Khalifa himself, or by his chief eunuch. As the wearing of silver jewellery was strictly prohibited by the Mahdi, mother-of-pearl buttons and oblong strips of red coral and onyx, threaded together, are worn round the wrists, ankles, and head. The hair is usually worn in innumerable small plaits, which are arranged in all sorts of different ways, and bedaubed with a quantity of oily and greasy scents ; and to European olfactory nerves the odour emanating from a Sudanese lady *en grande toilette* is repulsive in the extreme. For the last few years the wives of the upper classes have again taken to wearing gold and silver jewellery ; and the Khalifa's principal women indulge in these luxuries to a greater extent than the rest. The latter live in a series of large detached houses, something like barracks, surrounded by courts encircled with high walls. Special women are maintained to watch over their state of health; and they are obliged to report it to their master, the Khalifa, from time to time. When he wishes to summon any lady in particular to share his affections, he communicates his desire by means of little boy eunuchs. Occasionally he holds an inspection of his entire household, and makes use of such opportunities to rid himself of those of whom he is weary, in order to make room for new attractions. Those disposed of in this way he generally passes on to his near relatives, his special favourites, or his servants. The harem courts are carefully guarded by eunuchs and the Black mulazemin. The women are almost entirely cut off from intercourse with the outer world; and perhaps once a year their female relations are allowed to converse with them for only a short time.

The Khalifa's principal wife is called Sahra, and belongs to his own tribe. She has shared with him from earliest days all his joys and sorrows, and is the mother of his oldest children, Osman and Kadija. During the early years of his reign he would only eat the simplest food, cooked by her or under her superintendence. It consisted, as a rule, merely of asida, roast meat, and chickens; but as his household increased he began to try the various sorts of cookery known to his new wives, many of whom were acquainted with the Turkish and Egyptian methods; and now, in place of the simple food, he indulges in far more luxurious fare, though to outward appearance he still pretends to lead a life of simplicity and abstinence. These innovations brought about a quarrel between him and his wife Sahra, who pointed out that the new dishes might be bewitched or poisoned, and might end in his death, with the result that he twice sent her letters of separation, but on the strong representations of his brother Yakub and the other members of the family, he was induced to cancel them.

He has in his service in all some twenty eunuchs, chief of whom is a certain Abdel Gayum, who is also charged with the superintendence of large quantities of land which are cultivated by slaves for the use of the household, and it is his duty to purchase the necessary supplies of grain, and have in readiness the sheep and cattle required for domestic purposes. He also draws from the Beit el Mal the necessary amounts required for the payment of the women and servants of the harem. He has also charge of considerable sums of private money with which the Khalifa purchases the presents he secretly makes to his Emirs and other influential persons. To assist him in carrying out his multifarious duties, he has a staff of clerks and servants, who are always eunuchs or slaves, as the Khalifa will on no account allow any stranger to get an insight into his harem.

Abdullahi's dress consists of a jibba made of superfine white cotton cloth with a coloured border, loose cotton drawers, and on his head a beautifully made Mecca silk skull-cap, around which a small white turban is wound. Around his body a narrow strip of cotton, about five yards long, called wassan, is worn, and a light shawl of the same material is thrown across his shoulders. He formerly wore sandals, but latterly he has taken to wearing soft leather stockings of a light-brown colour, and yellow shoes. When walking, he carries a sword in his left hand, and in his right a beautifully worked Hadendoa spear, which he uses as a walking-stick. He is invariably accompanied by twelve or fifteen little boy-slaves as his personal attendants. Many of these are children of Abyssinian Christians seized by Abu Anga and Zeki Tummal. Their duty is to remain always near him, and act as his messengers to various parts of the town. They usher into his presence all visitors, and must be ready day and night to carry his orders. When they reach the age of seventeen or eighteen they are drafted into the ranks of the mulazemin, and their places taken by others. The Khalifa thinks that by employing young boys his secrets are less likely to be betrayed; and in this he is not far wrong, when one considers the extraordinary amount of bribery and corruption which prevails amongst the older

classes. Within the house, into which these young boys
are never admitted, he employs young eunuchs, who wait
upon him, whilst the more advanced in age of this unfortunate class are relegated to the outer dependencies of the
household. Even these juvenile domestics suffer considerable brutality at his hands. The slightest mistakes are
punished by flogging, or the offenders are thrown into chains
and starved.

Upwards of three years ago he conceived the idea of
augmenting his mulazemin by a species of body-guard, and
for this purpose he selected a number of Jehadia from
Mahmud Ahmed's and Zeki Tummal's armies. In addition
to these, he called on the Emirs of the western tribes to
provide a number of recruits for his mulazemin; but his
orders were only partially obeyed. He selected a few of the
sons of the best Jaalin families for incorporation in the
body-guard; but he rigorously excluded all Danaglas and
Egyptians, in whom he has no confidence. In this manner
he created a force of from eleven to twelve thousand men,
who, with their wives and children, are all quartered close to
his and his son's houses, and within the newly-erected wall.
This force is subdivided into three corps, under the respective commands of his son Osman, the Khalifa's young
brother Harun Abu Mohammed, who is barely eighteen
years of age, and his cousin Ibrahim Khalil, who has been
recently replaced by an Abyssinian named Rabeh, who has
been brought up in the Khalifa's household.

Osman, in all matters regarding the mulazemin, is looked
upon as the Khalifa's representative. The corps are subdivided again into sections of one hundred men, over each
of which an officer called Ras Miya (head of the hundred),
who has several assistants, has command. Over every five
or six Ras Miya an Emir presides, who is also provided
with an assistant. The Black soldiers, or Jehadia, are in-
corporated in the subdivisions, not with the free Arabs, but
under the special command of the Emirs, who have therefore under their respective orders two or three hundred

Jehadia, and the remainder Arabs. Almost all these are armed with Remington rifles, which, however, are kept in store, and are only issued on special feasts. The monthly pay of the mulazemin consists of half a Dervish dollar, and every fortnight one-eighth of an ardeb of dhurra. The grain is received fairly regularly; but the cash payment is merely a nominal one, and is very seldom issued. The salaries of the Ras Miya and Emirs are proportionately higher, and they receive frequent gifts of women and slaves from the Khalifa. The duty of the mulazemin and body-guard is to protect the person of the Khalifa, and all must accompany him when he rides out or holds reviews. Even when making a comparatively small expedition into the town they must proceed with him. They have always to remain in readiness in the open square in front of his house. Although the Khalifa has forbidden all Egyptian music, he has collected the former Black buglers, two of whom invariably accompany him. The call for a Ras Miya is that of captain; for Emir, that of major; and for commander, that of colonel. Abdullahi frequently inspects the mulazemin at night, in order to see that they are in occupation of the posts allotted to them, and he pays special attention to the outposts. Owing to this unusually hard service, the Ras Miya and Emirs, under the pretext of illness, frequently go secretly to their houses, and great discontent prevails amongst them.

The Khalifa's public duties consist in saying the five prayers daily in the large mosque. At early dawn he begins with the morning prayers, after which the Rateb is read in various groups, as enjoined by the Mahdi. This consists of a selection of verses and special prayers from the Kuran, and occupies about an hour. The Khalifa then returns, as a rule, to his private apartments, but sometimes walks about in the mosque in order to see for himself whether the inhabitants of Omdurman comply with his orders to attend prayers regularly. He holds mid-day prayers at about two o'clock, and two hours later follows the Asr, or evening prayer, after which the Rateb is repeated. Prayers are said again at sunset, and three hours later night prayers are held. On all these occasions the Khalifa attends in his mihrab (niche), which has been erected immediately in front of the lines of believers. It is a square-shaped structure, consisting of a series of columns connected by open iron-work, through which he can see all that is going on around him. Immediately behind him are the seats of his son, the Kadis, and a few persons specially selected by himself. The mulazemin take up a position to the right and left, whilst the Black soldiers occupy large open enclosures, which are separated from the mosque by a wall. On the right of the mulazemin are the places of Yakub, the Emirs, and most of the western tribes, whilst to the left are some of Yakub's followers, a few of Khalifa Ali Wad Helu's Arabs, and the Jaalin and Danagla. Behind these the people are seated in ten or twelve rows, and repeat the prayers in unison after the Khalifa. On all occasions there are several thousand persons present, and the Khalifa is most particular that all the principal Emirs and influential people should assist him. If he bears any special dislike or ill-will to any persons, he invariably condemns them to regularly attend the five daily prayers in the mosque, under the supervision of people specially selected for this purpose. In making these strict regulations regarding prayers, the Khalifa is by no means actuated by devotional ideas, but utilizes these occasions to keep his followers together under his own personal control. As several of the people live a considerable distance away from the mosque, they are generally so tired and exhausted after these frequent journeys to and fro, that they do not collect in the evening in each other's houses, a practice which the Khalifa specially abhors, for his object is to destroy as far as possible what he is pleased to call 'social life'—that is to say, social gatherings—for he is perfectly well aware that his deeds and actions on such occasions are invariably discussed and criticised, and not generally very favourably.

If for any reason, such as illness, he is prevented from attending prayers, his place is taken by one of his Kadis, or by a very pious mulazem of the Takruri tribe ; but on such occasions the substitute Imam is never allowed to occupy the mihrab, but stands outside. Khalifa Ali Wad Helu, who, in accordance with the religious law, should on such occasions represent the Khalifa, is scarcely ever permitted to do so.

In the afternoon, or between afternoon and evening prayers, he receives reports, news, and letters, and interviews the Kadis and Emirs whose names have been previously submitted to him, as well as any other persons whom he specially wishes to see.

His postal arrangements are very primitive. He keeps up from sixty to eighty riding camels, with a specially selected staff of postmen, and these he despatches to different parts of his Empire with orders and instructions. Ibrahim Adlan had suggested to him that he should make special stations for the posts along the various main roads, and establish a more regular and less expensive system ; but he utterly refused to entertain the idea, saying that he placed special value on the verbal accounts of the postmen who were despatched direct, and he frequently obtained from them important information concerning the attitude and behaviour of his Governors. The Emirs of the various districts also have a similar postal system of their own, and despatch camel-men with important information to Omdurman. There is no system of postal communication for private persons, though sometimes the camel-postmen convey letters secretly. The Khalifa being intensely suspicious of all intercourse with strangers, any communications between his subordinates and the outside must be carried out with the greatest circumspection and secrecy. Utterly ignorant of reading and writing, the Khalifa orders all letters that arrive to be handed over to his secretaries, Abu el Gasem and Mudasser, who are obliged to explain the contents, and write replies in accordance with his orders.

These two individuals lead a wretched life ; for they know that he will not forgive the slightest mistake, and should he have the least suspicion of their having revealed any of his secrets, even through carelessness, he would not hesitate to treat them as he treated their comrades Ahmedi and his four brothers, who, having been accused of communicating with the Ashraf, were executed.

He converses principally with his Kadis, who are, for the most part, willing tools in his hands, and serve to give a veneer of justice to his despotic actions. These myrmidons, submissively seated in a semicircle on the bare floor, their heads bowed down, listen to his orders, which are generally given in an undertone ; and rarely any one of them dares to open his mouth or make a suggestion, no matter how necessary he may think it. In addition to the Kadis, he occasionally interviews Emirs and other influential persons, from whom he ascertains the condition of the country and tribes ; but he invariably stirs up intrigue, and tries to pit one against the other. He generally consults, immediately after night prayers, with Yakub and some of his near relatives, and these meetings often last till long past midnight. They are usually convened for discussing the ways and means of ridding themselves of persons who are objectionable, or who are in the smallest degree a menace to their authority.

Occasionally, he makes short riding excursions to various parts of the town, or visits his houses in the north or south of Omdurman. The melancholy notes of the ombeya and the beating of war-drums announce to the inhabitants that their master is about to appear in public. Horses are at once saddled in the large thatched enclosure immediately behind the mosque. The doors are thrown open, and the mulazemin stream out from all directions, and, last of all, follows the Kalifa, mounted, as a rule, on horseback. A square is immediately formed round him, and the men advance in front of him in detachments, ten or twelve abreast. Behind them follow the horse and footmen of the town population, while on the Khalifa's left walks an immensely powerful and well-built Arab named Ahmed Abu Dukheba, who has the honour of lifting his master in and out of the saddle. On his right is a strongly-made young Black, who is chief of the slaves in the royal stables. The Khalifa is immediately preceded by six men, who alternately blow the ombeya by his orders. Behind him follow the buglers, who sound the advance or halt, or summon, at his wish, the chiefs of the mulazemin. Just behind these follow his small personal attendants, who carry the Rekwa (a leather vessel used for religious ablutions), the sheepskin prayer-carpet, and several spears. Sometimes, either in front or rear, as the case may be, follows the musical band, composed of about fifty Black slaves, whose instruments comprise antelope-horns, and drums made of the hollow trunks of trees covered with skin. The strange African tunes they play are remarkable rather for the hideously discordant noise they make than for their melody. These rides are generally undertaken after mid-day prayer, and the Khalifa returns at sunset. Whilst he is advancing in this solemn state, the mulazemin generally indulge in displays of horsemanship. Galloping four abreast, with their spears poised high in the air, they dash up towards him at full speed, drawing up their horses almost on their haunches. They then slowly retire to repeat the operation.

During the early years of his rule, the Khalifa was present every Friday on the large parade ground where the ceremony of trooping the colours is performed; but now he attends only four times a year, viz., on the birthday of the Prophet, on the Feast of Miraj, the Feast of Bairam, and the Feast of Kurbam Bairam; on this last date all the troops in the neighbourhood, as well as the Darfur and Gedaref armies, are assembled during peaceful times. On the first day of the Feast of Bairam the Khalifa holds prayers on the parade-ground, and retires himself within a zariba in which a small mud-brick house has been built. A

few special favourites, and a number of mulazemin, remain
with him; but the rest of the troops and populace range
themselves in long lines; and when the prayer is over he
mounts a wooden pulpit, and delivers a sermon, which is
generally specially prepared for him by his secretaries.
This over, a salute of seven guns is fired, and all those who
can afford it kill the sacrificial lambs prescribed by the
religion; but, owing to the prevailing distress and poverty
of the inhabitants, very few of them are in a position to
bear this expense, and are obliged to content themselves
with a sort of porridge which takes the place of a
sacrificial dish. During the three following days a review
is held. Long before sunrise the Emirs, with their flags
and followers, collect and march to their allotted positions
on the parade-ground, which is an almost perfectly flat
sandy plain, with a few stones here and there. The troops
are marshalled in long lines in rear of each other, facing
east.

Yakub has the principal flag—an immense piece of black
cloth, which is hoisted exactly opposite the Khalifa's zariba,
and about four hundred yards from it. To the right and
left are ranged those of the different Emirs, while on the
north side flies the green flag of the Khalifa Ali Wad Helu,
on either side of which are the flags of his Emirs. On the
left flank the horse and camel-men are drawn up, while on
the right flank are ranged the riflemen, consisting partly of
Jehadia, and partly of men belonging to the various Emirs,
who are only specially provided with arms for the time
being. Immediately after sunrise, the Khalifa comes out of
the zariba, and, mounted on his horse, stands surrounded by
his mulazemin and body-guard, whilst the entire army
passes in review before him, the troops being generally
provided with new jibbas and turbans in honour of the
feast. Sometimes the Khalifa mounts on a camel; and, on
one occasion, he drove in the carriage of one of the former
Governors-General which had been captured in Khartum,
and which was kept stored away in the Beit el Mal. Two

horses were specially trained to draw this vehicle, which the Khalifa ordered to be driven at a foot pace, as he feared being upset ; but latterly he has given up this plan, and generally rides on horseback direct from the mosque along the road leading due west towards the black flag, and, on reaching it, he solemnly contemplates it for a few moments, and then rides to the zariba, at the south front of which a small shelter, consisting of trunks of trees lashed together and covered with palm-mats, has been erected. Here he dismounts and reclines on an angareb, surrounded by his Kadis, whilst the troops file past. Occasionally he starts from his own house, and, taking a southern road, marches out of the town, then turns west and rides along the front alignment of his troops, after which the usual march past takes place. At these reviews the horsemen are generally clad in coats of mail, of European or Asiatic origin, whilst on their heads they wear heavy iron helmets and curious cotton caps of various colours and the most grotesque shapes, round which a small turban is wound. The horses are clothed in large padded patchwork quilts, somewhat resembling those worn by the knights of old at tournaments ; and one might almost imagine one was gazing at one of those old mediæval displays. These reviews terminate at the end of the third day ; and the troops brought from beyond Omdurman are permitted to return to their respective garrisons.

I propose now to briefly consider the Khalifa's political ntentions and ideas.

As I have already stated, when the Mahdi first declared himself, he nominated three Khalifas, viz., Abdullahi, Ali Wad Helu, and Mohammed Sherif, who were to succeed him in this order, if they survived. On his death, Abdullahi succeeded as arranged ; but from the moment he took over the reins of government he did everything in his power to increase his personal ascendancy and make it hereditary in the family. The mutinous Ashraf, who prided themselves on their relationship to the Mahdi, afforded him a welcome pretext for compassing their downfall; and he did not hesitate to possess himself of the Black troops belonging to both his rival Khalifas. An obscure member of a western tribe, he was a complete stranger in the country; and he knew that he could not reckon on the Jaalin, Danagla, inhabitants of the Gezira, and other Nile Valley tribes to support his authority. He therefore sent secret emissaries to the western Arabs to induce them to make a pilgrimage to the Mahdi's tomb, and emigrate to the Nile Valley. His agents drew a tempting picture of the magnificent country to which they had been invited, telling them that they were the Lord's chosen people, and that they should go out to possess the land, the inhabitants of which were rich in cattle and slaves, which should be theirs. Tempted by these glowing accounts, many of these tribes emigrated of their own free-will to Omdurman; but as this contingent was not sufficient, the Khalifa instructed his Emirs in Darfur and Kordofan to enforce his orders; and, in consequence of this, an immense emigration took place, and continues, on a reduced scale, down to the present day. By this means the Khalifa has surrounded himself with hordes of strangers who have ousted the rightful owners of the soil, and have made themselves absolute masters of the situation. All offices and important situations are filled by them and his own relatives, the majority belonging to the Taaisha section. Almost the only one of the old Emirs left is Osman Digna; and the reason for this is that the eastern Arab tribes he governs speak a language which is unknown to the western Arabs. Besides, many of these tribes are gradually coming under Egyptian and Italian influence, and the few that are left are merely attached to Osman Digna because he is one of them. Thus the Taaisha tribe has acquired all the power and authority in the land; and they fill their pockets with the waning revenues of the impoverished Sudan.

Years ago, the Emirs of Dongola and Berber had been instructed by the Khalifa to weaken the local population as much as possible; and, in consequence, firearms and weapons of all descriptions were taken from them, and they were reduced to a condition of complete harmlessness. Moreover, in the actions of Toski and Tokar numbers of Jaalin and Danagla were killed, whilst large contingents of them had been sent to Darfur and Gallabat in the hope that they might be eventually exterminated. In this manner the Khalifa has secured their countries, and rendered any attempt to oppose his authority almost impossible. The same may be said of the inhabitants of the Gezira, who have also been drafted off into various remote parts of the country, or have been forced to come to Omdurman with their families, where they have endured the greatest hardships and privations. Moreover, they were called upon to give up more than half their cultivated lands, which were distributed amongst the western Arabs; and all their best fields are now possessed by the Khalifa's own relatives and favourites. The former owners are often obliged to till the soil for their new masters, who have annexed their servants, slaves, and cattle. Thus the cultivable area of the Gezira, which in former times was the most populous and prosperous part of the Sudan, has been reduced by at least a half; and such commotion prevailed in the districts that the Khalifa was himself obliged to intervene on behalf of the inhabitants, who were ill-treated, tyrannised over, and oppressed to an incredible extent.

As I have before stated, his own tribes are preferred on all occasions. Not only do they hold all the best positions and posts, but the greater part of the money and spoil which passes into the Beit el Mal from the provincial treasuries at Darfur, Gallabat, and Reggaf finds its way into their hands. For their special benefit he has imposed a horse tax, which must be paid in kind, and in this manner he has provided the majority of the Taaisha with chargers. His own section (the Jubarat) of course gets the lion's share of everything.

He never hesitates to make use of every description of intrigue in order to strengthen his own side and weaken the other. For example, on the defeat and death of Nejumi, whose flags belonged to those of Khalifa Sherif, and from whom Abdullahi had withdrawn all power of command over other Emirs, the remnant of the defeated force was placed under the direction of the Emir Yunes, and in order to replace those who had been killed, he appointed fresh Jaalin and Emirs as well as men from Omdurman. These he first placed under the command of their compatriot, Bedawi Wad el Ereik; but instead of sending them to Dongola, they were despatched to Gedaref, and as an unavoidable delay occurred in their departure, he made out that this was a proof of disobedience, and condemned Bedawi, with six of his Emirs, to be banished to Reggaf, and in their place he nominated other Emirs, whom he placed under the direct command of his cousin, Hamed Wad Ali.

It is human nature to seek the protection of the most powerful, and now, instead of being desirous to serve under their own Emirs, the greater number of the so-called opposition party vie with one another in their efforts to be placed under the direct command of the Khalifa or of Yakub; even the adherents of Ali Wad Helu come under this category. As an instance of this, I will quote the case of Hamed Wad Gar en Nebbi, who was the principal cause of the destruction of the Batahin. He belonged to the Hassanab tribe, which was commanded by Ali Wad Helu. Recognising how matters stood, he wished to place himself and his tribe under Yakub's command, but he was short-sighted enough to tell Khalifa Ali's relatives of his plans. He even went so far as to state in public that, on the death of Abdullahi, he would be succeeded by his brother Yakub or his son Osman, and that, as they had all the power in their hands, Khalifa Ali could expect nothing, and was, moreover, a weak man, without energy. Several of the bystanders retorted that the Mahdi had nominated Khalifa Ali to be Abdullahi's successor, to which he replied that times had changed, that Abdullahi was all-powerful, and that the Mahdi's commands were never attended to or taken into consideration. When this interview came to the ears of Khalifa Ali, he charged Gar en Nebbi before the Kadi, and it was proved beyond a doubt that the latter had actually made these statements. He was consequently convicted of being ' irreligious,' having doubted the maintenance of the Mahdi's doctrines and instructions. Abdullahi could not therefore publicly interfere. Had he done so he would have revealed his own intentions, which were in reality well known, and would have corroborated Gar en Nebbi's assertions. The judges sentenced him to death, and although Abdullahi did all in his power to induce Ali Wad Helu to grant a reprieve, the latter insisted that the sentence should be carried out, and Gar en Nebbi was publicly executed in the market-place as an unbeliever and a disturber of public tranquillity. All the tribes under the command of Yakub, as well as the Khalifa's immediate followers, received instructions to show general dissatisfaction with the execution by openly absenting themselves from it.

Whenever it is a question between himself and his opponents, the Khalifa invariably relies upon his arms, which are far more than sufficient to overcome with ease any attempt to dispute his authority, whether it be in Omdurman itself or in any other part of the country. Within the Sudan, therefore, he is all-powerful, but he is not in a position to offer determined resistance to outside enemies. His leaders are neither capable nor sufficiently instructed to ensure victory. His men are not now loyal enough to fight with that determination which early fanaticism had inspired. They have little or no faith in the cause for which they are supposed to be fighting, and there is little doubt that the Khalifa's forces could not resist the advance of a foreign power bent on reoccupying the Sudan.

The table on the next page shows approximately the forces at present at the Khalifa's disposal. Of the forty thousand rifles shown in the table there are not more than twenty-two thousand Remingtons in good condition. The remainder consist of single and double barrel smooth-bores,

POSITION AND GARRISONS.	EMIRS.	ARMED STRENGTH.			GUNS.	RIFLES AND SMOOTH-BORES.
		JEHADIA.	CAVALRY.	SWORDS. SPEARMEN.		
Omdurman (mulazemin)	Osman Sheikh ed Din	11,000	..	..	..	11,000
"	Yakub	4,000	3,500	45,000	46	4,000
" (in store)		6,000	..	..	..	6,000
Reggaf	Arabi Wad Dafalla	1,800	..	4,500	3	1,800
Western Sudan:						
El Fasher						
El Obeid	Mahmud, etc.	6,000	350	2,500	4	6,000
Shakka, etc.						
Berber	Zeki Osman	1,600	500	1,300	6	1,600
Abu Hamed	Nur en Nau	400	100	700	4	400
Eastern Sudan:						
Adarama	Osman Digna	450	350	1,000	..	450
Gedaref	Ahmed Fedil	4,500	600	1,000	4	4,500
El Fasher		1,000	200	500	..	1,000
Asubri	Hamed Wad Ali	900	400	1,400	..	900
Gallabat	En Nur	50	..	200	..	50
Dongola	Yunes ed Degheim	2,400	500	5,000	8	2,400
Suarda	Hammuda	250	100	1,000	..	250
Total		34,350	6,600	64,000	75	40,350

and other guns of a variety of pattern. Several of the Remington barrels, however, have been cut short, with the object of lessening the weight, and with entire disregard to the altered trajectory thus occasioned. Of the sixty-four thousand swords and spearmen, at least twenty-five per cent. are either too old or too young to be considered effective for a campaign. The seventy-five guns comprise six Krupps of large calibre, and for which there is only a very small amount of ammunition, eight machine-guns of various patterns, and sixty-one brass muzzle-loading guns of various shapes and sizes, the ammunition for which is manufactured principally in Omdurman, and is of a very inferior quality, the range being little over six or seven hundred yards.

Let us now consider for a few moments the present limits of the Khalifa's influence.

Until a few years ago Dervish authority extended from near Wadi Halfa in a south-easterly direction towards Abu Hamed, thence eastwards to the Suakin neighbourhood, including Tokar and the Khor Baraka, thence in a southerly direction, including Kassala, Gallabat, and the south-eastern slopes of the Beni Shangul and Gulli mountains, and from here it trended in a south-westerly direction towards the White Nile, and included Fashoda, Bohr, and Reggaf. On the west it extended in a south-westerly direction through the southern Libyan desert, including Selima, the Dongola, Kordofan, and Darfur Provinces, up to the Wadai frontier, and thence southward across the Bahr el Arab through Dar Runga, and included Dar Fertit, the Bahr el Ghazal, and a portion of Equatoria.

The defeat of Nejumi obliged the Mahdists to evacuate the northern portion of the Dongola Province; and their most northerly outpost is now Suarda, some three days' march from Dongola.* The Egyptian victories at Tokar and Handub gave back to the local tribes the districts in

---

* In 1896 an Expeditionary Force succeeded in driving the Dervishes out of the Dongola Province, and re-establishing Egyptian authority as far south as Merowe.

the immediate neighbourhood of Suakin and Kokar, whilst the capture of Kassala threw into the hands of the Italians all districts lying east of that town, in consequence of which the river Atbara may now be considered the Khalifa's eastern frontier. The main force originally stationed at Gallabat under Ahmed Fedil has been moved to Gedaref, and only an insignificant force is maintained at the former station. The chief of the Beni Shangul districts, Tur el Guri, and many of the neighbouring Sheikhs have declared themselves independent.

In the extreme west the Massalit, Tama, Beni Hussein, and Gimr tribes, who formerly paid tribute, have now revolted against the Mahdi's government, and until lately were independent. They entered into an offensive and defensive alliance with Sultan Yusef of Wadai, and the Khalifa was about to despatch an expedition with the object of bringing them into subjection, when the alarming news, to which I have already referred, regarding the appearance of Europeans in the Bahr el Ghazal induced him to alter the destination of Khatem Musa's force to that neighbourhood. After the retirement of the Dervishes orders were sent to Khatem Musa not to proceed further south until he had received reinforcements from Omdurman.

CHAPTER XVI.

MISCELLANEOUS REMARKS (*continued*).

Administration of Justice—Religion in the Sudan—Enforced Pilgrimage to the Mahdi's Tomb—Limits of the Mahdist Empire—Caravan Roads — Trade and Commerce — The Slave Trade — The Slave Market—Industries—Immorality—Unpopularity of the Khalifa— His Ignorance and Cruelty—His Private Apartments—Principal Buildings in Omdurman—Description of the City—The Prison and its Horrors—Death of Zeki Tummal and Kadi Ahmed.

THROUGHOUT the preceding pages I have frequently referred in general terms to the Khalifa's system of administering justice. The Kadis, or judges, are ready tools in the hands of their astute master. They are only permitted to act independently in trivial cases, such as family disputes, questions of property, and the like; but in all matters of importance they must invariably refer to the Khalifa for final decision, in giving which the latter invariably consults his own immediate interests; but at the same time his earnest endeavour is to appear before the public to be within the bounds of justice. The judges, therefore, have a somewhat difficult task to perform : that is to say, they must invariably carry out the Khalifa's wishes, and give them the appearance of being legally correct; whereas, in nine cases out of ten, they are entirely contrary to the first elements of justice and right.

Religion in the Sudan, as far as my experience goes, is governed by the principle that the end justifies the means. Proclamations and pamphlets enjoining strict attention to the performance of religious duties, and urging the abandonment of all earthly pleasures, are despatched to the remotest parts of Africa and Arabia, to Bornu, Dar Fellata, Mecca, and Medina. The Khalifa, if his health permits it, attends the five daily prayers most regularly; and yet, at heart, no man could be more irreligious. During all the years in which I have been in the closest communication with him, I have never once seen or heard him say a prayer in his own house. Should any religious rite or ceremony interfere in the smallest degree with his wishes or ambitions it is instantly abolished, but in doing so he is careful that the proposition for its abolition should emanate in the first instance from his Kadis, who declare it necessary for the 'maintenance of the faith,' and the astuteness with which these obsequious myrmidons twist and turn matters in order to suit the Khalifa's will is deserving of a better cause. Whenever it is quite impossible to create some pretext for the execution of an unusually gross piece of injustice, Divine interposition and inspiration is invariably called to the rescue.

Abdullahi often addresses his followers from the pulpit

in the mosque, but as he is entirely ignorant of theology, and knows little or nothing about the rudiments of religion, the scope of his sermons is excessively limited, and consists of a repetition of stereotyped phrases.

He has forbidden pilgrimage to Mecca, having substituted for it pilgrimage to the tomb of the Mahdi, who is the Prophet's representative.   Although the Sudanese intensely dislike this innovation, they are perforce obliged to accept it, and as it is now impossible for them to return to the orthodox faith, which they so unwittingly cast aside, they now accept the situation, and carry out their mock religious duties in the most business-like manner, but without the smallest belief in their efficacy.

Education and religious instruction are practically non-existent.   Some boys, and occasionally a few girls, are taught to recite the Kuran and the Rateb in the mesjids (religious schools attached to the mosques), of which a few are allowed to be privately kept up.   A small percentage of these children, when they have completed their course in the mesjids, are sent to the Beit el Mal, where they become apprentices to the old Government clerks, and learn a certain amount of business correspondence.   The system of theological instruction which obtains in most Moslem countries, but which was never much in vogue in the Sudan, has now ceased to exist altogether.

The once extensive commerce of the Sudan has now sunk down to comparatively nothing, and the roads which were formerly traversed by numberless caravans are now deserted, obliterated by sand, or overgrown with rank vegetation.   The principal routes were :

1. The Arbaïn, or forty days' road, from Darfur to Assiut, or from Kordofan through the Bayuda desert to Dongola and Wadi Halfa.

2. From Khartum, *viâ* Berber to Assuan, or *viâ* Abu Hamed to Korosko.

3. From Khartum, *viâ* Berber or Kassala, to Suakin.

4. From Gallabat, Gedaref, and Kassala to Massawa.

At present the only roads used by occasional caravans are from Berber to Assuan and Suakin. Shortly after the capture of Khartum, the Sudan merchants imported to Assuan considerable quantities of the captured gold and silver ornaments; and partly owing to this fact, and partly to the amount of spoil accumulated in the Khalifa's private treasury, the supply of these metals has become so reduced that Abdullahi has given strict orders to the merchants that they shall on no account take with them to Egypt any gold or silver except what is absolutely necessary for the expenses of the journey. This amount is fixed by the Beit el Mal, and has to be taken in old currency, the value of which is inserted in the passport.

As the sadly diminished trade with Egypt began to revive, natural products, which had been the former wealth of the Sudan, were again made the medium of commerce. Gum, ostrich feathers, tamarinds, senna-leaves, etc., were collected in the Beit el Mal, as well as ivory, and were sold by auction at local currency rates; but as the majority of these products came from the western districts, which owing to war, famine, and disease had become almost de-populated, the supply was scanty. In exchange for these, the merchants brought from Egypt Manchester goods, which are greatly in demand in the Sudan. Gum is a monopoly, and the price paid for it varies greatly. The Beit el Mal purchases at the rate of twenty to thirty dollars (Omla Gedida), and sells to the merchants at the rate of thirty to forty dollars. The purchaser generally receives permission to take it to Egypt, and is taxed at the rate of a dollar a hundredweight at Berber, where the amount is carefully checked with the bill of lading. If he wishes to take it to Suakin or Assuan, he is obliged to pay a tax of a further dollar a hundredweight; but in this case it is a Maria Theresa dollar, which is equivalent to five Omla Gedidas, and thus already a sixth of the original cost has been added in taxation.

Ivory comes from the Equatorial regions in considerable

quantities about once a year, and generally finds its way to Suakin, and as these districts appear to be gradually passing out of Mahdist control, it is hardly probable that the amount will increase in future years. Occasionally a few tusks are brought from the Southern Darfur districts; but unless the Dervishes reoccupy the Bahr el Ghazal in force, their ivory trade stands in danger of dying out altogether.

Goods can only be imported from Egypt by the Assuan and Suakin roads. Formerly a certain amount of trade was carried on between Suakin and Kassala, and Kassala and Massawa; but since the occupation of the Eastern Sudan by the Italians, it has almost entirely ceased. The goods imported are generally of an inferior quality, and consist mostly of material for women's dresses and men's jibbas; but to the inhabitants of the Sudan this is a matter of little consequence, for they much prefer gaudy and tawdry material to the more durable fabrics. Indeed, it would be very difficult, if not impossible, to find purchasers for a better class of goods in the Sudan.

One of the principal imports is scent of every variety, such as sandal-wood oil, cloves, scented seeds, etc., for all of which the Sudanese ladies have a strong predilection. A certain amount of sugar, rice, inferior jams, and dried fruit also find purchasers amongst the more wealthy of the population. The importation of all articles made of iron, brass, tin, copper, etc., has for some time past been rigorously prohibited by the Egyptian Government, and now it is almost impossible to obtain a pair of scissors or a razor. Copper cooking utensils have risen to an enormous price, and most of those which previously existed have been bought up by the arsenal for the manufacture of cartridges. Consequently food is now cooked almost entirely in earthenware vessels.

The tax of ushr (a tenth) is levied on all goods imported to the Sudan. It must be paid in either money or kind, and is frequently taken more than once along the road. All goods on arrival in Omdurman are taken to the Beit el Mal and stamped ; and here the ushr is again taken. Merchants, therefore, owing to the heavy taxes imposed, in addition to the presents they have to make to the various chiefs, have generally paid half as much again over and above the value of their goods. They are therefore obliged to considerably raise the price, and even then the total profit is by no means a large one. Several of the more wealthy inhabitants of the Sudan have taken to trading with Egypt, not so much with a view to making money, as to spending a few months away from the atmosphere of the Khalifa's authority. It is by means of trade alone that any of the unfortunate in-habitants of the Sudan can temporarily escape from the hands of that tyrant, whose rule is more detested than ever. Most of the merchants, having their wives, families, and relatives in the Sudan, are obliged eventually to return ; and, were it not for these ties, I think that few men who have the chance of leaving the Sudan would ever return.

But if trade in general is in a state of depression, there is one trade to which the advent of the Mahdi and Khalifa has given a great impulse. I refer, of course, to the slave-trade. As, however, the export of slaves to Egypt is strictly pro-hibited, this trade is confined entirely to the provinces under the Khalifa's control. In prohibiting the export of slaves, the Khalifa acts on the wise principle that he should not increase the power of his adversaries at his own expense. It is, of course, quite impossible for him to absolutely pre-vent slaves being taken occasionally to Egypt or Arabia; but the slave-caravans which were formerly sent from the Sudan have now almost completely stopped. A few years ago quantities of slaves were sent from Abyssinia by Abu Anga, and from Fashoda by Zeki Tummal, as well as from Darfur and the Nuba mountains by Osman Wad Adam, and were generally sold by public auction for the benefit of the Beit el Mal or the Khalifa's private treasury. The transport of slaves is carried on with the same execrable and heartless cruelty which characterizes their capture. Of the thousands of Abyssinian Christians seized by Abu Anga,

the majority were women and children, and under the cruel
lash of the whip they were forced to march on foot the whole
distance from Abyssinia to Omdurman. Wrenched from
their families, provided with scarcely enough food to keep
body and soul together, barefooted, and almost naked, they
were driven through the country like herds of cattle. The
greater number of them perished on the road, and those
who arrived in Omdurman were in so pitiable a condition
that purchasers could scarcely be found for them, whilst
numbers were given away for nothing by the Khalifa. After
the defeat of the Shilluks, Zeki Tummal packed thousands
of these wretched creatures into the small barges used for
the transport of his troops, and despatched them to Omdurman. Hundreds died from suffocation and overcrowding
on the journey, and on the arrival of the remnant, the Khalifa
appropriated most of the young men as recruits for his body-
guard, whilst the women and young girls were sold by public
auction, which lasted several days. Hungry, and in many
cases naked, these unfortunate creatures lay huddled together in front of the Beit el Mal. For food, they were
given an utterly inadequate quantity of uncooked dhurra.
Hundreds fell ill, and for these poor wretches it was also
impossible to find purchasers. Wearily they dragged their
emaciated bodies to the river bank, where they died, and as
nobody would take the trouble to bury them, the corpses
were pushed into the river and swept away.

But a worse fate than this befell the slaves who had the
misfortune to be sent from Darfur along the broad stretches
of the waterless desert which lie between that province and
Omdurman. These miserable creatures were mercilessly
driven forward day and night, and it would be impossible
for me to describe here the execrable measures adopted by
these brutal slave-drivers to force on their prey to their destination. When the poor wretches could go no further their
ears were cut off as a proof to the owner that his property
had died on the road. Some of my friends told me that on
one occasion they had found an unfortunate woman whose

ears had been cut off, but who was still alive. Taking pity on her, they brought her to El Fasher, where she eventually recovered, whilst her ears had been duly exposed in Omdurman as proof of her death.

Latterly, no large caravans of slaves have arrived in Omdurman, because the majority of the slave-producing districts, such as Darfur, have become depopulated, or, in some cases, the tribes, such as the Tama, Massalit, etc., have thrown off allegiance to the Khalifa. Consignments, however, still come from Reggaf, but, owing to the long and tedious journey, numbers of them perish on the way. As the supplies from Gallabat, Kordofan, and Darfur have considerably diminished, the Khalifa now allows the Emirs to sell slaves to the itinerant Gellabas, and the latter are obliged to sign a paper giving a descriptive return of their purchase, and the amount paid. They are permitted to resell on the same conditions.

There is, of course, a daily sale of slaves in Omdurman ; but the purchase of male slaves is forbidden, as they are looked upon as the Khalifa's monopoly, and are generally turned into soldiers. Anyone wishing to dispose of a male slave must send him to the Beit el Mal, where a purely nominal price is paid for him, and he is then, if likely to make a good soldier, recruited for the mulazemin, but if unsuitable, he is sent off to work as a labourer in his master's fields. The sale of women and girls is permissible everywhere, with the proviso that a paper must be signed by two witnesses of the sale, one of whom, if possible, should be a Kadi, certifying that the slave sold is the actual property of the vendor. This system was brought into force because slaves frequently ran away from their masters, and were caught and sold by other persons as their own property, and thus theft of slaves was a very common practice in Omdurman. They were frequently enticed into other people's houses, or secretly induced to leave the fields, then thrown into chains and carried off to distant parts of the country, where they were sold at very low rates. In accordance with the

Mohammedan law, slaves cannot be witnesses, and being well aware of their inferior position, these stolen creatures, as long as they are kindly treated, are not dissatisfied with their lot.

In Omdurman itself, in an open space a short distance to the south-east of the Beit el Mal, stands a house roughly built of mud bricks, which is known as the Suk er Rekik (slave market). Under the pretext that I wanted to buy or exchange slaves, I several times received the Khalifa's permission to visit it, and found ample opportunity for closely observing the conduct of the business. Here professional slave-dealers assemble to offer their wares for sale. Round the walls of the house numbers of women and girls stand or sit. They vary from the decrepit and aged half-clad slaves of the working class to the gaily-decked surya (concubine); and, as the trade is looked upon as a perfectly natural and lawful business, those put up for sale are carefully examined from head to foot, without the least restriction, just as if they were animals. The mouth is opened to see if the teeth are in good condition. The upper part of the body and the back are laid bare, and the arms carefully looked at. They are then told to take a few steps backward or forward in order that their movements and gait may be examined. A series of questions are put to them to test their knowledge of Arabic. In fact, they have to submit to any examination the intending purchaser may wish to make. Suryas, of course, vary considerably in price; but the whole matter is treated by the slaves without the smallest concern. They consider it perfectly natural, and have no notion of being treated otherwise. Only occasionally one can see by the expression of a woman or girl that she feels this close scrutiny; possibly her position with her former master was rather that of a servant than a slave, or she may have been looked upon almost as a member of the family, and may have been brought to this unhappy position by force of circumstances, or through some hateful inhumanity on the part of her former master. When the intending purchaser has completed his scrutiny, he then refers to the dealer, asks him what he paid for her, or if he has any other better wares for sale. He will probably complain that her face is not pretty enough, that her body is not sufficiently developed, that she does not speak Arabic, and so on, with the object of reducing the price as much as possible; whilst, on the other hand, the owner will do his utmost to show up her good qualities, charms, etc., into the detail of which it is not necessary to enter here. Amongst the various ' secret defects ' which oblige the dealer to reduce his price are snoring, bad qualities of character, such as thieving, and many others; but when at last the sale has been finally arranged, the paper is drawn out and signed, the money paid, and the slave becomes the property of her new master. Payment is always made in local currency (Omla Gedida dollars), and runs approximately as follows :

For an aged working slave, fifty to eighty dollars; for a middle-aged woman, eighty to one hundred and twenty dollars; for young girls between eight and eleven years of age, according to looks, one hundred and ten to one hundred and sixty dollars; and for suryas, according to looks, one hundred and eighty to seven hundred dollars. These rates, of course, vary also according to market value, or special demand for a particular race.

There are practically no industries in the Sudan, as, with the exception of the articles I have already mentioned, there are no exports. Formerly, gold and silver filigree work was sent to Egypt; but, owing to the scarcity of these metals, and to the Mahdi's edict against wearing jewellery, this export has altogether ceased. There is a considerable manufacture and trade in long and short spears of various shapes, stirrup irons, horse and donkey bits, knives for fastening on the arm, as well as agricultural implements. Wooden saddles for horses, camels, and mules, angarebs, boxes for carrying clothes, and doors, windows, and shutters of a primitive description are also made. Formerly, boat-building was extensively carried on; but, owing to the

Khalifa's confiscation of all boats on the Nile, it ceased almost entirely, till about a year ago, when, with the Khalifa's permission, it recommenced. As, however, all new boats are taxed highly by the Beit el Mal, there is little induce ment to the builders to undertake such profitless work.

There is a certain amount of leather-work in red and yellow shoes, sandals, saddles of different sorts, harness, amulets, sword scabbards, and knife sheaths, etc., whilst whips in large quantities are made from the hide of the hippopotamus. There is also a considerable cotton industry. Every woman or girl spins for her own use or for sale, and in every village there are numbers of weavers who work the spun-yarn into a variety of materials. In the Gezira are woven common cotton stuffs—such as tobs, damur, and genj (names of cloths)—in lengths of about ten yards. These are brought to the market in large quantities, and are principally used for the clothing of the commoner classes. The finest yarns are spun in the province of Berber. Strips of coloured silk are frequently interwoven in the material, which is used principally for turbans and hazams (the strips of cotton which are used to bind round the body), as well as coverings of various sorts, and shawls. A certain amount of cotton stuff is made in the Dongola province ; but that district is chiefly noted for the manufacture of sail-cloth. Materials from Kordofan are noted for their durability rather than for their beauty.

In addition to spinning, the women occupy themselves largely in plaiting mats of various shapes and sizes from the leaves of the dom palm, which are sold largely in all parts of the Sudan. The best quality of these mats is made from the narrow strips of the palm leaves, barley straw, and thin pieces of leather. Mats of a similar description are also made for placing under dishes on the dinner-table. The workmanship of some of these is so fine and good that a certain quantity find their way to Egypt, where they are sold as curiosities. The Darfur women are specially clever in making these mats, into which are interwoven various sorts of glass beads, and the result is sometimes extremely pretty.

In the preceding pages I have endeavoured to give a brief outline of the Khalifa's life, and the existing state of affairs in the country; but this would not be complete without a few remarks regarding the moral condition of the people. The attempted regeneration of the faith by the Mahdi, who disregarded the former religious teaching and customs, has resulted in a deterioration of morals, which, even at the best of times, were very lax in the Sudan. Partly from fear of the Khalifa, and partly for their own personal interests and advantage, the people have made religion a mere profession, and this has now become their second nature, and has brought with it a condition of immorality which is almost indescribable. The majority of the inhabitants, unhappy and discontented with the existing state of affairs, and fearing that their personal freedom may become even more restricted than it is, seem to have determined to enjoy their life as much as their means will allow, and to lose no time about it. As there is practically no social life or spiritual intercourse, they seem to have resolved to make up for this want by indulging their passion for women to an abnormal extent. Their object is to obtain as many of these in marriage as possible, as well as concubines; and the Mahdi's tenets allow them the fullest scope in this direction. For instance, the expenses in connection with marriage have been greatly diminished. The dowry for a girl has been reduced from ten to five dollars, and for a widow, five dollars, a common dress, a pair of shoes or sandals, and a few scents. Should a man desire to marry a girl, her father or guardian must consent, unless there are some very cogent reasons for not doing so. Under any circumstances, they are held responsible that their daughters or wards become wives as soon as they reach a convenient age. The acquisition, therefore, of four wives—which is the number authorized by the Kuran —has become a very simple matter, and in most cases is considered merely a means of acquiring a small amount of personal property. Moreover, a large proportion of the women are quite agreeable to this arrangement, and enter into matrimony, either with the object of obtaining some clothes and a little money, or temporarily changing their mode of life, being well aware that, in accordance with the law, they can dissolve marriage ties without difficulty. If a woman seeks a divorce, she retains her dowry, unless the separation rises from aversion to her husband, in which case the dowry is returned if the man wishes it. I know many men who, in the space of ten years, have been married forty or fifty times at least; and there are also many women who, during the same period, have had fifteen or twenty husbands, and in their case the law enjoins that between each divorce they must wait three months at least. As a rule, concubines, of whom a man may legally have as many as he likes, lead a most immoral life. They rarely live in the same house as their master, unless they have children by him, in which case they cannot be sold; but in the majority of cases they are bought with the object of being retained merely for a very short time, and subsequently sold again at a profit. This constant changing of hands leads to great moral deterioration. Their youth and beauty quickly fade, and, as a rule, they age prematurely, and then enter upon a life of hardship and moral degradation which it is almost impossible to conceive.

It is a common practice for merchants to make pecuniary profit out of the immorality of their slaves. They buy young girls, permit them to enjoy a certain amount of freedom by seeking a shelter and livelihood in the manner which suits them best, and for this privilege they refund to their masters a percentage of their gains.

The greatest vice exists amongst the slaves of the mulazemin. The latter entice women to their quarters, where they remain a short time with them as their wives, but the freest interchange takes place between them. The Khalifa does not seem to think it worth while to check this immorality, as he imagines that by allowing them to please themselves, his own slaves will become more attached to him, and will not wish to leave him. It may be readily conceived that the result of this moral laxity has led to the prevalence of the worst sort of disease, which has taken such a hold of all classes of the population, both free and slaves, that were it not for the warm and dry climate, the ravages would be terrible. As it is, the general state of health is very unsatisfactory, and is considerably aggravated by the complete absence of medicines necessary to check the malady.

A certain number of people also indulge in unnatural love, and at first the Khalifa made some attempt to check this by banishment to Reggaf; but latterly he has given up doing so. He has come to the conclusion that it is much easier to rule by despotism and tyranny a degraded nation than one which possesses a high standard of morality. For this reason he both hates and fears the Jaalin, who inhabit the Nile banks between Hagger el Asal and Berber, because they are almost the only Arabs in the Sudan who maintain a well-regulated family life, and hold morality in high esteem as a necessary condition for a healthy and contented existence.

The widows of the Mahdi are forcibly prevented from leading a corrupt life, as, immediately after his master's death, the Khalifa, in honour of his memory, confined these women in houses surrounded by high walls in the immediate vicinity of his tomb, where they are strictly guarded by eunuchs. Much against their will, not only the wives and concubines, but also many of the young girls—most of whom were daughters of former Government officials, and who were taken into the harem when quite young, in order to become his future wives—have been thus forcibly deprived of the possibility of re-marrying, and are so closely guarded that they are only permitted to see their female relatives once a year. They are supplied merely with the bare necessaries of life, and long for their freedom. Let us hope that before very long it may come!

In spite of his despotism, the Khalifa is in considerable fear of his life. He ruthlessly evicted all the local inhabitants of those portions of the town in the immediate neighbourhood of his own residence, and their places have been taken by his enormous body-guard, whose numbers he daily seeks to increase. These he has surrounded by an immense wall, within which he and his relatives live, while all persons of whom he is in the slightest degree suspicious are forced to reside without the enclosure. Within, however, all is not peace and contentment. The constant duties he imposes on his body-guard have produced a feeling of irritation. They grumble at the small pay they receive, and do not appreciate the restrictions imposed on their social life. Thousands of these who belong to the free Arab tribes are prevented from having any intercourse whatever with their relations. They are scarcely ever permitted to quit the enclosure, and their smallest offences are punished with appalling severity. Abdullahi is surrounded day and night by his own specially appointed guard, and by numbers of faithful servants, and no persons—not even his nearest relatives—are permitted to approach him with arms in their hands. Should anyone be commanded to see the Khalifa, his sword and knife, which he invariably wears, are taken from him, and he is generally searched before being admitted to the audience-chamber. This general mistrust has added to his unpopularity, and, even amongst his most devoted adherents, remarks are frequently let fall in an undertone, commenting on his despotism and his personal fears.

In spite, however, of all this undue severity, the Khalifa has not succeeded in keeping his own tribe in hand. On their first arrival in the Nile Valley they indulged in wholesale raids on the local population, seizing their grain, ravishing their women, and carrying off their children. Indeed, affairs became so serious that the Khalifa was obliged to issue an order that no Taaisha Arab would be permitted to leave the town without special permission; but his instructions were practically ignored, and lawlessness is even more rife than before. The conduct of these Arabs is unbearable. They openly boast that their relationship with the Khalifa has made them masters of the country, and that they intend to assert themselves. They have seized all the best pastures for their cattle and horses, and they live on the fat of the land, a state of affairs which has caused considerable jealousy amongst the other western tribes, who view the Taaisha with no very friendly feelings. Of all this the Khalifa is well aware, but I do not think he realizes how unpopular he really is, and his constant effort is to retain the sympathy of his Emirs by frequently sending them secretly by night presents of money and slaves. The latter do not hesitate to accept these gifts, which they know have been unfairly gained, and their opinion of the Khalifa, instead of being improved, remains as it was before.

The Khalifa has not moved out of Omdurman for upwards of ten years. Here he has centralized all power, stored up all ammunition, and gathered under his personal surveillance all those whom he suspects, obliging them to say the five prayers daily in his presence, and listen to his sermons. He has declared Omdurman to be the sacred city of the Mahdi. It is strange to think that ten years ago this great town was merely a little village lying opposite to Khartum, and inhabited by a few brigands. It was not for some time after the fall of Khartum that the Mahdi decided to settle there. Mimosa-trees filled up the space now occupied by the mosque and the residences of the three Khalifas. Abdullahi took as his own property all ground lying south of the mosque, whilst that on the north side was divided between Khalifa Sherif and Khalifa Ali Wad Helu. During his lifetime the Mahdi had declared that Omdurman was merely a temporary camp, as the Prophet had revealed to him that he should depart this life in Syria, after conquering Egypt and Arabia; but his early death shattered all his plans and the hopes of his followers.

From north to south the new city covers a length of

about six English miles. The southern extremity lies almost exactly opposite the south-west end of Khartum. At first everyone wanted to live as near the river banks as possible, in order to facilitate the drawing of water, consequently the breadth of the city is considerably less than its length, and it is in no place over three miles in width. At first it consisted of thousands and thousands of straw huts, and the mosque was originally an oblong enclosure, surrounded by a mud wall four hundred and sixty yards long and three hundred and fifty yards broad; but this has now been replaced by one made of burnt brick, and then whitewashed over. After this the Khalifa began building brick houses for himself and his brother, then for his relatives, whilst the Emirs and most of the wealthy people followed his example. I have already described the construction of the Mahdi's tomb, but before I left Omdurman much of the whitewash had been knocked off by the weather, which spoilt its general appearance. Above the apex of the dome are three hollow brass balls, one above the other, connected together by a lance, the head of which forms the top ornament of the structure. I have often heard people say that the Khalifa erected this spear to show that he is perfectly prepared to declare war against the heavens if his wishes are not carried out. Occasionally Abdullahi shuts himself up for hours in this mausoleum, probably with the object of obtaining some special inspiration; but since the execution of the Mahdi's relatives his visits are much less frequent, and it is generally supposed he dreads to be alone with the body of his dead master, whose tenets and influence he has, not in words, but in deeds, so persistently overturned. Every Friday the large doors in the surrounding enclosure are opened to admit the pilgrims, and as every Mahdist is ordered to attend on these days to repeat the prayers for the dead, thousands are to be seen in the various attitudes of prayer, beseeching the protection of the Almighty through the intermediary of the saint (?) who lies buried there; but I doubt not that many fervent prayers ascend to the throne of God for relief from the terrible oppression and tyranny of his despotic successor.

South of the tomb, and adjoining the great mosque, lies the enormous enclosure of the Khalifa. It consists of a high wall built of red bricks, which is subdivided into several smaller courts, all of which are in communication with each other, and nearest to the mosque are his own private apartments, to the east of which are those of his wives, the stables, store-houses, quarters of the eunuchs, etc. In the centre of the eastern face of the mosque is a large wooden door (the other entrances to the mosque have no doors), through which admission is obtained to the Khalifa's private apartments and reception chambers. On entering the main gate one passes through a sort of porch, leading into a small court, in which are two rooms, one side of each of which is left completely open, and it is here that the Khalifa receives his guests. A door leads out of this court into the private apartments, and the youthful attendants are the only persons allowed to enter. The various houses within the enclosure are constructed in the shape of large detached halls, on one or both sides of which are verandas. On the roof of one of these buildings a second story has been added, on all four sides of which are windows, from which a complete view of the town can be obtained.

The reception chambers are furnished with the greatest simplicity. An angareb, over which a palm-mat is spread, is the only article of furniture; but his interior apartments are provided with all the luxuries it is possible to procure in the Sudan. Brass and iron bedsteads, with mosquito curtains—the spoil of Khartum—carpets, silk-covered cushions, door and window curtains of every variety of colour and texture, are the principal articles of furniture, while the verandas are provided with the universal angareb and palm-mat. Compared with the Khalifa's early mode of life, these articles constitute the most extreme luxuries.

To the east of the Khalifa's enclosure lies the house of his son, which is furnished much in the same style as that of his father, but with even greater luxury. Several large brass chandeliers from Khartum are suspended from the ceilings, and there is an immense garden made from earth transported from the banks of the Nile, and in which hundreds of slaves are employed daily. The latter are justly irritated with the great love of show which is the distinguishing characteristic of their young master, whilst they themselves are provided with scarcely enough food for their maintenance.

The Khalifa and his son spend much of their time in building and furnishing new apartments, and in making their lives as pleasant and comfortable as possible. Yakub follows their example, and every day numbers of workmen are to be seen streaming towards these two houses, carrying beams, stone, mortar, and other requisite building material. Khalifa Ali Wad Helu's house is very much smaller, and is furnished with great simplicity.

In addition to his principal residence, Abdullahi possesses houses in the northern and southern districts of the city ; but they are built and furnished on much simpler lines, and are merely used by him as rest-houses when he despatches troops on expeditions from the capital, or goes out to inspect freshly arrived detachments from the provinces. He seldom stays in these houses more than a day or two at a time. He has also built a house near the river, and close to the old Government fort, the ditches of which have now been filled in. He generally goes to this house when steamers are about to start for Reggaf, in order that he may personally superintend embarkations.

The Beit el Amana, or arsenal, is separated from Yakub's house by a broad open space. It consists of a large building enclosed by stone walls, and here are stored the guns, rifles, ammunition, and other warlike material, as well as the five carriages belonging to the Governor-Generals and to the Catholic Mission. At intervals of every few paces sentries are posted in small sentry-boxes, and they are charged to allow no unauthorised persons to enter the building. Just north of the arsenal lies a building in which are stored the flags of all the Emirs residing in Omdurman, and beside it is a semicircular building about twenty feet high, provided with stairs, where the Khalifa's war-drums are kept. A little further to the east is the cartridge and small-arms manufactory.

On the north side of the city, and close to the river, is the Beit el Mal, which is an enormous walled-in enclosure subdivided into a variety of courts, in which are stored goods coming from all parts of the Sudan and from Egypt, as well as grain stores and slave courts. A little to the south of the Beit el Mal lies the public slave-market, and in close proximity the Beit el Mal of the mulazemin has been erected.

The town of Omdurman is built for the most part on fairly level ground, but here and there are a few small hills. The soil consists mostly of hard red clay, and is very stony, with occasional patches of sand. For his own convenience the Khalifa has driven large straight roads through various parts of the town, and to make way for these numbers of houses were levelled, but no compensation was given to their owners. A glance at the rough plan attached to the end of the book will give the reader an approximate idea of the extent and general situation of the town and principal buildings, and its relative position with reference to Khartum, which is now a complete ruin, the dockyard alone being kept up, and communication between it and Omdurman maintained by a submarine cable worked by some of the former Government telegraph officials. Outside the large unfinished wall built along the road leading to the Beit el Mal are a number of shops belonging to the various trades, all of which are kept quite distinct—such as carpenters, barbers, tailors, butchers, etc. The Mehekemet es Suk (market police) are charged with maintaining order in the town, and the gallows erected in various parts of the city are a very evident indication of the system of government of the country.

The population of the city is located entirely according to tribes. The western Arabs live for the most part in the southern quarters, whilst the northern portion has been allotted to the Nile Valley people; and in addition to the market police, the various sections of the populace are obliged to supply a number of watchmen for the preservation of public security in their respective quarters, and they must report any disturbances to the night patrols.

With the exception of the few broad roads which the Khalifa has made for his own convenience, the only communications between the various quarters consist of numbers of narrow winding lanes, and in these all the filth of the city is collected. Their wretched condition and the smells which emanate from these pestilential by-paths are beyond description. Dead horses, camels, donkeys, and goats block the way, and the foulest refuse lies scattered about. Before certain feast-days the Khalifa issues orders that the city is to be cleaned; but beyond sweeping all these carcases and refuse into corners nothing further is done, and when the rainy season begins the fetid air exhaling from these decaying rubbish-heaps generally produces some fatal epidemic, which sweeps off the inhabitants by hundreds.

Formerly there were cemeteries within the city, but now all the dead must be buried in the desert north of the parade-ground.

Fever and dysentery are the prevailing maladies in Omdurman, and between the months of November and March an almost continuous epidemic of typhus fever rages.

Of late years numbers of new wells have been made. Those north of the mosque give good water, but those in the southern quarters of the city are mostly brackish. They vary in depth from thirty to ninety feet, and are generally dug by the prisoners under the direction of the saier.

'He has been taken to the saier,' is an expression one frequently hears, and it means that some wretched creature has been carried off to the prison. The mere mention of this word awakens feelings of horror and dread in the minds of all who hear it. The prison is situated in the south-eastern quarter of the city, near the river, and is surrounded by a high wall. A gate, strongly guarded day and night by armed Blacks, gives access to an inner court, in which several small mud and stone huts have been erected. During the daytime the unhappy prisoners, most of them heavily chained and manacled, lie about in the shade of the buildings. Complete silence prevails, broken only by the clanking of the chains, the hoarse orders of the hard-hearted warders, or the cries of some poor wretch who is being mercilessly flogged. Some of the prisoners who may have specially incurred the Khalifa's displeasure are loaded with heavier chains and manacles than the rest, and are interned in the small huts, and debarred from all intercourse with their fellow-prisoners. They generally receive only sufficient nourishment to keep them alive.

Ordinary prisoners receive no regular supply of food; but their relatives are allowed to provide for them. It often happens that long before a meal reaches the person for whom it is intended, a very large portion of it has been consumed by the rapacious and unscrupulous warders: and sometimes the prisoner gets nothing whatever. At night, the wretched creatures are driven like sheep into the stone huts, which are not provided with windows, and are consequently quite unventilated. Regardless of prayers and entreaties, they are pushed pell-mell into these living graves, which are generally so tightly packed that it is quite impossible to lie down. The weaker are trampled down by the stronger, and not infrequently the warder opens the door in the morning to find that some of his victims have succumbed to suffocation and ill-usage in these horrible cells. It is a painful sight to see scores of half-suffocated individuals pouring out of these dens, bathed in perspiration, and utterly exhausted by the turmoil of the long and sleepless night. Once emerged, they sink down, more dead than alive, under the shade of the walls, and spend the remainder of the day in trying to recover from the effects of the previous night, and gain sufficient strength to undergo the horrors of that which is to follow.

One would think that death was preferable to such an existence. Still these unfortunates cling to life, and pray to God to relieve them from their sufferings. In spite of the prison being invariably overcrowded, and notwithstanding the horrors of prison life, I do not ever remember having heard of a case of suicide amongst the unfortunate inmates.

Charles Neufeld has spent some years in the Saier, often ill, subject to the greatest privations, and merely kept alive by the occasional supplies which reached him through the Black servant he brought with him from Egypt, and who, in turn, was assisted by the other Europeans in Omdurman. He managed to survive, though heavily chained by the neck, and wearing two large irons round his feet. On one occasion, he refused to spend the night in one of the stone huts, which he aptly described as ' the last station on the way to hell,' and for this act of disobedience he was severely flogged ; but he bore it without a murmur, until his tormentors—amazed at his powers of endurance—cried out : ' Why do you not complain ? Why do you not ask for mercy ?' ' That is for others to do, not for me,' was the stronghearted reply which gained for him the respect of even his gaolers. After enduring three years of imprisonment his irons were lightened, and, with only a chain joining his ankles, he was removed to Khartum, where he was ordered to refine saltpetre for the manufacture of gunpowder, under the superintendence of Wad Hamednalla. Here his condition was much improved, and he received a small monthly remuneration for his work, which sufficed to provide him with the bare necessaries of life. As the saltpetre refinery adjoins the old church of the Mission, the latter has thus been saved from destruction. After his daily hard work is over, Neufeld is allowed to rest in the mission gardens ; and here, no doubt, his thoughts often revert to his family at home, and he must in his heart curse the evil day which induced him to quit Egypt, and thoughtlessly venture into the clutches of the Khalifa. For him Fate has indeed been cruel; and most fervently do I hope that ere long he may be reunited with his relatives, who have not abandoned all hope of seeing him again. In Europe there is no lack of friends who are ready to do all in their power to help him; but it rests with God alone to release this poor captive from his misery.

It makes my heart ache to think of all the horrors that have been enacted in that dreadful prison. There was the sad case of poor Sheikh Khalil, who had been despatched from Cairo with letters to the Khalifa, informing him of the number and names of the prisoners who had been captured at the battle of Toski, all of whom, he was assured, were being well cared for, and would eventually be set free; and he was requested to hand over to the Sheikh the sword and medals of General Gordon, which, it was assumed, were in his possession. Khalil's companion, Beshara, was sent back with the letters unanswered, whilst the unfortunate emissary, who was an Egyptian by birth, was thrown into chains, under the pretext that he had been sent as a spy. Ill-treated, and deprived of nourishment, he became so weak that he could not rise from the ground. His tormentors even refused him water to drink; and at last death came to him as a happy release from his sufferings.

Malech, a Jewish merchant of Tunis, who had come to Kassala with Abu Girga's permission, was seized by the Khalifa's orders, and brought to Omdurman, where he remains in captivity in the Saier to this day. He is as thin as a skeleton, and is driven almost to despair. He is kept alive by the efforts of his own community, who have been forced to become Moslems, and who succeed in providing him with small quantities of food.

Two Ababda Arabs, arrested on suspicion of carrying letters to Europeans in Omdurman, were seized and imprisoned, and died soon after of starvation. The alarm in the European colony was great; but fortunately it tran-

spired that the letters were for a Copt from his relations in
Cairo.

The great Sheikh of the Gimeh tribe, Asakr Abu Kalam,
who had shown such friendship and hospitality to the
Khalifa and his father in early days, was ruthlessly seized
and thrown into chains, because it came to the Khalifa's
ears that he had spoken disparagingly of the present condition of the Sudan, and had expressed regret at having taken
up arms against the Government.   He was eventually
exiled to Reggaf, whilst his wife, who was a well-known
beauty in the Sudan, was torn from the arms of her husband
at the hour of his departure, and carried off to the Khalifa's
harem.

The well-known Emir, Zeki Tummal, on being seized,
was thrown into a small stone building the shape of a
coffin, the door of which was built up.   He was given no
food whatever, but a small amount of water was handed to
him through an aperture in the wall.   For twenty-three
days he suffered all the horrors of starvation, but no sound
or complaint was heard to issue from that living grave.
Too proud to beg, and well aware of the futility of doing so,
he lingered on till the twenty-fourth day, when death carried
him out of reach of his tormentors.   The Saier and his
warders watched through the aperture the death agonies of
the wretched man, and when at length he had ceased to
struggle, they hurried off to give their lord and master the
joyful news.   That night Zeki's body was removed to the
western quarter of the city, and there buried amongst a
heap of old ruins with his back towards Mecca.*   The
Khalifa, not content with having tormented him in life,
thought thus to deprive him of peace in the world to come.

I have already described how the Khalifa disposed of his
most trusted adherent, the Kadi Ahmed.   On reaching the
Saier, he was thrown into the hut in which Zeki had been
interned, and a few days after he was visited, at the command of the Khalifa, by two other Kadis, who asked

---

* All true Moslems are buried facing Mecca.

where he had hidden his money. 'Tell your master, the Khalifa,' said he, 'that I have settled my account with this world, and I know of no place where gold or silver can be found.' To their further inquiries he remained perfectly silent, and the two myrmidons returned crestfallen to their master. This happened only a few days before I quitted Omdurman. Since my return to Egypt I have ascertained that he died shortly afterwards, under similar circumstances to those of Zeki.

One could fill a volume with descriptions of the horrors and cruelties enacted in the terrible Saier, but it is useless to weary the reader with further accounts of the atrocities committed by order of that merciless tyrant, the Khalifa.

CHAPTER XVII.

PLANS FOR ESCAPE.

European Captives in Omdurman—Artin, the Watchmaker—Friends in Cairo—Efforts of my Family to help me—Difficulties of Communication—Babakr Abu Sebiba's Failure—Efforts of Baron Heidler and the Egyptian Intelligence Department—Constant Failures— Osheikh Karrar—Abderrahman matures his Plans—Hopes and Fears—My Plan to gain Time—I quit my Hut never to return.

IN keeping me constantly close to his person the Khalifa had a twofold object. He knew that I was the only remaining high Egyptian official who had a thorough knowledge of the Sudan, had traversed almost the entire country, and was complete master of the language. Utterly ignorant of the political situation, he imagined that, if I succeeded in escaping, I should induce the Egyptian Government, or some European power, to enter the Sudan; and he well knew that in that case I should form a link between it and the principal tribal chiefs who were disaffected to him, and longed for the return of a settled form of government. On the other hand, it flattered his vanity to have practically as

his slave the man who had formerly governed the whole of
the great province of Darfur, including his own country and
tribe. He never attempted to conceal his feelings in this
respect, and frequently said to the Western Arabs, ' See,
this is the man who was formerly our master, and under
whose arbitrary rule we suffered. Now he is my servant,
and must obey my commands at all times. See, this is the
man who formerly indulged in the pleasures and vices of
the world, and now he has to wear an unwashed jibba and
walk barefooted. God indeed is merciful and gracious!'
He paid much less attention to the other European captives,
who gained a small livelihood by working at various trades
in a quarter near the market-place, where they had built
their own huts, and were left almost undisturbed by the
other inhabitants of the city. Father Ohrwalder lived by
weaving. Father Rosignoli and Beppo Rognotto (a former
Mission brother) kept a cook-shop in the market-place, and
the Sisters lived with them until (with the exception of
Sister Theresa Grigolini) they succeeded in escaping. Then
there is Giuseppe Cuzzi, one of A. Marquet's former clerks,
and a number of Greeks, Syrian Christians, and Copts—in
all some forty-five men, who have married either Christians
born in the country or Egyptians. The entire colony is
termed the Muslimania* quarter, and they have elected
from amongst themselves an Emir, under whose orders they
agree to live, and who is responsible to the Khalifa for
every member of the colony. The present Emir is a certain
Greek called Nicola, whose Arabic name is Abdullahi. No
one is on any account allowed to quit Omdurman, and they
are obliged to guarantee each other. Consequently, when
Father Rosignoli escaped, his companion Beppo was thrown
into prison, and was in chains when I left the town. After
Father Ohrwalder's flight, a much stricter surveillance was
exercised over all these unfortunates. A place has been

* The term ' Muslimani ' is generally given to the descendants of
' unbelievers '; it is an opprobrious epithet, and is applied by the
Mahdists to all so-called renegades.

allotted to them in the north-eastern portion of the mosque, where they have to attend prayers daily; but not being under special control, they take it in turns to be present, so that, in case of inquiry, the colony shall always be represented. Their huts are built adjoining each other, and in this way they can communicate without difficulty, and thus derive some alleviation of their sad lot by mutual sympathy; but their children are obliged to live in the various tekias (religious rest-houses), where they are taught the Kuran.

I have already described my own surroundings and mode of life, and it now remains for me to add that I was only permitted to converse with a few of the body-guard who were, like myself, either under surveillance or specially employed as spies by the Khalifa to watch and report our every action and word. I was seldom permitted to enter the town, and I was strictly forbidden to make any visits.

The Khalifa is very fond of watches and clocks, and one of my many duties was to wind them up, and generally look after them. I availed myself of this privilege to occasionally visit an Armenian watchmaker named Artin, on the pretext that a clock or watch required repair. His house was situated near the market-place, and here I used to arrange meetings with some of the people I particularly wished to see. I never confided in Artin, and those who came to the shop invariably made some small purchases, and in doing so we succeeded in exchanging, as it were quite casually, a few words. Most of my time was spent at the Khalifa's gate reading the Kuran. I was not permitted to write, as Abdullahi thought it unnecessary for me to practise an art of which he himself was ignorant. I invariably accompanied my master to the mosque, or when he appeared in public, and on these occasions my duties were somewhat those of an aide-de-camp. Being in receipt of no salary, my food was of the simplest, and consisted generally of asida, various sorts of sauces, and occasionally a little meat purchased in the market.

Abdullahi knew perfectly that I longed for freedom, and, in spite of all my efforts to conceal it, I could not overcome his very rational suspicion of me. By constant gifts of slaves, by offers of marriage with his family, and various other expedients, he did all he could to make ties which he thought would hold me down; but my continued refusal of these very questionable benefits only confirmed his suspicions that I intended to escape on the first possible occasion. After the fall of Khartum, my family had done all in their power to obtain news of me, but fortunately they realized how careful they must be. Herr Von Gsiller, the Austro-Hungarian Consul-General in Egypt, spared no pains to get news of me, and his efforts were heartily seconded by the officers attached to the Egyptian army and other officials. It was at his suggestion that my relatives had communicated with me through the Governor of Suakin in 1888, and I have described in the preceding pages how I was eventually forbidden by the Khalifa to hold any further intercourse with the outside world. Already my relations with the Khalifa had become much strained owing to these events, and they became much more so when a letter reached the Khalifa from Herr Von Rosty (who had succeeded Herr Von Gsiller), asking his permission to send a priest to minister to the members of the Mission, who, he stated, were Austrian subjects. At the same time he had written to me, asking for information on the present situation in the Sudan. The Khalifa, of course, took no notice of Herr Von Rosty's letter, and accused me of duplicity and disloyalty, because I had previously informed him that the members of the Mission, with the exception of Father Ohrwalder, were Italians. I had deliberately done this, as I feared that Abdullahi, in one of the sudden outbursts of passion against me, might vent his rage on those whom he believed to be my compatriots, and whom I was anxious to save; but now this letter, stating directly the contrary, was a heavy blow. It was quite beyond the Khalifa's capacity to understand that members of various nationalities could

be, for the purpose of the Mission, under Austrian protection, and for a long time he incessantly upbraided me for
having deceived him.

My family had placed a considerable sum of money at the
disposal of the Austrian Consul-General with the object of
assisting me, and they, through the kind intervention of the
various Sirdars of the Egyptian army, and of Major Wingate, the Director of Military Intelligence, succeeded in
sending me occasional sums by the hands of trustworthy
Arabs. Of course, I invariably received considerably
smaller sums than those which had been originally confided
to them, though I was obliged to give receipts for the full
amounts. However, I was truly thankful for what I
received, and, by the system which was established, I was
enabled to send my relatives scraps of information about
myself and my affairs. I was obliged to exercise the most
extreme caution in spending the money thus received lest
suspicion should be aroused, and therefore I continued to
live as simply as possible, and expended all I could spare in
cementing my various friendships.

My friends in Cairo had fully realized that, after I had
been prevented from holding any communication with the
outside, it was quite impossible for them to secure my
release from the Khalifa's hands by ordinary methods.
They therefore spared no efforts to afford me the means of
effecting my escape should an opportunity occur. From
the earliest days of my captivity I had realized that my
only hope of freedom lay in flight, and although the rise
and development of this great movement interested me
considerably—especially as I had exceptional means of
watching it—I never for an instant abandoned the idea of
succeeding in my object, though I little dreamt that twelve
long years of hardship, misery, and humiliation must elapse
before it could be accomplished.

For years I did not confide my secret to a soul, but
eventually I told Ibrahim Adlan of my intentions, and he
promised to assist me to the best of his ability. Unfortu-

nately, the Khalifa executed him soon afterwards, and in
him I lost a true and kind friend and protector. On his
death I confided my secret to two influential individuals, on
whose silence I could rely, and though I knew that—partly
owing to their liking for me and partly owing to their hatred
of the Khalifa—they would have willingly assisted me in
the accomplishment of my object, our negotiations came to
nothing. The money required would, I knew, be forth-
coming ; but they dreaded that after my escape their names
might be eventually divulged, and as they were tied by
their families to live in the Sudan, they knew that, in the
event of discovery, the Khalifa would wreak his vengeance
on their defenceless wives and children.

Meanwhile, my family had not been idle, and no sacrifice
was too great for their love. Living in Vienna, ignorant of
the real state of affairs in the Sudan, and not aware of how
they could best help me, they trustfully continued to place
considerable sums of money at the disposal of the Austrian
Agency in Cairo, the representative of which received instructions from the Minister of Foreign Affairs to utilize it
to the best of his ability. His Excellency Baron Heidler
von Egeregg — now Ambassador and Minister Plenipo-
tentiary, and who has been for some years Consul-General
in Cairo—took a personal interest in my affairs, and did
everything in his power to facilitate my escape. But it is
only possible to secure the services of reliable persons
through the intermediary of Government officials, and, with
this object in view, he enlisted the sympathies, first of
Colonel Schaeffer Bey, and subsequently of Major Wingate,
who had on several previous occasions endeavoured to
assist me ; and it is to his and to Baron Heidler's incessant
efforts that I owe my freedom. Without their intervention,
it would not have been possible to procure reliable Arabs to
bring me occasional sums of money, and I owe to them my
heartiest thanks for their frequent attempts to effect my
rescue ; and although, with the exception of the last, they
all failed, the arrangements were such that the Khalifa

and his myrmidons never had the slightest suspicion of them.

Early in February, 1892, the former chief of the Dongola camel postmen, Babakr Abu Sebiba, arrived in Omdurman from Egypt. He was an Ababda Arab, and when brought before the Khalifa, he asserted that he had escaped from Assuan, that he sought the Khalifa's pardon, and begged to be allowed to settle down in Berber. As he had letters of introduction to the Emir of Berber, Zeki Osman, permission was accorded to him; and when going out at the door of the mosque he nudged me, and whispered, 'I have come for you; arrange for an interview.' 'To-morrow after evening prayers, here in the mosque,' was my reply, and he then disappeared. Although I had not given up hope of escape, I never dared to be very sanguine; for I had had much experience of these Arabs and Sudanese, and knew that often their words go for nought, and their promises are more frequently broken than kept. I therefore spent the following day much as usual, though I could not help wondering what would be the upshot of the interview.

After evening prayers, and when all the people had left the mosque, Babakr passed the door at which I had seen him the previous day.

Cautiously I followed him, and together we entered the thatched portion of the building, which was in deep shade. Out of sight and out of hearing, Babakr now handed me a small tin box, which, from the smell, seemed to contain coffee, saying, 'This box has a double bottom. Open and read the papers enclosed in it; and I shall be here again to-morrow at the same hour.' Concealing the box under my jibba, I returned to my place, and, as chance fell out, was summoned that evening to sup with the Khalifa. Imagine my feelings, for the box was sufficiently large to be seen under my clothes; and here was I seated opposite my master with his lynx eyes fixed on me. Fortunately he was rather tired, and only talked on general subjects, though he did not fail to caution me to be loyal, or he would

punish me unmercifully. Of course I assured him of my
fidelity and affection for him ; and, after having partaken
of a little meat and dhurra, I feigned sudden illness, and
obtained permission to withdraw.   Hurrying home with all
speed, I lit my little oil lamp, tore open the box with my
knife, and there found a small piece of paper, on which the
following words were written in French :

'Babakr Wad Abu Sebiba is a trustworthy man.
            '(Signed)   SCHAEFFER, Colonel.'

On the other side of the paper were a few lines from the
Austrian Agency confirming this. The writers had wisely
omitted my name, fearing that it might fall into the hands
of enemies ; and now I had to exercise more patience until
the following evening.

As agreed, I met Babakr as before ; and he briefly informed me that he had come to arrange my escape, and
that, having seen me, he would return to Berber to complete his preparations. As the Emir Zeki Osman had been
ordered to come to Omdurman in July for the manœuvres,
he proposed to accompany him, in order to carry out his
object. I assured him that I was ready at any time to
make the attempt ; and, after imploring him to do all in his
power to help me, we parted. He returned, as arranged, in
July, with Zeki Osman ; and, in a secret meeting, he told
me that, in order to disarm suspicion, he had got married in
Berber ; that he had brought four camels with him, but
that he had not yet arranged about our crossing the river.
Should I, however, decide to risk flight, he would guide me
through the Bayuda desert and by El Kaab (west of
Dongola) to Wadi Halfa ; but I knew that the camels
could not possibly perform such a journey in the height of
summer. I soon saw that the man wanted to spend a few
more months in the Sudan, probably with his newly
acquired bride ; and so we agreed to postpone the attempt
till the month of December, when the long nights would be

more favourable to the enterprise. Months passed; and I heard from secret sources that Babakr was still at Berber. December went by, and the year 1893 had begun. Still no sign of my friend. At length he returned in July, and told me that the messenger whom I had despatched to Cairo asking for £100 had been delayed on the road; and that as he had arrived there at a time of year when the journey would have been impossible, the authorities had refused to supply him with the funds. He added, however, that he had brought two camels, and that if I would risk flight, he would try to procure a third. I saw that the man had been making inquiries, and had ascertained that at most it would only be possible for me to obtain a few hours' start, which would not be sufficient to insure success; besides he knew that it was out of the question starting in July. When therefore I proposed again postponing flight till the beginning of the winter, he readily acquiesced, merely for form's sake. His constant visits to Omdurman had aroused the Khalifa's suspicions; and one of the Kadis notified him that he must attend the mosque five times daily, and should not leave Omdurman without the Khalifa's permission. Alarmed probably at the turn affairs had taken, he escaped and returned to Egypt. Three days after he had left, his absence was discovered. On his arrival in Cairo, as I subsequently learnt, he informed those who had sent him that he had frequently come to Omdurman; but that I had persistently refused to risk flight with him. Baron Heidler and Major Wingate, however, realized that the man's statement was untrue; and some time later I had an opportunity of informing them, through a trusty agent, of the man's behaviour.

These gentlemen subsequently made an agreement with a merchant named Musa Wad Abderrahman, promising him £1,000 if he succeeded in effecting my escape, while at the same time he was furnished with what was necessary for the undertaking. In the winter I received information of this fresh enterprise; but it was not till June, 1894, that one of Musa's relatives, named Ahmed, told me that some Arabs had been secured who would arrive in a few days, and would attempt to fly with me. He also told me that a station had been prepared in the desert, where a change of camels would be in readiness, and that, in spite of the great heat, there was every prospect of the success of the undertaking.

On 1st July Ahmed warned me that the camels had arrived, and that I should be ready to start the next night. That evening I told my servants that one of my friends was dangerously ill, and that I had obtained the Khalifa's permission to visit him, that I would probably stay the night, and that therefore they need not be uneasy if I did not return. That night, when my master had retired to rest, accompanied by Ahmed, I quitted the mosque ; and, with bare feet and armed only with a sword, we hurried along the road leading towards the parade ground, and then turned off in a north-easterly direction.

The night was dark. During the day the first showers announcing the beginning of the rainy season had fallen ; and as we crossed the cemetery I put my foot into an old grave, which had been washed out by the rain, and my foot got twisted in the bones of the skeleton on which I had stepped. It seemed as if the dead as well as the living were conspiring to throw difficulties in my path ; but, in spite of the pain, I struggled on, and reached Khor Shambat. We crossed to the other side, where it was arranged the camels would await us. We searched up and down the banks. Ahmed even called out in a low tone ; but not a sign of them was to be seen. The night was cool, but our efforts had bathed us in perspiration, and after wandering to and fro for hours in our vain search, we were at length obliged to give up and retrace our steps. What could have happened to our men ? Could they have been noticed by some Dervishes, who had perhaps arrested them on suspicion ? Full of doubts and fears, we reached our homes in safety. I had parted from Ahmed on the parade-ground, and I had begged him to let me know in the evening what had happened. At the same time, I repeated that I was prepared to renew the attempt at any time. The dawn was just breaking as I reached the threshold of my hut, which I had quitted a few hours before, as I thought, for the last time, and my feelings can be better imagined than described. I had scarcely been back more than a few minutes when one of my fellow mulazemin, named Abdel Kerim, arrived with a message from the Khalifa to inquire the reason of my absence from morning prayers. I replied that I had been ill, and, indeed, my wretched appearance almost warranted such an assertion.

In vain I waited that evening for news from Ahmed ; but I did not learn from him till two days afterwards that the Arabs had reconsidered the matter, and had come to the conclusion that the risk of recapture was too great, and had returned to their homes instead of coming to the place of rendezvous. So we had completely failed, and considered ourselves lucky to have returned unnoticed from our midnight ramble.

Again I informed my Cairo friends of what had happened. They were unsparing in their efforts, and had now the valuable aid of Father Ohrwalder, who, when in Vienna, had visited my family, and had obtained from them some ether pills, which are very strengthening on a journey, and ward off sleep. They had been prepared by Professor Ottokar Chiari, and had reached me safely. They were in a small bottle, which I had buried carefully in the ground.

I now made a confidant of Abderrahman Wad Harun, whom I despatched to Cairo with a message to Baron Heidler, to place at his disposal the requisite means for my escape. Again an agreement was made between this merchant and the Austrian Agency, with the concurrence of Major Wingate, and the assistance of Milhem Shakkur Bey and Naum Effendi Shukeir, of the Intelligence Department. If successful Abderrahman was to receive £1,000, and he was also given the necessary outfit and £200 in advance.

Meanwhile Major Wingate, who had been despatched to Suakin as acting Governor, fearing another failure, made a similar agreement with a local Arab named Osheikh Karrar, who, it was arranged, should attempt my rescue *viâ* Tokar or Kassala. One day a Suakin merchant in Omdurman handed me a small slip of paper, on which was written :

'We are sending you Osheikh Karrar, who will hand you some needles, by which you will recognise him. He is a faithful and brave man. You can trust him. Kind regards from Wingate.

'(Signed)   OHRWALDER.'

Soon afterwards I heard from one of Abderrahman Wad Harun's relatives that the latter had arrived at Berber from Cairo, and was making preparations for my escape ; but, in order to avoid being suspected, he had decided not to come to Omdurman, and in this I fully concurred.

The 1st of January, 1895, had dawned. How many weary years of deprivation and humiliation I had spent in closest proximity to my tyrannical master ! And would this year come and go like the rest, leaving me still in his clutches ? No. I felt sure that the time was at length approaching when my friends would be able to break asunder the bonds which held me down, and that I should once more see my relatives, fatherland, and the friends of my youth.

One evening, about the middle of January, a man I had never seen before passed me in the street, and made a sign to me to follow him, and as I brushed up against him he whispered, 'I am the man with the needles.' Joyfully I led him in the dark to a little niche in the outside wall of my hut, and begged him to tell me his plans quickly. He first presented me with three needles and a small slip of paper, and then, to my dismay, told me that at present flight was impossible. 'I came,' said he, 'with the full intention of taking you to Kassala, but now that military

posts have been formed at El Fasher, Asubri, and Goz
Regeb on the Atbara, which are in constant communication
with each other, flight in this direction is not possible.' He
added, further, that one of his camels had died, and that
he had lost money owing to bad trade, and in consequence
he had not sufficient means to arrange for the escape. He
therefore begged that I would give him a letter to Major
Wingate, asking for a further sum of money, and promising
to return again in two months. I felt sure that the man
did not really mean to risk his life for me; and as he
informed me he wished to leave without delay, I told him
to meet me the following evening at the mosque. We then
separated, and I returned once more to my post at the
Khalifa's door. The note from Suakin contained a few
lines of recommendation from Father Ohrwalder, to which
I wrote a reply, briefly describing what had taken place ;
and the next night, when we met, I handed to Osheikh the
letter, which he hurriedly thrust into his pocket, hoping that
it would be the means of obtaining more money.

Bitterly disappointed, I was returning disconsolately to
my house, when I suddenly came across Mohammed, the
cousin of my friend Abderrahman. As if by mere chance I
found him walking at my side, and in a whisper he said to
me, ' We are ready. The camels are bought ; the guides
are engaged. The time arranged for your escape is during
the moon's last quarter next month. Be ready !' And
without another word he left me.

This time I felt convinced that I was not to be doomed
to disappointment. Towards the end of January Hussein
Wad Mohammed, who had also been engaged by Baron
Heidler and Major Wingate, arrived in Omdurman, and
secretly told me that he was ready to help me to escape.
He begged me to let my friends in Cairo know what I had
decided to do, and said that one of his brothers, who was
about to proceed to Egypt, would be the bearer of the
letter. As I was bound to Abderrahman, I decided to wait
and see if his efforts would succeed, and should they fail I

decided I would try Hussein; but I merely told the latter
that at present I was not well enough to attempt so long a
journey, and that at the end of February I would let him
know definitely my decision. At the same time I gave him
a letter to my friends, telling them that I intended to
attempt escape with the assistance of Abderrahman; and
in case of failure, from which I prayed the Almighty to
preserve me, I would seek the help of Hussein. I was now
in some alarm that so many people being in the secret, the
Khalifa might suspect something. Had he obtained the
slightest clue to what was going on I should have certainly
paid for it with my life.

On Sunday, the 17th of February, Mohammed, in a few
hurried words, told me that the camels would arrive the
next day, that they would rest two days, and that the
attempt would be made on the night of the 20th. He said
that on Tuesday evening he would communicate with me
by a sign by which I should know that everything was
ready, and that I should then do all in my power to arrange
that we should have as long a start as possible.

At last Tuesday night arrived, and I found Mohammed
waiting for me at the door of the mosque. In a hurried
whisper he told me that all was ready, and, after arranging
a rendezvous for the following night, when the Khalifa had
retired to rest, we separated.

I confess that I passed the greater part of that night in a
state of fevered excitement. Would this attempt also fail
like the others? Would some unforeseen event frustrate
this effort, too? These thoughts kept me awake and restless, and it was not till towards morning that sleep, which
was so necessary to keep up my strength during the journey,
came at length, and I had two or three hours of sound
repose.

The next morning, when before the Khalifa's door, I
feigned sickness, and asked the chief of the mulazemin for
permission to absent myself from morning prayers, as I
proposed taking a dose of senna tea and tamarind, and

remaining quietly at home the following day. The necessary permission was accorded, and Abdel Kerim promised to make my excuses to the Khalifa should he inquire for me. I felt sure that my master, when he knew that I was not present, would, under the pretext of solicitude for my health, send to my house to see if I was really there; but I could think of no other way of accounting for my absence.

Before sunset I assembled my servants, and, after making them promise to keep secret what I was about to say, I told them that the brother of the man who had brought me letters, money, and watches from my relatives seven years before, had arrived with a further consignment, and that, as he had come entirely without the Khalifa's knowledge, I had decided to keep his arrival secret. I told them that I intended visiting him that night, as I wished to arrange with him without delay and let him return at once. My good domestics, of course, believed the story implicitly, and I knew the thought that they would share some of the good things which were supposed to have come would make them keep the secret. In continuation of my imaginary scheme, I ordered my servant Ahmed to meet me the next day at sunrise at the north end of the city, near the Fur quarter, with my mule. I told him not to be impatient if I happened to be late, as the business in hand was important and might take some time to arrange, but that on no account was he to leave the rendezvous, as I intended to give him the money I received to take home. I impressed upon the others the necessity of maintaining perfect silence, as I ran a great risk of being discovered. Should any of the mulazemin ask for me, I told them to reply that I had been very unwell during the night, and had ridden off, accompanied by my servant Ahmed, to seek advice of some man whose whereabouts they did not know, but that they supposed he was someone who could cure illness. To make my story appear more real, I gave my servants to understand that I should receive a considerable sum of money the next day, and in anticipation I presented them with several dollars

apiece. My object in making these arrangements was to
secure a few hours' delay before the hue and cry that I had
escaped should be raised. My servant Ahmed would probably wait for some hours with the mule, while those in the
household would anxiously expect my return with the
money. I naturally concluded that, should the Khalifa
send to inquire for me, the reply which my servants were
to give would avert suspicion for a time; and then it would
take more time for them to find Ahmed, and his story of
the arrival of the supposed messenger would still further
perplex them. Of course, they must eventually find out the
deception; but to me every moment's delay in sending out
search parties was of the utmost importance. After afternoon prayers I once more returned to my house, again
impressed on all my servants the immense importance of
keeping the secret, and, with repeated promises of reward,
I stepped across the threshold praying fervently to God that
I might never set foot within my hut again.

CHAPTER XVIII.

MY FLIGHT.

I escape from the Town by Night — My Guides, Zeki Belal and
    Mohammed—A Scare—130 Miles in Twenty-four Hours—Our
    Camels break down—Hiding in the Gilif Mountains—Precautions
    against Surprise—Arrival of Fresh Camels—Our Journey to the
    Nile—The Crossing—Friendly Sheikhs—Narrow Escape from a
    large armed Party of Mahdists—Difficulties with my Guides—
    Hamed Garhosh the Amrabi—Out of Danger—Assuan at last—
    Congratulations and Welcome—Arrival in Cairo—Meeting with Old
    Friends.

IT was three hours after sunset. We had offered the
evening prayer with the Khalifa, and he had withdrawn to
his apartment. Another hour passed without interruption.
My lord and master had retired to rest. I rose, took the
farwa (the rug on which we pray) and the farda (a light

woollen cloth for protection against the cold) on my shoulders, and went across the mosque to the road that leads north. I heard a low cough, the signal of Mohammed, the intermediary in my escape, and I stood still. He had brought a donkey. I mounted, and was off. The night was dark. The cold, northerly wind had driven the people into their huts and houses. Without meeting a soul we reached the end of the town, where a small ruined house stands obliquely to the road, from which a man led out a saddled camel. 'This is your guide. His name is Zeki Belal,' said Mohammed. 'He will guide you to the riding camels that are waiting concealed in the desert. Make haste. A happy journey, and God protect you.'

The man sprang into the saddle, and I got up and sat behind him. After about an hour's ride, we arrived at the spot where the camels were hidden among some low trees. All was ready, and I mounted the animal assigned to me.

'Zeki,' said I, 'did Mohammed give you the medicine?'

'No. What medicine?'

'They call them ether pills. They keep off sleep and strengthen you on the journey.'

He laughed. 'Sleep!' said he. 'Have no fear on that account. Fear is the child of good folk, and will keep sleep from our eyes, and God in His mercy will fortify us.' The man was right enough. We rode in a northerly direction. The halfa grass and the mimosa-trees, which in places grew rather close together, prevented the camels from making rapid progress in the darkness. At sunrise we reached Wadi Bishara, a valley extending here to a breadth of about three miles, which is sown in the rainy season with millet by the Jaalin tribes who live along the Nile.

With daylight I was now able to see my guides. Zeki Belal was a young fellow, with his beard still downy; Hamed Ibn Hussein, a man in the prime of life.

'Of what race are you?'

'We are from the Gilif mountains, master, and if God will, you will be satisfied with us.'

'How long a start have we got from our enemies? When will they miss you?' the elder one asked me.

'They will look for me after the morning prayer; but before all doubt is over as to my escape, and before the men and the beasts are found with which to pursue me, some time must elapse. We may, at least, reckon on twelve or fourteen hours' start.'

'That is not very much,' answered Hamed. 'But if the animals are up to their work, we shall have left a good bit of ground behind us.'

'Don't you know our animals? Have they not been tried?' I asked.

'No. Two of them are stallions of the Anafi breed, and the third a Bisharin mare, bought expressly for your flight from friends,' was the answer. 'We must hope the best of them.'

We drove the creatures at their swiftest pace. The country in these parts was flat, broken now and then by solitary shrubs, with here and there small stony hillocks. We rode without stopping until near mid-day, when suddenly my guide called out:

'Halt! Let the camels kneel down at once. Be quick!'

I stopped. The camels knelt.

'Why?'

'I see camels a long way off and two led horses, and fear we have been seen.'

I loaded my Remington to be prepared for any issue. 'But if we have been seen,' I said, 'it is better to ride quietly on. Our making the animals lie down will excite their suspicion. In what direction are they going?'

'You are right,' said Hamed Ibn Hussein. 'They are marching north-west.'

We rose, and changed our line of march to the north-east, and were almost confident that we had passed unobserved, when, to our despair, we perceived one of the party, which was about two thousand metres away from us, jump on his horse and gallop swiftly towards us.

'Hamed,' said I, 'I will go slowly on with Zeki. Do you stop the man and answer his questions, and in any case prevent him from seeing me close. You have the money on you?'

'Good; but march slowly!'

I rode on quietly with Zeki, hiding my face with my farda, so as not to be recognised as a white man.

'Hamed is greeting the man, and has made his camel kneel,' said Zeki, looking back. After about twenty minutes, we saw the man remount his horse and Hamed urging his camel on to rejoin us.

'You must thank God for our safety,' he cried, as he came up. 'The man is a friend of mine, Mukhal, a Sheikh, on his way to Dongola with camels to bring dates to Omdurman. He asked me where I was going with the "white Egyptian." The man has the eyes of a hawk.'

'And what did you answer?'

'I adjured him as my friend to keep our secret, and gave him twenty Maria Theresa dollars. We Arabs are all a little avaricious. The man swore a sacred oath to me to hold his tongue if he happened to fall in with our pursuers, and his people are too far off to tell black from white. Urge the camels on; we have lost time.'

At sunset we passed the hills of Hobegi, and camped nearly an hour later in the open country, about a day's journey west of the Nile, so as to give our exhausted animals some rest. We had been riding twenty-one hours without stopping, had eaten nothing all day, and only once drunk water. In spite of fatigue, we ate bread and dates with a good appetite.

'We will feed our beasts and then get on,' said n guide. 'You are not tired?'

'No,' I replied. 'In Europe we say time is money Here one might say time is life. Make haste.'

But to our despair the beasts refused the food which was placed before them. Hamed made a little fire, took a piece of burning wood and a little resin, which he laid on the wood, then walked round the camels muttering some words which I could not understand.

'What are you doing?' I asked him with some surprise.

'I fear the fikis of the Khalifa have bewitched our camels, and am trying the Arab's antidote.'

'For my part,' I replied, 'I fear that they are second-rate market camels, or are sick. Let us give them a little more rest. Perhaps they will pick up.'

As, after another half-hour's rest, the beasts still refused food, and longer delay was out of the question, we tightened up the saddle-girths again and mounted. The tired animals refused to trot, would only walk at a good pace, and as the sun rose we found ourselves on the high ground to the north-west of Metemmeh. The diminishing strength of our mounts filled us with anxiety, and it became clear to us that they would never hold out till the spot—about a day's journey north of Berber, on the edge of the desert—where we were to change camels. Towards afternoon we let the exhausted animals rest in the shade of a tree, and agreed to make for the Gilif range, distant a good day's journey to the north-west, where I should remain concealed in the un-inhabited hills until my guides could succeed in securing other mounts.

About sunset we struck camp. The animals had so far recovered that they could walk at a good pace, and we reached in the early morning the foot of the Gilif mountain, which at this spot is quite uninhabited. We dismounted, driving our camels before us after an extremely difficult march of about three hours in a valley hemmed in by sheer rocks.

My guides, Zeki Ibn Belal, as well as Hamed Ibn Hussein, both belong to the Kababish tribe. The Gilif mountain is their own country, and they were familiar with every path. We unsaddled the camels and concealed the saddles among the boulders.

'We have come into our own country, and she will protect her son,' said Hamed Hussein. 'Have no fear, as

long as we live you need have no misgiving. Remain
quietly concealed here. A little way off there is a cleft in
the rocks containing water. I will water the animals there.
Zeki will bring you a water-skin full. I will also hide the
beasts elsewhere, that our halting-place may not be betrayed
by the vultures circling above. Wait for me here, and we
will see what our next step must be.'

I was alone and somewhat depressed. I had hoped to
make a straight dash for the Egyptian frontier and to out-
distance my pursuers by speed, and now a crowd of unexpected obstacles was gathering round me. About two
hours later Zeki arrived with the water-skin on his
shoulders.

'Taste the water of my native land,' he cried. 'See
how fresh and pure it is. Take confidence. God, if He
will, will bring our enterprise to a happy end.'

I drank a deep draught. It was delicious indeed.

'I am full of confidence,' I said to Zeki, 'but a little put
out by the delay.'

'Malaish kullu shai bi iradet Illahi ("It matters not.
All happens as God ordains"), and perhaps this delay has
its good side too. Let us wait for Hamed Hussein.'

Soon after mid-day Hamed came. We ate our frugal
meal of bread and dates, and while doing so arranged that
Zeki should ride to the friends who were privy to my escape,
a brief two days' journey, and fetch new animals.

'I will ride the Bisharin mare,' said Zeki. 'She is strong,
and has not yet got to the end of her tether. This is
Saturday evening. I shall ride all night and to-morrow,
Sunday. Monday morning early, please God, I shall reach
our friends. We must allow one to two days there, because,
it may be, no animals will be ready. But Thursday or
Friday I should get here with fresh camels if no misfortune
happens to me.'

'It is better to put it a little later,' I answered. 'We
will wait for you here till Saturday. If you arrive sooner,
all the better ; but remember that our life is in your hand.

Above all, be cautious in bringing the animals that you arouse no suspicion.'

'Trust in our good fortune and my goodwill,' and he grasped my hand in farewell.

'God protect you, and bring you back right soon.'

He tied a few dates up in a cloth as provision for the journey, and took the saddle on his shoulders. Hamed described the spot accurately to him where he would find the mare. As he turned he enjoined us to be careful not to be seen, and in a few moments he was lost to sight. We cleared the ground which was to serve as our night's resting-place of stones, and were in the best of spirits as to our success.

'I have a proposal to make to you,' said Hamed to me after a long interval. 'A relation of mine, Ibrahim Masa, is Sheikh of this district, and has his house at the foot of the hill, about four hours' distance from here. Now, though, as I hope, no one has seen us, still, it would be better to warn him of our arrival, so that he may be prepared for any eventuality. I will describe our situation to him without mentioning your name. As my kinsman, he is bound to give us asylum, and would warn us in time of pursuit, if it should be that our track is followed to the base of the hills, though, indeed, this is scarcely to be feared. If you agree, I will go during the night, so as to see him without being observed by other people, and will be back with you early in the morning.'

'The plan is good; but take twenty more dollars with you, and offer them as a small contribution to his house, and, as you have said, do not mention my name.'

Hamed left me at sunset, and I was alone with my thoughts. I thought of my housefolk and companions, to whom, in spite of the difference of race and of many unattractive qualities, I had grown accustomed in the long course of years, and whom I had just left behind me in the hands of the enemy. I thought of the dear ones I was now on my way to meet, of my sisters, my friends, and well-wishers. If only my adventures have a successful issue! Exhausted with fatigue, I fell asleep on my hard bed. I woke while the dawn was gray, and shortly afterwards heard the sound of approaching footsteps. I knew it must be my guide.

'All goes well,' said he as he came up. 'The Sheikh, my kinsman, greets his unknown guest, and bids God protect you. Fortify yourself with patience. For the present, we have nothing else to do.'

He sat down between two blocks of stone, from which his dark skin was hardly distinguishable, and kept watch. I sat a short distance below in the shade of a little tree which struggled for existence among the rocks, and we talked in low tones of the present and the former condition of the country. It was past mid-day when I suddenly heard behind the noise of footsteps, and, turning round, I saw, to my disgust, a man about one hundred and fifty yards off, climbing the slope opposite me, trying to draw the end of his farda, which was twisted round his loins, over his head. Judging from the direction he had come from, he must have seen us.

'In any case it is a fellow-countryman,' said Hamed, who had heard the sound, and had perceived him. 'Anyhow, it will be better that I should overtake him and speak with him. Or do you not agree?'

'Certainly; make haste, and, if necessary, give him a small present,' I answered.

My companion left his seat, and followed the man at a swift pace. He had now reached the crest of the hill and passed out of my sight. A few minutes later I saw them both approaching me with smiling faces.

'We are in luck,' Hamed cried from a distance. 'He is one of my numerous relations. Our mothers are children of two sisters.'

The man came up to me and offered his hand in greeting.

'The peace of God be with you. From me you run no danger,' he said as he sat down on the stone at my side.

I gave him a few dates, and bade him taste our travelling fare. 'Who are you?'

'They call me Ali Wad Feid,' he replied, 'and, to be honest with you, my intentions were not well disposed to you. I was changing my pasture ground, and arrived a few days ago with my flocks at the foot of those hills which you see from here to the south. I went to the cleft in the rocks to see if there were much water there, because we might need it, although we also get drinking water in the plain. There I found traces of a camel, and followed them up. When, in the distance, I saw the white skin of your feet which were sticking out of your hiding-place, I realized that a stranger was concealed here, and tried to get away again unobserved, so that,' said he, smiling, ' I might return again with a few comrades by night and make your further journey easier by removing your superfluous luggage. I thank God that my cousin here caught me up. By night I should not, perhaps, have recognised him.'

'Ali Wad Feid,' said my guide, who had listened in silence, ' I will tell you a little story. Listen! Many years ago, when I was a little fellow, in the days when the Turks ruled in the land, my father was Sheikh of these mountains, which then were thickly peopled. One night there came a man, a fugitive, who sought asylum with my father. He was closely pursued by Government troops, under suspicion of being a highway brigand who had murdered some merchants. His women fell into the hands of his pursuers, but he himself sought and found protection with my father, who kept him in concealment. A long while after my father went to the seat of Government at Berber, and by money and fair words succeeded in obtaining pardon for the man, against whom there existed no definite proofs of guilt. He went bail for him, and set free his women, who were in prison. That man's name was Feid——'

'And he was my father,' interrupted Ali, whose face had grown grave during his narrative. ' I was born later, and heard the story from my dead mother, on whom God have mercy. My brother, let me give you good tidings. What your father did for mine, his son will do for your father's son. In peace or in peril I am with you. But follow me, and I will show you a better hiding-place.'

We went some two thousand yards back round the hill towards the south, and reached a sort of little grotto formed of rock slabs, large enough to hold two men.

' When evening comes bring your baggage here, although there is nothing to fear, since the hills are uninhabited ; but under the cover of darkness you can choose some other spot in the neighbourhood to sleep in. It is impossible to be quite sure that someone may not have perceived you, and have the intention which I confessed to have had, of return-ing after dark. I have lost time, and my road is a long one. I will go, pick up what news I can, and return to-morrow when it is dark, announcing my presence by a low whistle. Farewell till then.'

As Ali Wad Feid had advised us, we selected a place to sleep in, and early in the morning, before the sun rose, retired again to our cave. Throughout the day Hamed Hussein kept watch from a high point of vantage, like a sentry on a tower, and only came to me when driven in by hunger. Our bread came to an end this day, and we had only dates to eat.

In the evening, two hours maybe after sunset, we heard a low whistle. It was Ali Wad Feid, who, faithful to his promise, had come to visit us. He brought some milk in a small vessel of gazelle-skin (the skin of young gazelles is tanned by the Arabs, and now much used for carrying milk in), and had rolled up some bread (millet cakes) in his farda.

' I pretended to my wife that I was going to visit the caravan folk, and show them hospitality,' he said, after greeting us. ' I cannot trust her with the truth; she is such a chatterbox.'

' A feminine quality which many married men complain

about in our country at home,' I remarked, with a smile, delighted at the prospect of such a grateful meal.

'I made inquiries at the well,' he continued, 'and heard of nothing to cause you uneasiness. Eat and drink your fill. I have every confidence in your good luck.'

After we had done honour to his good fare, I begged him to return so as not to awake suspicion with his own folk by remaining out unduly long, and whispered to Hamed to give him a present of five dollars before he went.

'Do not return,' I said to him in taking leave. 'Your comings and goings may excite suspicion among your people, and your footsteps may perhaps leave traces on the ground which would betray our hiding-place to others, unless, of course, you hear any really disquieting news. Farewell. I thank you for your loyal friendship.'

Hamed Hussein accompanied his kinsman some little way.

'Ali would not take the money,' he said, when he returned. 'I had to press him very hard, and it was only the fear of offending you which induced him at last to accept it.'

We once more selected our couches, and rested undisturbed till the morning, when we returned to the cave, or, rather, I did, for my companion had to go back to his post as watchman. This day went by equally without event, but how slowly the time seemed to pass! The hours grew to days, and thoughts succeeded thoughts in weary sequence. My patience was severely tried, but there was no help for it, and nothing to do but to bear it.

As our water-supply threatened to fall short, Hamed Hussein went with the skin to the cleft in the rocks. At the same time he intended to look up the camels, which had been hobbled, and were getting what food they could from trees and bushes.

'I shall return in about four hours. Meanwhile remain quiet in the cave,' he said to me, 'and should anyone appear —which God forbid! it could only be one of my own countrymen, for no stranger gets so far as this—detain him, and tell him that Hamed Wad Sheikh Hussein is coming in a little while. But do not yourself enter into any negotiation, and above all do not spill blood.'

'I will follow your counsel whatever happens,' I replied; 'but I trust you will find me here undisturbed when you return.'

My guide returned with the water-skin full even before the time he had indicated.

'I found the camels somewhat recovered—at any rate in appearance,' he said, with evident satisfaction. 'Give me a few dates; I am hungry, and must return to my watch-tower.'

The rest of the day passed slowly, but without episode. At night we betook ourselves to our sleeping-place, talked for awhile in a low voice, and prayed that our patience might not be put to too hard a trial.

On Thursday morning Hamed had gone as usual to his post of observation, and it must have been about mid-day when I suddenly saw him climb down from his seat. I clutched my rifle.

'What is the matter?'

'I see a man running in the direction of our former hiding-place. It must mean news. Remain here till I come back.'

I sat down and waited for what seemed an eternity; then I rose with caution to have a look out, and saw a long way off two people approaching me. My eyes could make out Hamed, and with him was Zeki Belal. As I stepped from my hiding-place he perceived me, and ran up.

'God give you greeting, master. Here is good news for you,' said he, shaking my hand. 'I have arrived with two fresh camels, and have hidden them some way behind. I will be off and fetch them.' And he hurried back again.

About an hour later he arrived with the new animals.

'You have been quick!' I cried with delight. 'Now tell your story.'

' It was Saturday evening when I left you,' he replied ' I rode all night and all day. My Bisharin mare went splendidly over the ground, which was tolerably level, and on Monday morning I reached our friends. They sent immediately for the beasts you now see, which were at a considerable distance. They came in early on Tuesday. I started at mid-day. I rode slowly, so as not to wear them out, and now we can start at once. And, oh, I had almost forgotten to tell you that your friends, after discussing it with me, went off to the camp on the edge of the desert to warn their people there to be ready. I promised we would reach the tryst on Friday, or at latest on Saturday after sunset.'

' Did you bring bread ?' I asked the youth, who was talking away in high spirits. ' We have got nothing but dates to eat.'

' Good heavens ! I forgot that in my haste.'

' No matter,' I replied, seeing him look rather crestfallen. ' Even without dates we could hold out for this short ride.'

' Zeki,' said Hamed, ' saddle the light-coloured camel, go with our friend and brother to the hollow rock, and give the camels water. Wait for me there. I will take the other saddle and follow with my own camel, which has recovered sufficiently to stand this comparatively short march. But it will be better,' he added, turning to me, ' that you should not go right up to the spring, but remain hidden in some suitable spot near till we fetch you. One never can be too sure ; there are so many thirsty folk in the wide world.'

I went with Zeki, leading one of the camels, towards the cleft where the water was, and hid myself in a place my guide suggested, among the boulders of rock.

About two hours before sunset, Hamed and Zeki came with the three camels that had just been watered, and the skins all filled. We mounted and rode east-north-east across hills, which at times were very steep to climb, till, as darkness gathered round us, we arrived in the plain without having been observed.

Throughout the night we rode without a halt at a slow trot or a walk, and at daybreak Hamed calculated we had left half the road behind us.

'This is the most critical day of our journey,' said my guide. 'We come into the neighbourhood of the river, and cross pasture grounds of the river tribes. God grant we reach our destination unobserved!'

The aspect of the country does not change. The veldt, as one may call it, is covered with a thin mat of grass, with here and there clumps of half-dried mimosa bushes. The ground is sandy, and at times covered with stones. We rode on without stopping, and ate our frugal meal, which consisted of nothing but dates, as we rode. When the sun was at the zenith, we saw in the distance a flock of sheep with its shepherds. We turned a little aside from our straight course, and Zeki rode off to them to ask for news ; but when he rejoined us he said he had learned nothing of interest. Though we came upon constant tracks of camels, donkeys, sheep, etc., in the soil, our eyes detected nothing which caused us concern, and the country had become quite flat again.

'Do you see the broad gray band in front, crossing from south to north-west?' Hamed asked me. 'That is the great caravan track which leads from Berber to Wadi Gammer and Dar Shaigia. If we pass that without being seen, we have nothing more to fear, for between this and the river there is only stony ground, without a vestige of vegetation, and quite uninhabited. But now you must follow my directions closely. Let the camels advance at a slow pace, and each some five hundred paces from the next till we reach the big track. When we get there we will turn into the road and proceed for a few minutes in the direction of Berber. Then we will leave it again, and march in an easterly direction. Do you see that stone hillock about three miles away? There we will join again. This is the only way to put anyone who may be pursuing us off our track.'

We did as he had instructed us, crossed the caravan road, which is at most times tolerably frequented, without seeing a trace of anyone, and met again at the spot indicated.

'And now urge the animals on. Don't spare them. Let them do us their last service,' said Hamed, with a merry laugh. 'All has gone well.'

Since I left Omdurman I had not seen a laugh upon his face, and I knew that on this side of the river we had nothing more to fear.

So on we went, driving the weary camels forward with the stick without much mercy, till, leaving a range of hills on our right, we reached the Kerraba.

The Kerraba is a plateau with a sandy soil. The surface is covered with black stones, ranging from the size of a man's fist to that of his head, packed closely together. Single blocks of rock are seen at a certain distance one from another. The animals could scarcely make any progress over the rolling level. It was a break-neck march. Towards evening we saw the Nile in the far, far distance, like a silver streak across the landscape. Climbing down from the plateau in the darkness, we reached a valley lying between stony hills. We halted and took the saddles off. The river was about two hours' march away.

'Our mission is near its end,' said Hamed and Zeki, as they sat on the ground munching dates. 'Stay here with the animals. We will go to a spot we know near the river; and there we shall find your friends, who will escort you on.'

I was left alone, looking forward in the highest spirits to the future. Already in imagination I saw my own people, saw my fatherland. I awoke after midnight. No one had come, and I began to feel somewhat concerned at the delay, for if they did not soon return I could not cross the river that night. It was not till some two hours before dawn that I heard footsteps. It was Hamed.

'What news?' I asked impatiently.

'None!' was the despairing answer. 'We could not find

your friends at the place indicated. I returned because you cannot remain here after daybreak. You are too near human habitations, and exposed to the risk of being seen. I left Zeki behind to look for your people. Take the water-skin on your shoulders and some dates. I am too exhausted to carry anything. We must go back on to the Kerraba. There you must stay till the day is over, hidden among the stones.'

I did as I was bidden, and reached the plateau in about an hour. After we had marched a little further in the darkness, Hamed stood still.

' Stop here,' he said. ' Make a ring of stones as camel-herds do in winter to protect themselves from the cold, and lie down between them. You know how to do it. You are just as much an Arab as one of us. In the evening I will come again to fetch you. I go back to the camels. The people of these parts know me, and I have nothing to fear. If they ask me any questions I shall say I have come from Dar Shaigia to look up some people who are settled here. Luckily I have some relations here also.' He went back. I stood upon the rolling plain alone—abandoned.

I piled the stones on top of one another to a height of about half a metre, leaving just room enough between for myself, my water-skin, and my gun. Morning began to grow gray, and I crept into my hiding-place. The ground beneath was sandy. I dug it up with a flat, pointed stone, and heaped up sufficient between the piles of slabs to prevent my being seen from without. I flung myself on my back in weariness, and stretched out my limbs. Again reflection came and thoughts thronged past. I looked back again to the past, and pictured to myself the Khalifa's anger at my flight. My imagination sped once more towards my dear ones. I longed to be united to them again, and, unanticipated, almost insuperable obstacles seemed to be springing up round me. What change has come over me ? Where is my motto of ' Never despair ' ? However desperate the circumstances in which I may have found myself

I have never lost courage, never abandoned confidence in
my ultimate good fortune. To-day a sense of fear is pressing on me. Perhaps it is that I am already lying in what
will be my grave. But that is, after all, the end of every
man. Be his days long or short, he can go no other way.
And yet to die in a strange land forsaken! God, up there
in heaven, have mercy on me—have mercy on a miserable
man who, if he has sinned, has surely bitterly atoned for
his transgressions. God have mercy on me! Let me see
my friends and dear ones, my fatherland again!

Then I grew calm once more. After all, I thought, in
spite of a few little delays, affairs are not so bad. To-night
I shall cross the river. To-morrow I reach the desert. In
two or three days I shall be beyond the reach of danger,
and fly towards those I crave to see. I smiled once more,
and grew full of confidence and hope. The sun was burning
hot. I had brought my farda, and held it up over me to
keep my face in the shade, waiting in patience for what
would follow.

A little after mid-day I heard a low whistle, and raised
myself to look out over the stones. It was Hamed, who
approached me smiling.

'Good news!' he cried. 'We have found your people.'

A sense of joy possessed me as I caught his words, and
my lucky star was once more in the ascendant. When he
came up to me he sat down outside the stones.

'You may make yourself more comfortable,' he said. 'I
have kept a good look-out all round. You have nothing to
fear. Zeki found your people before daybreak, and just now
one of them came over to us to find out where we were.
They are ready. In the evening they will come to fetch
you. But you will have to take great care, for your flight
is known in this part of the country. Come with me now,
or, better still, wait till darkness comes on. I am going now.
Can you find the way alone, or shall I come back for you?'

'It is not necessary for you to go over the ground again.
I know the place, and will join you in the evening.'

The sun had disappeared from the horizon when, with gun and water-skin slung upon my back, I left the spot which had cost me such bitter hours of reflection. When I reached my companions, I found myself in the presence of two men who were strangers to me.

They greeted me, saying, 'We are sent by your friend Ahmed Wad Abdalla, and are of the Gihemab tribe. We will take you down to the river. He himself will cross the stream with you. On the other side the camels are waiting ready to take you across the desert. Take leave of your guides. Their task is done.'

I shook my old friends by the hand, and thanked them with words which came from the heart for their devotion. ' Farewell, and may we meet again in better times of peace.'

We saddled two camels and left the third to my former guides. I mounted, and one of the new-comers got up behind me.

' What is your name ?' I asked him.

' They call me Mohammed, sir, and my companion's name is Ishaak.'

' Do you go with me across the desert ?'

' No ; there are others told off for that. Let the camel walk slowly, and it will be better to cover your face in spite of the darkness. Orders came from Berber three days ago to have all the roads closely watched ; and the ferries have been put under observation. Still, in our country you have nothing to fear.'

After proceeding for about two hours in an east-north-east direction, we approached the river. We could hear the groaning of the water-wheel, the cries and laughter of the slaves and their women at work. As we came up to a small clump of bushes, Mohammed, who was riding behind me, sprang down, and said, ' Make the camel kneel down slowly —gently, that he may not grunt, and so attract attention.'

They knelt down without a sound.

Bidding me remain there till they returned with Ahmed, they disappeared into the darkness. I waited about an

hour, and then saw four men approaching. The tallest of
them came up and embraced me. Pressing me to his breast,
he said, in a low voice :

'God be praised! Welcome to the land of my fathers.
I am your brother Ahmed Ibn Abdalla, of the tribe of
Gihemab. Believe my words, you are saved. Mohammed,
Ishaak, take the saddles off the camels quietly. Make no
noise. Ride a good way on along the stream. Blow the
water-skins full of air, and tie them round the camels' necks.
Then cross the river at different spots, and to-morrow await
my orders near the stones of the " Fighting Bull." Meantime, do you follow me,' he said, turning to me.

He himself, with the fourth man, took the saddles on
their backs, and I followed. A few minutes later we reached
the shore of the sacred Nile, and found, in a little hollow
washed out by the current, a tiny boat constructed by my
friends themselves, scarcely large enough to hold us. We
climbed down the steep bank, got into the boat, and pushed
off. It took us more than an hour to cross the stream.
When we reached the far side, the other man, who had
remained in the little boat, guided it back into the river,
and bored a hole in the bottom, swimming to the land while
the boat sank in the stream, and with it disappeared all
traces of our crossing. We marched for about half an hour,
and then Ahmed Abdalla bade me wait there while he went
away, to return soon after with a dish of milk and bread.

'Eat and drink,' said he, 'and have no more fears as to
the success of your flight, for I swear to you by God and
the Prophet you are saved. I had intended that you should
start to-night, but the hour is already too late. It will be
better that you should wait till to-morrow evening. Besides,
to-morrow is the day when your camels should be watered.
As we are here too near to human habitations, my nephew,
Ibrahim Ali, will conduct you to a place some distance off
which is difficult of access. Wait for me there. I will
bring you an animal to ride, or do you feel strong enough to
go on foot ?'

'I am strong, and can walk,' I replied. 'Where is Ibrahim Ali ?'

'He is here, and he will be your guide through the desert.'

It was a black night. Ibrahim went first with an empty water-skin in his hand along the caravan track leading beside the river to Abu Hamed, and I followed. After proceeding about three English miles, he went down to the river, filled the skin half full, and then changed the direction, turning inland. The march was very difficult. The big stones with which the hills were covered hindered one's progress. I was dead beat, and staggered about to right and left like a drunken man. At last we halted by a hollow in the ground.

'This is the spot which my uncle indicated,' said Ibrahim, who had kept silence up till now. 'Remain quietly here without misgiving. To-morrow evening I shall bring the camels, and we will start. Here is water and bread. I will return now to make my preparations.'

Once more I was alone. Once more I was exposed for a long day to the scorching sun ; but now it was easy for me to bear, for I was near to the goal I had longed for so wildly. At last the sun disappeared from the horizon, and, after waiting about an hour more, I heard the sound of hoofs moving quickly over the stones. I rose, and recognised Ahmed Abdalla, accompanied by two men on donkeys.

Springing off in haste, he pressed me warmly to his breast. 'God be thanked that you are safe! These two men,' pointing to his companions, 'are my brothers, and have come with me to wish you luck.'

I pressed their hands in greeting, and, turning to Ahmed, said : 'But I do not understand *you* ; your tremendous spirits——'

'Of course not,' he replied, 'for you do not know the great danger you have escaped. Listen ! Three days ago the Emir of Berber, Zeki Osman, learned, we know not how, that the Egyptian garrison at Murrat had received important reinforcements, and intended to attack the Mahdist station at Abu Hamed. Zeki Osman is sending reinforcements, and to-day at noon sixty horsemen and about three hundred foot soldiers passed our dwellings. You know these wild bands who call themselves Ansar [defenders of the faith]. We had killed a sheep, and were busy preparing a portion for you to take with you on the road, when they suddenly came upon us by surprise. They consumed what was intended for your provision, and then scattered in search of loot. We were in terrible anxiety on your account, fearing one of these wild fellows might find his way to your hiding-place. Now they have marched on. The curse of God go with them! Thanks be to Him who has protected you!'

And I also humbly thanked my Creator, who had saved me from this great and unexpected danger. As I learned later, the Commander-in-Chief of the Egyptian Army, General Kitchener Pasha, had come to Wadi Halfa to conduct the usual manœuvres. Captain Machell Bey marched with the Twelfth Sudanese Battalion and two hundred of the Camel Corps from Wadi Halfa to Korosko by Murrat, and this accounted for the rumour of a strengthening of the garrison at Murrat, and the contemplated attack on Abu Hamed.

'The camels will be a little late,' said Ahmed, continuing. 'I sent them hastily away into the interior when the Dervishes came in, for fear they might press them into service to carry their ammunition or other baggage. If, however, you feel inclined to rest in patience till to-morrow, we should be able to procure fresh provisions.'

'No; I want at all hazards to start at once, and want of provisions will not alter my resolve,' I replied. 'I trust the camels will come soon.'

It was towards midnight when they brought in the three animals. Ahmed Abdalla presented my two guides to me. 'Ibrahim Ali, the son of my brother, and Yakub Hassan, also a near relative of mine. They will conduct you to Sheikh Hamed Fedai, the head of the Amrab Arabs, who are subject to the Egyptian Government. He will assist you in getting on to Assuan.'

We filled the water-skins and took our leave.

'Forgive the failure of provision for your journey,' said Ahmed Ibn Abdalla. 'It is not my fault. You have meal and dates enough to keep hunger off, though there are no luxuries.'

We rode three hours and a half east-north-east before the sun rose, and as the dawn grew gray found ourselves east of Wadi el Homar (the Vale of Asses), which, though called after the wild asses which inhabit it, is in a great measure devoid of vegetation. As we proceeded, the country assumed the genuine characteristics of the desert— wide stretches of sand, with here and there, at long intervals, ridges of hills, but never a tree or trace of grass. After riding for two days, almost without a halt, we reached the hills of Nuranai, formerly occupied by the Bisharin Arabs. The valley, running in a north-easterly direction for the most part, between ridges with very steep walls, grows mimosa-trees along either side, and in one lateral valley are trees which take their name from the hills.

Ibrahim Ali got off and took an observation from the heights, and, finding that the valley was quite unoccupied, we entered it, hastily watered our camels, and partially filled our water-skins.

The well lies in a hollow some twenty-five yards across, and some eighteen feet deep, dug out with a sharp decline towards the centre. Down this sloping plane there are slabs of rock and stones, serving as steps, by which one descends to the water-hole in the middle. As wells are always places where people are apt to collect, we left the spot and rested in the plain, after crossing the hills of Nuranai in about three hours.

There was a great difference between my former and my present guides. The first were brave, devoted fellows, ready even to sacrifice their lives for me, whereas these new ones were just the contrary. They grumbled at the service which it seems their relative Ahmed Abdalla had forced upon them, and were for ever complaining of want of sleep and hunger, and at the danger of the enterprise, the reward for which would go to others. Through their carelessness they had dropped my sandals and tinder-box on the road, and the loss of the former was destined to cause me much trouble later on.

The next day, a Thursday, we reached the groves of Abu Hamed an hour before noon, and though the tribes who at present live in these parts are hostile to the Mahdists, I preferred to remain hidden. Ibrahim Ali and Yakub Hassan had been ordered by Ahmed Abdalla to guide me to Sheikh Hamed Fadai ; but this did not suit their views.

They came to me in the afternoon, and represented to me the risk they would incur if their people missed them for many days. Since it was certain everything would come to the Khalifa's ears which was calculated to throw light on the question of who had helped me in my flight, and since their tribe was already under suspicion of being friendly to the Egyptian Government, there was danger not only for them, but also for my friend Ahmed Abdalla. In conclusion, they begged to be allowed to go and look for a man who was well known to them both, and living in these parts, who would conduct me further. I saw that their reluctance would prove of more harm than service to me as I proceeded further, and agreed to their proposal almost with alacrity, so distasteful had both my guides become to me, and bade them settle the matter as quickly as possible according to the best of their powers.

It was not yet sunset when they brought back the man in question. He was an Amrab Arab named Hamed Garhosh, and considerably the wrong side of fifty in years.

' Every man looks to his own advantage and profit,' he said curtly to me after the greeting. ' Your guides, whom I know well, wish me to show you the way from here to

Assuan. I am ready to do so, but what shall I earn by the job ?'

'On the day of my arrival I will pay you there one hundred and twenty Maria Theresa dollars, and, in addition, a present which I shall calculate according to the manner in which your duties are accomplished.'

'I accept,' said he, giving me his hand. 'God and the Prophet are my witnesses that I trust you. I know your race. A white man does not lie. I will bring you to your own folk across untrodden mountain ways known only to the fowls of the air. Be ready. After the sun is down we start.'

I selected the strongest of the three camels for the remainder of my journey, took two water-skins, the greater part of the dates, and a portion of dhurra for my provision. As the darkness closed in Hamed Garhosh arrived.

His son had gone away on the only camel which he possessed to the country of Robatab near the river to fetch grain, and he was therefore obliged to perform his functions as guide on foot. Since the road was most of it mountainous, however, and the camel could only go at a foot's pace, he would not be any the worse off on that account. It was merely a question of goodwill and stout legs. I took leave of Ibrahim and Yakub with few words, and, there was no doubt about it, we were mutually glad to part company.

After a march of more than two days, crossing, for the most part, bare ridges and stony hills, we reached on Sunday morning a small well, nearly dried up, called Shof el Ain, and though presumably it was not likely to be visited by anyone, I waited for my guide, as he desired, at a spot an hour's distance from it.

Our food consisted of dates and bread which we baked ourselves. That is to say, an apology for bread, for I am convinced, though my guide prided himself particularly on his talent, that the stuff which he produced would give our European bakers a proper sense of disgust, both on account

of its appearance and its taste. To prepare it, my guide
piled together a lot of stones about the size of pigeons' eggs,
and laid dry wood on top of them. Then he kneaded dhurra
mixed with water in a wooden vessel, and lighted his pile of
fuel with flint and tinder. When the wood had burned out,
he removed the embers from the glowing stones, poured his
dough over them, and then replaced the embers on the top
of that again. A few minutes after he rescued his work of
art from its fiery grave, beat it severely with a stick to
remove the superfluous ashes and stones which stuck to it, and
served it up. This abortive production we ate, if not quite
with pleasure, at any rate with hearty appetite, and realized
the truth of the proverb. After resting a little while, we
left the neighbourhood of the fountain, and in a few hours
reached the first slopes of the Etbai mountains.

These mountains (El Etbai), stretching between the Red
Sea and the Nile, are inhabited in the southern portion by
Bisharin and Amrab Arabs, and in the north by the Ababda
tribe. Between lofty black cliffs, absolutely bare of vegetation, rising in sheer perpendicular, stretch broad valleys
well wooded, which the camel-breeders of these tribes
pasture in. We traversed a well-nigh impassable road,
moving on without resting, impelled by my desire to see
my own folk and to finish the weary journey as quickly as
possible. Though we had nothing more to fear, for we
were by now out of the power of the Mahdists and on
Egyptian territory, my guide insisted on the importance of
not being seen. He was afraid of being recognised by the
people, who have commercial relations with the Sudan.
Since his home lay on the border, and he was often obliged
for various reasons to go to Berber, the knowledge that he
had served me in my flight might be fraught with most
serious consequences for him.

But with him the spirit was willing though the flesh was
weak. Being already advanced in years, the want of proper
food and the overtaxing march had their effect on his health.
In addition to this, he felt the cold, which was often severe,

so much that he fell ill, although I had made over to him my
jibba, and had nothing myself upon my body but the farda
and hezam (a strip of woollen cloth to wind round the body,
eight to nine yards in length). In order to get on I made
over the camel to him for the last four days, and walked
behind him with my bare feet over the stones, for my
former guides had lost my sandals, and this was therefore
for me, from the physical point of view, the hardest part of
my journey.

Even our camel seemed to be going to leave us in the
lurch. He had got a raw place on his off fore-foot, and had
besides injured it so severely with a pointed stone that the
unfortunate beast could hardly walk on it. I was obliged
to sacrifice one of my hezamin, with which, by binding it in
quadruple fold, I made a kind of shoe for him, which had,
however, to be renewed every twenty-four hours. I had
seen this done by camel-herds in Darfur, though they use
leather for the purpose, and the old experience now stood
me in good stead.

At last, on Saturday, the 16th of March, in the morning
at sunrise, descending from the heights, I saw the river
Nile and the town of Assuan along its shore. I cannot
describe the feelings of joy which possessed me. My woes
were at an end; saved from the hands of fanatical barbarians, my eyes beheld for the first time the dwellings of
civilized people in a country governed with law and justice
by its ruler. My heart went out to my Creator in thankful-
ness for His protection and His guiding hand.

I was received in the most friendly manner at their quarters
by the English officers in His Highness the Khedive's service
and the Egyptian officers, who only just then learned the
surprising news of my arrival, and each vied with the other
to do all that was in his power to help me to forget the
miseries I had gone through.

The commanding officer and Governor of the frontier,
who happened to have arrived almost at the same moment
in Assuan, Colonel Hunter Pasha, as well as his officers,

Majors Jackson, Sidney, and Machell Bey, with Bimbashi Watson, and others whose names I cannot at this moment call to mind, generously placed their wardrobes at my disposal, and I availed myself of their kindness for what was strictly indispensable.   Before, however, I changed my clothes, my excellent friend Watson, who is a capital artist, asked leave to make a sketch of me, a request to which I was delighted to accede.

As to my guide, Hamed Garhosh, with the assistance of a former acquaintance, Butros Bey Serkis, who is now British Vice-Consul in Assuan, I at once paid him the one hundred and twenty Maria Theresa dollars.   He also received from me a present of money, clothes, and arms, while over and above this Hunter Pasha presented him with a gift of £10 as a token of joy at my safe arrival; and so, having suddenly become a 'man of means,' he took a touching farewell of me and departed.

A short time afterwards telegrams of congratulation arrived.   The first was from Major Lewis Bey on behalf of himself and the garrison of Wadi Halfa.   The second, from the chief of the Austrian Diplomatic Agency in Egypt, Baron Heidler von Egeregg, who had been so indefatigable on my behalf.   Then from my devoted friend Major Wingate Bey.   Baron Victor Herring and his sons, who were travelling on the Nile, were the first of my own countrymen to greet me.

As it happened that the postal steamer was starting that afternoon, I was recommended to avail myself of it to continue my journey.   Escorted by all the officers, to the tune of the Austrian national hymn (played by the band of the Sudanese battalion), which it brought the tears into my eyes to hear, I went on board the steamer, amid the hurrahs of a number of tourists of all nations assembled on the bank.

I was deeply moved.   Though I have ever tried to live up to my standard of honour in whatever circumstances I have been placed, which, indeed, any officer in a similar position would surely do, I had done nothing to prepare me for, still less to deserve, this public expression of sympathy, and it made me feel very humble.

I travelled in company with Machell Bey, who commands the Twelfth Sudanese Battalion, and whose march during the manœuvres from Wadi Halfa by Murrat to Korosko had been the cause of my provisions being eaten up, and of the short commons I had to put up with in the desert. I took a terrible vengeance. He had to submit unconditionally to all my whims in food and drink, and endured his martyrdom with extraordinary good nature and soldierly fortitude.

When I arrived on Sunday evening in Luxor, I was again the object of a lively demonstration of sympathy from the European travellers, and here received, through Baron Heidler, a telegram from my dear sisters, and from my native city of Vienna. Sisters and native city! How sweet the words sound!

On Monday, at five in the afternoon, we reached Girga, the southernmost station on the Egyptian State Railway, and proceeded to Cairo, which I reached at six in the morning, on Tuesday, the 19th of March. In spite of this early hour, Baron Heidler von Egeregg, with his staff, and the Austrian Consul, Dr. Carl Ritter von Goracuchi, had come to the station to meet me; and there, too, was my dear friend Wingate Bey, to whom I can never sufficiently show my gratitude in word or deed. The *Times* correspondent was also there; and Father Rosignoli, with a number of others, and, of course, a photographer taking snap-shots.

We drove to the Austrian diplomatic agency, where I was for a long time the guest of the warm-hearted Baron Heidler, who had worked so hard for my freedom, and whose actions were not only prompted by a desire to do his duty as a representative of the Government, but who was actuated by a deep sympathy for the sufferings of a fellow-creature held down in miserable bondage.

On arrival I found my rooms adorned with the flags of my dear fatherland, and decked with roses and flowers, whilst above the door was written, 'A hearty welcome home.' On the same day I received telegrams of congratulation from my family, friends, fellow-students, and from several newspapers. I also met with a hearty welcome from His Royal Highness Duke Wilhelm of Würtemberg, and His Serene Highness General Prince Louis Esterhazy, both of whom had been in the Bosnian campaign when I had served there with my regiment, and who greatly honoured me by their expressions of genuine sympathy with me in the hardships I had undergone, and in the joy I now experienced at having escaped at last from the tyrannical thraldom of the Khalifa. I was received in audience, soon after my arrival, by His Highness the Khedive of Egypt, who conferred upon me the title of Pasha. I had entered the Sudan sixteen years before as a first lieutenant of the Austrian army, and, whilst Governor of Darfur, had been granted the Egyptian military grade of lieutenant-colonel, and now, on my return, I was promoted to the rank of colonel, and posted to the Egyptian Intelligence Department.

A few days after my arrival, when seated on the balcony of the Agency, and looking down on the garden all fresh with the verdure of spring, I espied a tame heron stalking across the flower-beds. Instantly I thought of Falz-Fein of Ascanea Nova, in Tauride, South Russia, and I hurried to my room, and then and there wrote to him a full account of the crane which he had released in 1892, and which had been killed in Dar Shaigia. It was the greatest pleasure to feel myself in a position to give the former owner of the bird an accurate account of what had happened; and soon afterwards I received a reply from Mr. Falz-Fein, who possesses a large estate in the Crimea, thanking me warmly for my letter, and inviting me to pay him a visit, which, unfortunately, the numerous calls on my time have hitherto prevented me from accepting.

A series of official and private calls, numerous invitations, and other social duties, so occupied my time that some weeks elapsed before I could undertake any serious work. My first duty was, of course, to submit a detailed official report to my military superiors, and it was not till some time later that I began to describe the story of my life during the last sixteen years.

My old friend and comrade in captivity, Father Ohrwalder, who is now a missionary at Suakin, took an early opportunity of coming to Cairo to welcome me. Our meeting was indeed a happy one, and I rejoiced to be able to thank him personally for all the assistance he had given in arranging for my escape.

The contrast between my past and present life, the influence of fresh impressions, the many changes I see around me, sometimes make my head feel heavy—heavy, as though I had just woke up from an evil dream. Twelve years' captivity—a long dream indeed!

It was long before my excitement subsided, but gradually I began to settle down and collect my thoughts. Now again in the midst of civilized society, once more a man among men, my thoughts often turn back to the fanatical barbarians with whom I had to live so long, to my perils and sufferings amongst them, to my unfortunate companions still in captivity, and to the enslaved nations of those remote territories. My thanks are due to God, whose protecting hand has led me safely through all the dangers behind me.

CHAPTER XIX.

CONCLUSION.

Africa, Past and Present—The Sudan, Past and Present—Rise, Progress, and Wane of Mahdism—How long will it last?—The Khalifa's present Position—European Encroachment—' Whites' in the Bahr el Ghazal—Important Strategical Position of the Province—Time and Tide wait for no Man—I recover my long-lost Sword—A last Word.

AFTER more than sixteen years in Africa, including twelve years of captivity, during which I was cut off from all communication with the civilized world, I have at length had the good fortune to return to Europe. How Africa has changed within this period! Regions in the exploration of which Livingstone, Speke, Grant, Baker, Stanley, Cameron, Brazza, Junker, Schweinfurth, Holub, Lenz, and hundreds of others risked their lives, are now accessible to civilization. In most of these, in which the explorer had formerly to encounter the greatest dangers, there are now military posts and stations to afford security, and facilitate the trade, which is constantly becoming more active. From the east Italy, England, Germany, from the west the Congo State, France, and England, are daily enlarging their spheres of influence, and are now on the point of joining hands in Central Africa. Wild tribes, who in their modes of life are nearer to beast than to man, are beginning to know new wants, beginning to understand that there are beings mentally superior to themselves, and who, through the appliances of modern civilization, are unconquerable even in foreign lands. The more northerly of the still independent Mohammedan States —Wadai, Bornu, and the Fellata kingdoms—will doubtless sooner or later be compelled to conclude alliances with some of the advancing powers, perceiving that only in this way can their hereditary rule be secured.

In the middle of Africa, between the lands just mentioned and the powers advancing from east, south, and west, lies the former Egyptian Sudan, now under the rule of the Khalifa Abdullahi, the despotic head of the Mahdists. No European can venture to cross the limits of this land, cut off from civilization, extending in the south along the Nile to Reggaf, and east to west from Kassala to near Wadai; death or lifelong captivity would be his lot. Yet it is only within the short period of ten years that the land has been subjected to these miserable conditions. For more than seventy years, since the time of Mohammed Ali, it remained under the rule of Egypt, and was open to civilization. In the chief towns were found Egyptian and European merchants. In Khartum itself the foreign Powers had their representatives. Travellers of all nations could pass through the land unharmed, and found protection and help through their aid. Telegraphs and a regular postal service facilitated intercourse with the most distant countries. Mohammedan mosques, Christian churches and mission schools looked after the religious and moral education of the young. The land was inhabited by the most diverse tribes, many of which lived in hostility with one another, but were compelled by the strength of the Government to keep the peace.

Discontent no doubt prevailed in the land, and in the preceding pages I have shown how the avarice and misgovernment of the officials brought about a condition of affairs which rendered the country ripe for revolt. I have endeavoured to explain how Mohammed Ahmed took advantage of the mood of the people, and, well knowing that only a religious factor could unite the hostile tribes, he maintained that he was the Mahdi sent by God to deliver the country from foreign yoke, and to regenerate religion, thus bringing into existence that element of fanaticism which throws such a lurid glow over those dark episodes with which the history of the past twelve years of the Sudan has been so replete. Without fanaticism the revolt could never have been successful, while with it one is brought face to face with a condition of warfare and religious enthusiasm, to find a parallel to which one must go back to mediæval history, and even further.

In the preceding account of my life and adventures, in the vortex itself of this mighty religious movement, I have endeavoured to briefly trace, step by step, the principal causes which have led to the present situation—changed greatly, it is true, from the time in which the Mahdi and his successor were in the zenith of their power, but nevertheless a situation requiring careful handling, and a thorough knowledge of details, in order that those concerned may be enabled to grasp accurately the conditions necessary to restore to civilization this vast expanse of country which has now fallen into an almost indescribable state of moral and religious decadence.

In the Sudan we have before us a terrible example of nascent and somewhat crude civilization suddenly shattered by wild, ignorant, and almost savage tribes, who have built over the scattered remnants a form of government based to some extent on the lines they found existing, but from which they have eradicated almost every symbol of right, justice, and morality, and for which they have substituted a rule of injustice, ruthless barbarity, and immorality. Nor can I recall any other instance in modern times of a country in which a semblance of civilization has existed for upwards of half a century, falling back into a state so little removed from absolute barbarism.

But let us consider for a moment what is this new power which has suddenly grown up, and which seems to the European world to block so completely all their civilizing efforts, which have during recent years made such startling strides in almost every other part of the vast continent of Africa.

I have endeavoured to show how, on the Mahdi's first rise to power, the entire country was with him heart and soul, how on his death real fanaticism gradually waned, and gave place to a temporary power wielded, under the cloak of religion, with reckless severity by the Khalifa and his western Arabs, who, taking the place of the Egyptian garrisons they had destroyed, ruled the unfortunate populations with a rod of iron, and with such oppression and tyranny as to make them long for a return to any form of government which would give them rest and peace. It is needless for me to recapitulate the horrors and cruelties which have been enacted by the Khalifa and his followers in order to maintain their position of ascendancy; but it will be sufficient for my purpose to recall here that at least seventy-five per cent. of the total population has succumbed to war, famine, and disease, while of the remainder the majority are little better than slaves; and that terrible scourge, the slave-trade, with all its attendant horrors, is rampant in the land, and includes amongst its victims numbers of Abyssinian Christians, Syrians, Copts, and Egyptians.

The extent of country now governed by the Khalifa is little altered, it is true, from that occupied originally by the Egyptian Government, but with what a difference! Prosperous districts with a teeming population have been reduced to desert wastes. The great plains over which the western Arabs roamed are deserted, and their places taken by wild animals, while the homesteads of the Nile dwellers are now occupied by those nomad tribes, who have driven out the rightful owners of the soil, or enslaved them to till the land for the benefit of their new masters. Deprived of the means of self-defence, reduced by oppression and tyranny to a condition of hopelessness of relief from their foreign taskmasters, their powers of resistance crippled, the comparatively small river populations which are left are little better than slaves. What can they do of themselves against their despotic rulers? It is folly to imagine that the country can right itself by internal revolt. The helping hand must come from without; and the local populations must realize that the first step to re-establish Government authority having been taken, there will be no drawing back. They must be convinced that the Khalifa's power is doomed, and that the bright era of civilization is assuredly returning. Then, and not till then, will they heartily throw in their lot with the advancing forces, and lend their aid in breaking down the power of the now waning Mahdist Empire. Let it not, however, be supposed that although I describe this power as declining, it is likely of itself to become extinct within a comparatively short period. A careful perusal of the last few chapters will, I think, make it clear to all that the means taken by the Khalifa to render his position secure against his internal enemies have been most thoroughly effective, and, assuming that his authority is not threatened by external influences, I see no cause why, as long as he is alive, he should not maintain his ascendancy. With his death it is more than probable some internal convulsion will take place, which might under certain circumstances displace the dynasty he has attempted to found, but which would not necessarily bring that unfortunate country much nearer to civilizing influences than it is at present. Considered, therefore, from this point of view, the necessary palliative still lies in the introduction of external aid.

The above hypothesis does not, however, entirely meet the conditions of the case. Those who wish to study the present situation in the Sudan must not think of that country as it was in the days of Ismail Pasha, when the civilizing influence was represented by the Egyptian Government, and when the various countries lying immediately beyond the Egyptian sphere were barbarous or Pagan states, in which Europeans were almost unknown, and the Arab slave-hunter had barely penetrated; that condition has been little else than reversed. The Mahdist authority, as I have already shown, is at once intolerably obstructive and dangerously insecure. The once comparatively civilized Sudan is now occupied by a barbaric power hostile to both European and Ottoman influence. It blocks the way from the central plateaus along the Nile valley to the Mediterranean, it seals up districts which were at one time fairly tranquil, and open to the influences of commerce and civilization, while the various countries by which it is bordered are now being gradually opened up. Intercourse between them and the outside world is becoming easier, trade is pushing obstacles out of the way, risk to life is lessened by the protective action of European governments, and the savage races by which they are peopled are beginning to learn the folly of fighting against the resources of civilization.

To turn from generalization to details, what do we find to be the present situation ? On the east Egyptian influence is slowly—very slowly—recovering its lost ground in the vicinity of Suakin and Tokar. To the south-east the Italians have captured Kassala, and have forced the

Mahdists to take up a strong line of defence on the west
bank of the Atbara River. Further south the Abyssinians
show no present intention of altering the relations which
have previously existed between them and the Dervishes.
In the mountainous districts of Fazoglu and the Blue Nile
the inhabitants have thrown off allegiance to the Khalifa.
Far away to the south, at the sources of the Nile, British
influence is beginning to make itself felt in those regions
where Speke, Grant, Baker, and others gained imperishable
renown by their magnificent explorations, and by their
efforts against slavery and the slave-trade—regions which
will ere long be connected with the coast by a railway
which will open up, not only the country it traverses, but
will also give an exit to the trade of Southern Equatoria
and the adjacent countries. Next to these British
possessions comes the Congo Free State, which within the
last few years has made such gigantic strides in bringing
under its influence large tracts of country, not only in the
vicinity of the Mbomu and Ubangi, but in many districts of
the Bahr el Ghazal Province and in Equatoria, almost to
within striking distance of the Dervish advanced post at
Reggaf in the Nile Valley, while behind them, in the Haute
Ubangi, or even in juxtaposition with them, the enterprising
French pioneers are striving to give effect to their colonial
dreams, which have of late years been so fully realized in
various parts of Africa. Still further to the north-west the
Khalifa's authority in those districts is menaced by hostile
tribesmen, who may, sooner or later, become subject to the
guidance of European influence, penetrating from the west
and north of Africa; and on the extreme north lies the
Egyptian power, which Abdullahi is gradually learning to
dread, as being that most likely to be the first to interfere
with the uncertain tenure of his empire.

Such, then, is briefly the present defensive and offensive
position of the Mahdist Sudan. All-powerful within his
dominions, but threatened from all sides from without, there
is little doubt that before the onward march of civilizing

forces the whole empire of the Khalifa must crumble and collapse—and what then? Will Egypt once more become the actual possessor of the country of which she was the legitimate owner? Will all those civilizing Powers who are marching forward unselfishly realize that, should they establish themselves on the banks of the navigable Nile, they must not attempt to cut off or minimize the life-giving water-supply of Egypt by introducing skilled irrigation within the territories they may have acquired? Will they unselfishly abandon the advantages which they may have secured through the expenditure of blood and treasure, in order that the legitimate rights of Egypt may not be interfered with? All these questions enter into the domain of practical and current politics, with which it is not my province to deal. I am merely in the position of expressing my views on the importance and value of the Sudan to Egypt, and on this subject I hold a strong opinion. The reasons which first prompted Mohammed Ali, three-quarters of a century ago, to take possession of the Sudan still hold good. As the Nile is the life of Egypt, so every effort must be made to preserve the Nile valley from intrusion. Any advance, therefore, of civilizing influences towards that gigantic waterway must naturally be viewed with alarm by those authorities who are fully alive to the danger which would arise by the creation on the banks of the river of colonies whose personal interests would predominate over their regard for the preservation and advancement of Egyptian welfare and prosperity.

Here and there in the preceding pages I have referred to the immense importance of the Bahr el Ghazal, and it is perhaps not out of place here to recapitulate once again the peculiar position which this province holds in regard to the remainder of the Sudan. It is a most fertile district, extending over an enormous area, watered by a labyrinth of streams, and covered with mountains and forests in which elephants abound, while the low valleys are subject to inundations. The soil is exceptionally good, producing quantities of cotton and indiarubber. There are cattle in abundance, and I estimate the population at between five and six millions. They are capable of making excellent soldiers. Moreover, the continual feuds between the various tribes prevent any combination of the inhabitants as a whole, hence the ease with which foreigners can obtain an ascendancy in the province, and create an efficient local army.

The port of the Bahr el Ghazal was Meshra er Rek. To this place steamers periodically ascended from Khartum, but were often stopped by the floating vegetation which from time to time blocks the passage of the Upper Nile. Just south of Fashoda, the river emerges from what may have been the bed of an ancient lake. Into this wide marsh trickle a great number of winding streams which are often completely blocked by the suds, and through these dense barriers travellers must at times cut their way with swords and axes. Sir Samuel Baker's expedition (1870-1874) was delayed a year from this cause.

The geographical and strategical position of the province, therefore, with reference to the rest of the Sudan, renders its possession of the greatest importance. The presence of foreigners, unconcerned in the preservation of Egyptian interests, having at their command the vast resources of this great country, which are estimated at a much higher value in both men and materials than those of any portion of the Nile valley, would place them in such a predominating position as to endanger any occupation by Egypt of her lost provinces.

In the preceding pages I have described all I know of the movements of Europeans in these districts, and it is possible an attempt in force on their part to reach the Nile *via* Meshra er Rek, or the Bahr el Homr, or Bahr el Arab, might meet with some opposition from the Mahdists; but if well conducted it would, in all probability, result in their losing their province.

If, therefore, the Khalifa were to learn that the ' Whites ' in the Bahr el Ghazal were in greater force than his present information leads him to suppose, he might engage in a campaign against them, and in this case he would be obliged to send reinforcements from Omdurman, a matter of some difficulty, as the drain on his resources caused by the maintenance of large forces at the threatened points on the Atbara opposite Kassala and in the Dongola province is considerable.

Reverting to the Dervish situation in Darfur and Kordofan, it should be noted that the present force of the Emir Mahmud amounts to some thousands of rifle and spear men, scattered in garrisons at El Fasher, Shakka, and El Obeid. Mahmud himself resides at El Fasher with the bulk of this force, and is constantly at war with the Dar Gimr, Massalit, Tama, Beni Hussein, Hotir, and other tribes of the Kebkebia and Kulkul districts. Recently, one of Mahmud's lieutenants (Fadlalla) was killed, and his force of six hundred men heavily defeated in a contest with these revolted tribes, and, just at the time I left Omdurman, permission had been given to Mahmud to send out a punitive expedition from El Fasher, which appears to have been partially successful. These tribes, although nominally independent, owe a certain allegiance to the Wadai Sultanate. It is therefore erroneous to suppose that they are acting under the direction of Rabeh Zubeir, whose hostility to Wadai is well known, and whose authority does not extend so far to the east, and now appears to be centred in the districts lying south and south-west of Lake Tchad.

Such, then, was the state of affairs in these southern and western districts when I left the Sudan; and, since my arrival in the midst of civilization, I have frequently seen many strange and conflicting reports in the press as to the situation in these distant regions, and although concurring with the view that the onward march of civilizing forces must eventually cause the collapse of the Mahdist Empire, I feel that my unique position in the centre of Dervish authority entitles me to give a word of warning to the country whose interests I endeavoured for long years to uphold, and whose eventual welfare and prosperity, in a recovered Egyptian Sudan, I earnestly long to see. I would merely impress upon her the fact that time and tide wait for no man ; that whilst she is contemplating with longing eyes the recovery of her lost provinces, there is always the possibility that they may fall into the hands of others who may prove more difficult to dislodge than the Khalifa, and who, by bringing engineering skill on the life-giving waters of Egypt, may endanger its very existence, and who would, though it is undoubtedly the lesser of two evils, deprive that country of the rich blessings of trade and commerce which, under a beneficent administration in the Sudan, would give wealth and prosperity both to the parent Egypt and her recovered Nile provinces.

With these few words of friendly advice to the country to whose services I rejoice to have returned after twelve long years of captivity, I now end this narrative. But ere I close I will relate yet one more incident which, were I superstitious, I would consider presaged well for the recovery of what has been lost. In December, 1883, when force of circumstances obliged me to surrender to the Mahdi, the sword of Austrian pattern which I had received on entering the Austrian army, and on which I had had my name engraved in Arabic characters, was taken from me. In August, 1895, when I came to London to attend the Geographical Congress, it was returned to me by Mr. John Cook, senior, of the firm of Thomas Cook and Son, at his office in Ludgate Circus. It appears that Mr. John Cook had, in 1890, purchased this sword from a native of Luxor, on the banks of the Nile, his attention having been attracted by the Arabic inscription on the blade, from which my friend, Major Wingate, whom he met shortly afterwards, was able to decipher my name. It is, I think, likely the Mahdi had presented my sword to one of his followers who had taken part in the invasion of Egypt by Nejumi in 1889; and when that redoubtable Emir was overthrown by General

Sir Francis Grenfell on the field of Toski, it is probable that the wearer of my sword fell too, and the long-lost weapon was taken from the field by a villager, from whom Mr. Cook purchased it. To have lost my much-prized first sword in the wilds of Darfur, and to find it again in the heart of London, is almost more than a coincidence.

During the last sixteen years I have led a life of strange vicissitudes, and I have endeavoured to narrate as simply as I could my unique experiences, in the hope that my story may not only prove of interest to those who have shown sympathy with the hard fate of the European captives in the Sudan, but with the most earnest desire that these, my experiences, may prove of some value when the time for action may arise, and when, if God wills, my services may be utilized in helping to abolish the rule of my tyrannical master and life-long enemy, the Khalifa Abdullahi, and re-establish in that country the Government authority I struggled with some measure of success, but, alas! vainly, to uphold.

Baron Rudolf Carl Slatin Pasha,

G.C.V.O., K.C.M.G., K.C.V.O., C.B., C.V.O., M.V.O.

1857-1932

British Inspector-General of Sudan 1900-1914

Two biographies of the life of Slatin Pasha are:

Slatin Pasha by Richard Hill
Published by Oxford University Press, 1965

Between Two Flags: The Life of Baron Sir Rudolf von Slatin Pasha, *GCVO, KCMG, CB*
by Gordon Brook-Shepherd
Published by Weidenfeld and Nicolson, 1973

INDEX

The following letters appended to names of persons signify : *A.* Ashraf, descended from the Prophet ; *C.* Commander ; *D.* Danagla or Dongolowi ; *E.* Emir ; *G.* Governor ; *J.* Jaalin ; *K.* King ; *Kfa.* Khalifa ; *M.* Mahdi ; *P.* Pasha ; *S.* Sultan ; *Sh.* Sheikh.

ABAKR, *S.* Begu, 92
Abba, Island of, Mahdi's home, 45, 48, 59
Abd el Kader, Mahdi's uncle, *P.*, *G.* Gen. Sudan, his advice, 69, 125
Abderrahman ben Naga, 159
Abdul Kerim to Sennar, 236
Abdullahi bin Sayd Mohammed, Khalifa el Mahdi, *W. Arab,* early history, 49, 308 ; proclaimed Khalifa, 156 ; succeeds Mahdi, 230 ; tyranny, 257 ; Mahdi's Dome, 258 ; Dr. Wahrmund's letter, 269 ; brethren arrive, 270 ; illness, 297 ; fortifies Atbara, 303 ; fiendish character, 311 ; harem, 314 ; postal service, 321 ; how he rides abroad, 322 ; reviews, 324 ; present army, etc., 330 ; frontiers, 331 ; timidity, 346 ; house at Omdurman, 349 ; his ' blackholes,' 353
Abdullahi Dudbenga, Harun's cousin, *S.*, 110
Abdullahi om Dramo, *Sh.* Messeria, 94
Abu Anga, *E.* of Blacks, befriends Slatin, 196 ; reduces Kordofan, 242 ; marches to Omdurman, 254 ; beats Abyssinians, 255 ; dies much lamented, 256
Abu es Saud, attacks Abba, 58
Abu ' Falja ' (Mahdi), 162
Abu Gemmaisa, his rebellion, 265
Abu Girga, *D. E.* Gezira, 156 ; besieges Khartum, 171 ; repulsed, 169 ; joins Osman Digna, 260 ; sent to Reggaf, 297
Abyssinians take Gallabat, 245 ; beaten by Abu Anga, 256 ; King John's death, 264
Adlan, Ibrahim, in charge of Beit el Mal, 236 ; hung, 277
Afifi Wad Ahmed, *Sh.* Habbania, 73 ; killed, 106
Agordat, battle of, 302
Ahmed ed Dalia, executioner, 258, 268
Ahmed Fedil, Khalifa's cousin, 302
Ahmed Wad Ali at Kassala, 260 ; routed by Italians and killed, 301

Ahmed Wad Ali, ' Kadi el Islam,' 125, 356
Ahmed Wad Suleiman, *E.* Beit el Mal, 82-125 ; discharged, 236
Ala ed Din, *P., G.* Gen. Sudan, 3
Ali Bey Sherif, *G.* Kordofan, 7 ; *G.* Darfur, 31
Ansar, ' helpers,' 64, 178
Arab clothes, 38 ; courage, 69, 73, 74, 106, 120, 248, 268 ; customs, 38 ; food, 16, 38 ; greed of gain, 10 ; oath of fealty, 100 ; tactics, 43 ; treachery, 133
Arabs : *Batahin,* 267 ; *Bedeyat,* 36, 39 ; *Beni Helba* chastised, 120 ; *Gehéna,* 69 ; destroyed, 254 ; *Habbania* rise, 70 ; *Hawazma,* 9, 69 ; *Homr,* 9 ; *Khawabir* restless, 104 ; *Maalia* rise, 70, 72, 85 ; *Maheria* rise, 136 ; *Mima* restless, 104, 107, 138 ; *Misseria,* 9, 84 ; *Rizighat,* 9 ; rise, 70 ; *Shaigi* loyal, 69 ; to Khartum, 171 ; *Tagu,* 85 ; *Taaisha* masters, 346 ; *Zagawa,* 84 ; *Zayedia,* 136
Arabs, animosity between E. and W. tribes, 235
Artin, Armenian watchmaker, 359
Ashraf starved and beaten to death, 289 ; property confiscated, 295
Atbara River, 407

Babakr Abu Sebiba, 363 ; Black population, 8 ; recruiting ground, 304 ; penetrated by Congo State, 305 ; its importance to Egypt, 409
Bairam, 185, 323 ; trooping colours at, 324
Bara captured by Mahdi, 80
Batahin, execution of, 267
Bazingers, 7
Begu, *S.*, 92
Beit el Mal, 124, 134
Berber, fall of, 162
Beresford, Lord Charles, 216
Beshari Bey, 120
Black babies, 28

Calamatino, George, Gordon's messenger, 173, 188, 200
Camel besieged by Waganda, 30

Also from Greenhill Books

WITH KITCHENER TO KHARTOUM
by
G.W. Steevens

Nearly fourteen years after Gordon had been murdered in Khartoum, the British fought their way through to bury him. Under Sir Herbert Kitchener, later 1st Earl of Khartoum, an Anglo-Egyptian army at last in 1898 managed to conquer the fearsome forces of Mahdism under Mahmud. In April came the Battle of Atbara, when Mahmud's forces, hitherto unresisting, chose to stand firm. Kitchener's forces, arranged in a huge bow with the British on the left and the Egyptians on the centre and right, opened the battle with artillery and then advanced. The dervishes defended the Fort vigorously, but by the end of the day Atbara had fallen to Kitchener and Mahmud was a prisoner.

Pressing along the Nile, and now reinforced, Kitchener faced the last and greatest stand by the Mahdi forces. Early in September he attacked at Omdurman. At first the dervishes fell back, but then forces hidden in the hills fell upon Kitchener's army with renewed vigour and the outcome looked in doubt. Kitchener's men prevailed, but as Steevens writes: 'The Dervishes were superb - beyond perfection. It was their largest, best and bravest army that ever fought against us for Mahdism and it died worthy of the huge empire that Mahdism won and kept so long.' Over 11,000 dervishes died to a few hundred on the British side.

This classic and stirring account relives those days with vivid descriptions of the combat, of the way of life in the Soudan and above all of the men who lived and fought there.

6 illustrations and 8 maps
ISBN 1-85367-067-7

Also from Greenhill Books

FIGHTING THE FUZZY-WUZZY
DAYS AND NIGHTS OF SERVICE WITH
SIR GERALD GRAHAM'S FIELD FORCE AT SUAKIN
by
Major E.A. De Cosson, FRGS

'Too late, it is true, to save Gordon, we may still rescue our gallant comrades from their perilous position on the Nile and, joining hands with Wolseley, deliver a crushing blow to the power of the Mahdi.'

These were the high aspirations, so writes the author, of the men who set out with such high hopes on the Suakin expedition. Written as soon as he returned home, this is his story of the campaign, which has often been overshadowed by the exploits of Gordon and Wolseley. Here, dramatically told, is a day to day account of what happened when the British Tommy came face to face with Kipling's Fuzzy-Wuzzies, the 'first class fighting man'.

When news first came through to England of General Gordon's plight, besieged in Khartoum by the forces of the Mahdi, such was the public outcry that Lord Wolseley was sent with an expeditionary force to relieve him. Through tragic delays and miscalculations, it arrived too late, and in the ferment of public outrage at Gordon's horrific death, the Government hastily despatched the Suakin expedition under Sir Gerald Graham to come to Wolseley's aid by engaging the forces of the mighty Osman Digma. They left England with high aspirations in February, and the story of what happened is told graphically from the author's eye-witness accounts, from the official despatches he saw at HQ and on contemporary reports from newspapers. Holding their own against Osman Digma, constantly luring him to the battlefield, their aim was to construct a railway through to Berber, as the key to regaining the Soudan. It was forging ahead when in May the Government decided to withdraw from the Soudan.

This is a first class memoir of a little known Victorian campaign.

6 illustrations and 1 map
ISBN 1-85367-066-9